Send 'e

Vincent Power

Kildanore Press

Kildanore Press, Blanchardstown, Dublin 15, 1990
Send 'Em Home Sweatin'

Cover design: Fran Dempsey
Design consultant: Willie Finnie
Photographer: Denis O'Farrell
Location: Rolestown Community Centre, Co Dublin.
Doorperson: Pat Ryan
Editing: Joanne McElgunn

With special thanks to Liam Moher, Fran and Margaret Dem-
psey, Cork Examiner Publications, Albert Reynolds TD,
Larry Gogan, Joanne McElgunn, Gerard Sweeney, Dr. John
O'Mahony, Kate T. O'Mahony, Michael Heney, *Irish Press*,
Independent Newspapers, *Sunday World*, Colin McClelland,
Kevin Sanquest, *The Belfast Telegraph*, John Coughlan *Spot-
light*, Donal Gallagher, Brian O' Brien, Cork City Library,
Joe McCadden, John McCarthy, Niall Stokes (*Hot Press*),
Lynn Snyder and David Wild (*Rolling Stone Magazine* ®),
In Dublin magazine, Justin Nelson RTE, John Kennedy
(Green Studios, Dublin), J.A. Phelan, Sean Dunne, T.P.
O'Mahony, Fr. Brian D'Arcy, Andrew McLoughlin, and
Robert Ballagh.

Typesetting: Terence Riley and Kildanore Press
Colour separations: Litho Studios, Dublin.
Printed and bound by the Guernsey Press Company.

To Mary, Stella-Marie and Vance

" The Clippers, at that time, meant precisely the same thing as U2 means to the present generation..." **Gay Byrne**

" The whole thing happened accidentally..." **Brendan Bowyer**

"Some people said that we were mad in the head. The ballroom thing was supposed to be a joke. It couldn't be done. Everybody thought we were lunatics to build a ballroom where there was no population... "**Albert Reynolds TD**

" I saw girls refusing to dance with fellows with drink taken. It would be nearly a mortal sin if a fella came in tipsy — the girls wouldn't go for him. But, the Pioneers were in great demand..." **Eileen Reid**

" I'd have crawled over broken glass to be part of this; just to see and hear the Capitol..." **Phil Coulter**

" T.J.(Byrne) was as talented a manager as I have ever met in any field. He would be fully capable of managing a major world-wide act today..." **Jim Aiken**

" Brendan Bowyer jumps around the stage, Joe Dolan jumps around the stage, but I *move* around the stage..." **Dickie Rock**

" I have mixed feelings about showbands. I learned a lot and had good fun. But, ultimately, what's the point in being a 'copy band'?..." **Rory Gallagher**

"When I met him (Tom Jones), he knocked me flat. He was everything that I hoped he was going to be. I could have fallen flat on my heels in love with him..." **Eileen Kelly (Kelley)**

" Fellows were coming out from under motor cars and down from trees to become showband managers overnight..." **Des Kelly (Capitol Showband)**

" They lived well, drank a lot, and fornicated at a great rate..." **John Coughlan, editor, *Spotlight* magazine**

" This phenomenon was exploding all over the place. Big halls were being built. There was money to be made. You didn't have to be all that great a musician to be involved. Then, suddenly, it was all gone..." **Phil Coulter**

Vincent Power is a thirty-year-old senior journalist with Cork Examiner Publications. A native of Limerick city, he is married with two children and lives in Cork. This is his first book.

2.20a.m. Dublin: Sunday, August 28th 1966.

The city centre is calm. Pubs, cinemas and theatres are as dead as the night. The curtain has fallen on the final performance of *More Gaels of Laughter* with Maureen Potter and Milo O' Shea at the Gaiety; Jack Cruise has completed a fifth week of *Cruise Inn* at the Olympia, and Omar Sharif has sent female hearts fluttering in *Doctor Zhivago* at the Metropole. Suddenly, the calmness is shattered. The streets burst into life as thousands of people criss-cross the capital in cars, taxis and 'special' buses. A queue forms at the taxi rank outside the Gresham Hotel in O'Connell Street. Fast food vans open for business, and the smell of deep-fried chips and burgers hangs in the air. Two lone Gardai at the corner of Abbey Street chat quietly as they observe the bustle. The rush from the ballrooms is on. The last notes of the national anthem have sounded and the showbands have once more succeeded in their mission to *"send 'em home sweatin'..."*

THE STAGE IS SET

The roots of the showband story go back to the dark days of the early fifties. Unemployment and emigration ravaged the country: The choice in rural Ireland was the boat or the farm. For those left behind, the radio — or wireless as it was then called — and newspapers provided the only link with the outside world. In most houses, the wireless was off-limits to the younger family members, with the exception of the weekly *Hospitals Requests'*. Record players and television were somewhere in the future. Home entertainment was simple: cards, storytelling and draughts. Farmhouses hummed nightly to the sound of the Rosary. A Catholic upbringing captured a soul for life. The power of priests in country parishes was absolute. When annual church collections came around, it wasn't uncommon for priests in some parishes to read out a list of names of those who contributed — and how much they paid. Weekend entertainment was the classic 'Ballroom of Romance' situation in church dominated and sexually repressed Ireland. Over zealous priests kept a lookout for courting couples after dances... up lanes and boreens, behind ditches and the marquee.

The first half of the fifties was the heyday of the big band orchestra, and the front runners were Mick Delahunty, Maurice Mulcahy, Gay McIntyre and Johnny Quigley. However, orchestras lacked the glamour and excitement that came later with the showbands. Big band leaders were not expected to be flamboyant public figures who caused fan hysteria. Their job was to provide acceptable dance music. Communication with the dancers was strictly musical. The gentlemen of the orchestra sat and concentrated on their music sheets. The only break in the pattern came when a featured musician stood up, showed what he could do and sat down to polite scattered applause.

Dancing took place in established commercial ballrooms, town halls, parochial halls, carnivals and marquees. Many dances were fund-raisers organised by social and sporting organisations. Parish festival committees ran dances in the country where marquees were erected at crossroads and these canvas monsters peeped into the clouds. Funds went to aid the church and/or local village community. Dancing in the early fifties generally lasted from 9pm to 2am, or 3am on big nights. Admission was usually five shillings (25p), and sometimes more. Special events that merited double bills inevitably raised the price. For instance, when Teddy Forster and his orchestra appeared with Jimmy Rohan and his orchestra at the Maple Ballroom at Millstreet, Co. Cork, in late October '55, the admission was ten shillings (50p).

By the late fifties the social climate was changing rapidly. When the ballrooms sprung up, they threatened the parish dances. It wasn't uncommon for the local priest who saw funds drying up to warn congregations to stay away from the nearest ballroom. Such was the case at Woodford in Co. Galway where a ballroom called the Waldorf opened. The clergy saw that the days of the parochial hall dance were numbered. The warning was duly delivered from the altar at Sunday Masses: stay away from the Waldorf. Generally, church edicts were dutifully obeyed in rural Ireland: anyone opposing the priest was said to be possessed by drink or the devil. On this occasion, however, the excitement offered by the new ballroom was too much to resist.

Two local girls who cycled to their first dance at the Waldorf were mesmerised by the lights, the music and the glamour. As they gazed down on this new world from the balcony, a press photographer took pictures with the aid of a flash bulb. As the flash went off, one of the girls took fright and imagined that the wrath of God had come down on top of them. She blessed herself, turned to her friend and said: "We're done for..." Indeed, as parochial halls lost ground, the Devil made guest appearances in ballrooms around the country. Ireland was a land of superstitions. Those who tempted fate paid the price: one successful orchestra folded because it was said to have gone ahead with a performance on the night that the mother of one of its musicians died.

The showband phenomenon was invented in Northern Ireland by the Clipper Carlton. The Strabane band lit the fuse that led to the showband explosion of the sixties by literally putting a show into their stage routine. It was known as *Juke Box Saturday Night*. While orchestras provided the musical accompaniment to the dancefloor, the Clippers became the centre of attention. They became entertainers, wore colourful suits, got rid of the music stands and moved around the stage. The Clippers transformed the dancing ritual simply by becoming themselves. The younger Royal Showband, who studied them every time they played in Waterford, were snapping at their heels by the dawn of the sixties.

Outside the ballrooms, the winds of change were sweeping the country. Sean Lemass — who as Minister for Supplies had kept the country going during World War Two — succeeded Eamon de Valera as Taoiseach in 1959. He aimed to modernise the country and prime its industrial potential. He gave the people confidence and created desperately needed employment. *Time* magazine spoke of "a new spirit in the ould sod." The new sense of optimism was reflected socially in the ballrooms where bands and their followers were ready for something different.

The communications revolution was the critical factor. Economic prosperity alone would not be enough to create the changes in social behaviour that fostered showbands as a force for public entertainment. The invention of the transistor radio aided the revolution enormously: youngsters listened to Radio Luxembourg under the bedcovers and tuned in to rock'n'roll. Radio Eireann introduced morning radio, a new concept, and then came the sponsored programmes. Television opened up new horizons and brought the world into Irish living rooms. Mass communications transformed Irish life. The country became smaller. Fr. Brian D'Arcy, the showbands' chaplain, reflects: "The Second Vatican Council happened. Elvis happened. We wouldn't have known about any of them were it not for communications. That's the big key to it all. It's impossible to explain to people today the kind of hysteria generated by the showbands. You see, nothing can compare to it now. Today's generation doesn't know what it was like to live in an era of no communications."

T.J. Byrne saw Brendan Bowyer and his friends in action at the Olympia Ballroom in Waterford and sniffed a success story.

Bowyer worshipped Elvis Presley. When he sang, his limbs started to flay, almost involuntarily.

It was no cheap imitation, and revolutionised the traditional notion of a 'live' performance. Byrne taught the Royal to think big — and they did. It was their meteoric rise that encouraged other bands, such as the Dixies, to turn professional. The Clippers started it all, but the Royal took it away from them — and from everybody else. Throughout the '60s, there was the Royal — and the rest. They had youth, vigour, talent, good looks, a slick repertoire and a natural zest for the stage. Tom Dunphy went on bended knee, Bowyer leapt into the air over Dunphy's head and slipped into pelvic thrusts and twirls. He personified rock'n'roll and its central force, Presley, before Ireland really knew what it was all about. His sex appeal was enormous: the girls went to watch Brendan and the boys went to watch the girls watching Brendan.

Showbands didn't explode onto the scene overnight — the change was something of a gentle simmer from '56/'57 that boiled over in '60/'61. Businessmen and building contractors with an eye for an opportunity built ballrooms all over the country to cater for the droves who wanted to follow the new craze. Huge sheds capable of holding between 2,000 and 4,000 mushroomed all over Ireland. The Munster and Leinster Bank — now AIB — backed Albert and Jim Reynolds, and the country's first ballroom chain was built. They began with the Cloudland near their home in Roosky, and an empire was born. Profits from one built the next and so on. Con Hynes from Portumna built his first ballroom, the Las Vegas, at Templemore in 1961. He followed a similar pattern. Hynes was later partnered by band leader Donie Collins, who was involved also with Jack O'Rourke in the Majestic Ballroom, Mallow. This trio ultimately combined as Associated Ballrooms. They came later than the Reynolds chain but wielded easily as much influence.

There was also a growing number of independent owners. In Cork, Jerry and Murt Lucey built two enormously successful ballrooms at Crosshaven and Redbarn. Packie Hayes ran a plant hire business at Dromkeen, a crossroads between Tipperary and Limerick. He built a ballroom on a site beside his premises. The Oyster, as he called it, became part of the social life for whole communities in North Cork, Tipperary, Clare and Limerick. It was jammed every Sunday night. Twelve buses brought dancers from Limerick city alone. In the boom, there were about 450 ballrooms countrywide.

The showband craze changed Irish courting habits forever. In rural areas, the ballrooms created the opportunity to meet others away from the narrow confines of the parochial hall. Youngsters cycled to local dances in the '50s, and drove to ballrooms miles away in the '60s. Boys and girls could be more anonymous at a dance fifty miles from home — away from the prying eyes of neighbours. A boy from Clare could meet a girl from Tipperary in Dromkeen. If things worked out, he met her there again the following week. Registration plates from three and four different counties could be seen in the car park at Dromkeen any Sunday night. Similarly, it wasn't uncommon to find Galway car plates at the Jetland in Limerick. Twenty buses lined up in the Grand Parade, Cork, to take dancers to the Majorca, Crosshaven.

The Majestic in Mallow attracted large numbers from Killarney, Millstreet, Fermoy, Cork, Doneraile, and Midleton. Redbarn in Youghal brought them from Dungarvan, Clonmel, Cork city and all parts of East Cork. Distances meant nothing. The top bands brought people from a fifty mile radius.In Cork city, the Arcadia's Peter Prendergast frequently had one thousand tickets sold before the box office opened on Saturday night. Dancers got lifts from all parts of the county. On Sunday evenings in the early '60s, queues formed from 8.30pm outside the doors of ballrooms all over Ireland.

Ballroom owners had the power to put bands on the road to fame and fortune. They had the venues and the market. For example, Kerryman Bill Fuller ran a thriving dancehall business in Dublin. He introduced bands to audiences abroad through his chain of ballrooms in Britain and the U.S. If a top band wanted to have a crack at Las Vegas, Fuller had the connections to get an audition that could lead to lucrative bookings. The ballroom oligarchy was all powerful and decided whether or not there was room for a new band on the circuit.

The new wealth in Ireland was the industrial wage. Young people developed a lifestyle based on spending what they earned each week. Ballrooms gave them a social outlet. It's remarkable now to recall that people spent hours squashed together without access to alcohol. All ballrooms had a minerals bar, usually on the balcony, and they did great business. Drink was frowned upon: those were the days before women frequented pubs. Michael Coppinger, leader of the Royal Showband, once saw two girls ordering bottles of lager at a pub in Lisburn, and he nearly fell off the stool with shock. That would never have happened back home in Waterford.

The ballroom was classless; it brought together people from all walks of life. In the '50s, class structures were more pronounced, particularly in rural Ireland. The big farmer's daughter wouldn't dare be seen going out with the farm labourer's son. In the '60s, ballrooms ended the social divide.

These venues were the platform for what appears now to have been a bizarre mating ritual: men on one side, women on the other. Separating the sexes was the intimidating territory known as 'No Man's Land'. Early on, only couples doing steady lines were on the dancefloor. Young men crossed to the other side at their peril. A solo journey was made with the trepidation of a soldier attempting to tip-toe through a minefield. The result was always unpredictable. Success brought the chance to meet the girl of one's fancy. Failure brought rejection and humiliation. Rather than risk that kind of retreat, a common tactic was to ask out other girls in the vicinity of the first refusal.

It took time to build up courage to face the female masses. Novices usually stuck together. Their sanctuary was the balcony where they sipped minerals and teased each other about the girls below. Couples on the dance floor who craned their necks could see all the inquisitive voyeurs staring down at them from above. Nosey-parkers on the balcony kept a check on who was making headway with whom. Downstairs, anxious novices agonised over whether or not to "chance it." Often, two lads made a pact: "I'll ask her if you ask her friend." Frequently, one chickened out at the last minute and left the other suitor to go-it-alone. Refusals came with a litany of standard excuses... 'too tired'; 'not now'; 'maybe later'; 'my feet are sore'; 'my fella's gone to get me a mineral'; 'I've broken a heel'; and the old Dublin reliable, 'ask me sister, I'm sweatin'.

Girls stood back-to-the-wall as the boys crossed the floor, walked slowly up and down and assessed the selection on offer — the 'cattle mart' syndrome. The prettiest girls were snapped up; the wallflowers stood patiently, pretending not to care. The toilet was the ladies' conference centre. They elbowed for position around the mirror where they discussed the male 'talent'.

The '60s was a remarkable period in contemporary Irish history. There was a hint of affluence for the first time ever. Young people aspired to things that their parents could never have imagined. Social attitudes were challenged: working class kids could aspire to a university education. The policies of Lemass and his economics guru, T.K. Whitaker, encouraged initiative and enterprise. Hard work was rewarded with hard cash. Men sweated blood working all-night shifts to meet deadlines and collect generous bonus payments. Housing estates mushroomed in the cities. The showband business was a perfect feast for entrepreneurial appetites. The take-away was fast and fulfilling. It was a business that mushroomed at country crossroads all over Ireland, and on the outskirts of every half-sized town.

Lemass and Whitaker altered the image of Ireland as portrayed by Honor Tracy who wrote of "this boggy little piece of land with its few inhabitants, lying forlorn in the ocean, washed by rain and curtained by mist, in grave danger of being overlooked by the outer world were it not for its frequent and lively toots on the horn." De Valera's pastoral vision was taking one hell of a battering; his "comely maidens" were fleeing the fields and villages for Brendan Bowyer in the nearest ballroom and the "athletic youths" were chasing them chasing him. His countryside — "bright with cosy homesteads" — was at the mercy of money men who filled it with ballrooms. People devoted their leisure not to the "things of the spirit" but to romance on the dancefloor.

Politics failed to touch the young soul. True popular appeal rested not with the politicians but with the showbands — young leaders of a generation chosen by box office ticket. In Ireland, it was the showbands who set the tempo for the 'swinging sixties'. They were a phenomenon peculiar to this country, and, after little more than ten years, had virtually disappeared. The top bands were once bigger than the Beatles and the Rolling Stones. It's hard to imagine now that the Beatles played support to the Royal in Liverpool where Bowyer advised them to stick together; that the Waterford singer won the admiration of Elvis Presley — as did Belfast showband the Witnesses who performed for the 'King' in the Bahamas; that Mick Jagger admired the smart uniforms worn by Eileen Reid and the Cadets; that Rory Gallagher played support with the Impact Showband to the Dixies; and that Van Morrison began his career in a Belfast showband, the Monarchs.

Bands like the Royal, Capitol, Miami, Drifters, Dixies, Cadets and Freshmen could pull crowds of between 1,800 and 3,000 on Sunday nights, the highlight of the week's dancing programme. In their glory days, the Royal drew crowds of 3,500. Bad weather once forced attendances down to 1,900 at the Royal Ballroom, Castlebar. The manager, Jerry McDonald, counting the take at the end, said: "The Royal are finished boys. They've dropped below the two" (thousand). Bowyer himself said that if crowds went under 1,000, he'd retire.

On a Sunday night, the Olympic ballroom in Newcastlewest, Co. Limerick, was marooned by floods. The buses from Ballybunion never made it, but the Royal still managed to draw 1,950. Connie Lynch, a sardonic Cavanman who succeeded T.J.Byrne as band manager, remarked: "That was tremendous boys. I never thought we'd do it." Lead guitarist Jim Conlon refreshed his memory. "Yerra, Connie, when *The Hucklebuck* was number one we played here on a Wednesday night to 3,100."

Larry Cunningham and the Mighty Avons smashed records by performing to 6,000 Irish emigrants at the Galtimore, Cricklewood, London. On a St. Patrick's night at the Majorca in Crosshaven, Co. Cork, Dickie Rock and the Miami played to 4,000, and they could draw 3,000 on a Saturday night at the Arcadias, Cork and Bray. In Cork, the Dixies were local heroes who could pack 3,000 into the Arcadia. The Dixies ranked second only to Jimmy Shand for pulling the record attendance to that ballroom — 4,000.

Dancing was a religion. Top bands frequently closed the doors at the peak of the boom from '61 to '66. They played to an average of 2,000 on Sundays. Typically, Saturday was a city date while Friday and Sunday night gigs drew the biggest crowds in the country. Fleets of buses carried hundreds to the ballrooms. Dublin was the dancing capital. Doors opened seven nights a week at the Irish Club, the National, Ierne, Town and Country Club, Crystal, 4 Provinces (later Television Club), Olympic, Barry's Hotel, Metropole and Kingsway. Each did a roaring trade and attracted their own clientele. On St. Stephen's night, Ireland danced like a nation possessed. Top bands could draw 4,000. The experts — that is, those who collected the money — estimated a total dancing population of 731,700, aged from 15 to 34 on Stephen's night...a quarter of the total population. Lent brought the other extreme — but people again flocked in their thousands to ballrooms on Patrick's night and Easter Sunday night.

But there was another side to the showband story. Fortunes were made — and squandered. The biggest lie of all was that "nobody really made much money". Officially, casual sex didn't occur either. No married showband member strayed while away from home. The dark side, in truth, was adultery, marriage break-up, business ruthlessness, scams, and bitter internal band strife.

Quite a number of bands fell into at least one of these categories. Greed was a common cause of showband disputes. Jealousies fuelled the fires of discontent. Line-ups changed like the weather. Money set friend against friend, musician against musician, managers against their proteges and vice versa. Most bands were paid flat fees for performing five and six hours a night in the late '50s. That changed as the money rolled in. Popularity gave the bigger names more clout; they demanded 50% of the take, and more, in proportion to drawing power. Bands were envious of others on higher percentages. Musicians in a band who saw stacks of money being made became disenchanted with weekly wages — particularly if the 'star' of the act earned more. Bands argued; cliques formed and secret meetings were held. Then came the split. A common move was for one or two of the front men to re- group and hire salaried musicians, thus creaming off most of the earnings for themselves. Occasionally, the money men coaxed a 'star' away from his colleagues, promised the moon, and put a new band under him. Or else they scouted the ballrooms for a good looking 'image' man and put him to work with the band. Musicians who wanted to form a band, or else quit an existing outfit to start another, needed cash. That's where rich backers came in. It could cost from £5,000 to £10,000: advertising, equipment, organisation, making the right contacts and greasing the right palms. Without their 'stars', bands folded overnight — others lingered to die slowly. It wasn't uncommon for the manager of one band to attempt a financial killing by wrapping his arms around a few other bands. Business empires were built. The original outfit — once his bread and butter — was sometimes neglected. Some rows were never patched up.

The business was a bastion of male supremacy. A showband man would be considered chauvinistic by today's standards. One woman band member loathed her days traipsing around the country. "What did the men tell you?" she asked me. "They all had fond memories," I replied. "Of course they had," she said, "sure weren't some trying to screw every bimbo in the country." Women in the business were expected to take the rough with the smooth, just like the men. It wasn't a job for the faint-hearted.

The top bands lived like royalty, but the pressures were enormous... pressures to remain competitive... domestic pressures... pressures of travelling five and six nights a week... pressures to keep control. Huge earnings made many of them look like children let free in a candy shop. They were musicians — not businessmen — so taking care of business did not come naturally. The bigger the band, the more muscle could be applied to ballroom owners, especially if the band had a record in the charts. A simple calculation, based on the Consumer Price Index, reveals the comparative scale of the profits in 1967.

Two thousand dancers on a busy night at ten shillings a head, paid £1,000 gross: The equivalent figure for a similar night in 1990 would be **£9,691.45**, of which a band on 60% would earn **£5,814.87**. The average industrial weekly wage in 1967 was

£12.47. Powerful band managers flexed their muscles when they talked percentages with dancehall owners. The percentages started at 50/50 and went as high as 70/30, and occasionally 80/20. Little known bands had to be satisfied with the crumbs, a flat fee.

Ironically, the big earners had little time to indulge themselves. Success meant being on the road five and six nights a week. A band didn't rate unless it played a minimum of five. The day was for sleeping. Typically, bands rested on Mondays and caught up on paper work. On a night off, some moneyed musicians thought nothing of flying to London and returning the following day. Others became legendary for their meanness: today they're still living off money made in the '60s. It was a cash business that survived on a steady flow. Some Irish dance-band musicians of the '60s were the highest paid in the world, and the taxman rarely got his hands on the spoils.

Although dancehalls served only minerals, booze became a big temptation for bands, backstage and in their hotels. Drink was a showband accessory that claimed all too many casualties. It gave the perfect 'lift' before going on stage and after coming off. It was a habit that became a deadly addiction. Booze broke up bands and marriages. Some who remember the '60s only through an alcoholic haze are still paying the price.

The showband explosion catapulted young men from poorly paid jobs to big bucks, from dreary existences to stardom. It was a lot to handle. Brendan Bowyer was a clerk in Waterford Paper Mills who became a nationwide sex symbol; Joe Dolan was an apprentice compositor on the *Westmeath Examiner* before he found fame with the Drifters; Dickie Rock was a youngster from Cabra West fronting his own band, the Echoes, who joined the Miami, and also found himself fighting off frenzied girls lined up under his stage.

Not everybody made it to the top. Out of five hundred fulltime bands criss- crossing the country in search of fame and fortune at the height of the craze, only ten formed the super-league: The Royal, Capitol, Miami, Drifters, Dixies, Freshmen, Plattermen, Cadets, Mighty Avons, and Clipper Carlton. Various layers of lesser bands profited from the success of the leaders and their drawing power varied from place to place. Some established bands rivalled the hot acts on their home turf: for example, Johnny Flynn in Tuam, Johnny Quigley and Gay McIntyre in Derry and Dave Glover in Belfast. Every county in Ireland gave birth to local heroes who became crossroad celebrities.

Church and school choirs spawned future showband stars who, as boy sopranos, sang like angels. Brendan Bowyer first raised his voice at Mount St. Alphonsus, the Redemptorist Church in Limerick, and later at the Dominican Church in Waterford; Dickie Rock at the Church of the Most Precious Blood in Cabra West, Dublin; Butch Moore with the O'Connell School Choir in North Circular Road, Dublin.

The showbands' *raison d'etre* was to entertain, pure and simple, and *send 'em home sweatin'*. Musical abilities were secondary to the stage spectacle. Songwriting flair was redundant because of audience desire to hear chart hits and dance music. There were extremes of musicianship: brilliant players competed on the same circuit as an army of three-chord-trick merchants. Gimmicks and image cultivation frequently masked a lack of the basic fundamentals. Many weren't true showbands, at least not by the criteria laid down by the Clipper Carlton, Royal and Dixies. Gifted musicians powered the best bands to the top of the business. Some great players, lost in the ranks of the lesser bands, went on to prove their worth in the '70s and '80s. Others faded into oblivion.

Musically, audiences got a *pot-pourri* : rock'n'roll, country and western, skiffle, dixieland, ceili, waltzes, Irish ballads. Versatility was the name of the game. Bowyer sang ballads and rock equally well. He could hit the high notes with *Boolavogue* or *Holy City* one minute and gyrate through *The Hucklebuck* the next. The Irish accepted ballads and rock'n'roll side-by-side. Music was never ghettoised, as in Britain. It's the same today: impresario Jim Hand wins bets at parties predicting an uncontrollable slide into *The Fields of Athenry* by the trendiest yuppies after a few jars. Bowyer covered Presley; O'Brien imitated Buddy Holly; the Freshmen sang like the Beach Boys.

Big Tom and the Mainliners followed the 'Country'n'Irish' assault launched by Larry Cunningham. Big Tom is still the

King of Irish music, but Cunningham and The Mighty Avons were the first country band to make it big in the urban ballrooms, attracting a huge following of rural exiles to dances in Dublin. Their appeal was enormous everywhere else: they drew 2,500 one Tuesday night in '66 to a carnival near Castlewellan, Co. Down, run by promoter Jim Aiken; and established unbroken attendance records at nine Irish ballrooms in Britain in the same year. Cunningham was the pioneer of 'Country'n'Irish' who exuded downhome charm. Asked on one occasion to state how many were in the band, he was reported to have said: "I don't know. I never looked behind me."

Dickie Rock was the master of the romantic ballad who left women weak at the knees. Butch Moore and the Capitol were the first Irish showband to be played on Radio Luxembourg in 1963. Joe Dolan and the Drifters became a hot dance ticket in the Reynolds' chain of ballrooms. They called Dolan the 'national aphrodisiac', and it wasn't difficult to see why. He projected a raw sexual energy on stage that captivated the ladies. Dolan's soaring voice could hit 'A' above the stave. Derek Dean of the Freshmen looked like a handsome student priest and women fell at his feet. His stage partner, Billy Brown, was one of the finest musicians in the land.

Authentic showbands had common ingredients that separated them from fakes or 'bengal lancers' — showband speak for 'chancers'. These were powerful brass and rhythm sections, slick showmanship, comedy routines, highly versatile repertoires, glamorous stageclothes, and neat haircuts. Showbands covered versions of well-known hits, sometimes even better than the original artistes. The test of a good showband was one that got closest to the record. In the days before nationwide TV, the clones gave young people a visual interpretation of what they heard on the airwaves. That's partly why they became such an important feature of youth culture in rural Ireland.

The beat scene offered a basement alternative to the showbands in the mid '60s. The beat boys were given a boost when the bands hired 'relief' groups to perform from 9pm till pub closing time. That was the environment in which Irish rock was born. The first Irish beat group is acknowledged to have been the Greenbeats who even took their sounds to the Cavern in Liverpool. Beat groups did covers, too, but also dared to experiment. No self-respecting beat fans went near the showbands. But the big money was still to be made in showbands who made six times more a week than the groups. One fundamental difference was that beat groups performed for love of music — as distinct from love of money. Showband members were earning a minimum of £60 a week compared to the average industrial wage of £10 a week. The big money lured many beat boys into showbands. The moneyed bands viewed groups with suspicion, and considered them to be pretentious. As Eileen Reid of the Cadets puts it: "The groups used to get up my nose. They used to go out and say...'listen to us, we're great.' They had that thing about them. Their approach was...'if you don't want to listen to us, then up yours'. They hated the showbands. The bands were making the bread, and yet the groups thought they were better musicians. They weren't showmen. They were very dull."

In showband-land, T.J. Byrne, the big Carlow man with the persuasive manner, managed the hottest dance ticket in the country, the Royal Showband. "T.J. always felt that he had the Beatles on his hands," recalls Bowyer. The business acumen of Ireland's first real band manager is acknowledged by Jim Aiken, the promoter who first brought the biggest rock acts in the world to Ireland. Big-name bands demanded and got the largest percentages — thanks largely to Byrne's negotiating clout. Some demanded a guarantee as well as a percentage.

The key figures in the industry — band managers and ballroom owners — were ruled by an unwritten code. Deals running into thousands of pounds were done on a handshake. Contracts didn't exist: your word was your bond. It was a 'world within a world'. They even spoke their own language, a slang that only insiders understood. The legitimate wheeler-dealers trusted each other, if only because they had to. Reputable businessmen played by the rules, and everybody went home with their pockets full. But the business also attracted a persistent breed of quick-buck merchants who wanted to take everybody else's money. There were strokers, rogues, chancers, bowsies and conmen at every crossroads, and it wasn't always easy to tell the good guys from the bad.

It was a lucrative business that gave those at the top the trappings of success, and a ticket to the good life. "In those days, when you'd have half a dozen suits hanging up in the wardrobe," says Connie Lynch, "I often took out a suit to put it on and found 40, 60 or 80 pound in the pocket of it, that you didn't know you had. You came home with a few jars in you, took off the suit, hung it up and didn't wear it again maybe for a month. All of a sudden you put it on you, and put your hand in the pocket and found forty... be Japers now if there was 50p missing I'd run around the floor lookin' for it!" Brown, Dean and the Freshmen became accustomed to the high life like others in the first division. They were the first band from the north to make the big-time down south. Brown recalls: "We lived like princes. I used to live in the Great Southern Hotel in Galway — all the time; shelves up, pictures on the wall." But it wasn't all fun and games.

Bands followed a punishing schedule on the road. They were packed like sardines into 'meat wagons' winding their way through bad country roads in the dead of night. Only the well-heeled band could afford luxurious transport. The aim was to make as much money as possible while fans, or 'punters' as they were called, stayed loyal. If that meant appearing at Redbarn, near Youghal, in Co. Cork, tonight and Caproni's in Bangor, Co. Down, tomorrow night, so be it. Generally, dates were linked up. It was a rough life that demanded the stamina of a lion. The money was great — if only there was time to spend it. "As far as I can remember," says Eileen Reid, "it was bed to stage and stage to bed...we worked that hard."

There were no borders to divide showbands' territory: cross-border travel was unrestricted. Bands played anywhere they got dates, from Cahirciveen to Ballymena. The Dixies were made to feel like stars in Belfast, just as the Freshmen were idolised in Cork. Dickie Rock was hugely popular in what are nowadays described as loyalist areas of Belfast. The business was non-sectarian: Catholics and Protestants played on the same stage, and frequently in the same band.

Pranks kept spirits up: the Dixies played music before an audience of cattle by the side of the road at 4am. Bands waged the egg and flour war — country roads became the battlefield as rivals fired eggs at each others' wagons. Flour was added to make the yellow mixture stick. Hostilities took place in the early hours between rival squads who met up on their way home from dances. Tactics were planned with military precision: One band, who knew that another played in town on the same night, ambushed them afterwards on the road. Apart from egg battles, bands let off steam by playing poker in ballroom dressing rooms, hotels and in the back of the wagons on the long road home. Musicians packed away their instruments and metamorphosed into card sharks.

Showbands were mischief-makers. They were the scourge of hotels, especially when several met under the same roof. Rooms were invaded, traps laid. Joe McCarthy of the Dixies was an outrageous practical joker. As he puts it: "We were out to do mad things." Joe Mac once smuggled a rabbit into a colleague's bed as he slept and waited for the reaction. "We were barred out of that hotel too."

Most stories are unprintable. Bands were awake while the rest of the country slept. Pranks were usually played in the hours after they came off stage, high as kites. A regular prank pulled by the Hoedowners involved the unconventional use of their long column speakers, which looked like coffins. The wagon was hidden down a side road near a graveyard, the speakers taken off the roof and brought to the gates. The band would wait for an approaching car. In full view of the oncoming motorist, two musicians dressed in long overcoats would carry the speakers across the road like body-snatchers. "You'd hear the car screeching to a halt," recalls Sean Dunphy. "People didn't know what to think." When the band once stopped in a town for petrol, the local priest approached and said: "Ye're the Hoedowners. Smart men. I was called out of my bed and told that somebody was taking coffins out of the graveyard." For another prank, Earl Gill, dressed in a duffel coat, stood on a wall and played the trumpet, while the band lit a fire beneath him and staged an impromptu 'seance'.

In the mid '60s, the sense of fun found expression on the sports field when the Showband/All-Stars' football matches gave fans the opportunity to see their heroes in a different setting. The matches raised many thousands of pounds for charity. The All-Stars' series was the brainchild of broadcaster Jimmy Magee. The first game took place on the night of June 6th, 1966 at Ballyjamesduff, Co. Cavan. Such was the public interest that gardai were ordered out on point duty in the town at 2am to control the crowds. There was a mixture of sports and showbiz stars. Magee was the link between celebrities. He says: "It was a success and the fellas said, 'we should do that again.' What I didn't tell them before Ballyjamesduff was that I'd arranged the whole season." The All-Stars survived decades after the last showband notes were played and the ballrooms closed. Magee's merry men drew all strands of the business together, from broadcasters to drummers. The story of the All-Stars is interwoven with that of the showbands.

When Lent closed the ballrooms, bands packed their bags and headed off to the Irish clubs and dancehalls of Britain and the U.S. The majority played for Bill Fuller, owner of Dublin's Crystal Ballroom and Town and Country Club, who also had a string of others in Britain and across America. Irish exiles flocked in droves to hear the sounds of home. A handful of bands tried their luck at the American bases in Britain and Germany. International tours were hyped to kingdom come: many were real, some fictional. The prize for the most imaginative trip goes to Jimmy Magee who compiled the first official Top Ten chart broadcast by Radio Éireann on October 2nd, 1962 and who once managed a band called the Boyne Valley Stoppers. While scratching his head to come up with a new publicity stroke, he invented an African tour. His dance diary in the papers read: "Due to African tour, the Boyne Valley Stoppers are unavailable. Thursday — Bulawayo; Friday — Salisbury; Saturday — Mombasa; Sunday — Nairobi; Monday — recording."

Britain became the bands' bread and butter during the slack times at home. Musicians there were staggered at the high earnings of their Irish counterparts. Touring bands were paid as much, if not more, than the Beatles and Rolling Stones during their early days. As a result, Irish musicians never envied upcoming stars that made the bigtime in Britain, and further afield. While touring Britain in '67, Kelley and the Nevada went on a Monday night to see the 'in' soul group, Geno Washington and the Ram Jam Band, at London's 100 Club, a famous jazz venue. The headliners were a top act and won widespread recognition through their TV appearances. The Nevada met them during the break.

"We discovered to our amazement that we were far better paid," says a former member of the Nevada. "Each of us were on £50 a week for four nights (£463.01 in '90). But they were broke, and we actually had to buy them drink." Artist Robert Ballagh, a former bass guitarist with the Chessmen, recalls that the band was paid £250 a night in '64 while resident at the Astoria Ballroom, Manchester. In the early '60s, as he says, "that was a fair crack of money". In '90 terms, that represented an equivalent take of £2,544.89 a night. On a night off, a few of the lads made the pilgrimage to the Cavern, Liverpool. "It was just after the time that the Beatles were playing, and it was still considered a very special venue. A group were playing who had a record in the Top 20. I can't remember their name. We got talking to them, and I asked what the money was like. They said, 'ten pounds'. I said, 'that's not very much to get paid'. It turned out that they had to pay the tenner in order to play."

Back home, even the weakest showbands, were paid union rates. The Chessmen were managed by Noel Pearson — later chairman of the Abbey Theatre, one of Ireland's most successful impresarios and producer of films *My Left Foot* and *The Field*. Ballagh says of him: "He was ahead of his time, the kind of management that Noel has a flair for. His originality was almost a handicap at that time. He did such innovative things for us. I remember he managed to persuade *Spotlight* magazine to run a glossy supplement on the Chessmen."

It was a multi-million pound business that flourished from nothing. Within a few years, the showband boom gave work to about 4,000 singers and musicians, and another 6,000 in dance-halls, marquees, recording studios, management offices, companies and magazines. The economic spin-off was enormous. Bands drew thousands of dancers to ballrooms in towns and villages. Communities benefited from their spending power in pubs, shops, cafeterias and petrol stations. The economic loss was incalculable when the business died...

The Clipper Carlton
Makers Of The Mould

8.30p.m. Cork: Saturday, October 8th, 1955.

"Next please." The rush is on. Crowds who waited patiently for two hours on the street descend on the box office at the Arcadia.

Hundreds more defend their places as if their lives depend on it — long queues stretching down Lower Glanmire Road. The Clippers are in town and nobody wants to miss them. News of their Cork performance had spread like wildfire in a city where the Strabane showmen were hailed as superstars of the '50s.

Tickets went on sale in music shops such as Kellys, Grand Parade, and Pigotts, Patrick Street. The Clippers are ready to go on stage, but people still queue to get in. Peter Prendergast, proprietor of the Arcadia, appeals for help to the Clippers' manager, Victor Craig. "It's no use, Vic," says Peter, who is dressed, as usual, in a tuxedo. "We can't hold them any longer. You'll have to open another door for me."

Craig, a post office clerk from Strabane, swings open an exit door onto the street, rolls up his sleeves at a makeshift table and collects the five bob (shillings) entrance fee from hundreds of outstretched arms. Long experience of handling money over the post office counter makes the job child's play. By 9pm, Peter is at the mike. As always, he makes the formal introduction. "Ladies and gentlemen. The stars of our show tonight... the wonderful Clipper Carlton." The band bounds on stage in bright suits to a crescendo of ear-splitting cheers and screams. Big Fergie O'Hagan talks to his "boys and girls" in a soft, deep voice. He has a rhythmic line in patter... "there we had rock'n'roll... and now Nat King Cole." Everybody loves Fergie.

Down by the Riverside is their signature tune: a favourite in Cork.

The Clippers are an antidote to the staid orchestras that dominate the dancehall circuit. They're like no other band in the country. It's almost like a concert. Bodies mass twenty deep in front of the stage. Heads tilted backwards, all eyes are on these colourful showmen from the north. The balcony is lined with people happy just to watch. The unconventional act draws couples towards the stage to stand and be entertained.

Relentlessly on the move, their performance shows that well-played music alone doesn't make for a memorable night's entertainment. Music gusts around the Arcadia for five hours — punctuated by breaks for dancers and musicians. What everybody wants to see, of course, is the visual climax: *Juke Box Saturday Night* — a twenty-minute piece of 'circus' in which the Clippers bring the house down with carefully-rehearsed comedy routines. It is mimicry *par excellence*, with swift costume changes. Art and Fergie O'Hagan become Laurel and Hardy; Don Shearer is Elvis Presley; Mickey O'Hanlon sends up Charlie Chaplin one moment and Jimmy Shand the next; Hugo Quinn does a clever Eddie Calvert routine, *Oh Mein Papa*.

It is a typical dixieland frontline: trombone, trumpet and clarinet. The Clippers amuse and entertain as well as delivering the pops, country numbers, dixieland jazz and their own favourites. By 2am, Prendergast is back at the mike again. "Ladies and gentlemen... what can I say... let's hear it once more for the wonderful Clipper Carlton... a big thank you to Fergie and the boys for putting on such a tremendous show." The ballroom erupts in applause. O'Hagan signs off and bids farewell to Cork.

As hundreds of dancers collect their coats and disappear into the night, the visitors collect their reward. The band is paid on a 50% deal for 2,867 dancers at 5/- a head. Their take comes to £358: the '90 equivalent, **£4,866.** It wasn't the Clippers biggest night. They generally played to about 3,000 in Cork, with three month intervals so that, in Craig's words, "we wouldn't kill the goose." Prendergast would have them down every month if he could get them. He couldn't. Hence, public interest was maintained and a good turnout guaranteed. Still, £358 was big money in 1955 — the average weekly industrial wage was only £5.89.

(Photo: Cork Examiner)

The Clippers were a unique combination of musical and entertainment talent who would alter the course of the dancehall business. It was their influence that sowed the seeds of the showband boom of the '60s. Nobody realised that history was being made... least of all the Clippers. They brought a dash of colour into people's lives in the decade before nationwide television. The Clippers lit the fuse that caused an explosion of bands. Led by trumpeter and singer, Hugo Quinn, the band took the featured spot routine a stage further by getting everybody involved.

They boogied to the music and developed co-ordinated steps. They played well, danced, wore bright suits and changed into funny costumes and donned wigs for comedy sketches. They dressed as women, acted the eejit for a few laughs and people lapped it up. It was pure pantomime. A show was based around simple songs: one of them dressed as *Liza* to send up *There's A Hole In The Bucket Dear Liza*. Or else Mickey O'Hanlon did great drum solos, threw his sticks in the air and pulled funny faces.

The majority were talented musicians: weaker band members compensated by cultivating roles as funnymen and impressionists. It seems fairly mundane stuff now, but in the mid '50s, this transformation from an ordered musical performance to a frenetic, often madcap show, was sensational in the dancehalls. The band created a rapport between themselves and the audience that left the orchestras led by Mulcahy, Delahunty, Jimmy Rohan, Brose Walsh, Chick Smith, Jack Ruane and the rest sitting — literally.

The barriers between stage and floor were broken down. The Clippers developed a show that 'stopped' the dancers, a revolutionary concept in the ballrooms. They were fresh and exciting. Their fast, eye-catching stage routines, glamorous image and flamboyant suits appealed to teenagers like Brendan Bowyer and Brendan O'Brien, who wanted to see something different. The Clippers paved the way by guiding dancehall entertainment away from the standard repertoire of old time waltzes, foxtrots or quick steps. They changed the danceband image and content, and there was no turning back. As dancers gradually expected to be entertained by 'shows', they began to pick out their favourite bands. They developed preferences and discriminated between the bands' 'shows'. Previously, it didn't matter *who* came on stage, so long as they provided a source of dance music.

Orchestras were not blitzed entirely from the landscape. Derry bandleaders Johnny Quigley and Gay McIntyre emerged from the big band era and adopted showband styles. Belfast bandleader Dave Glover also launched his career in orchestras, and built one of the North's most successful showbands of the late '50s and '60s.

Established orchestra leaders like Delahunty and Mulcahy remained big draws on the dance circuit. Contrary to popular belief, orchestras didn't always look down their noses at the whipper-snappers who threatened to take their business. Mick Del, a giant of his time, took the Royal Showband under his wing in their embryonic days. He gave an unknown band of youngsters the opportunity to play 'relief' to him, and they never forgot his interest in their careers.

In '55, the big band sound still reigned supreme. That's what made the Clippers such an oddity — and such a hit. The 'show' syndrome crept into northern dancebands. Bandleader Glover claims to be the first in Ireland to call his act a 'showband' in '55/'56. Glover had built a 'show' into his programme during summer seasons at the Arcadia Ballroom in Portrush. It was pure vaudeville and 'stopped' the dancers.

Like the Clippers, the Glover band abandoned music stands and stood up to play from memory. However, the Clippers were acknowledged as being the first to take their 'show' on the road the length and breadth of the country.

Quigley and his All Stars, also brought glamour and excitement to the ballrooms, and he too had power over the dancers. McIntyre was recognised as one of the finest musicians in the country. The Melody Aces, from Newtownstewart in Co. Tyrone, were contemporaries. They followed the tracks of the Clippers to ballrooms south of the border and quickly established an enormous following, particularly in the midlands.

The Melody Aces were acknowledged as the first 'Country'n'Irish' showband with sticking power. The Clippers brought vaudeville to the ballrooms, but the Melody Aces were primarily a dance band.

"If you wanted to look at a band, you went to the Clippers,"says Fr. Brian D'Arcy. "If you wanted to *dance* to a band, you went to the Melody Aces." The Aces didn't pretend to be a showband in the strict sense of the Clippers. The inheritors of the Aces' style were the Mighty Avons and, to some extent, the Mainliners. The Clippers had their critics. People who just wanted to hear dance music and didn't want a show went elsewhere. Four northern bands in particular made the grade down south in '55: the Clippers, McIntyre, the Aces and Glover.

The Clippers notched up an impressive string of firsts in the mid '50s... first to appoint a manager and road manager, first to introduce percentages, first to play with relief bands, first to tour America, first to buy a custom-built coach, first to distribute publicity photographs and postcards, and first to print their own headed notepaper. Victor Craig recalls: "To have seen the whole business unfolding at first hand was marvellous."

Despite the Clippers' success, Craig did not give up his day job in the post office. When the band broke up, he still had secure employment. Not everybody in the business was as wise.

The beginnings of the showband business can be traced to the late 40s when the Clipper Carlton was born. A group of friends living in Strabane got together and decided to form a band. They were no different to anybody else. They sat down and read music sheets — an ordinary band hustling for bookings. They played at the Pallidrome Ballroom in Strabane every Saturday night. They also got work at dances run by local cricket, rugby and football clubs.

"We started out as Hugh Tourish and the Carlton. One night in 1949, for a gimmick at a dance in Fintona, they ran a competition to find us a new name. A barman in the crowd came up with the idea of *Clipper Carlton* and won himself a tenner," said Hugo Quinn. The name conjured up images of transatlantic travel: all Pan American flying boats through Foynes in the late '30s, as well as their land planes through Shannon in the '40s, were known as Clippers; their most famous flying boat was called the *Yankee Clipper* ; Pan Am jetliners were all christened

Clippers afterwards. The extension of that name to a danceband was novel.

Craig entered the picture in '52. He was secretary of the cricket club and had links with the rugby club. A gifted sportsman in his day, he played cricket for Ireland and soccer for Strabane. Craig became friendly with Terry Logue, the Clippers' sax and clarinet player. Craig offered to double their money for appearances. In December '52, the band got an important break when booked to perform at a grand masquerade ball in the Guildhall, Derry. Tickets for the event gave notice that their 'famous' Jolson act would be featured. The admission was five shillings.

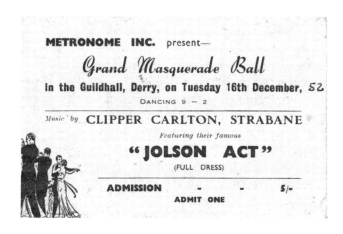

This was the first deviation from straight musical performance. In '53, Craig was working on what looked like becoming a successful formula. The dates were more regular — and the music stands would soon be pushed aside. Their popularity began to increase — and so did the fees. The line-up: Hugo Quinn, trumpet; Hughie Tourish, piano; Terry Logue, sax and clarinet; Mickey O'Hanlon, drums; Art O'Hagan, vocals and double bass, and his brother Fergus, M.C. and vocals. Victor Fleming joined the band in '54. He played trombone and piano and, significantly, arranged the music. That year, the band stood up and stayed on their feet.

"Previously, people danced around them. People paid no attention to the band. The lads didn't like it, and neither did I. So the boys decided to create a bit of excitement," says Craig. "The thing worked. They took it from there. They stood up completely. Chairs were provided, but they very rarely sat down. There was no such thing as a showband until we started it. We got the suits about '54. Every other band used to sit down. They looked like penguins in tuxedos. That didn't suit the image of our band. Moving around the stage with dinner jackets on didn't seem right somehow. Smart suits would be better. We got off-white and light grey suits. Then we graduated to blazers for a while. Sure, we had great ideas altogether."

Hugo Quinn's singing voice was once so bad he wasn't allowed into the local choir. In '63, he recalled: "We gave people something to watch as well as to listen to. Musical abilities were not so good at the beginning so we had to give them something different. We were full of the innocence of youth. One way of letting off steam was to get up on a stand and act the mickey. That's what we did in those early days. In some places we were nearly put off the stage. But, for the most part, it went down very well because people liked to watch other people enjoying themselves. People liked it because it was different and excited them. Their reaction surprised us."

Don Shearer joined the band as lead singer in '56. For two years now, Craig was thinking big... very big. When we brought Fergie in, we got twenty-five pounds for playing at a dance in Omagh. That fee was set. But I asked for an extra five pounds on account of bringing in the extra man. The dancehall promoter said, 'no way.' The date was fixed at twenty-five pounds. He wasn't going to give us thirty pounds. It turned out to be an expensive five pounds because we never played for him afterwards. On the following year, I told Hugo that I wanted to bump it up to a hundred pounds for Sundays and fifty for week nights. Hugo said, 'that's fine, if you can get it.' In 1955, I looked for percentages.

"We never sought a guarantee beyond the 50/50. We didn't think it was fair. We played the dance and took our 50/50 and that was that. We thought that we were doing fair enough. We were playing for promoters who were very good to us. I remember one night going to Tooreen to play a dance for Fr. Horan. There was a snowstorm. We had 70 people. It was just a freak thing. We played the dance and took our 50/50. It was just the way things worked out. You won some. You lost some. But mostly we won.'

The money was rolling in. By '54, the Clippers bought a new wagon. A year later, they could afford to order a custom-built bus. It was made by O'Dohertys, a coach-building firm in Strabane. Clippermania was cleverly cultivated by the distribution of thousands of pictures of the band and of individual members. These were autographed and handed out at dances. In Cork, Prendergast took a keen interest in the growth of the Clippers — as he did in the development of other bands.

Craig once showed him a copy of *The Chicago Tribune* that featured a news item written about them during an American tour. "I'll take it away, Vic, and do something with it," promised Prendergast. In fact, he cut out the article and had it reproduced on thousands of leaflets distributed nationwide. The Clippers were the only musicians in Ireland to have their own stamps. Four members of the band were depicted in a fairly typical moment of foolery for the camera. Hundreds of stamps were printed and stuck on official Clipper envelopes as an advertising gimmick. Clipper postcards were also available.

The band worked five nights a week. They took Monday and Tuesday off, left home on Wednesday, and returned to Strabane in the early hours of Monday. Maxie Muldoon — later to manage the Jetland ballroom in Limerick for the Reynolds' chain — was appointed road manager in '58. His function was primarily to take care of business on the circuit, collect the percentages and pay the hotel bills. "Dancehalls made us big by getting a relief band," says Craig. "We paid them ourselves. We did a three hour show. Whatever part of the country we were in, somebody got us a relief band and we paid them. That came out of our 50%. We didn't ask the promoter to pay it."

The Clippers had a regular booking at the Borderland Ballroom in Muff where they played to a crowd of 2,000. It was a fixed date on Patrick's Night and Stephen's Night. Craig's business approach was based on remaining loyal to a coterie of proprietors such as Jim Reynolds in Longford, Prendergast in Cork, Bill Kenny in Waterford and Tommy Nevin in Galway.

"If I established a good relationship with a promoter, then I stuck to him and stayed loyal," he explains. "Cork was just out of this world for us. There's no doubt about it. *Juke Box Saturday Night* ...och, the Cork people will remember that alright."

The Clippers were a huge draw south of the border, especially in Dublin, Galway, Waterford , Cork and Limerick. Up north, the band once caused such scenes of crowd mayhem at the Floral Hall in Belfast that they were banned by the City Council as being "too popular".

The Clippers took flight to Britain and the U.S. during Lent. The first British tour was in '55. Bill Fuller gave them dates at the Buffalo in Camden Town, as well as bookings in Coventry, Birmingham and Manchester. Three years later, Uncle Sam beckoned. The '58 American tour, organised by promoter Harry McGurk, opened at St. Nicholas' arena in New York, a major boxing venue of the '50s. It was billed as a 'huge' Irish night.

Immigrants flew in from Toronto, Cleveland, Chicago and Boston. The turnout — 6,300 — was astonishing. Craig relishes the memory of the first time that they took a large bite from the Big Apple: "I'll never forget it as long as I live. To hear the cheers of the crowd was like being at Wembley for the Cup final. There were mounted policemen patrolling outside, and big cops swinging truncheons. It was a fantastic night. We were treated like stars. They loved the Clippers." Half way through the dance, promoter McGurk was grinning like a Cheshire cat. He took the Irish band manager aside and said: "Vic, I don't give a damn how the rest of the tour goes. We have the 'ex's!" The Clippers had the time of their lives in New York. McGurk put them up at the flash Plymouth Hotel. He even made arrangements for them to dine every day in a restaurant owned by a former chef to President Eisenhower.

The Clippers also played Chicago and Boston. Their last performance took place before 2,000 people on a Sunday night in Queens, New York. Craig recalls: "Everybody knew that we were going home next day. I was with a crowd of Donegal people. It came to the last dance of the night. Don Shearer sang *Danny Boy*. Everybody started to cry. I couldn't believe it... just like a wake."

They subsequently toured America to play in Fuller's ball-rooms. During a further visit in March, 1959, *The Chicago Tribune's* Steve Schickel became a fan of the Clippers when he saw them in action at an Irish dance in The Keymen's Club ballroom. He was among a crowd of 1,500 knocked out by their performance. The dancers were treated to dixieland, jazz, rock'n'roll, waltzes, polkas and fox trots. "The Clipper Carltons are about the best showband your reporter has ever heard in his more than ten years of covering amusement events," wrote Schickel in his column on March 18th, 1959. "These guys sang like it was their main effort in life. They played all the instruments so well you couldn't possibly tell which instrument was their primary function. On top of all this, the guys paired up in twos, threes and fours to sing duets, trios and quartets. They even went so far as to imitate the Four Aces, Four Lads, Four Freshmen, the Everly Bros, Elvis Presley and Louis Armstrong. Their imitations were strictly top notch. Here's a tip to some enterprising entrepreneur. This group is good enough to put on the Steve Allen show and then follow up with a tour of the better theatres and clubs across the country with a possible booking in Las Vegas." Fuller got them an audition in Las Vegas in later years, but it didn't lead to any contracts.

At home, the Clippers' ability to generate hysteria and attract huge crowds was legendary. They inspired many youngsters to earn a living in the music business. Jackie Flavelle — who played bass with the Glover and Quigley bands, and now music and information producer with Downtown Radio, Belfast — first saw them perform at the Floral Hall, at the age of sixteen in the mid-'50s. Flavelle, who, like many others, played then in skiffle groups, was captivated. "It was like trying to get in to see superstars," he recalls. "The place was absolutely stuffed with people. The Clippers had it all."

Household names in Ireland today have vivid memories of the excitement generated by them in '54/'55. Broadcaster Gay Byrne went dancing with pals to the Clippers during these years at The Hanger Ballroom while on summer holidays to Salthill, Galway. "You had to queue half the day to get in," he says. "They would be packed for three or four nights running, absolutely crammed packed tight. The Clippers were all the go. I remember being in the place and you couldn't move. They were huge in the mid fifties. They were doing their *Juke Box Saturday Night* and their imitations and impersonations. These were wildly exciting times. I didn't have much time for showbands, quite frankly. I had been into jazz since I was fourteen or fifteen. I liked the Clippers because they played some jazz and were good brass players. The Clippers, at that time, meant precisely the same thing as U2 means to the present generation. They were just as novel and different, except they didn't write original material. They had a colossal following."

In 1960, the Clippers were still the most popular band on the circuit — even though the Royal had come on strong.

They were big enough to draw an average crowd of 2,000 at the top price of 7/6 (37.5p) per head to Redbarn, Youghal, on any good Sunday night. That generated £750 of which the Clippers, on 50%, took £375 (**£4,531.85** in '90). Based on a figure of 7,000 dancers a week at an average admission of 6/-, would have given the Clippers an estimated £1,050 a week (**£12,689.17** in '90 or **£634,458.40** per annum).

On October 1st, '60, word of their next American tour reached the Tempo column of the Evening Herald. The trip would take in New York, Chicago, Cleveland, Philadelphia, Boston and Toronto. In an open letter to Hugo Quinn, written tongue-in-cheek, columnist Frank Hall wished them luck abroad.

"You know what I think about showbands. Till my dying day I will always hold you and the rest of your crew totally responsible for what has happened in the last few years. All sorts of jokers are trying to revive all your old tricks. Give my regards to Hugh Tourish and the boys and tell them not to get into conversation with strangers. There are some terrible characters over there, I do hear."

When the Clippers returned from the U.S. they went on a major British tour in December. They played in Manchester, Nottingham, Coventry, Birmingham, Brighton and Leeds. A highlight of the last hours of '63 was their appearance at the Metropole Ballroom in Dublin for the Variety Club of Ireland. It was an 'International Pantomime Dance' to help raise funds for blind and underprivileged children.

But the bubble burst for the Clipper Carlton in '63/'64. By then, the showband business was in boom — due primarily to the enormous popularity of the Royal. Other top northern show-band attractions were the Freshmen and Platters (later Platter-men). The Clippers were now older than Bowyer, the young idol. The 'show' component that carried them safely through the '50s was about to be overtaken by other bands' emphasis on image and gimmickry. But few, if any, ever really matched the Clippers' 'showband' criteria.

The break-up in '63/'64 took Craig by surprise. "It was just sprung on me. It was all over. Of course, I was disappointed." He stayed away from the dancing business for two years before taking on the management in '65 of the Pallidrome, Strabane. Craig remained in the day job, as always. "I once did a lot of heart-searching about leaving the post office during the early days with the Clippers," he says. "It was lucky that I didn't." Hugo Quinn and the two O'Hagan brothers carried on with the Clippers while other members formed a new showband, the Santa Fe: included in the ranks were Mickey O'Hanlon, Victor Fleming, Don Shearer, George Galway, a brother of the famous James, and noted electric guitar player Barney Skillen.

Maurice Cassidy took over management of the Santa Fe at Easter, '64. He was introduced to the new band by Maxie Muldoon through a mutual friend, Charlie McBrien, who managed the Ohio at the time and later managed the Mighty Avons.

In 1966, the Clippers reformed. "The Santa Fe were on the road doing moderate business," Cassidy recalls. "I suggested that it might be a good idea for them to get back together again as the Clipper Carlton. Time had elapsed since the break-up and neither the old Clipper nor the Santa Fe was as successful as previously."

The Clippers returned to the road in the second half of the '60s.There was still money to be made.They rekindled some of the fire of the '50s but it was short lived. They lasted for nearly three years before collapsing amid tensions in the band. They broke up again in '69. A year later, Cassidy was running the Stardust Club in Derry, which featured dances and discos. He later returned to band management with Tony Kenny and the Sands. He now has extensive financial interests in the entertainment industry. He represents Phil Coulter, Colm Wilkinson, Maura O'Connell and Bibi Baskin. He is a director of Capital Radio with Jim Aiken. They are partners also in the HMV music stores in Dublin. A mutual friend once said of the duo: "They're both shrewd northerners, slightly suspicious of Dublin where talk is cheap and bullshit is plenty."

As Cassidy went on to manage other bands in the '70s, the Clippers packed away their instruments. But the showband forerunners came out of retirement and made a final return to the dancehalls on a wave of nostalgia in May, '85. It ended abruptly in October, '87 following the death of Hugo Quinn. They intended to do a summer season in '85, but continued for two years. They were given a one-hour RTE TV special in January '86 which gave the veterans a late boost. The comeback re- created some of the magic of the past with a new show to replace *Juke Box Saturday Night*. It was called *There's No Business Like Showbusiness*.

All the familiar mimicry was brought back... Chaplin, Presley, Laurel and Hardy.

There were new gestures to the '80s. Hugo Quinn did a send-up of Boy George. When they returned to play in Belfast, it was not to the Floral Hall, the Boom Boom Room or the Orpheus, but rather to the Thrupenny Bit at Balmoral. The only new face was Terry Duffy, who replaced trombonist and musical arranger Victor Fleming. The band adapted a new programme for the '80s. Quinn told the Belfast Telegraph: "In our heyday, one of our specialities was Sinatra's *Nancy With The Laughing Face*. Now we're playing his *New York, New York*, which is back in the charts. Most of us are in our fifties, a couple are 62 and 64. But we're enjoying ourselves. We never run out of puff."

The revival began when the Clippers were honoured in '85, at a civic reception in Lifford. They were persuaded to go on stage and do a few numbers... 'for old times' sake'. It went down so well the band agreed to do a short tour. "It was an incredible night and one we shall never forget," said Quinn. "We thought we were forgotten. But the people let us know in no uncertain terms this was not the case. We sang a few numbers and acted the cod a bit and, from that, came the reformation of the Clipper Carlton. For us it is all down to entertainment and that never changes. There are too many long faces on the stage nowadays. We are enjoying it more now than we ever did because we don't feel the pressure of competition on us anymore. The big changes are in the places we play and all the extra gear we have to carry. There are practically no ballrooms left. The conditions we work under are way ahead of what we were used to. We only play two hours a night, instead of five or six, and all this new PA makes you sound great.

"When we started off we had two twelve-inch speakers, a fifteen- watt amplifier, one mike and, in some places, a twelve-volt battery because there was no electricity. Our crowd is the over 35s, but the youngsters are getting interested. We still put on a good show, you see. They like that in between the whirls round the floor — just like the old days. People come up to us after a show and thank us for coming back on the road. It should be us thanking them for being there and allowing us to entertain them again. This is a pleasure we never dreamed of having. Never."

Joe McCadden, their last manager, got a glimpse of the once devastating appeal of the showmen. As a Dublin schoolboy, McCadden had been an avid admirer of the Clippers. He grew up in North Great Georges Street near Barry's Hotel Ballroom and collected showband pictures as a hobby. The collection mushroomed to over 2,000. Two days after completing the Leaving Certificate in '70, he was introduced to Mick Clerkin and Jimmy Magee by a friend, Eddie Masterson. Clerkin, Magee and Dermot Hegarty had just formed Release Records. McCadden worked with them in summer '70. He was bitten by the bug, went on to Ritz Records and managed bands since '73.

The prospect of managing the revived Clipper Carlton was a dream-come- true for the former showband fan. Sadly, the revival ended with the death of Quinn. It closed the book on the Clipper Carlton forever. "When Hugo died, it was the end for me," says McCadden. "He was the original one who started the band off. You could call him an anchorman. I couldn't see it continuing successfully without Hugo. He was the main man. He was missing."

The Clippers trend-setting brand of glam pop in the '50s was years ahead of its time. The modern day equivalent can be found in the entertainment lounges of Las Vegas. Under different circumstances, the Clippers would have been moulded for cabaret, entertaining a sit-down audience. The next logical step would have been to present an entire show, rather than just playing for dancers. But cabaret was unheard of in the '50s and early '60s. The dancehall was the only platform to reach an audience.

"I believe that they had international potential way back in the '50s," says Cassidy. "But they were never proximate to a world stage. They toured substantially in Ireland and operated in an Irish context. They were a rare and wonderfully entertaining item. The emphasis is on the word *rare* because all sorts of things are manufactured in this business now. At that time, it was an accidental circumstance. It was rare that an accidental circumstance could turn out that sort of talent. They were like the Beatles in their time. They fell together by accident. It wasn't invented by the industry.

"What goes on today, fortunately or unfortunately, has to do with selling records. It's a studio business. It doesn't necessarily have a lot to do with entertainment on stage. It has to do with the manufacture of recording content, geared towards tapping into an audience susceptibility."

Recording was alien to the Clipper Carlton. They concentrated on live performances that satisfied their desire for recognition and good earnings. "Today, you can't do anything worthwhile unless you have recording success," remarks Cassidy. "The entertainment content is largely irrelevant. The confidence did not exist for people like the Clippers to write and be successful. The industry wasn't bred on that basis. It was bred on a copycat scheme. Other people were being looked up to as the inventors. The entertainment equivalent today would be the likes of Christy Moore who, while being a singer, is primarily an entertainer."

There are no monuments to the Clippers. Just memories. During a British tour on their final comeback in the '80s, McCadden and Hugo Quinn ended up one night in an Indian restaurant in Birmingham. McCadden, who later managed the Fureys, wanted to know all about the old days. Were the Clipper Carlton really that big in the '50s? Was the money that good? Quinn gave him a rude awakening. "He told me they made so much money that, on a day off, they could afford to drive from Strabane to Dublin airport, take a flight to Paris, have a night out and fly back the following day. And that was a time when many people in Ireland didn't even have cars..."

First Royal Flushes

London, February 13th, 1961.

Mr Showman leans across the desk in his small office on the top floor of Mecca's headquarters in Southwark, England, and interrupts T.J. Byrne: "Not interested." He shakes his head as the manager of the Royal Showband tries to negotiate a date at the Hammersmith Palais on St. Patrick's night. "I've already booked the greatest band in the world. What do I want any other band for?" Byrne was fortunate to secure this meeting with Eric Morley, and wasn't giving up easily. A two-week British tour with dates in Manchester, Birmingham, Nottingham and London fell through following a last minute disagreement between the band and an Irish promoter. So, Byrne flew to London and mustered up the courage to approach the Mecca chain.

The Royal had played Irish ballrooms in Britain since turning professional in 1959. The band was popular in venues like the Garryowen beside the Hammersmith Palais, the Gresham in Holloway road and the Galtimore in Cricklewood. In 1960, they began annual tours of the United States during Lent when ballrooms at home were closed. Bill Fuller organised dates in his chain of ballrooms in cities with big Irish immigrant populations like New York, Boston and Chicago. They joined a planeload of Irish emigrants that took fifteen hours to reach New York on the first trip.

Mecca could give them a bigger platform in Britain. Morley's office is modestly furnished. It has big steel ashtrays, a battered television and an ancient electric fan. The only piece of modern equipment is a telephone. The simplicity belies the importance of the man behind the desk. Morley is the king of the ballrooms, and Byrne knows it. A showman, promoter and businessman with the Midas touch. A collector of bands, he had three hundred in his stable in 1969. A fast-riser in Mecca's nationwide chain of ballrooms with his sights set on the managing director's chair. He snaps: "Joe Loss is already booked to play. I don't need anybody else." Of course he didn't. Loss, the man who got Britain in the mood to dance, was the "Barnum of the big band world". He formed his first orchestra three decades earlier for the Astoria Ballroom, Charing Cross Road, London, and became the greatest bandleader in Britain. Loss would set toes tapping for another thirty years from the Hammersmith Palais to Buckingham Palace. The Royal were not in his league.

Byrne sweetens the bait. "Okay, so what about the greatest band in the world playing with the greatest band in Ireland on St. Patrick's night in London?" A smile creases Morley's face for the first time. "Now that's different; that's something to consider. Let's talk." They agree terms on a two-band session. It's a great ticket: big band leader Loss and an Irish showband sensation on St. Patrick's night at the biggest ballroom in Britain. The crowd-pulling potential is enormous. Byrne left Morley's office floating on a cloud, convinced that an appearance by the Royal at the Palais could pave the way for a future tour of the Mecca circuit.

St. Patrick's night at the Palais surpassed all expectations. Six thousand people confirmed Byrne's confidence in a double bill. The Royal ignited the Palais, and the big beat sound of the Loss orchestra kept thousands of feet dancing from the first notes of their signature tune, Glenn Miller's *In The Mood*. The Irish came in droves from all over London. Doors were closed. Hundreds more thronged the street outside, pushing and shoving to get in. The London Fire Brigade was called and firemen had to turn their hoses on the crowds. Loss was impressed too: he took a personal interest in the Irish showband and later introduced them to the EMI record company in London. The showman, whose band was voted Britain's No. 1 in '65, made over one thousand recordings for EMI. His influence helped to open up new opportunities for the Royal.

When Byrne returned later to Mecca headquarters, he expected to be talking to the converted. Not so. "That was a tremendous night," said Morley; "but it proves absolutely nothing." Then Byrne hit him with phase two of the game plan. "Give me a tour. We'll play Birmingham, Coventry, London and Manchester on any week. Just give me any week in about three months' time. I'll show you what we can do." Mr Showman replied: "Okay, you're on." Then, Byrne said: "One thing though, your normal dancing here is 2/- or 2/6. You'll have to charge 10/-." Morley shook his head. "Oh no," he said, "we couldn't do that." Then, he added in the same breath: "we might consider going to 7/6." They were two of a kind. They shared a nose for talent, a flair for publicity and, most significantly, a gut feeling for what the dancers wanted. Neither was afraid to charge for the privilege of giving it to them. Byrne did for Irish showbands what Morley had done for the beauty queen business: he taught them to reach for the stars.

The Morley connection made '60 and '61 pivotal years in the history of the Royal Showband. The future head of the Mecca chain understood ballroom entertainment better than most. He devoted his life to showbusiness from an early age. The former army bandboy became one of the wealthiest men in Britain by turning a '40s pin-up gimmick into an annual event watched by thirty million people — Miss World.

He was responsible for Come Dancing, the incredibly popular regional ballroom dancing competition series. It started in '49 and broke records as the longest running TV programme in the world. Morley's great achievement was to popularise ballroom dancing.

Morley recognised a marketable dancehall product in the exciting showmen from Ireland. That's why he agreed to give them a shot at the Mecca circuit. Morley's faith in the Royal paid rich dividends. "We played Coventry first," Byrne recalls, "and it was choc-a-bloc. You couldn't get into the Locarno in Birmingham; we closed the doors at the Ritz in Manchester and packed them in at the Hammersmith Palais." The Royal were a big hit at the Ritz. They played there on a Friday night when the normal attendance was between 600 and 700. The turnout for the Royal was 2,400. Towards the end of what became a record-breaking tour, the Royal were booked for a three- hour stint at the Liverpool Empire Theatre. It was a gamble because the support act was unknown.

"There's a group up there with a horrible bloody name — the Beatles," said Morley. "Don't worry. They'll draw the crowd to hear your band." He was wrong. The attendance did not live up to expectations. In those days, the Beatles were raw beginners whose main repertoire was other people's material. They opened with Bruce Chanel's *Hey Baby* — number one in the charts — and followed with *Twist and Shout*. The Waterford headliners acknowledged the enthusiasm of four Liverpool kids, but had no idea that it was the start of something revolutionary. Groups hadn't caught on yet. The emphasis was still on big solo acts: Elvis Presley, Cliff Richard, Billy Fury and Marty Wilde.

"We could see that they were talented," says Brendan Bowyer. "But we couldn't see where the vehicle was going to come from so that they would be successful." It wasn't one of the Beatles better nights. Afterwards, Paul McCartney ate a bag of chips in the car park of the Liverpool Empire and gazed admiringly at the Mercedes wagon that belonged to the star attraction. The Beatles had scarcely merited space on the publicity posters. The headline act was in giant lettering.

Bowyer caught McCartney, a kid with boyish good looks and infectious smile inspecting their Mercedes wagon. He declined the offer of a chip, put a reassuring hand on McCartney's shoulder and advised that if the Beatles stuck together, they could do well. It seemed the most natural thing in the world for Bowyer to give the Beatle some encouragement. After all, it wasn't so long ago since the Royal were in the same position themselves: a bunch of mates hustling for dates around Waterford, awestruck at the popularity of bands like The Clipper Carlton. Byrne puts it neatly into perspective: "We walked out the door that night to become the biggest thing in Ireland. The Beatles walked out to become the biggest thing in the world."

1961 was the year of the Royal Showband in Britain... a fact officially recognised when they were given the Carl Alan Award as the 'most outstanding modern dance band attraction' of the year. The recognition was based on their staggering box office achievements with Mecca. The award was presented to the Royal at a glittering Oscars- style ceremony at the Lyceum Ballroom, the Strand, London, on February 5th, '62. It was broadcast on BBC Television. The Royal joined a host of stars for rehearsals throughout the day before the TV cameras. Other awards for their contribution to entertainment went to Acker Bilk, Billy Fury and Adam Faith. As the Royal arrived at the Lyceum, they were handed a telegram from Strabane. It read: "Congratulations. We'll be watching. Vic and the Clippers."

Following a victory tour in Britain, the Royal returned home to Waterford as all-conquering heroes, honoured with a civic reception hosted by the Mayor and members of the Corporation. The prestigious award gave them status in the British entertainment world and confirmed their ranking as the number one Irish showband. It provided a major psychological uplift. The Mecca link was crucial to this success. The Royal became the first band to record in '62, and Tom Dunphy the first showband singer to record a single, *Come Down The Mountain Katie Daly*, for EMI. They broke into the Irish Top Ten with Presley's *Kiss Me Quick*, which shot to number one in '63.

The Royal resumed a money-spinning blitz on the ballrooms at home following the Mecca triumph, while the Beatles, their little known support act in Liverpool, became international superstars. Bowyer's acquaintance with the Liverpudlians would be renewed in Dublin on Thursday November 7, '63 — under very different circumstances. The Beatles already had a No. 1 hit in Ireland that summer with *From Me To You* and, in the fall, *She Loves You* went to No. 2 and stayed in the charts for 19 weeks. Bowyer met the Beatles at the Intercontinental Hotel where a reception was held for the distinguished visitors. McCartney's palate had become more sophisticated; not a chip in sight. "Everybody was having drinks and eating hors d'oeuvres," says Bowyer. "I said hello, how are you? Do you remember us?"

The Royal were undisputed kings of the Irish ballrooms. The band had come a long way since their embryonic days when, as youngsters, they played with the Harry Boland accordian band in halls around Waterford. Nobody could have predicted their meteoric rise. There was no turning back. The story began in '55/'56. Michael Coppinger, still attending the De La Salle school, played accordian part-time with the Sliamh Rua Ceili Band. He was persuaded by Boland to join him on some free nights. A convenient date was fixed for the fisherman's hall in Dunmore East. It paid a pound each. Coppinger convinced

Boland to take on a drummer, his friend Charlie Matthews, who lived around the corner from him in Ferrybank. Another pal, Jim Conlon from Sallypark, played the guitar and frequently came to Coppinger's house for "rehearsals." He was persuaded to join the Boland Band. And so was Jerry Cullen, the pianist, who also lived in Ferrybank.

Next came Tom Dunphy. "At the time, the skiffle stuff, Lonnie Donegan, was very popular," says Coppinger. "We said to Harry that we wanted somebody in who could sing. Tom's father had a big old double bass that he once played with Mick Del. We knew that Tom had a good singing voice and could get a double bass. That was the whole thing for a skiffle group. It was basically rhythm, bass, double bass, guitar and a washboard. Charlie used to play the washboard." The band experimented with pop and modern material, including songs in the charts...Dunphy sang *The Rock Island Line*, a hit skiffle number.

The kids in the Harry Boland Band went to see the Clippers perform at the Olympia Ballroom, Parnell Street, to pick up tips. The Olympia was Waterford's dancing mecca, attracting dancers from the city and county, many of whom travelled miles on bicycles in search of romance. It was where Coppinger and his fellow musicians came into contact at Easter, Christmas, Whit and New Year's Eve with the big bands: the Clippers, Mick Delahunty, Maurice Mulcahy and Gay McIntyre. The Clippers were the top draw: people went to dance but stood instead near the stage and watched the show. The Olympia was a magnet for top British bands: Joe Loss, the Dutch Swing College Band, Sid Phillips and Humphrey Lyttelton. Queues stretched back to Winston's Corner. On Tuesday night 'hops', the Olympia gave a platform to local bands: Frankie King, Paddy Power, Sadie Byrnes, Busty Griffin and Johnny Drohan.

Easter Sunday night and St. Stephen's night. Dances cost 6/6, with New Year's Eve dances being the highlight of the dancing calendar. It wasn't unusual for people to dance their way outside into Parnell Street, and join in a march with the Erin's Hope Fife and Drum Band around town as the minutes ticked away to midnight. The Olympia ranked nationally as a top dancing venue alongside the Crystal, Dublin; Redbarn, Youghal; the Arcadia, Cork; and the Hanger, Galway. Coppinger was impressed that the Clippers had brass: trumpet, trombone and sax. He stood in awe too at the big beat sound of the Strabane showmen. He wanted to entertain like them but, like the youngsters in the Boland band, felt restricted. The stage was getting too crowded: others wanted out as well. The end of the road was in sight.

Meantime, Brendan Bowyer had been playing trombone with another local band, the Rhythm Kings. He was also a keen student of the Clippers. "Brendan moved over to us," recalls Coppinger. "We knew that the Boland Band was breaking up anyway and that the lads wanted to go their own way. We decided to start our own band. But, before we finished with Harry, we approached Brendan and asked him if he would be interested. He said he was. We had another date to play in Waterford." The Boland band broke up in August, '57. The pieces were immediately picked up by Coppinger, Matthews, Cullen, Conlon and Dunphy. Bowyer, a trombonist, would later join the others to form the Royal Showband.

There was no hint that Bowyer — a tall, awkward, shy teenager — would become one of the great symbols of the '60s generation. He played trombone, and didn't raise his voice. On stage, he was self- conscious and lacked confidence. Bowyer was steeped in a family musical tradition. He was the eldest of his family; next came Olive, six years younger, then Patricia and Alison. "The fact that he was much older meant that we really looked up to him, both physically and in terms of our admiration," says Olive. "We really thought he was something special."

Their parents — Stanley, Yorkshire born, and Maura, a local woman — met through music. He taught piano, violin and voice at Bow Street in Waterford. She took singing lessons and became recognised as a fine metso soprano. They fell in love. Stanley Bowyer had moved to Ireland with his parents who ran the Bowyer Westwood operatic touring company. It was popular in theatres around the country such as the Coliseum, Limerick. Stanley liked Ireland. Later on, he decided to stay on after his father died at Omagh in '35. While working as an organist at the Cathedral in Ennis, he converted to Catholicism from the Methodist Church. He was formally received into the Catholic Church at Killarney Cathedral. He then went to work in Waterford where he met Maura Daniels from Dunmore East. They were married in Dublin on January 15th, 1938. Brendan was born on October 12th, 1938.

His first home was at William Street in Waterford. The Bowyers and their young son moved to Limerick and lived at Clareview Terrace near the Redemptorist Church where Stanley was organist. He again taught music, and also played the famous Compton organ at the Savoy Theatre, Limerick. Two of the three daughters were born in Limerick, Olive and Patricia. At the age of eight, Brendan was a boy soprano in the choir at Mount St. Alphonsus, the Redemptorist Church.

The Bowyers returned to Waterford in 1949 and bought a pub in Baileys New Street, the Steamship Bar. They lived overhead. A third daughter, Alison, was born. Stanley continued to teach and was closely involved with choirs in local schools, particularly De La Salle, Waterpark and the Sacred Heart of Mary Convent. He was organist and choirmaster — first at the Dominican Church and then at the Cathedral. Brendan joined the choir at the Dominicans, but his voice had broken by the time Stanley went to the Cathedral. Music teachers were not well paid, so the pub supplemented the household income. Located near the quay, it got a spin-off from trade through Waterford port and became a favourite haunt of dockers and ships' crews. The Bowyers were hospitable and threw memorable parties: sing-songs were invariably led by Maura, accompanied by Stanley on piano.

Brendan attended primary school at St. Declans CBS, and then secondary school at Waterpark. It was a middle-class background.As a father, Stanley was strict but affectionate. When any of the children misbehaved, they were referred to him. Brendan once fell through a neighbours glass roof while trying to gain entry to his house through an upstairs window. His father made him repay the full cost of the roof. It took him a year. Brendan was closest to his mother. "He really idolised her," says Olive. "And she idolised him. It was mutual. She did so much for him in terms of giving him confidence to do things that he wanted to do while my father would have been a lot more negative."

In his teens during the early '50s, Brendan leaned more towards sport than music. The playing field was his first love — not the stage. He played rugby, cricket, tennis and table tennis. He once mitched school to compete in the Munster final of the table tennis championships. There was consternation when he failed to return home after class. He finally turned up clutching a large cup, and announced that he was the new Munster Champion. The victory defused his father's rage. On the rugby field, he played in the back row. He got a cricket bat once for Christmas and liked to organise play on the beach in Dunmore East. Music was not a priority. "It was only with the greatest persuasion that he would practice," said his mother in '64. "You'd find him at the piano picking out the notes with a pained expression on his face and a pair of rugby boots over his shoulder." She often wondered how successful he'd have been as a rugby player if he stayed in an ordinary job. Bro. O'Donovan, one of his teachers at Waterpark College, took Mrs. Bowyer aside later on and said: "If I ever saw a potential cap for Ireland, Brendan is it. What a shame to lose him off the rugby field."

Sport dominated the lives of Bowyer and his teenage friends. Television did not exist. Youngsters competed in games on the playing pitches, and also on the streets. Soccer, hurling and cricket were popular. The kids' heroes were either on the silver screen or on the sports field. The Bowyer charisma was evident as a teenager. "People used to flock around him," recalls Olive. "In his own shy way, he attracted a lot of attention. He used to organise cricket teams of total strangers on the beach."

Young Bowyer was pushed towards classical music by his father, but rebelled. He was a "huge" fan of Elvis Presley. His house was full of Presley records, and his sisters became fans too. Favourite songs were *Heartbreak Hotel*, *Baby I Don't Care* and *Jailhouse Rock*. "When I was in the late stages of school, Elvis was like the U2 of that time," he recalls. "My father wanted me to be a classical musician, but I wouldn't have made it. I didn't have it. I learned all these things on the piano, and I was geared along that way mentally. But Elvis had the biggest effect on me. I started singing his stuff." At the same time, Bowyer began to follow the top touring bands that visited Waterford. Although turned on primarily by Presley's rock'n'roll, he studied the excitement generated by the Clippers at the Olympia, only ten minutes walk from his home. He began to think about the stage.

"I think Brendan first became interested in modern music when he sang a pop song at a friend's birthday party," says his mother. "The clap he got made him feel there was something to his own voice after all. Then, he was asked to join a newly-formed quartet. Their first date was at the old Arundel ballroom. I was passing by when I heard this awful noise coming out, so I thought I'd pop in and have a look. I saw this group on stage playing like mad with Brendan in the middle on the washboard. His cheeks were flushed with excitement. For the first time, I felt sure that his life was going to be music."

Bowyer, naturally a shy person, was never seen to practice before mirrors at home. His sisters were astounded when they saw him perform on stage. At fifteen, Olive watched her brother and the Royal for the first time at the Olympia.

"I remember being totally amazed. That's my brother! I was absolutely agog because he wasn't like that at home. The Olympia was jammed. You couldn't move on the floor. We stood up on the seats at the side."

Waterford of the '50s was a fairly bleak place. Working class boys fled in their droves. The established businessmen mapped out careers for their sons. It was a class ridden city like other small Irish cities. Emigrants returned on holiday to sunny days in Tramore and late-night drinking in Dooleys Hotel. The work ethic was important in the Bowyer household: during school holidays, Brendan worked part-time behind the bar at the Hotel Majestic in Tramore to earn pocket money. As a youth, he was clumsy — the tinkle of breaking glass became a familiar sound in the hotel. When he quit to take up a better paying holiday job at the Waterford Glass factory, the hotel manager remarked: "God help the glass." Bowyer nursed an ambition to be on the stage some day. His parents wanted to see him settled in a steady job, probably the bank. Apart from rock'n'roll, he wasn't sure

(photo: Sunday World)

what he wanted. Music and sport were his big interests. He wasn't academically-minded. He had no definite career plan. The Leaving Certificate was a passport to almost any white-collar job, and young Bowyer went to work at the Paper Mills. With his background, he landed an office job, rather than work on the factory floor.

"The whole thing happened accidentally," says Bowyer. "My parents couldn't afford to send me to college. We didn't have a university in Waterford. If there was one, they probably could have scraped it. But having to send somebody to Cork or Dublin would have been a different story. I don't know if I would have stayed on in the Paper Mills. I don't think so. In hindsight, I wouldn't have changed what happened for the world."Young Bowyer first met Dunphy at the Paper Mills where they both worked as clerks in the sales office. The pair were efficient employees, but music was their first love. Dunphy had played in the Boland band. Then, he and his fellow musicians decided to form their own outfit, the Royal.

Coppinger, the leader, asked Bowyer to join them as trombonist. They launched the Royal, as semi-professionals, on September 22nd, 1957. "We decided to incorporate 'showband' into the name," says Coppinger. "We thought of the names of cinemas in town: the Regina, the Regal. Then, there was the Theatre Royal...that's probably how we thought of the name." The boys wanted to base their concept on the Clippers. So, that meant brass, first and foremost. Coppinger played sax. Bowyer was the trombonist. Eddie Sullivan joined as trumpeter six months later.

The line-up was complete. The band was unknown, and found it easier to get work outside the city in places like Mooncoin and Portlaw. They couldn't afford to spend as much as bigger bands on advertising and publicity. They depended largely on word of mouth. The Royal actually started off with music stands on stage, but abandoned them to do the chart toppers.The first big local break came when Coppinger negotiated a date at the Olympia, Parnell Street, on St. Patrick's night, 1958 — one of the best dances of the year. It was unheard of for a local band to play on big nights; top bands were brought down from Dublin or the North. Even more surprising was the fact that band leader Coppinger, who took care of business in those early days, managed to secure a 60/40 percentage of the door takings. He got the idea from Maxie Muldoon, road manager of the Clippers whom, he knew, laid down the same terms. "I just copied him and it worked." The other big Waterford ballroom, the Arundel, was enjoying the best business. The Olympia wasn't doing well until Bill Kenny took it over. The Royal, at the Olympia, were competing against a two-band session at the Arundel on Patrick's night...Joseph Locke, the main attraction, supported by a popular Dublin band. The Arundel charged 6/3; the Olympia 3/9.

It was impossible to predict how things would go. Although the Royal were building up a local following, Locke's popularity was certain to draw big crowds from all over Waterford and Kilkenny. The Royal played for five hours, from 9 till 2. By 10pm, the Olympia was packed. The manager, Jimmy Quinn, wore a grin wide enough to tie behind his ears. He shouted to Coppinger on stage: "The queues are ten deep all the way down to St. John's." It was a fantastic night for the Royal Showband; a turning point in their career.

T.J. Byrne came on the scene in '58. A big Carlow man, he was a sales representative for Cotts of Kilcock, Co. Kildare. The company did a roaring trade in mail order, selling everything from muck spreaders to musical instruments. Byrne was a master at clever sales pitch. He discussed an order for a piece of machinery with a farmer — but always left an enticing catalogue of goods open on the kitchen table in the hope of catching his wife's eye. Byrne sold a guitar to Jim Conlon. He went to see the Royal play at the Olympia and decided that it was just the challenge he needed. Coppinger recalls being approached by Byrne at the Arundel Ballroom around this time. "He asked me if he could get a few bookings for us. I said, 'well if you can, okay, we'll give you ten per cent of whatever you get'".

Byrne knew nothing about showbusiness, and told as much to the band. Nevertheless, his attitude was that if he could sell musical instruments, then he could surely try 'selling' a band. Byrne saw tremendous potential in the Royal, and knew that he could market them. He offered to seek out dates in Carlow, Kilkenny, Carrick-on-Suir, Wexford and anywhere else. He went home to Carlow and told his wife, Betty, excitedly: "I'm leaving Cotts." The first date he lined up was in Carlow — for £25. The Royal were still part-timers, working by day and earning £5 each any night they played. At the start, they played on Friday and Sunday nights. "So we were getting £10 a week out of the band," says Coppinger, "and working for the week in our jobs for half that amount. When we went on the road full-time, our intention was to get £15 a man per week out of it. Remember, at that time, a good wage would have been £9 or £10 a week. So, we reckoned that if we got three nights a week and had £15 each out of it, we'd be doing grand."

Meanwhile, they remained part-time musicians. Bowyer and Dunphy built up a loyal following among colleagues in the Paper Mills. Indeed, it was the factory workers of Waterford who first made the Royal feel special. Eddie Wymberry — a chronicler of contemporary Waterford history and lore who worked in the sample department of the mills at the time — recalls the bond between Bowyer and Dunphy, and their popularity. "They were great chums. They were pals inside and outside the job. They were the most easy-going, approachable guys that anyone could hope to work with. There was no bullshit about them. They were just ordinary fellows who made it and never forgot their old friends. To this day, Brendan has never forgotten the fellows he worked with. He's on first name terms with every one of them." Dunphy was nicknamed 'Gunsmoke' by his close friends at work because "he used to drive us cracked singing cowboy country'n'western songs that were in vogue at the time. He sang all the Frankie Lane, Marty Robbins numbers." The Royal were called on to play at factory socials. Alec Casey ran the soccer team and could count on the band to do free concerts in the municipal theatre.

Curiously, while the Royal and U2 were certainly world's apart, they shared one important venue during their respective apprenticeships. A place where both won recognition while still struggling for public attention on their home turf. The Arcadia in Cork. A group of UCC students gave the Royal a booking at the 'Arc' in December '58. Coincidentally, in '78, exactly twenty years later, U2 got a bigger welcome there than in Dublin— a fact publicly acknowledged by U2 manager Paul McGuinness. "We were surprised on our first appearance that there was such a big crowd," says Bowyer. "It was hard for groups like us starting off to exist. We were making it in Cork before anywhere else. Likewise, the Freshmen came to the Arcadia later on and were popular in Cork before they were known nationally. In the '60s, we were used to crowds of 3,000 there on a Saturday night."

The Royal went full-time on Easter Sunday, 1959. It was a giant leap into the unknown for all members of the Royal. They held a meeting at the Olympia and took the momentous decision to hand in their resignations at work. Employers asked if they really knew what they were doing, and if they realised the consequences of turning their backs on steady wages. It was a traumatic period for their parents who questioned the wisdom of such action. Bowyer and Dunphy quit their jobs at the Paper Mills. "The office was a misery to me," Bowyer later recalled. However, his parents were strongly against the idea of

swapping the factory for the stage. Bowyer didn't resign immediately, and it took some time before his parents finally gave approval. Work colleagues recall how both agonised over whether to give up their jobs. "I remember they were into talking about the economics of a showband," says Wymberry. "For instance, they said that if the band travelled to Dublin, they'd have to pay a driver a shilling a mile. At that time, everybody's ambition was either to be in a band or else, if you couldn't make it, to own a car and drive a band. A shilling a mile was big money."

By October/November 1959, the Royal were playing five, and sometimes six, nights a week. Byrne was their permanent manager. His plan was to get as much exposure for the band as possible; first by supporting Mick Del, who always played to big crowds, and then by carefully selecting their own dates in strategic parts of the country where he wanted the band to be remembered. At the end of '59, Bowyer realised they were 'onto something', but wasn't sure what. Fortunately, their rise coincided with the construction of big ballrooms. People like the

Reynolds' brothers had the market, and Byrne had the product.

Word soon spread about the Royal. "We used to play for the students at the Arcadia in Cork," recalls Byrne. "That made us in Cork. It was great because we could expect crowds of 2,000 and 2,500. Students came from everywhere. They went home and spoke about us. We got to play too in Seapoint during the Galway Races. People from all over Ireland were there. So they carried the word. That's exactly what I wanted. I tried to pick venues and festivals where I knew that there would be a guaranteed crowd to hear the band. In the early days with Mick Del in Waterford, we always had a guaranteed crowd."

Before Dunphy and Bowyer became nationwide showbusiness personalities, the Royal, as a musical entity, enjoyed considerable success. The name alone was enough to pack the halls. Band members were asked by Spotlight later about their feelings on turning professional. Conlon had left temporarily to concentrate on finishing his accountancy exams. "I was sorry to leave but I was too far advanced in my accountancy to pack it in," he told the magazine. "When the boys asked me up again I just couldn't believe it. I had finished my exams then and gratefully accepted the opportunity." The drummer, Matthews, formerly an apprentice electrician, said that the chance to go professional represented a "wonderful opportunity to get away from a hum drum day-to-day routine."

Coppinger had no regrets either, but didn't intend to stay in showbusiness forever. In time, he wanted to start a business of his own. Dunphy said his ambition was always to be on stage, but he regretted not having more time with his family. Sullivan thought that playing in a brass band would be as far as he would go in the business. "The Royal has given me everything I ever wanted," he said.

Byrne went in search of headlines. He wanted the showbusiness columnists to take notice of his act. One important critic was Frank Hall of *The Evening Herald* who didn't approve of the showbands. His musical tastes leaned more towards Mick Del than to the Royal. Hall once received a letter from Byrne, "a great man who actually revolutionised the whole business."

He recalls: "T.J. referred to my wonderful influence as a musician and critic. These young lads were studying their trades. They had now reached the crossroads of their career. Would they continue at their trades or would they go into the showband business professionally? Would I come to the Olympic Ballroom one night and see them?" Hall delivered his advice in an article for his paper. "I said I'd seen these clean nice looking boys and they were a credit to their parents. They were very nice chaps. I left it like this...on reflection, Ireland has need for good tradesmen. It just goes to show you what a prophet I was!"

In Waterford, the Royal were special and emerged at the right time. The rise of the band on the eve of the '60s cannot be divorced from the changes sweeping the social and economic life of Waterford. The mediaeval city was energised as never before by an economic revival. Factories sprung up around the city in line with the national transformation from a rural, homogeneous society to an urbanised- industrialised society.

Housing estates were built in Waterford to cater for factory workers who, unlike the '50s generation, did not have to emigrate to make a decent living. They could afford to stay home for the first time. People had more money and were able to socialise on week nights. They wanted to dance to a different tune. Suddenly, a bunch of good-looking city kids were jumping around the stage and singing the chart hits. Young Bowyer was a rock'n'roller. Couples organised their dates around the movements of the Royal. She wanted to see Brendan, and he took her along.

The Royal were a city band. Everyone knew where they lived and recognised them by sight. Band members, and even their families, were in some way touched by stardom. They were celebrities in their neighbourhoods, symbols of the new sense of freedom, optimism and prosperity. People who walked past Dunphy's house, at St. John's Park, or past Bowyer's in South Parade, craned their necks in the hope of glimpsing a 'star'. That celebrity status was confirmed later when they began to make regular TV appearances. The Royal brought glamour and excitement to Waterford. "Everybody was delighted that, at last, we had something that we could take pride in," says Wymberry.

"The only other famous star from Waterford was Val Doonican who we'd hear occasionally on *Desert Island Discs* on BBC."

Later, when the Royal visited Miami on February 25th, '64, they went ringside to watch the world heavyweight title fight between Cassius Clay and Sonny Liston. They shared the excitement with a crowd of 8,297 as Liston refused to come out for the seventh round and Clay took the title. BBC commentator Eamonn Andrews spotted Tom Dunphy in the crowd and asked for his reaction to the result. Dunphy duly obliged, but took the opportunity to send home greetings to Waterford. At that time, it was unusual for someone to send good wishes over the airwaves in this way. A loud cheer went up across Waterford.

"The Royal were to Waterford what the Beatles were to Liverpool," says Wymberry. "People thought they were total superstars. But, at the same time, while everybody respected them, they couldn't appear to be big-headed. In actual fact, they were bigger everywhere else than they were in Waterford. A showband industry went up around them locally. At one stage, there were ten showbands in town when the Royal were big. Young fellows who wouldn't have thought of doing so before formed bands. The Royal broke the mould, went away from the conservative strict tempo dancing and brought in a new era. It cost 6/6 to see the band, a huge amount of money. It was big bread. Later, it went up 7/6. They could actually charge what they liked."

When the Royal began annual tours to the U.S. they were guaranteed rousing homecoming celebrations. Friends wanted to know what stars they'd met. The band regaled them with stories. Bowyer once met Wymberry coming out of Howards record shop on the quay. Wymberry asked him: "Well, Brendan, did you see anyone big?" Bowyer replied: "Eddie, I spoke to Ella Fitzgerald." Wymberry thought this sensational... "we only saw Ella Fitzgerald in the pictures, but Brendan *spoke* to her."

The majority of bands were happy to perform for a flat fee, regardless of the success of the dance. In theory, they were at least guaranteed money at the end of the night. The Royal had been playing for relatively small money in '58/'59 — from £25 to £50 per performance — because dancehall owners weren't prepared to pay more. But, at the turn of the '60s, the Royal were attracting big crowds, largely because of Byrne's clever management, flair for publicity and careful selection of dates to ensure maximum exposure. Queues formed everywhere they played: the anticipation was unprecedented.

Fr. Brian D'Arcy, then a student attending St. Michael's College, Enniskillen, waited for hours outside the town hall in order to see the Royal. "The two big talking points were their Mercedes wagon, as well as the fact that Bowyer could leap over Tom Dunphy on stage," he recalls. "Bowyer could physically jump over Dunphy. The excitement was enormous. You knew in your heart and soul that this was the closest you'd get to Radio Luxembourg. Bowyer was the big star coming to town. It wasn't just a local band that you went to work with next day. This guy was in showbusiness. He came from miles away to your town, and you were never going to see him again. I can still see Bowyer leap-frogging Dunphy. I've looked at the town hall stage since then and wondered how the hell did he do that?"

Bowyer once stopped the dancers when his stunt went wrong. It happened on stage at the Olympia, Waterford. As usual, Dunphy went on bended knee while playing the bass guitar. Bowyer leapt into the air over his head and crashed through the floor. "Tom went down, Brendan jumped...and bang, down through the boards," says road manager Brendan McGrath of the incident. "He wasn't hurt — just wounded pride. It was just laughed off. It went down a bomb with the dancers."

As the crowds swelled in '60/'61, Byrne told ballroom owners that if they wanted his band to play in their halls, then they would have to cough up a percentage of the door receipts. Coppinger had previously insisted on percentages too. The enormous popularity of the Royal meant that nobody was in a position to refuse. Byrne wouldn't settle for less than 60/40. "Look, it was sometimes difficult even to get a fee out of some people," says Byrne, explaining his business approach. "So, eventually, I said that we'd do it on a percentage basis. Some of the dancehall owners wouldn't come up with a fee.

They were scared. I said, 'okay, we'll do a percentage.' They wanted to know what that meant. 'Well, if we don't bring the crowd in, you don't pay us.' When we started out in the early days, dances were 1/6 and 2/6. Eventually, I said, 'look, you'll have to charge five shillings. We'd take 60% of the door. It worked like this: you had 2,000 people in at five shillings. So, that generated £500. On 60/40, you had £300. Dances remained at five shillings for a long time until they went up to 7/6 (37.5p). Eventually, we put them up to ten shillings. So, at fifty pence, 2,000 people meant £1,000, and that gave a cut of £600. It was good money. But good acts today can get £3,000 and £4,000 a night."

Byrne knew of bands who demanded a guaranteed fee on top of a percentage deal. That was too greedy, he thought. It was up to the band to draw the crowd and take the financial knocks with the windfalls. "We never insisted on any guarantees because it was our job to pull the people in," he explains. "I always stuck to a straight percentage. Some bands took their fees even if the crowd was down. That was hard on the ballroom proprietor. Anything could happen: a foggy or wet night could keep the crowd away. Brendan always thought that my way was the fairest. If we put them in, then we got paid. If we didn't, then it was nobody's fault.

"We accepted that the proprietor had spent money on advertising and everything. I always had a great relationship with the ballroom owners because they were never screwed. I had a thing that if I can't trust you, then you can't trust me. We shouldn't do business. If I have to spend the whole night looking over your shoulder, and you looking over mine, then we shouldn't be together. So I always trusted everybody. Anyone I did do business with were reputable people who could be trusted. You're talking about people like Jim and Albert Reynolds, Noel Finan of Seapoint, Galway, Jack O'Rourke of the Majestic, Mallow, Peter Prendergast of the Arcadia, Cork, Packie Hayes of Dromkeen and Con Hynes from Portumna. For example, Con was a very tough, but very straight, businessman. You took everyone you dealt with on trust and they took you on trust. There had to be trust when you worked on those percentages."

Byrne set standards that other showband managers tried to emulate. He was "a great man for marketing the band," says

Albert Reynolds. "T.J. introduced a whole lot of marketing skills that weren't apparent in the business." Top-drawing bands like the Capitol, Drifters and Dixies soon followed Byrne's example, and they too demanded 60% of the action. In '60, the Royal filled the ballrooms. Business was so good that they could pack the Showboat, Youghal, at 7/6 a head, on Easter Monday, one of the best dancing nights of the year.

High earnings gave the band a lifestyle they could never have imagined in their waged work in Waterford. They stayed only in top class hotels. They lived like kings and enjoyed life's luxuries. "We had money in an early stage of our lives when we might otherwise not have had it," says Bowyer. "None of the Royal went to college, or even had the chance to go to college because, being from Waterford, there was nothing there. We made a lot of money. I suppose we spent it too."

The Bowyers sold their pub in Waterford in 1960 and made a final move to an up-market Victorian house in Otteran Place near the park. This was made possible by the increased financial income to the household. Bowyer made good money, and shared it with his family. "He was really very good to us," says Olive. "My parents were working hard in the pub. His success afforded them the chance to move to a more spacious house. It was a beautiful house. My mother no longer had to work fulltime. We thought he was a millionaire." Bowyer's early success was a source of pride to his parents, although his classically-minded father "couldn't understand how people could make money singing that kind of music."

High income meant also that the Royal could afford the most modern instruments and equipment. They were the first band in the country to tour with a 'Binson' echo chamber. This revolutionary piece of equipment was hooked up to the amplifier and gave the voice an echoing effect. It added a new dimension to Bowyer's voice, and was particularly effective in the bigger ballrooms. It was the envy of other bands and baffled dancers who wondered how the effect was produced. When the Royal played at a hall in Caherconlish, Co. Limerick, one night in '60, a man at the foot of the stage couldn't keep his eyes off the echo chamber. He came to his own conclusion, and buttonholed Coppinger after the dance. "You can't fool me," he said with a knowing smile; "sure ye were only mimin' to taped music all the time."

Byrne looked abroad to keep the show on the road during Lent. The Royal played in Bill Fuller's ballrooms in Dublin, London, Manchester, New York, Chicago, Boston and San Francisco. He became a valuable friend to the Royal — and to Byrne. It wasn't unusual for the band to 'close the doors' at the Galtimore in Cricklewood, the Buffalo at Camden Town, the Harp in Birmingham or the Carousel in Manchester. The Carl Alan Award recognised their astonishing British box office achievements in '61. At home, the Royal began recording in '62 and made their TV debut in Easter '63 with a 45-minute *Royal Showband Show*. Bowyer and the Royal first broke into the Irish charts in late summer with *Kiss Me Quick*. It was No. 1 for seven weeks and stayed in the charts for fourteen. Then, they made a movie...

The Royal
Crowned Kings Of The Road

Cork, Wednesday September 18th, 1963.

Two chauffeur driven cars collect a party of celebrities at the Metropole Hotel in MacCurtain Street. Autograph hunters trap their quarry before the VIPs climb in. Their destination: the Savoy Cinema, Patrick Street. They turn into Bridge Street, cross the Lee and sweep into the heart of the city. It's eight o'clock on the third night of the Cork Film Festival. Flags of different countries flutter outside the Savoy as several internationally famous faces arrive. Crowds on the street go wild at the sight of the latest arrivals from the Metropole. People dash across the street to catch a glimpse of the hottest dance act in Ireland: the Royal Showband.

Inside, there's a double bill on the screen. First, *The One Nighters*, a Peter Collinson production shot on location with the Royal. Cameras follow "this bunch of extremely nice lads" into their homes and the dance halls. They perform before 5,000 in the Ulster Hall. Viewers meet their mothers, wives and families.

Next on the bill is the world premiere of *The Leather Boys*, produced by Raymond Stross. It's the story of a couple who wed in their teens, and end up on the rocks.

The Royal follow their film with a personal appearance on stage. They get the loudest and most prolonged applause of any showing over the eight-night festival. "Their diffidence obviously went down extremely well in the presence of a more adult audience than they usually play to," the Cork Examiner reported next day. That week the Royal were riding high in the charts with Elvis Presley's *Kiss Me Quick*.

The festival programme painted a snow white image of the Royal and their place in the Irish music business. "Harps, flutes and unaccompanied singers are the expected form of entertainment," it said. "But there is also a driving beat of pop commercial music all over Ireland. The Top 20 means as much to this scene as anywhere else in the world. The gods of this form of entertainment are the hundreds of showbands that tour the dance halls of Ireland, playing and singing to thousands of elated fans. An ideal example of this scene are the Royal Showband. They play six nights a week to an average of 4,000 to 5,000 people a night. They have taken the biggest pop music award in England and they tour America annually. But the difference between them and any other international stars is that they refuse anything that usually goes with the money and the fame.They live in ordinary little houses in a quiet little town in Ireland."

The blurb is transparently innacurate: average audiences of 4,000 to 5,000 a night were not the norm, and it's also stretching credulity to suggest that Irish bands weren't interested in the things — desirable or otherwise — that money could buy. Despite the crude attempt to project a holy and a wholesome image of the Irish at play, the handout does convey a sense of the environment in which the Royal flourished.

The One Nighters was an acclaimed piece of work by Collinson who wrote the script and experimented with TV techniques in his treatment of the film. It portrayed an innocent picture of young heroes who could take on the world but still come home untainted by corrupting influences. The film took a festival award, and was described as "charming" by the Cork Examiner. Not so charming, apparently, was a Swedish film called *The Mistress,* which was shown on the night before the Royal performance. Protests were made to newspaper offices about it's "immoral nature." Fr. John Burke, of the Catholic Film Office, described it as evil. Leave it to the Royal to set the right moral tone in an environment fraught with temptation. The band stepped into the limelight of their film premiere at a time when they had the Irish entertainment world literally at their feet. Within five years, they had reached the dizzy heights at home. In '63, the Royal were as important to the young people of Ireland as U2 were more than a quarter of a century later when they attended the film premiere of their own Rattle And Hum in Dublin.

(Photo: Cork Examiner)

Bowyer's chart success with *Kiss Me Quick* won him recognition as *Spotlight's* Showband Personality of '63. Presley's version of the song was rush released by RCA on a single in Ireland only — but failed to effect sales of Bowyer's recording. Bowyer was the undisputed king of the ballrooms: girls fell at his feet; boys envied his good looks and sex appeal; promoters worshipped the ground he walked on and sang his praises all the way to the bank. He was the best thing that ever happened to the dancing business. Everything he said or did was newsworthy: fans waited eagerly for his messages, delivered via the columns of *Spotlight*. The adulation was unprecedented. Bowyer could do no wrong and could aspire to achieve anything he wanted. He even considered a later career in politics:

"I love Ireland, and it's people. I think that at the moment we are enjoying a boom economically and socially. I have certain ideas of my own which I would like to find an outlet for. I also feel politics is a very interesting career and has a lot to offer for a young man who feels he has initiative. I hope to contest the Waterford Municipal elections, gain experience in the Corporation and then run for Dail Eireann when I am ready."

The political career never materialised. In the same *Spotlight* interview, he regretted the lack of a university education..."I feel the opportunities to study and go to college, while having a job, are tremendous in the United States." On marriage..."I often think about getting married. I do feel that no man should end up a bachelor."

Bowyer was idolised. It was almost a sin to criticise him. One eighteen-year-old Dublin schoolgirl, Barbara Culle, provoked the wrath of fans by daring to suggest he wasn't a good singer in a letter to *Spotlight*. "Are the people of Ireland going mad, or have they already gone mad," she wrote. "Surely nobody could possibly consider Brendan Bowyer, Sean Fagan etc. good singers. It makes me, and all my friends, absolutely sick to read how great these singers are. Even if you have no idea of a good singer, surely the public shouldn't have to read all this trash you write about 'the great Brendan Bowyer'." Angry replies flooded the *Spotlight* offices for weeks.

At twenty-five, Bowyer was an Irish superstar. It was a lot to handle. Hundreds of fan letters poured into the family home every week. His mother acted as personal secretary, replied to letters and sent off pictures of the band. On Monday, his night off, Bowyer signed letters and autographed publicity pictures. Fame reflected on the family who enjoyed celebrity status in Waterford. "Our father's name was already quite well known in music circles," says his sister, Olive. "When Brendan became famous, we were hugely proud. We told everybody that Brendan Bowyer was our brother. People stopped us in the street and asked if we could get his autograph. From the female point of view, he was quite a hunk. He was tall, strong and good looking. He had a lot of appeal for the girls. I remember that there were always letters, telephone calls and a big buzz around the place."

Bowyer and the Royal followed the success of *Kiss Me Quick* with four successive No. 1 hits. *No More* entered the charts just before Christmas '63, shot to No. 1 on December 27 and stayed in the charts for ten weeks. The next No. 1 was achieved on July 3, '64 with *Bless You*; it stayed in the charts for eleven weeks. Spotlight described the Waterford heroes as the million dollar showband: readers were told that this was the massive offer given to them to spend twelve months in the U.S. For the moment, however, the Royal concentrated on the lucrative Irish dancehall circuit.

In August 1964, the band released their first LP, *The One Nighters,* named after the Collinson film. The Royal went on their first English tour in over three years in November '64. "Thousands were turned away at ballrooms we played in," says Coppinger. "At one London ballroom, dozens of extra police were called to prevent the crowds from smashing down the doors." At home, the band maintained the momentum. "All the time we were pressured to keep the show up front to stay the number one act, or to be classed as the number one showband in the country," says Byrne. "Voting in the Spotlight charts proved that we stayed on top year after year." Bowyer, Dunphy and the Royal opened new ballrooms all over the country, some of which were even named after the band.

There was a driving force within the Royal during these vital years that pushed them to the top rung of Irish showbusiness and, eventually, to the entertainment lounges of Las Vegas where the opposition came from greats like Frank Sinatra, Sammy Davis Jnr, Dean Martin, Tom Jones and Neil Diamond. That meant a gruelling weekly schedule criss-crossing the country. The manager was on the road too, taking care of financial dealings. "We normally got back to the hotel where we were staying about 3am, had a cup of tea and a chat and stayed up talking until 4am or 5am," says Byrne. "But I had to be up at 10am because people would be calling my home in Carlow looking for me. Betty, my wife, would tell callers what hotel to contact between 10am and 1pm. So, I was working all the time. I had to be available, and I also had to be with the lads. If I wasn't there and anything went wrong, I'd feel responsible. When we were on percentages, I felt that it was only right to be there. The lads had their job to do, and I had mine.

"Wednesday you could be in Sligo; on the Thursday night at the Ags in Dublin; you might nip home because you'd be in Waterford on Friday; at the Arcadia in Cork on the Saturday; and off to Dromkeen on Sunday. I'd get home about 5am or 6am on Monday, the band's day off. I was supposed to be off too. But, all those people who didn't catch me during the week were 'phoning at 10am or 11am on Monday, even though I'd have only returned home at 5am. I averaged four to five hours sleep every night."

Byrne kept the marketing campaign in top gear, and culti-vated media contacts. His achievements at this time were moni-tored by lesser known managers in the business — among them Derryman Maurice Cassidy. He managed the Santa Fe and the reformed Clipper Carlton and looked up to the master handler. "I think that T.J. had the quality that should be important to managers: flair," says Cassidy. "He was a gifted publicist, always keeping his act in public attention. All these tasks are split now: a manager, a business manager, an agent and a publicist."Coppinger gave fans an insight during late '64 into his life as leader of the most successful band in the country. "It's not a bed of roses as some people would like to make it out," he insisted. "It's an endless round of travelling, playing and sleeping. Personally, I dislike the travelling most of all. It can be very boring hanging around hotels in the afternoons. I miss my home life very much when I'm away. I take my own car to most dances. Providing we're not more than 100 miles or so from Waterford, I try to return home after a dance whenever possible. We usually spend two days a week at home. We get a fair share of begging letters. Only in exceptional cases do we take any notice of them. It's extraordinary the number of people who think we must be all millionaires. We've certainly earned very good money for the past couple of years but our expenses are high and we've got to think of the future by saving."

By Christmas 1964, the Royal had scored three successive No..1 hits and spent four successful years at the top. Bowyer was restless and publicly admitted "things have reached a stalemate." He said: "We have done everything that can be done in Ireland: topped the charts three times (we hope to do a fourth time shortly); made a number of TV appearances; made a film; we hold the record for attendances in 99% of Ireland's ballrooms; and have won the coveted Carl Alan Award. The question is...where do we go from here? What more can we do? Well, my ambition is to break into the English and American charts."

1965 was the year that Ireland did *The Hucklebuck.* Bowyer discovered the song on an album while on a trip to New York.Amazingly, it was first considered as a B-side. It became an anthem of the showband era with the kind of enduring appeal that brought disco dancers to their feet generations later.It entered the charts on January 4th and went to No. 1 on January 18th. It stayed on top for seven weeks and in the charts for twelve, also charting in Britain. The Irish twisted with the Royal during their electrifying performances of *The Hucklebuck* on Telefís Éireann's *Showband Show.* Bowyer and Dunphy wriggled and waddled alongside two women dancers. The women wore polo-neck blouses with the words *Hucklebuck* and *Royal* written across their chests, below-knee- length white skirts and white bobby socks. Teenage girls who watched on TV envied Bowyer's *Hucklebuck* dancers. The record was hyped with a big publicity campaign: Bowyer's youngest sister, Alison,joined him in photographic sessions to promote the record.

At that point, Bowyer was to the '60s generation what Bono was to the '80s generation, says Gay Byrne. "It was a very important record for the Royal," he says. "It still sounds damn good." Astonishingly, *The Hucklebuck* still had enough popular appeal to reach No. 4 in the charts when released again in '76... and to reach No. 10 in 1981.

Dunphy was next to strike No. 1 in the charts with *If I Didn't Have a Dime* on March 22nd, '65. The song, hummed in every office and factory floor in the country, remained in the charts for nine weeks. It was released again eleven years later and reached No. 4. Bowyer achieved his fifth No. 1 on September 6 — *Don't Lose Your Hucklebuck Shoes.*

Five No. 1 hits in a row ensured a special place in the pop history books for Bowyer. His last single of '65, Presley's Wonder of You, reached No. 2 in October and stayed in the charts for six weeks.

The Royal pulled the biggest crowds, demanded and got the highest fees. They played to 4,000 at the Jetland Ballroom in Limerick on St. Stephen's night '65 with the Firehouse Five as support band. It was a year that returned huge earnings for the band. One estimate puts their annual income at £112,500. This calculation is based on an average dance attendance of 2,000, five-nights-a-week at 7/6 (37.5p), and the band's 60% cut. That gives a weekly income of £2,250, or £112,500 annually. The equivalent in 1990 would be **£1,106,435.**

Similarly, for '67, when admission was ten bob, dance attendances of 2,000 five-nights-a-week yields an annual income of £150,000 — or **£1,475,246.83** in '90. These projections do not take account of factors that swelled their earnings even further, or else reduced them: fluctuations in crowd numbers caused by severe weather; earnings on international tours during Lent; percentage cuts that went higher than 60% on big nights in major ballrooms; record-breaking attendances on key dancing dates like St.Stephen's Night, New Year's Eve, St. Patrick's Day and Easter Sunday; royalties from record sales, etc. Nevertheless, despite the many variables, the calculations do reveal the scale of the income.   The Royal made fortunes, and remained high earners for longer than anyone else in the business. The colossal income was the envy of lesser bands who, occasionally, got glimpses of the bonanza. One incident two years earlier graphically revealed the hefty cash flow of the Royal and their generosity.The band were due on stage at the Ulster Hall, Belfast, on a big night promoted by Jim Aiken in '63. Tom Dunphy was delayed in Manchester en route to Belfast. His appearance was in doubt. Aiken needed a replacement. He telephoned Jackie Flavelle of the Dave Glover Showband, who was on a night off. He said: "Listen, Jackie, Brendan and the boys are stuck. Will you come down and play bass?" Flavelle dashed to the Ulster Hall, "for my chance at stardom." He was about to strike up the first chords when

Dunphy arrived late after having chartered a plane. Dunphy thanked Flavelle, opened his wallet and gave him 70. Flavelle was dumbfounded. He asked: "What's that for, Tom?" Dunphy replied: "That's for your trouble for coming down, Jackie."

At the time, Flavelle was earning £35 a week with Glover. Dunphy had just given him two weeks wages — for not playing! The '90 equivalent of that handshake is **£764.46.**

High earnings enabled band members to buy nice homes and prestige cars, enjoy good living standards and make investments in property. They even invested in a racehorse, trained by Paddy Norris at the Curragh and re-named *Royal Showband*. Norris bought the horse, on their behalf, from top trainer Paddy Prendergast. Bought originally as a jumper with strong potential, the horse showed form immediately while gaining flat racing experience: *Royal Showband* won a two-mile race at Mullingar, ridden by T.P. Burns. But the unfortunate animal was injured over hurdles shortly afterwards while schooling at the Curragh, and had to be destroyed. At one point during their money-spinning days, the Royal were hit with a big tax demand, and the shock was felt throughout Waterford. "Everybody nearly died when news spread," says Wymberry. "There was a claim in for something like £25,000. People shuddered because no one could visualise that kind of money. There was no PAYE at the time. Everybody thought... how can anybody pay that money?"

1966 ushered in a mini-recession for the showband business.It was weathered. The business was swamped by two-bit bands,and the poorer ones were being squeezed out. For dance-halls,it was still a highly commercial environment. Associated Ballrooms continued to expand: for example, they opened the Caroline Ballroom in Drimoleague on St. Patrick's Night and sponsored their own Radio Éireann show at 2.30pm every Thursday.But new sounds were being heard on Radio Luxembourg. Chas Chandler discovered Jimi Hendrix at The Cafe Wha in Greenwich village. The age of the electric guitar was born. The Experience and Cream consolidated rock's electric revolution.Folk was merging with rock: Bob Dylan did it in America; at home, experimental bands were trying traditional music variations on electric instruments. Sweeney's Men, of which Andy Irvine formed part, pioneered electric folk in Ireland. They had a number one hit with *Old Maid in the Garret* in '67.

Only the better showbands would survive the dying '60s and crossover into the '70s. The Royal were taking stock too after six glory years. They decided to tap lucrative markets in the U.S. They spread their wings and flew to the neon of Las Vegas for annual stints. Thus, the band could straddle markets at home and abroad. "We were looking for an outlet where we wouldn't have to do twelve months of the year in Ireland," says Bowyer. "At that stage, we were at our height alright. But we figured that you couldn't do twelve months of the year in Ireland. At that time, we were just trying to get in the door."

Bill Fuller introduced Bowyer, and the Royal, to Vegas in '66, a year in which they had two Top Ten hits — *The Fly* at No. 6 in April and *I Can't Get You Out of My Heart* at No. 4 in September. Byrne and Coppinger were friendly with Fuller. The Royal had played in his dancehalls across the U.S. since the beginning. Fuller set up an audition for them in Vegas. The call-up took them by surprise. The Royal were actually on a Fuller tour when summoned to Las Vegas. Coppinger picked up the phone in a New York hotel room. He recognised the Kerry accent immediately. Fuller said: "Get all the lads out to the airport, Mike. Get them there by twelve. All the tickets are waiting."

"Where are we going? Coppinger asked." Fuller replied: "We're going down to Vegas. We'll have a go, Mike." Coppinger was stunned and told him: "Bill, we wouldn't have a chance down there." But, the promoter insisted: "Look, just get the lads up out of bed and get out to the airport. I'll take care of the rest." The Royal auditioned in Las Vegas before a booking agent for the Desert Inn and the Stardust, a squat Italian/American named Rocky Sennes. He was watching another group rehearse as the Royal arrived. He was giving them hell. Coppinger recalls: "They'd obviously gone down badly the night before. He was stopping them in the middle of their song and ticking them off. We had to wait about half an hour before we went on stage. We said we could do twenty minutes right through. At the time, we didn't really care because it was Lent in Ireland, which meant we were away anyway. We treated it as a holiday going to Vegas. Brendan did a Tom Jones number, "Delilah". He used to do that number very well. Tom Dunphy did a yodelling song. Charlie Matthews did something that was popular at the time over there."

The audition was successful. The Royal got their first bookings in Las Vegas. They developed a polished cabaret show and brought in female dancers to create the right image for the entertainment lounges. The Royal returned in the autumn of '66 and played at the Desert Inn for four weeks. That November, Charlie Matthews had his first No. 1 with the Royal, *Somewhere My Love*. It stayed in the charts for twelve weeks. The band returned during Lent '67 to do the ballroom circuit in the U.S. and secured another short-term residency in Las Vegas. On this occasion, the venue was the Stardust Hotel on the Strip. It was the year when James Brown tried to crack Las Vegas too. The Godfather of Soul first played at the Flamingo. It wasn't easy: audiences were older, and wary of his raw funky sound. The biggest problem was how to connect with the changing faces. The same challenge faced Bowyer, Dunphy and the Royal. For Brown, Vegas was so different to a theatre or stadium — just as it was world's removed from the Irish ballroom circuit for the Royal.

The culture shock was, of course, enormous. The Strip was like nothing the Royal had seen before, a dazzling collection of luxury hotels and mammoth casinos on either side of South Las

(Photo: Sunday World)

Vegas Boulevard. On one of their first night flights into Vegas, Byrne turned to Jim Conlon and said: "It's like a big Christmas tree lit up." At home, Bowyer's *Holy City* reached No. 7 in the charts at Christmas '67. The Royal began a six-month contract at the Stardust in '68 and pioneered the Irish showband programme in Las Vegas. Offstage, the band went to the big shows to see some of the hottest acts in the world. They attended big-name boxing fights. Fuller, who retained a strong interest in the band, went ringside regularly with Coppinger. The ballroom business was booming for Fuller. He talked a lot about work. One of the band leader's indelible memories is of a conversation with Fuller on the Strip around this time. "Sold a ballroom today Mike," said Fuller out of the blue."How did you do?" asked Coppinger. "Yerra, not so bad," replied Fuller, understating his gains in unmistakable Kerry tones. "I got half a millun."

As the Royal made progress in Las Vegas in '67, the Irish entertainment business was rocked by news of the resignation of their long-time manager, T.J. Byrne. He had always been linked in the public mind with the top-drawing showband since their discovery. His influence on the entire business had been enormous. When he quit, it was the showbusiness shock of the year. Yet, he never strayed too far away from his wonder boys and would later make a comeback when Bowyer and Dunphy formed the Big 8 in '71. After nearly a decade managing the Royal, Byrne handed his letter of resignation to Coppinger, the leader. "T.J. wanted to go on his own," says Coppinger. "He wanted to manage other acts. I said, 'no, you have enough to do to manage the Royal.'

"We were recording up in Dublin in studios at Henry Street when T.J. came in to see me. He handed me a letter. I took it from him. It was his resignation. I put it into my pocket straight away and said, 'fair enough.' I don't think he expected that." Byrne says that he suffered ill health around this time, and doctors warned him to slow down his hectic lifestyle. "It was a big decision for me to leave the Royal," he says. "But I got this warning and that frightened the daylights out of me." During the intervening years before he returned to manage the Big 8, Byrne was involved in the management of Maxi, Dick and Twink. He also ran The Top Hat ballroom in Dun Laoghaire.

Byrne stepped out — and Connie Lynch, a Cavanman, stepped in. Lynch had been working in London as area manager for Electrolux when encouraged by his country singer friend, Larry Cunningham, to try band management at home. Connie took over Pat Lynch and the Airchords in '66. "They were doing poorly," he recalls. "I worked on them and gave them a bit of a lift. They were in the red. I got them out of the red into the black. I did very well with them." The Airchords had a No. 1 hit on December 16th, '67 with *Treat Me Daughter Kindly*. The band had made it to No. 3 earlier that year with *Irish Soldier Boy* that stayed in the charts for an amazing twenty-five weeks. Connie's golden opportunity came when the Royal job was up for grabs. A lot of well-known names were mentioned by the media as contenders. Lynch says he didn't look for the job — because he didn't think he had a hope of getting it. He was friendly with Bowyer and Dunphy.

He was selected for the post and took over at Easter 1967. The Royal were still hot property and looked like breaking new ground in Las Vegas.Lynch never had to hunt for dates. By Easter, he knew that the diary was full till St. Stephen's night of the next year.Lynch operated on a 60/40 basis — no guarantee. "Unlike a lot of acts today, the Royal took 60% but they left 40% behind them. So a proprietor never had to go to the till to pay them at the end of the night. They left 40%, whatever the takings were. If it was up, it was up. If it was down, it was down. On a Sunday night, you wouldn't be playing to less than 1,500, and from there upwards. Packie Hayes in Dromkeen would do 3,000 with the Royal in their heyday. On a Friday night in Mallow, we would do 1,500 or 1,600. The money varied from place to place. We were getting 7/6 in Castlebar. On St. Stephen's night in Athy, Jim Reynolds was able to get 12/6. But you wouldn't get 12/6 in Castlebar. It was just the area. A busy Sunday night on 60/40 could net anything up to £600. In those days, that was big money boy."

Lynch's style of management was to link up dates as much as possible on the five-nightly schedule to avoid, for instance, a hop from the Borderland in Muff, outside Derry, down to Millstreet. "You'd play Cashel on a Wednesday, then go home;Millstreet on Thursday, then go home; on Friday, you'd be in Dundalk; on Saturday, in Dublin, and on Sunday, in Kingscourt. That would be a nice handy week. Two nights at home and two nights away. Nowadays, a band has to play Derry one night and Maudie Macs, outside Mallow, the next night." Money was rolling in — more than Lynch could ever make working for Electrolux. He scoffs at the image of lavish lifestyles: "Not lavish. Not at all. We never stopped to realise. Of course we took in good money. But we spent it. Nobody spent it more so than Brendan. He was a fellow who took a drink. You'd drive a good car. You kept up a pretty good lifestyle." The Royal continued to record and achieved two Top Ten hits in '68 — *Lady Willpower* and *Same Old Song*, both at No. 9.

Meantime, Byrne took on a young up-and-coming Northern band, the College Boys. It was an unhappy alliance. "I came to the conclusion that they were more interested in their hobbies than in into the job as professional musicians," says Byrne. "The band was just a hobby. It wasn't a living. You'd get them a booking but, you didn't know whether they were going to turn up and play or not. I didn't stay that long with them. It wasn't my scene to have people who weren't that interested."

The Royal, under the guidance of their new manager, divided the year between Las Vegas and Ireland, bridging the cultural gaps back and forth. They flew out just after the Christmas celebrations and returned home in early July. They missed the Irish winter and came home to blue skies. It was a shrewd marketing move too. "Vegas made them scarce," says Lynch. "It was great because when the band came home, they did colossal business. We'd go to England and do a tour, and it was marvellous. We'd stay home till Christmas. Then it was away again." The band brought a touch of vaudeville to the ballrooms on their return from a stint in Las Vegas. The crowds still flocked to see Bowyer and Dunphy. The Royal sang the same songs that made their name a decade before. Road manager Brendan McGrath, of Gracedieu, Waterford, didn't go to Las Vegas because of union restrictions there. The pace was frenetic from the moment the band stepped off the plane on their return home.

"It was go the whole time," says McGrath. "The whole band were stars. They went in and out back doors of ballrooms...the usual high profile stuff." He was amazed that the Royal could make the same songs sound fresh and exciting night after night. "That always intrigued me," he says. "Everybody gets bored or browned off with their jobs sometime. But these fellows had to motivate themselves to do the same thing over and over and sing those songs as if it was for the first time." Soon, bags were packed again for Las Vegas. The band took flight.

The Royal played their last gig together at the Stardust Hotel, Las Vegas, in July, '71. They came home and announced the departure of Bowyer and Dunphy. The writing had been on the wall for a year. Concerted efforts were being made by businessmen to lure Bowyer away. Although their allegiance to band colleagues was strong, Bowyer and Dunphy felt they had outgrown the Royal.Thirteen years earlier, the Royal were seen as pioneers. But, in 1971, they were being overtaken by younger bands and by new musical forms. One year before the star duo quit, a consortium of Dublin moneymen made Bowyer an offer to leave and form a new band. He gave them a verbal commitment that he would go. But the Royal came to new terms with him. He changed his mind. Before Bowyer's change of heart, Paddy Cole of the Capitol was asked to go in as leader of the new band, the Big 8. Cole met Dunphy at a ballroom in London.

"To keep it all above board, I told Tom I'd been approached to join up as band leader," says Cole. "Tom told me not to make any arrangements because it wouldn't happen. They then renegotiated a deal with Brendan." The consortium took legal action against Bowyer for pulling out of the deal, and he suffered a financial setback as a result.

The attempt to poach Bowyer from the Royal caused predictable tension in the band. It was a big shock. Coppinger's theory is that the consortium believed that by signing up Bowyer,they would have the lucrative contract in Las Vegas and, perhaps,even bring out other bands. Bowyer was well-established there: a lot of bands got auditions, but very few got work. "When Brendan was made a big offer to leave, naturally he was up in a heap about what to do," says Coppinger. "It was hard for him to turn it down. That started the rut. He didn't want to go with these fellows. Yet, he had to fix his own future. One thing led to another. We had the remaining six months to do in Vegas. Bill Fuller came in and said, 'look, whatever you want to do, why not finish out the six months anyway'. That's what we did. As a matter of fact, before we split, I had done all the negotiating myself for the new contract in Las Vegas with Rocky Sennes. I got that contract for the next two years before the split. My idea was that I might hold the band together if I got extra money, which I did." Byrne says that he was approached in 1970 by Bowyer and Dunphy who told him they were thinking of quitting the band. He said they were crazy. "I told them to cool it for the time being.I said they had everything going for them...the contract in Vegas. They asked me if I would look after them if they left the Royal. If they knew that I would, then it would give them more encouragement. I didn't encourage them one bit to leave the Royal. After another few months, they came back again and said they'd had it and just wanted to get out on their own. It was a big decision for them."

Following the first approach to him a year earlier, Cole got another phonecall. It was from Dunphy and Bowyer in Las Vegas. They had finally decided to leave the Royal and wanted him as their new band leader. "I remember asking them if this was really going to happen, or would it be like the last time," recalls Cole. "They said no, it was definite." The Royal came home from Las Vegas and disbanded in July '71. The Big 8 was launched three months later and returned to the Stardust Hotel in Las Vegas in January '72. Just before their departure, Bowyer and The Big 8 broke into the Top Ten with*You Gave Me A Mountain*. The record reached No. 6 over that Christmas. Fuller, a man with considerable influence in Las Vegas, was the guiding light behind the Big 8. He favoured the appointment of T.J. Byrne as manager.

The resignation of Bowyer and Dunphy had a traumatic effect on the Royal. It was the hot gossip all over Waterford. "It was a tough break up," admits Coppinger. "There were a few little things that the fellows felt a bit sore about. I think that was to be expected anyway. But, remember, we got on very well together for fourteen years. We never had any serious rows — maybe the odd few arguments. As a matter of fact, we got on exceptionally well. If it didn't break up that year, it would have broken up the following year anyway. It was going to happen one way or another." Bowyer believes the Royal had run their course and a new direction was necessary for him and Dunphy.

Another mainstay of the band, Jim Conlon, emigrated to New York with his American wife.

The loss of the frontmen left Lynch, as manager, picking up the pieces. He had five years "of the best of it." Now everything was falling apart. Although under contract to the Royal, he considers it a major mistake to have stayed on. He admits to an error of judgment in assuming that the duo would not leave.

"Brendan and Tom gave me the option to leave with them," he recalls of the break. "I had the job. But I had one thing in the back of my mind all the time: it's never going to happen. I could never, when the crunch came, see the boys leaving. I hesitated because I didn't think it would happen. I didn't want the fellows in the Royal turning to me and saying, 'you're a turncoat — when Brendan and Tom went, you ran with them'. I didn't want that said. T.J. came back to manage the Big 8. It's funny the way that the wheel turned. I remained with the Royal, which lasted about a year. It did no business. It just went downhill. It was like taking Big Tom out of the Mainliners. It was a joke. The Royal couldn't continue without Brendan Bowyer and Tom Dunphy. We brought in replacements. But it didn't work out. I went down the line to manage a lesser attraction. Instead of managing one band, I managed two or three. They were middle of the road bands. In those days, there was work for middle of the road bands." The Royal lingered on, a pale shadow of its former self, and never recovered. Bowyer and Dunphy were replaced by Lee Lynch as lead singer and Billy Hopkins as vocalist/bass guitarist.

The Big 8 were launched in the Stardust, Las Vegas, in 1972. It gave manager Byrne a lease of life and the opportunity to return to the big time. The new band was brighter and more up-to-date than the Royal. He was fascinated by the numeral '8'. In his mind's eye, he could visualise what their posters and advertising would look like. The Big 8 — it sounded catchy! Byrne was credited with solid promotional work that achieved results. The Big 8 was the ultimate showband, in the best sense: it combined the enormous experience of Dunphy and Bowyer; inspired management; the cream of Ireland's musicians; a big brass sound; advanced sound and lighting systems; the glitter of Vegas; the vital 'show' component which was nurtured in the Royal and now enhanced by the glamour and comic talent of Twink. The Big 8 represented a logical progression from the traditional 'showband' foundation. It had everything. Musicians were handpicked. As leader, Cole, selected the nucleus. The line-up was: Bowyer, (ex-Royal) vocals; Dunphy, (ex-Royal) bass and vocals; Twink, (ex-Maxi, Dick and Twink), vocals; Michael Keane, (ex-Johnny McEvoy) piano; Jimmy Conway, (ex-the Strangers) guitar; Dave Coady, (ex-Real McCoy) trumpet; Cole, (ex-Capitol) saxes, clarinet and vocals; Mickey O'Neill, (ex-Capitol and Swarbriggs) drums. All were top names in their fields.

The combination of talent and glamour, exploited by Byrne's marketing instincts, proved a winning formula. As part of their Vegas show, the band did a fifteen-minute Irish set: Cole played tin whistle, Irish dancers came on stage in traditional costume, and Bowyer sang *Danny Boy*. Irish Americans lapped it up. The programme had to be fast-moving and slick to hold the attention of audiences with other things on their minds. To complement the cabaret-style show, four glamorous dancers were added to the line-up: Phyllis O'Brien, Angela Larney, Maureen Carter and lead dancer Rita Houlihan. The Big 8 caused scenes of wild excitement on their first trip home. Fr. Brian D'Arcy recalls one memorable night at the National Ballroom, Dublin. People climbed on tables at the back of the hall to catch a glimpse of what was happening on stage. Bowyer and Dunphy were sensational. The band sounded terrific. Byrne, as always, stood in the wings with a torch in his hand. He flashed signals to indicate whether the volume needed to be increased or reduced. A red light meant that sound levels were too high; a white light that everything was okay. Back in Las Vegas, the Big 8 remained at the Stardust till '75. They transferred to the Aladdin with a reformed band after Dunphy's death in '75 and stayed in residence there till '80. Then, new owners came along with different ideas about lounge acts. The prospect of a contract next emerged at the Barbary Coast, situated beside the Flamingo Hilton which houses 'Kitty O'Shea's' casino and is directly adjacent to Caesar's. It was owned by Michael Gaughan, who became a friend of T.J. Byrne's. The Big 8 manager flew out to the Barbary Coast to meet Gaughan about a contract. "I went out and spoke to the man and we clicked," he says. "We had a great relationship. I came back with the contract for the Barbary Coast and the band started that in '82." The Big 8 were exiled in Nevada, playing three shows a night, six nights a week.

The band that spawned them, the Royal, had long since passed into history. The home-grown heroes who once took the highest pop honour in Britain went back to their day jobs when the business died in the '70s. There are no monuments to the Royal — just memories. The band who led a posse of showbands along a well-worn track were trapped by commercial success. Musical creativity was not encouraged: original material was sacrificed because audiences paid to hear the Top 20 and watch a clever show. The Royal never felt the need to write.

Neither did other bands. Even if songwriting was encouraged, recording was in its infancy in the early '60s. The showbands didn't have access to studio masters of the future. As Jackie Flavelle puts it: "If there had been a proper recording industry in Ireland during the boom years of the bands, who knows what would have happened to the Royal. They might have been as big as the Tremeloes, the Hollies or even the Beatles." The Carl Alan Award is proudly displayed in Coppinger's living room. It is a talking point when young friends of his family come to visit. He tries to explain what the Royal meant to the parents of the U2 generation.

Bowyer — The Irish Elvis

Las Vegas, January, 1983.

A road accident interrupts the afternoon flow of traffic through a busy junction in Las Vegas. Broken glass is scattered everywhere. Four smashed cars sit motionless. Drivers are dazed, but nobody is hurt. Someone calls the cops. The cause of the accident is immediately apparent. A motorist drove through a red light. He struck a car which came from a turning lane. Both careered across the street and ploughed into two cars stopped on the other side. The pile-up clogs traffic until the police arrive to untangle the mess. The offending motorist, Brendan Bowyer, is under the influence of alcohol.

The stakes were rising ever higher for Bowyer during the early '80s. He re-entered the real world on that January afternoon in Vegas while waiting to be freed from his wrecked car. An error of judgment could have cost him his life. Bowyer tried to beat the lights. He watched the sides, not the turning lane, and accelerated into another car. The fact that two other vehicles were then implicated meant it was a one- in-a-million stroke of good fortune that nobody was injured, or worse. For Bowyer, it could have been the end of the road.

It was the first time he thought seriously about the condition no-one ever wants to admit: alcoholism. Bowyer had been in tight corners before and always managed to stay in control. This time, he almost blew it all. "I was only up out of bed," he recalls. "I had two beers with my lunch. But certainly I had alcohol in my system from the night before. So I was well over the legal limit when the police came. I would have to say that it was responsible for the accident. The police brought me in. I got out a few hours later after signing all the things. I had to go back to court and pay my fine. I was very lucky. I was very fortunate because, a month later, there was a big turnover in all state laws about driving under the influence of alcohol. I was fined; but I was very lucky. I didn't even lose my licence, which I should have had. It was probably due to some Irish influence in City

Hall. I escaped. I was fined about five hundred dollars. The car crash could have been far more serious. I tried to give it up after that. I found that I would go for days without it. Then I would go back because of the withdrawal symptoms. I wanted to calm my nerves. That's how far the alcohol got at my nervous system."

The crunch came in November, '83, as he prepared for a family winter vacation in Hawaii. He was given an ultimatum by his doctor. Hawaii would still be there in six months — but he wouldn't. He agreed to spend four weeks undergoing treatment at a hospital care unit in Vegas. It was the foundation of his sobriety after years of addiction. Bowyer 'probably realised' before 1982 that he was hooked. But booze never created a problem — as long as he got enough of it. The addiction worsened in Las Vegas during the late '70s. It "escalated" from 1982. The problem developed gradually to a point where it dominated his life.

Bowyer was twenty-two before he touched a drop. He could take it or leave it. In those days, alcohol was the only drug available to showbands. Many frowned on it and were content with pots of tea and sandwiches after dances. Drink became more popular and acceptable as the decade progressed. By the age of twenty-seven, Bowyer was already on the way to becoming a veteran in Irish showbusiness. Since eighteen, he had been a big box office draw: a creation of rock'n'roll. The voice had unique qualities. Ireland's first rocker had people wriggling and twisting in ballrooms from Cork to Belfast with powerful interpretations of Presley's greatest hits like *Jailhouse Rock* and *Hound Dog*. Equally, he commanded ovations for a masterful delivery of beautiful ballads like *Love Thee Dearest*.

He could handle the emotional peaks that came with the climax of each stage performance six nights a week and, of course, the comedown afterwards. Pills could be acquired to calm nerves or else pump the adrenalin if someone desperately wanted them, but they weren't popular. Whiskey, gin or vodka did the trick just as well. Ireland was largely untouched by the drug-oriented hippie movement sweeping the U.S. Dope did not exist for the Irish showbands. Marijuana was the only drug around, but the bands preferred alcohol. If the lads felt like a few jars before or after a dance, why not? They deserved it. Alcohol wasn't regarded as a drug; it gave the right buzz before going on and helped to relax afterwards. Although the ballrooms were dry, proprietors who wanted to show their hospitality to bands left bottles backstage in the dressing rooms. Bands were never tired coming off stage. They were wound-up from the electricity generated by thousands of applauding and cheering fans squashed into a ballroom. It took time to unwind — and a couple of hours before they felt like going to bed. Band members stayed up in the hotel talking about everything under the sun. Some drank tea; others kept the night porter in training running to the residents' lounge with trays of drink.

It was almost inevitable that Bowyer would make a friend of alcohol like many of his contemporaries. For one thing, he has always been known in the business as a sociable fellow. He enjoys good company. Booze was the perfect ice-breaker. It helped to make friends easily. Bowyer made himself available to everybody. He was never struck by superstar delusions. He had a no-nonsense attitude to fan adulation: they were the 'punters' who paid his wages. He was a relatively moderate drinker up to the '70s. The problem worsened under the Nevada sun. Somewhere along the line booze took over. He planned his life around it. It got to the point where alcohol was nearly always in his system — as when he caused a four car smash in '83. Everybody could see he had a problem — everybody, that is, except himself. Friends say a crucial turning point was the untimely death of his stage partner. It had a shattering effect. He lapsed into a depression. His drinking became noticeably heavier. Tom Dunphy had a steadying influence, and Bowyer respected him. Dunphy was like his brother. They came from similar backgrounds, grew up and worked together and shared the same ambitions during the early days with T.J. Byrne. Later, they made the agonising decision to quit the Royal and start the Big 8. Dunphy watched out for Bowyer; he knew his strengths and weaknesses.

"Tom actually cared for Brendan," says Fr. Brian D'Arcy, a friend of both men. "He looked after him. He brought him to gigs. He took him home. Brendan was shy. Tom was low-key, not hyper, peaceful. He kept the band in order. Tom was the punters' man. He'd spot you a mile coming in the hall. He was the band's announcer, the MC. Brendan couldn't spoof himself, so Tom sold Brendan on stage. Once Brendan grabbed the microphone, he sold himself." Dunphy's loss was incalculable.

"Tom's death broke his heart," recalls Brendan's sister, Olive. The grim news came as Bowyer and Byrne finished dinner at the Great Northern Hotel, Bundoran, on Tuesday evening, July 29th, 1975. They were waiting for the band to arrive to play at the Mary of Dungloe Festival. Dunphy and fellow Big 8 Band member Noel Ryan were travelling from Waterford. Dunphy was driving. The Big 8 had just returned from their six-month stint at the Stardust in Las Vegas and were doing a series of one-night stands around the country. They were always guaranteed a good welcome home by their Irish fans. Bowyer had decided earlier that week to go to the Galway Races. Otherwise, he probably would have been in the car on that ill-fated evening. Bowyer and Byrne were chatting at their table in the hotel restaurant.Bowyer remarked that the boys were late. Byrne was paged to answer a phone call. He was still in the middle of dessert — so Bowyer offered to take it. He returned white-faced with his hands shaking. "Tom is gone...Tom is gone." Byrne asked: "Gone where?" Bowyer replied: "He's dead." Byrne will never forget the look of fright on his face.

Paddy Cole, who had just quit as leader of the Big 8 to form the Superstars, passed Dunphy on the road that day. "We saw each other passing in Kilbeggan: he was going one way, we were going the other. That night we went down to Ballybunion. We were just in the hotel ready to play when we got the word that Tom was killed."

On the Thursday before the fatal accident, Fr. D'Arcy took Dunphy to see country singer Ray Lynam at the National Ballroom, Dublin. "We spoke about the whole scene that night," he recalls. "It's one of the nicest memories I have of him. We had a great chat. At three in the morning, Tom always got really serious and talked about life. He'd been to the Waterford Glass factory that day. He was amazed that everywhere he went in Waterford on that trip home, people started singing *If I Didn't*

Have a Dime. He told me he wished he'd get another hit like that." The song was still remembered in his home town... ten years after it went to No. 1 in the charts.

Those closest to Dunphy during the Royal years describe him as a talented entertainer and a warm, good-humoured individual. He liked to play practical jokes too. Coppinger tells a story about one performance at the Arcadia in Cork in which Dunphy deflated the hopes of a diligent suitor. The band had noted a charmer who, by the last slow dances of the night, was making rapid progress with the woman of his desires. They were dancing by the stage, gazing into each other's eyes. Dunphy, as it happened, knew who he was. For a laugh, he took the mike and announced a special request for 'Mr. X', to mark the birth of his son! The lady stepped back and walloped her hapless dance partner across the face. The Royal exploded in laughter.

Dunphy had just bought a new house in Waterford. He left behind his wife, Maura, and four children. He was forty. A tragic car accident robbed a family of a good husband and good father, and the Big 8 of its heart and soul. Ryan, lucky to escape serious injury, was taken to the County Hospital in Longford. Newspaper reports said that Dunphy died instantly when his Ford Granada car collided with a lorry on the Carrick-on-Shannon/Longford road at 6.30pm.

Gardai said the accident happened as the singer was rounding a bend. A simple memorial stone today marks the spot at Drumsna. The story made front page news in the following morning's papers. Ironically, Dunphy's career was going from strength to strength. He was a gifted singer and guitarist who pioneered country'n'western music in Ireland. He had number one hits with *Come Down From The Mountain Katie Daly* and *If I Didn't Have a Dime*. He had recorded a number of best-selling solo LPs, including one produced in Nashville, the home of C&W. Dates were cancelled as the showband business mourned with the bereaved family and also with Bowyer, the Big 8 and Royal. It was the blackest week for showbands. Two days after Dunphy died, three members of the Miami were senselessly gunned to death in a terrorist ambush after a dance at the Castle Ballroom in Banbridge.

On the night of Thursday, July 31st, 3,000 lined the streets of Waterford as the Dunphy funeral cortege arrived from Carrick-on-Shannon. On reaching Ballytruckle, the hearse was surrounded by a guard of honour comprised of members of the original Royal Showband on one side and those from the Big 8 on the other, led by Dunphy's lifelong friend, Bowyer. The two managers associated with the singer's career, Byrne and Lynch, were in the line-up, as was former Royal lead guitarist Jim Conlon, who flew in from New York. He had returned to the U.S. on the previous Sunday after a holiday at home. Next day, the remains were laid to rest. But the show resumed — as Tom would have wished. The band reformed. The Big 8 had already lost Paddy Cole, Twink and some of the musicians before the fatal accident.

Cole tired of the Vegas routine. "We were doing a show three times a night six nights a week for six or seven months at a time," he recalls. "It would put you off your game. It would put you around the twist doing the same thing night after night. That's what eventually got to me. I just couldn't hack it any more, not blowing new numbers. Also, my eldest son, Pearse, had started going to school in Vegas. We came home and decided not to go back. I started the Paddy Cole Superstars and got the nucleus of the Big 8 in with me on that. I didn't go after them. I just told them I was leaving." Twink had been replaced by Kelley who left the Nevada to join the Big 8 in '74 at the invitation of Dunphy and Byrne. But Kelley felt frustrated too by the monotony of the routine, and she suffered ill-health in Las Vegas. She decided to leave the Big 8 when the band came home in summer '75. The Big 8 returned to Las Vegas for six months in '76 — this time to the Aladdin. Replacements were brought in to fill gaps. Dunphy was replaced by bass guitarist Frankie Carroll, who joined the Big 8 from Frank McCaffrey and the Country Folk. He was enlisted by Bill Fuller who telephoned him in Manchester from the Bahamas. D.J. Curtin, who had fronted the successful Kerry Blues, joined three years later. The fresh start in '76 failed to conceal the enormous loss. That year, The Hucklebuck was released again and went to No. 4 in the Irish charts. Dunphy's absence left a void that was impossible to fill. Bowyer felt lost without his friend and singing partner of so many years.

A gloom hung over the Big 8 on their return to Las Vegas. Bowyer took the loss hardest of all, and his drinking got heavier. Las Vegas was a social universe from Waterford of the '50s when Bowyer came of age. It was a custom-built resort in the middle of the desert. It began as a small Mormon mining town in the mid 1800s. In 1905, it became a railroad junction. Civic leaders in the 1930s dreamt up a plan to turn it into a resort city. Gambling was legalised in Nevada. The resort didn't take off, however, until the '40s when Bugsy Siegel, a Los Angeles gangster, opened the Flamingo Hotel. Rates for accommodation, food and entertainment were rockbottom. Siegel recouped losses on the gambling tables. The formula still works. Las Vegas attracts fifteen million visitors annually. Seven hundred organisations from all parts of the U.S. hold conventions there. Sixty thousand people work in the tourist industry, the city's biggest employer. Big production shows feature technical feats of wizardry with waterfalls, explosions, fireworks and casts of hundreds.

Bowyer watched Las Vegas mushroom into a resort city. It is the most garish of the world's oases — a playground for the Hollywood motion picture set. Las Vegas was the ideal outlet for the showmanship of the Royal — and later the Big 8. They spent six months making good money there — and then home for summer tours: the best of both worlds. Once home, they went straight on the road and, suddenly, farmers were being treated to a slick Vegas-style cabaret show in places like Newcastle-west. On his return to Nevada, Bowyer joined the troupe of resident entertainers who were well-paid to play their part in the tourist fantasy. For resident entertainers, the nightly schedule was demanding. Audiences constantly changed. Performers like Bowyer never knew what they wanted till the band got through the first half hour. Bowyer's formula was tailor-made for the tourists; the show was packaged to contain something for everybody. Residents lead routine daily lives far removed from the Strip and the hedonistic exploits of visitors.

A normal life does exist away from the neon glare: there are shopping centres, churches, schools and a university. Establishing a home life wasn't easy for Bowyer's wife, Stella. The initial six-month split between Ireland and Vegas was hard. Later, she had the task of raising three young children during the mid-70s. Friends say that their commitment to Brendan Jnr, a talented tennis player, Aisling and Clodagh, is absolute. Bowyer says that drink did not impinge on family life. "It was my problem really; nobody else's. I didn't let it interfere with the children, luckily enough, because they were sleeping while I was working and I was in bed when they were in school. So when I was up everything was fine." Bowyer made his name impersonating Presley in the Irish ballrooms and, later on, in the entertainment lounges of Las Vegas. Their friendship was cemented in Nevada. They first met for five minutes in '66. It was a dream come true for Bowyer. Presley was making a movie in Hollywood. Bowyer had his picture taken with him. Presley listened politely to what the young Irishman had to say. It went no further than that.

Bowyer sensed 'a kind of innocence' about him; the Southern boy unsure of how to handle fame and fortune. By summer '69, Bowyer's reputation for his Presley routines had spread among the showbusiness jet-set in Las Vegas. Presley was launching a comeback at the International Hotel — his first appearance in Las Vegas since '56. Those shows were used later as the opening event in the '79 movie, *Elvis*. Presley was intrigued to hear of the performer who replicated him as part of his act. He went to see Bowyer and the Royal Showband at the Stardust. "Elvis came into the audience and jumped up on stage," recalls Bowyer. "He gyrated a bit, laughed, ran out again and left a message that he'd be back the following night. He was. This time, he brought his entourage. We went back to where he was playing that night. He had a penthouse at the International, now the Las Vegas Hilton. We had a good conversation. I got to know him reasonably well."

Bowyer later developed the friendship to the point where he enjoyed rare access to Presley during the early '70s. Anytime the King hit Vegas, Bowyer was allowed backstage. He could even introduce relatives and friends from Ireland. He once introduced his youngest sister, Alison, to Presley, when she came over on holidays. Alison was whisked off to a party attended by Presley and his wife, Priscilla. The king sipped water. Presley was "ordinary and chatty." Bowyer introduced Alison as his little sister and, trembling, she said: "Hello, Elvis."

Suddenly, Bowyer was sent to Siberia in 1974. The access was ended. "In hindsight, I think that Elvis was starting to get aloof for many reasons," he says. "Even before that, he was cut off from the general public. His life was changing; he was changing. I really thought that he was the humble country boy. I never saw anything different in him. He seemed to be very sincere and intelligent. I don't know why he allowed himself to become so cut off from the world. I don't think it was really necessary for him." Bowyer's memories of him are indelible... like the time that Tom Dunphy mustered up enough courage to ask Presley why he made such second rate movies. The question came out of the blue during one of several meetings between Presley and the Royal. Bowyer was taken aback, and thought that Presley might take offence. He didn't. With typical honesty, Dunphy asked: "We all know, Elvis, that you had ambitions to be a movie star. Why did you make all those grade-B movies?" Presley was equally frank. "When I made *King Creole*, and some of the early ones, I thought that I might improve," he replied. "But we got millions of dollars a piece and it became an assembly line." Presley admitted he had made a mistake — but the movies swelled his bank accounts. Later on, Bowyer recorded his personal tribute, *Thank You Elvis*. The record climbed to No. 4 and stayed in the Irish charts for eight weeks following Presley's death on August 16th, 1977.

Bowyer has had his own share of suffering and can understand better than most what made Presley turn to prescription pills. "When we first met Elvis, we were having a couple of beers at the time. He said that he used a Bloody Mary once in a very seldom while. If he had two, he got a rash. He had some kind of resistance to alcohol. So he took prescription pills. I can understand what might have happened to him. You just get hooked on something. You try something once to give you a lift when you go on stage. You get hooked on it. Simple as that." Presley was moulded into the 'biggest goddamn industry' in America — as Bowyer was during the early '60s on an infinitely smaller scale in Ireland. Presley had a seminal role in the birth of rock culture.

BRENDAN and ELVIS

Bowyer was its personification for the Irish people. Both performers paid a high price. Presley got hooked on prescription drugs: Bowyer became an alcoholic. But the Irishman stopped short of making what was later cynically described as a great career move by Presley: he died. Presley was worth 4.9 million dollars when he passed away; twelve years later the estate was valued at more than 75 million dollars. Estate revenue alone in 1989 exceeded 15 million dollars — more than Presley made in any single year during his career. Yet, as Michael O'Riordan of Ritz Records points out, before Presley died "you couldn't give his records away."

Despite years of heavy drinking, Bowyer survived. He speaks with authority on the subject of addiction. "I am an alcoholic." The admission comes a lot easier now. It is a relief to roll out the four words that once caused such distress, threatened his career and, indeed, his life. People in the business who watched him put away vodka still wonder how his system coped. In the mid '70s, it wasn't unusual to pick up a strong smell of alcohol in Bowyer's dressing room. Friends became accustomed to seeing the two Bowyers — one drunk, the other sober. A dark period of career pressures and bereavements took a combined toll on Bowyer. His mother died on April 21th, 1974. Tom Dunphy died just over a year later. "There was a lot of upheaval in his life at that point," says his sister Olive. "I think perhaps all those things did have an effect on his drinking. He's quite sentimental, you know."

By the late '70s, the drinking reached alarming proportions, but all efforts to convince him that he needed help failed. "As with most alcoholics," says Olive, "he didn't realise the damage he was doing to himself. To be fair, he was a good husband. He provided for his family and made sure that they wanted for nothing."

Bowyer's daily routine revolved around alcohol. "I got to the stage where I couldn't exist with it and I couldn't exist without it," he admits. "It was a vicious circle. I didn't take a drink until I was about twenty-two or twenty-three in the first place. Then it was easy for me to take it or leave it. When I got into the forties, I started tanking up between the three shows a night in Vegas. I think that the drinking problem snowballed there. It might have been latent alcoholism all the time. Now I am an alcoholic, and that's it. During the last stages in '82, I would probably have four double vodkas and maybe a beer between shows. Then I'd go out, do the show, come back and repeat that again. Easily a litre of vodka a day. I maintained the buzz by having a beer here and there as the day went on. Even while out playing golf — that is, if I could see the ball properly — I had a beer. I used to plan my whole day whereby I wouldn't be too far away from it. I wouldn't go on boat trips if I didn't think that there was going to be drink because it meant that I would be away from it. I had it hidden around the house.I had it everywhere."

It is impossible to pinpoint any single cause. A combination of circumstances carried Brendan Bowyer over the edge. "You can't blame anything for things like that," he says. "It's a drug. It's a lethal drug. It's legal, but it's lethal. I probably felt a bit insecure as I was growing older. That prompted me to drink a little bit more than I had been.Now it's a relief that I don't have to worry about it. It doesn't bother me. It was hard during the first year or so probably. There are times when I would like a glass of wine with a meal. If it was an awfully hot day, a cold beer would taste great. But, sure a cold Ballygowan would probably taste just as good. If you're an alcoholic, you're an alcoholic. There's nothing to blame for it. It's something that grew on me and I didn't realise what was happening. I don't think it had any toll on my marriage. Everything was moderate until the late '70s. I just got a bit insecure going on stage and drank more. The volume of drink increased. The type of blackouts I had were not remembering things. Maybe I made an appointment or maybe I had a conversation with somebody the night before and promised to do something. I never blacked out and fell down. But lapses of memory, yes.

"I didn't touch pills or drugs at any stage. I found that having a couple of drinks before I went out made me ready to go. But it got to be more and more. Alcohol gave me that pick-up initially. Advancing years probably had something to do with it. I don't mind being fifty. I remember feeling far more traumatic at thirty. Forty didn't bother me so much, but then I really started to feel it. Once I made up my mind to go into hospital it was a relief. A big relief for me. We were on vacation so I wasn't missing work or anything. I felt much better afterwards. It was a relief not to have to worry about where the next drink was coming from." Now he takes one day at a time. He knows that one drink could obliterate all the hard work. "You can never say never," he says. "But as far as I'm concerned, it *is* never. I'm clean and sober and that's the way I want to stay."

His vision of the present is clearer. Recollections of the past are, at times, hazy. He remembers events in the '60s more readily than the '70s. "I remember the earlier parts of my life better than the '70s. The '60s and growing up in Waterford. I'll never forget that side of it." Bowyer has an exceptional memory for peoples' names and faces. He still surprises his sisters by recalling the names of childhood friends from the tennis club.

I first met Brendan Bowyer in August, 1989. The Big 8 were on their annual month-long Irish tour before settling into Clontarf Castle in Dublin for September. They played two nights at the Mary from Dungloe Festival on the previous weekend. It was Bowyer's first return to the Donegal event since Dunphy's death. Summer '89 marked the Big 8's fourth annual trip home. Previously, they remained in the U.S. from '82 to '85/'86. Initially, the Big 8 had a 50 week-a-year contract at the Barbary Coast. That was reduced by mutual agreement to 38 weeks. This allowed time for other projects: an Irish tour or else performances in New York or Boston. The residency at Clontarf Castle was the brainchild of Connie Lynch who, in his own words, "got back" with Bowyer five years ago. They had kept in touch over the years. Bowyer liked the idea of a two-week slot at the Castle. At first, it was a working holiday.

The venue was booked solid for the entire two weeks. It was a runaway success. Fans who hadn't seen Bowyer for five years wanted him to go on tour. This encouraged the Big 8 to return home for two months: one on the road and the second playing dinner shows at the Castle. Lynch's strategy was to pick twenty venues around the country where he hoped to draw crowds.

Professionally, Bowyer's bread and butter has been made in Las Vegas. The Big 8 performed three sets a night, six nights a week at the Barbary Coast hotel. Although hard work, the money was guaranteed, and so were the "punters." Bowyer got to bed by about 4am and was up by noon. His typical work day started around 9pm. On time-off, he played golf, tennis and enjoyed walking. The Big 8's eight-year-relationship with the Barbary Coast ended in March, 1990. The band played in other hotels before returning to Ireland for their annual summer tour. Negotiations were underway for thirty-six weeks' work in '91 spread over three hotels — the Aladdin, Four Queens and Holiday Inn. As the Big 8 returned to the U.S. in autumn 1990, Frankie Carroll announced his resignation from the band to take up a post as a marketing executive in Chicago.

Bowyer still gets a kick out of performing after over three decades in the business. He dismisses any talk of retirement. Age doesn't matter, he says. It's the performance that counts. He'll quit when he sees no further point to it all. "I won't proceed with the flogging when the man is dead." The accent is sort of mid-Atlantic these days, but Bowyer insists he'll never be fully Americanised. He has spent over twenty years with Uncle Sam, but protects his Irish identity. "We say we live there. But we never call it home. We live for the time when we can come home." Bowyer's father, Stanley, who remarried, died in 1980. His stepmother, May, lives in Waterford.

He can vividly freeze-frame the moment in his career that gave him most pleasure. It was the Royal's appearance at a Royal Variety Performance in London shortly after their Carl Alan victory in '61. "That's when I got the most excitement." Regrets? He's had a few. "I regret that because of our economic success — and I think this is where U2 scored — we neglected getting into original material. We were an economic success, so we sat on our laurels. Because we were an economic and financial success, we didn't go further ahead into trying to be original. The Beatles did that, and so did U2." The greatest tribute which can be paid to Bowyer is that he lasted in a crazy business while an endless stream of 'stars' rode the merry-go-round and disappeared into oblivion. Alcoholism took a toll, but he survived when all the odds were stacked against him and when lesser men would have fallen. The eyes may have lost some of the glitter, but the will to go on is as strong as ever. At the end of the day, it's all that really matters.

The Ballroom 'Land'lord

Co. Longford, July 5th, 1962.

Thick fog blankets the road. It's six in the morning. Albert Reynolds is nodding off at the wheel. Nearly home: another five miles to go. Smash! The accident happens in a dip on the road between Edgeworthstown and Longford. Reynolds crashes head-on into a lorry, skids and ends up in a ditch. The right wheel of his car is torn off: the drive shaft pushed out through the boot. The road is littered with broken bottles and money: whiskey flows everywhere; paper money scatters like confetti. The crashed car reeks of booze. The lorry driver assumes he's been struck by a drunk. Reynolds is charged later with drunken driving, reduced to careless driving. Reynolds, in fact, never touched a drop in his life.

He points today to a slight scar over his right eye. "You see that; that's where the mirror cut me." The Minister for Finance resembles a soldier discussing an old war wound as his private secretary enters the inner sanctum on Merrion Street, Dublin, with a document to be signed. The civil servant waits for his boss to finish the story before laying the document before him. "I nearly killed myself. I didn't come back to Kathleen on the first night after our honeymoon. She had to find me in hospital. Some start to married life, eh?"

Reynolds was driving home from a dance in Athy when the collision occurred. His night's earnings were scattered all over the road. "You'd throw a bag of money into the boot at that time. You'd drive across the country. Sometimes you wouldn't even take it out of the boot when you got home. You're talking a thousand, maybe two: a lot of money. You wouldn't even think about it. That was the society that time. It was a different country then." Reynolds had returned from his honeymoon in Majorca and went straight to a show dance in Athy. It was a big night in the area, one of the few occasions when the Reynolds' chain had to provide a bar. Kielys of Waterford were enlisted to provide the drink, and a team of barmen to serve it. The promised barmen never showed up. There was only one thing to do: roll up the sleeves and get behind the counter. Reynolds and his brother, Jim, assisted by an employee who travelled with them from Longford, ran the bar. "At the end of it all, we were jacked," says Albert. "Out for the count." He packed leftover bottles of whiskey in the boot, tossed in the bag of money and took to the road exhausted in the early hours...but the ballroom mogul came to grief.

It's easy to see why Albert is so well-liked, not just across the political divide, but in all walks of life. He shares many attributes with Brian Lenihan, who, when asked to take sides in one political controversy, described himself as "the X in OXO." Reynolds also possesses the "X" factor. He is gregarious, disarming, self-mocking when needs be. Reynolds never shies away from publicity, and is a practised media game player. Friends say that the yahoo went out of him years ago: the suits got darker, and more conservative. But he's still an old trouper at heart. His face lights up at tales of the good old days: a young entrepreneur selling sweets to schoolmates; a Bord na Mona clerk who footed turf to make an extra few bob; a CIE biro-pusher by day, and dance promoter by night; fortune-seeker in the ballrooms of romance; bingo king; and the thread that tied it all together...the gambler who loved to raise the stakes.

Each story is laced with humour, boyish enthusiasm and the right mix of self-congratulation or self-criticism. He smiles at the success of schemes that others denounced as madness. He guffaws at the spectacular failures. Reynolds' entrepreneurial flair was given full expression in the boom years of the '60s. People had money to spend, and he gave them something to spend it on.

The future Minister for Finance left school in Sligo at seventeen, quit a secure job in CIE at twenty-three and, by thirty-five, had made a sizable fortune in the ballroom business. Reynolds was born in Roosky, Co. Roscommon, in November, 1935. He and his predecessor at the finance ministry, Ray MacSharry, both attended Summerhill College, Sligo. By the mid '50s, Reynolds was working as a clerk with Bord na Mona at Ballydermot, Co. Kildare. The pay was £4 a week. He occasionally made a further £5 by working on his own plot of turf during time off. He lived in a hostel at Ballydermot that cost twenty-five shillings a week.

In 1955, Reynolds moved on to CIE and worked, once again as a clerk, at Dromod, a few miles from Roosky. Twenty five years later, he would become Minister for Transport in charge of the company. Young Reynolds was elected secretary of a carnival committee in '55/'56, running marquee dances to raise funds for the church building fund at Roosky. He liked the dancing game: the wheeling-and-dealing, booking bands and manning the box office. It was the perfect antidote to mundane clerical tasks for CIE. He learned how to run marquees: make the bookings at least six months in advance, handle the advertising, hire teams of workmen to erect the huge tent, lay the floors, and pay the wages. He relished the challenge of following a project through to the end, from booking the band to counting the take at the end of a dance. It was more rewarding than moving paper around Bord na Mona or CIE. Still, the transport authority was steady employment when jobs were hard to come by. Most of his friends were taking the boat.

Reynolds ran the marquee, successfully, for two years. On the third year, as he put the finishing touches to a festival programme, the local priest announced with gratitude that the fund-raising mission had been accomplished. However, the budding entrepreneur had already made agreements with bands. The last thing he wanted to do was to call it off. His inclination was to press ahead independently, but he didn't have the money to back up that kind of risk. "I went to my eldest brother, Joe, who was home. I asked him if he wanted to share the risk and, between us, we'd have a go. That's what we did. I ran the marquee for two years. It was very successful. During the second year my brother, Jim, came home from Australia. We sat down and discussed the whole business. We were all single. It looked like an opportunity."

It all began in 1957 when they bought a site for a ballroom beside the house where they were born and reared. It would be called the Cloudland. Within twelve months, the ballroom was up and, in Albert's words, "away it went from there."

The Reynolds' pooled their resources and made use of their individual talents. A third brother, Joe, stayed on the farm. Jim had been in the building business in Australia, so he took charge of construction. Albert had sufficient experience to deal with bands and handle the money. He had built up a relationship with many bands and their managers since the marquee days. The Clipper Carlton and the Melody Aces were the hottest dance tickets. The Rhythm Boys from Buncrana were a big draw also in the midlands. The big bands of Quigley, McIntyre, Delaunty and Mulcahy were in demand too. "Some people said that we were mad in the head," recalls Albert. "The ballroom thing was supposed to be a joke. It couldn't be done. Everybody thought we were lunatics to build a ballroom where there was no population. But people travelled forty and fifty miles to dances if the attraction was good enough. Knock Airport was a bigger joke. And, when I started to build a factory in Longford for cat and dog food, people thought I'd gone around the bend. Nobody buys food for cats and dogs, they told me. You feed them on scraps off the table."

The Reynolds' had a habit of confounding the critics. The Cloudland was an instant success. Next came the Roseland in Moate, followed by the Fairyland, Roscommon; Dreamland, Athy; Danceland, Portlaoise; Jetland, Limerick; Lakeland, Mullingar; Barrowland, New Ross; Rockland, Borris-in-Ossory; Borderland, Clones; Moyland, Ballina, and so on. The expansion was fast and furious. The Reynolds' brothers soon monopolised the business. "I was booking the bands, paying the wages and paying for the building of the new ballrooms," says Albert. "Jim was the contractor, the building man. He'd get the sites. We'd identify them on a map first and decide where to go next strategically. The construction was Jim's business. He'd go off and get the site and build the ballroom. It took about three and a half months from start to finish. I'd tell him to give me a date for completion. Everything had to be finished for the opening night and I would do the rest."

At the peak, the Reynolds' empire stretched to fourteen ballrooms. The chain leased other ballrooms, adding even more dance dates to the Reynolds' diary. Their influence was enormous; the architects of a minor social revolution that changed the recreational patterns of part of rural Ireland. They were talent scouts as well as businessmen, spotting new acts and giving them a platform before huge audiences. Some of the biggest names in the business were given their first break by the brothers. Friends from that period describe Albert as a workaholic, capable of turning his hand to any task, from selling tickets at the door to hanging up coats in the cloakroom. He expected others to shape up, too. Perfection was demanded and dedicated workers were rewarded.

Showbands, caught the imagination of the young. Astute businessmen like the Reynolds' housed the explosion. Ballroom owners provided the venues where the bands and their fans came together. The proprietors reaped a rich harvest. "Of course, it was big money in those times, " says Albert. "But, remember, we started off with very small money. Let's be honest about it, I was a clerk in CIE. My brother came home from Australia after spending four years there. We went to the Munster and Leinster Bank (now AIB) in Longford. I was able to show figures from the marquee to prove the potential of the business. Jim had a certain amount of money home from Australia. So, we put it up and the bank matched it and we got the first ballroom built. The cash flow was very good. We used the cash flow from the first ballroom to build the second one and the flow from those two to build a third, and so on. In fairness, the bank kept running with us. Unless you have a bank to run with you in this type of business, you just can't operate. But, to this day, it's the same for anybody in business. Your word is your bond. If you give a commitment to a bank, you keep it. Banks will run with you. We would never have gotten off the ground if it wasn't for the Munster and Leinster. Cash flow became a buzz phrase fifteen years later. But that's how we built the ballrooms — on cash flow."

The management structure was simple. Albert ran the growing chain of ballrooms from their hotel, the Longford Arms, assisted by a secretary. He worked with a local man in each area. In some places, such as Limerick, full-time managers were employed: Maxie Muldoon managed the Jetland on the Ennis Road. Sunday was the busiest night in rural ballrooms. The brothers picked two or three halls each and criss-crossed the

(Photo: Cork Examiner)

country to make sure everything ran smoothly. The economics were simple. Take a busy night in any of the bigger ballrooms such as the Roseland or Jetland: the profit from the mineral bar paid the band; the cloakroom paid the staff; the door takings were for the Reynolds. Advertising costs took little out of the pay off. It was a bonanza.

By 1966, the Reynolds' chain was at full stretch. They competed with a rival chain, Associated Ballrooms. Both chains had first call on dates from the cream of the showbands. Bingo sessions were introduced at some of their ballrooms to keep business going on slack nights. Jim and Albert knew the strengths and weaknesses of each unit in the chain. For example: Tuesday was good night in Mullingar; Wednesday in Portlaoise; Thursday in Roscommon; Friday in Limerick and Athy, and Saturday also in Limerick. A showband that could close the doors in Roosky may not have done so in Limerick. Musical tastes varied from county to county. The Reynolds' developed their knowledge to such a degree that they could match bands to specific areas. They could predict what bands would draw the best crowds at any particular venue.

The Melody Aces were a big draw in Roosky, Moate and Mullingar — but were just 'reasonable' in Athy where they weren't suited to a 'city- type' audience. They weren't to be risked in Limerick. The Dixies were a major draw in the south — but not quite as strong in the midlands. "I could count the numbers that those guys would put in at different ballrooms," says Albert. "I got it down to that fine an art."

The first band to demand percentages from the Reynolds were the Clippers. The Strabane showmen wanted 50% of the take. The majority of bands were paid flat fees that varied in proportion to drawing power. The Capitol, for instance, started with the Reynolds' for £50 a night, but the fee rose to £100 and, finally, £150. T.J.Byrne, manager of the Royal, talked percentages too. Albert was against percentages in principle, but eventually had to pay up. He explains: "I felt that we were the ones who made the investment in the business. T.J. really pushed it around the country and wouldn't play without a percentage in the end. Everybody followed suit then. If I wouldn't pay a percentage, he could go to maybe a single ballroom guy whom they normally wouldn't play for anyway. Everybody was looking for the Royal. He'd give that ballroom owner a date for 60/40 in my catchment area. Pressures of business dictated, so I had to follow suit. I kept most bands on a straight fee basis as much as I could. It was all fees for a long time until the Royal went big."

Reynolds had a few other tricks up his sleeve: "I was the first one to introduce a £1,000 bingo session in Ireland. It was banned afterwards." The first session took place at the Roseland, Moate, ten days before Christmas '63. One thousand pounds was big money. It was a localised version of the National Lottery that appealed to one of the oldest human failings: greed. The rules were straightforward — a pound a book, buy as many as you like. The house was packed. The session generated £2,200 (the '90 equivalent — **£23,331.01**).

He recalls the night: "I collected the money at the door. I sold the books of tickets. I went up and switched on the microphone and called the numbers. Together with a young chap who was with me, we did the mineral bar at the break. We sold sweets, minerals and bars of chocolate for ten or fifteen minutes in the middle. I opened the ballroom. I sold the tickets. I called the numbers. I ran the mineral bar. I closed my bag and went home. I made about £1,100." The equivalent of that profit in '90 would be a staggering **£11,727.74**. The bingo king was at it again after Christmas — this time in Mullingar. The operation was the same. He whipped up local excitement. His thinking was that people would be broke after Christmas and anxious to pick up some easy money. He offered them the opportunity with another £1,000 top prize. Nothing could go wrong — or so he thought. But it snowed heavily for two days before the much-hyped bingo night. Roads were impassable. Reynolds chuckles when he recalls the small number of people who bought books that night — 315!

"I was on risk for £1,000 top prize and supplementary prizes of 180 quid. Then there was the cost of advertising and the buses I employed to bring people in and out. I was on high risk. I knew that I had such a small crowd that everybody was watching me and wondering whether this guy was going to pay out the money.

I decided to pay out 150 quid more than I was committed to. When I was losing anyway, I decided to lose big. At least the customers were going to be satisfied. I knew they would go away and talk about it, and I was right. The word went around like wildfire. To be honest, I lost about £1,100 that night, but it set up the one pound bingo for me for all time. I had it every night after that in Moate and Mullingar."

Profit in the ballrooms depended on getting bands at the right price before a competitor. That meant developing a nose for talent and moving in first to make bookings. Talent scouting was part of it all. Reynolds subscribed to *Melody Maker* magazine to keep track of up-and-coming acts in Britain. "You had to spot what you believed to be the rising talent and take a chance on it," he explains. Reynolds booked Kenny Ball and his band during a jazz phase in the early '60s for a tour at £35 a night. The booking was made nine months in advance — and six months before Ball reached No. 1 in Britain. Reynolds ended up with a chart-topper on his hands at a rockbottom price for ten nights.

"I did it on my own, purely as a personal promotion and not part of the Reynolds' company," he recalls. "I finished up after ten nights being able to buy my house in Longford from the profits." On the final night, Ball and Reynolds had a meeting. The jazzman was paid the agreed £350 fee. They discussed the success of the tour. "Sure we'll have ten nights again next year," said Reynolds. Ball replied: "Fair enough: you gave me a break when I needed it. I appreciated that." As Reynolds offered a farewell handshake, Ball had the final word. "One thing, though. Next time it'll be £100 a night." Deal done. Ball had two Top Ten hits in Ireland at the end of 1962 with *So Do I* and *The Pay Off*.

The Reynolds' had a policy of booking international acts to supplement the big bands at home. They brought Acker Bilk to Ireland for the first time. "I booked Roy Orbison once for a Tuesday night," says Albert. "I took a real flier on it. Jim Hand was promoting him on behalf of somebody else. He talked me into taking him on a Tuesday night in Mullingar for 500 guineas. That was high risk stuff. I wasn't so sure about it. I took a chance.

Quite candidly, I think I was charging ten shillings or else 7/6. I had it worked out that if I got 100 quid, then that was it. Okay, it was good advertising and good PR for the ballroom. It lifted the standard: people thought this is the place to go to... *All the big names play here*. I did investments like that at times to give a ballroom a boost. Roy Orbison pulled in almost 1,800 people, so I think I made two or three times more than I anticipated. But it was a real flier, high-risk stuff on a Tuesday night."

On another occasion, Reynolds booked Jim Reeves to play for two nights, but an act of God intervened to force a cancellation. "One of the dates was the night that the Pope died. We called off the dance. That was expected. Reeves waived the contract. I had great admiration for that man. After all, I had signed a contract with him for 650 pounds for two spots."

Reynolds' ballrooms packed in an astonishing number of people — as did the independently-owned halls. Was there no limit to the numbers squashed in? The Jetland was one of the biggest links in the chain. It attracted thousands every Saturday night from a wide sweep of counties Limerick, Clare and north Tipperary. "There were big nights in the Jetland with the Royal," says Albert. "You had to close the doors...between three and four thousand people. I wouldn't like to be talking in today's terms about the fire regulations. I remember collecting from 3,500 people in Athy one night. Totally unreal. You just didn't know where the people came out of. We opened all the fire exit doors for ventilation purposes. The ballroom wasn't built to accommodate those numbers. Inevitably, people might get in for nothing. But, at that stage, you had enough. It didn't matter."

The success of the Reynolds chain meant success for the business generally. The brothers fostered talent and brought it to public attention. Joe Dolan got a break from Reynolds — but not, the singer says, without persistence. As the ballroom chain lengthened, the Reynolds' discovered that they no longer had to chase talent. "Most people starting out in the business wanted to get to me," explains Albert. "That's because I could give them a week's bookings. I could give them ten bookings or I could give them fifty because I had so many ballrooms. I could give them one night a week spread across fourteen ballrooms. Individual ballrooms could only offer one. I used my own judgment as to whether I thought they'd make it or not. We made the bands that time."

Another act to come to his attention was Larry Cunningham and the Mighty Avons. "They came to hear the Royal Showband in Cavan one night. They were starting off and wanted a break. It was Brian Finlay I spoke to. He said that they were a mixture of everything, a bit country and western. I told him that I'd be opening a ballroom in Roscommon in two months time. The Clipper Carlton were playing. If they wanted to do the relief, to do an hour for them, then the Clippers would be happy. They were beginning to look for relief bands at the time. So, that's how the Mighty Avons got their break. They played in the ballroom at Roscommon and never looked back. We gave them other dates as well afterwards. There are so many of these guys around that it's hard to remember them all."

A nationwide business boom developed around the ballrooms — and around the Reynolds'. Booking bands was straight-forward. "There were no contracts," says Albert. "Your word was your bond. When you booked a date with a guy, he'd produce his diary and I'd produce my diary. We'd write in the dates and check them at the end. End of story. A full year's booking could be done with a particular band. No problems. The most dangerous thing for anybody was to run two diaries. The rule was you kept one diary, and one only. That way you don't make any mistakes. What's in the diary, that's it. Occasionally, some of the managers kept two diaries. They carried one with them and had the other at home. Naturally, they'd forget to transfer a date. It meant that a double booking might show up. Basically, it was a very simple structure and a very simply-run business. We kept it that way."

The Reynolds' prided themselves on their treatment of bands. "A lot of them will tell you that they went to a lot of single ballrooms where they only got tea and sandwiches. We always made sure that bands had a hot meal no matter where they travelled from. Steak or whatever they wanted. Look after your bands; look after your customers; make sure you give the customer what he wants. I followed the same philosophy in

(Photo: Sunday World)

business. It's the very same thing: look after your customers; look after your workers, and the profits will look after themselves."

There was competition for bookings between the Reynolds' and ballroom owners such as Con Hynes, Packie Hayes, Jack O'Rourke, Donie Collins, Bill Fuller, Peter Prendergast, the Byrnes, Caseys, Luceys and, of course, the irrepressible Mgr. James Horan. The big chains gobbled up dates: the smaller proprietors took what they could get. The Reynolds' were always accused of having a monopoly, but Msgr. Horan believed there was room for the small operator who knew the market and did his business properly. That brought him into competition with the Reynolds' empire.

The monsignor booked top bands for his hall at Tooreen. He ran a thriving business and threatened the survival of other halls in the region. He took crowds away from McGarry's Ballroom in Ballyhaunis. But McGarry's fought back by offering their premises to the Reynolds'. The idea was that Albert would transfer some of his bands to boost the Ballyhaunis ballroom. Then, news spread that the devil, no less, had been sighted in Horan's ballroom in Tooreen. The finger of suspicion pointed in one direction. "I was credited with it as an opposition tactic," says Albert. "I never took away from the fact. Mgr. Horan even said it to me on the day that we talked about building an airport in Knock. I don't know whether he really believed it — but he certainly remembered twenty-five years later. I was always blamed for it."

Profits from the fourteen ballrooms were to be seed money. Albert saw the writing on the wall, got out on the high tide in late '66 and set off on other adventures. He sensed that the bonanza was "tapering off" and wanted out in good time. Jim retained the Longford Arms and continued to operate the ballrooms successfully until the business faded in the '70s. The brothers went their separate ways. "I thought that ten good years in the business was enough," recalls Albert. "It took a downward trend, but was still a good business for another four or five years after. Many people made very big money and thought that their day would never end. They spent it as they got it. What they

(Photo: Cork Examiner)

failed to appreciate, or realise, was that they were going to have their period of making big money and then the bad days were going to come. They thought that this thing was going to go on and on. I didn't share that view. Some people who were probably better trained or had better management intuition knew that it wasn't going to last forever. Others thought that they could make money again next week and the week after that."

Albert went in search of other opportunities — among them Kehoe's bacon factory in Dublin, the *Longford News* and C&D Foods. That same business eye saw huge potential in pet foods because of the overseas demand for waste offal from his meat factory. C&D had its ups and downs, including a legal battle over shares in 1976, but it subsequently underwent investment on a scale that made it one of the most modern plants in Europe.

In politics, the old touch was evident. When Charles Haughey was elected Taoiseach in December, '79, Reynolds was one of his key supporters. He was rewarded with a Cabinet post. His elevation to Finance in 1988 was his fourth ministry, and it made him the most powerful political figure in the State after the Taoiseach. Only eleven years after his election to the Dail, Reynolds, the former clerk, held the nation's purse strings and, in the opinion of many, stood only a heartbeat away from the Taoiseach's office.

It's difficult to gauge how ruthless he is politically, but he was tough in business — or, as he puts it himself, "firm and fair."

Reynolds once bought a hotel in Athy, and he drove down one night to close the deal. He went to a solicitor's office, signed the contracts and paid the deposit. After a celebration drink with the outgoing proprietor and his wife, he returned to Longford. On his arrival home, an urgent message awaited him. The hotel's ex-proprietor had suffered a heart attack and dropped dead soon after Reynolds had left. It may well have been caused by the shock of changing business. Reynolds recalls: "His wife had three small kids. She was in a terrible state. I told one of the lads to go back in the car to Athy and tell her that if she wanted to throw the contract into the fire, then she could. And that's what she did." Reynolds was a latecomer to politics, but the former ballroom king made up ground fast. Financially secure, friends say that politics are his form of sport. He was first elected to Longford County Council in '74 and to the Dail, for Longford-Westmeath, in '77. He has since regularly topped the poll with highly personalised election campaigns. Longford town was once described as being a virtual one-party state. Power and wealth have not gone to his head. Asked if being a top politician had changed Reynolds, Joe Dolan's road manager, Tommy Begley, told me: "Albert? no way; flows off him like water off a duck's back."

Reynolds depends on his own judgment in politics and relies upon the experience which he gained along the road to riches. His friends include many top names from showbusiness such as Noel Pearson, Jim Hand and Oliver Barry, with all of whom he kept step during the ballroom of romance days. "The friendships and relationships built up during those years still last," he says. "It was that kind of business. Huge personal relationships are never forgotten. The qualities I developed in that period stand to me today. I'm still dealing with people. It's all down to your ethic and trust and how you treat people."

Reynolds doesn't hesitate when asked what he would choose as an alternative way of life: "I'll tell you what I'd like to be doing. The wheel has turned full circle. All through the '60s, I searched the world for well known artistes to bring to Ireland. I once had the Beatles booked for two shows for an outdoor concert in Dublin. I couldn't get an outdoor venue big enough, so I had to forego the dates. I dealt with their manager, Brian Epstein. I knew him well. However, twenty- five years later, Irish artistes are world leaders in many spheres. If I was in the business again, I'd love to be out there around the world promoting Irish international artistes, and bringing more up with them. If you have a successful artiste, you can build more underneath him. I think that Irish artistes have a lot of potential."

Who would he most like to manage? "I'd pick U2. I'd love it. That must be a very exciting job. You could build an international industry behind them... merchandising, marketing, all the skills that are there. It's easier to get to the market now than it was before. It's all marketing today. We have the product in

Ireland. We've a lot more U2s. I was in the business of spotting talent. That's where you could build a big international industry behind them. I'd market U2 all over the world, bringing other acts up underneath them and building an industry that we could be proud of internationally. We were proud of the business that we created from the green fields. But you could be equally proud today because we have the material and U2 have broken through. The breakthrough is always the most difficult part." But, U2 is already a major international business force... "right, so what do you do when you reach the zenith? You maximise it. U2 will live on in their records, but their day will come. You have to recognise that you'll need to replace U2 at some stage. Tastes change." Paul McGuinness knows who to watch.

The Star Trek

Gentleman Jim refuses to budge. He sits in Jack O'Rourke's car near Mallow in the dead of night. The town is choked by traffic. O'Rourke abandons the car and asks the star attraction to walk with him the rest of the way to his ballroom, the Majestic. Jim Reeves insists on being driven to the door. O'Rourke has just driven Reeves and tour manager Nelius O'Connell from an earlier dance in Listowel. They're already late arriving in Mallow where 3,500 — who paid ten shillings a head — are waiting impatiently in the Majestic for the star of the show. Life as a ballroom proprietor isn't always a bed of roses — as O'Rourke discovers tonight.

Reeves fails to understand why he cannot be dropped at the door like any other VIP. Walk? Stars don't walk: they're chauffeur-driven. In exasperation, O'Rourke takes O'Connell aside, and says: "For God's sake do something. Use your influence on him." He does — but to no avail. So far, the opening five concerts of a twenty-nine date countrywide tour had gone reasonably smoothly. Reeves was in big demand. His song, *Welcome to My World*, was No. 1 in the Irish charts. The itinerary was planned so that he could perform in two venues each night. Associated Ballrooms — of which O'Rourke formed a part — had to double up on dates like everyone else. That meant the timing had to be perfect. Reeves went on stage at the Las Vegas Ballroom in Listowel at 10pm and sang for about 50 minutes. O'Rourke immediately whisked him to Mallow where he was scheduled to appear in the Majestic at 12.30pm. O'Rourke put the boot down, but got caught in heavy traffic outside Mallow around midnight. The sensible thing was to park the car and continue the rest of the short journey — for a mile or so — on foot. "We appealed and appealed, but he wouldn't listen," recalls O'Rourke.

Faced with the prospect of not being paid his £3,000 fee for the night, Gentleman Jim decided reluctantly to stretch his legs.

They arrived at the ballroom on foot half an hour behind schedule. Michael O'Callaghan and his band, from Buttevant, were still on stage. "I'll never forget Michael for the tremendous job he did," says O'Rourke. "People were shouting 'where's Jim Reeves, what's keeping him?'" As the relief band carried on regardless, the star of the night hopped up on stage, played a few notes on the piano and retreated to his dressing room. The piano was out of tune, Reeves protested. He refused to go on. His fixation with badly-tuned pianos was legendary. O'Rourke had gone to considerable lengths to make sure Reeves could find no grounds to complain in Mallow.

"I took care of it personally. We knew of the problem from other ballrooms where he condemned the pianos. There was a well-known piano firm in Cork at the time called Shanahans. I got music sheets from Jim Reeves' agency. I gave them to Shanahans who sent a man out from Cork to tune the piano that very afternoon. I didn't want any cribs."

When Reeves complained backstage, O'Rourke called his bluff by producing the music sheets from an inside coat pocket. They were signed by Shanahans as proof that the piano had been tuned properly. The tables were turned on Reeves. He glanced at the sheets and threw them to one side. After a further twenty minutes persuasion, he went on. His introduction provoked the wrath of the crowds. "My Goodness, I've been in Ireland for the past week, but never have I seen so many faces under one roof. Unfortunately, my performance tonight will not be on a par with other performances. You might well ask 'why?' It's because of that goddamn piano over there. Totally out of tune." The remarks were greeted by a chorus of boos and hisses. Some people at the front of the stage — already fed up at his late arrival — threw orange and apple skins. Gentleman Jim sat at the piano, sang six songs and left the stage. He bolted out the door and got a lift to the Central Hotel in town.

"His performance was a disaster," recalls O'Rourke. "It would have been a wonderful occasion if the guy had just co-operated. I don't want to be ungracious to Jim Reeves, now that the poor man is dead, but he was the most un-cooperative performer I've ever met. I think it had something to do with the fact that he was the top artiste in the world at the time. You'd compare him to Neil Diamond today. He was such a superstar in his own mind that he literally did what he liked. I saw the other side of Gentleman Jim — the nasty side." O'Rourke's experience was not unique. Con Hynes, another prominent ballroom owner, also got an opportunity to witness that paranoia about pianos. "He'd stand at the door and listen to the piano. If he thought that it wasn't in tune, he'd go away and leave you there. He didn't give a damn what the people did. Then you were in dire straits."

Reeves' Irish and British tour began on Saturday, May 30th, at the Oyster Ballroom in Dromkeen. It included concerts at the National Stadium in Dublin, the Ulster Hall in Belfast and the Arcadia in Cork. It ended on June 19th at the Flamingo Ballroom in Ballymena and the Royal Ballroom in Omagh. Sandwiched between dates the length and breadth of Ireland were six in Britain at American bases and Irish clubs. Reeves did not do a full tour of Britain. He refused to play there without his own backing group, The Blue Boys. No reciprocal agreement could be reached for a British group to tour the U.S., so the British Federation of Musicians would not allow Reeves' backing group to tour with him. Hence, his performances at U.S. bases and Irish clubs were outside the jurisdiction of the British Fed. Britain's loss was Ireland's gain. Reeves swopped American highways for Irish boreens. He was shocked to discover that he had to perform in two different halls each night — in some cases sixty miles apart. It meant a break-neck dash by car from one venue to the next. "I certainly would not have undertaken it if I thought things were going to be like this," he complained loudly during the tour.

Below is a reproduction of the original itinerary for the Reeves Tour 1963... complete with misspellings!

```
30th   May Dromkeen,Oyster Ballroom
       Ennis ,New Hall.
31st   Galway, Hanger Ballroom.
       Ballinasloe.
1st    June Cork, Arcadia Ballroom.
2nd    Listowel
       Mallow
```

3rd	Arklow, Ormonde Ballroom Dublin, Town and Country Ballroom.
4th	Mullingar, New Ballroom Port Leix,Coliseum Ballroom.
5th	Youghal, Redbarn Ballroom. Tramore.
6th	Sligo Kiltamagh
7th	Lifford, Mecca Ballroom. Donegal, Pavesi Ballroom.
8th	Belfast, Ulster Hall (2 concerts)
9th	Templemore Kilkenny.
10th	West Ruislip (American Base)
11th	Ipswich, Bentwaters.
12th	London, Douglas House American Club.
13th	High Wycombe, American Base.
14th	Alconbury ,American Base.
15th	Lakenheath, American Base.
16th	Dundalk, Adelphi Ballroom. Portadown, St Mary's Hall.
17th	Londonderry, St Columb's Hall. Port Stewart.
18th	Dublin ,Dublin Stadium (two concerts)
19th	Ballymena. Flamingo Ballroom. Omagh, Royal Ballroom.

The Lucey brothers — Murt and Jerry — awaited his arrival with some trepidation at their ballroom in Redbarn, Youghal, on Friday, June 5th. Eleven previous concerts by Reeves had given them some idea of what to expect. "I heard all the rumours about him," says Jerry. "I was scared of my life when he came to Redbarn. We were very nice and very easy with him." The performance went smoothly before a packed ballroom. Reeves was booked to do an hour on stage, but ended up doing an hour and a half. Later, he left the ballroom and walked outside to get some fresh air. Fans followed him in pursuit of autographs. Jerry, anxious to protect the star from the crowds, ran out and began to push them back. Reeves did not recognise him, and assumed that he was just another fan trying to get close. "I'll never forget his eyes; they went through me and I stood back because he was god. It was a most withering look — the kind that says who in the hell are you...get out of this place."

Reeves disappointed fans when he appeared, briefly, at the Orchid Ballroom in Lifford on Sunday, June 7th, before dashing to the Pavesi Ballroom in Donegal on the same night. Larry Cunningham, who played support with the Mighty Avons to Reeves in Lifford, recalls that the crowd turned angry when the superstar left the stage after singing only half a dozen songs. Reeves cut short that show, and headed off for Donegal. "We were privileged to be doing relief for him in Lifford," says Cunningham. "He only sang a medley of five or six songs but the sound he got, with poor amplification and not the best of acoustics in the hall, was as good as you'd hear on a stereo today. There was uproar after he finished. They'd have burned the place down only we went out and I tore into a few of his songs and settled the crowd. He didn't give them value for money because he didn't stay on long enough. He went on to Donegal town the same night and did a powerful show."

Reeves told *Spotlight* that he'd like to return to Ireland, *but on different terms*. "The pianos in many of the ballrooms I've sung in were in a terrible condition. In some places they had to borrow the instrument from a private house. My act depends on the piano, as the Blue Boys are only a quartet, and I cannot put on a really good show without one. The audiences here are the best I've ever come across but the pianos are the worst." Sadly, just over a year after Reeves toured Ireland, he died in a plane crash in Tennessee. The forty-year-old former member of the Grand Ole Opry — who exchanged a baseball career for country and western music and became a household name with *Mexican Jo* in 1953 — was killed with his pianist manager an Manuel. They were returning home to Nashville from Batesville, Arkansas, in a single-engine Beechcraft four-seater plane. There were no other passengers aboard. The wreckage was found on Sun-

day, August 2nd, 1964, in a thickly-wooded area ten miles south
of Nashville.

Reeves, the singer with the velvet voice, had an enormous
influence on the Irish showband scene. Larry Cunningham, Sean
Dunphy and, later on, Jim Tobin, followed his style and were,
at one time or another, each regarded as Ireland's answer to him.
Cunningham's *Tribute To Jim Reeves* became the first Irish
entry to break into the British charts in 1965. Cunningham never
wanted to be stereotyped and says that his No. 1 hit, *Lovely
Leitrim*, took him away from being modelled on Reeves. It was
Jim Tobin of the Firehouse Showband who came closest to
sounding like him. Tobin — a sand and gravel contractor who
was discovered by Firehouse leader Donie Cassidy — had a hit
in 1970 with a Reeves' song, *This is It*, and he recorded an LP
of Reeves' numbers in 1972.

Gentleman Jim was one of a host of international stars to play
in the Reynolds' and Associated chains in the '60s: Engelbert
Humperdinck, Tom Jones, Chubby Checker, Johnny Cash,
Johnny Dankworth, Helen Shapiro, Kenny Ball, Dusty Spring-
field, Bachelors, Hank Locklin, Victor Sylvester, Sandie Shaw,
Jimmy Shand, Marian Faithfull, Chuck Berry, Acker Bilk, Joe
Loss, Syd Lawrence, Freddie and the Dreamers, Mary Wilson
and the Supremes and Roy Orbison.

Many performed also in ballrooms owned by independent
operators like Finan, Prendergast, Kenny, Fuller and Luceys.
Leading showbands played double bills with the top international names. The excitement that gripped towns and villages in
the run-up to their arrival was unprecedented in those dark days
before TV invaded every parish in Ireland. Instead of depending
solely on showbands to give them the hits, dancers now got the
opportunity to see the stars themselves in the flesh. The sense
of anticipation was akin to the buzz generated by Michael
Jackson, and Prince decades later. The ballroom chains were in
a strong position to do business with overseas tour managers
because they could offer a nationwide network of venues. The
Reynolds' brothers and Associated Ballrooms had access to the
market place: full houses in their halls were virtually guaran-

teed. Stars closed the doors in all Irish ballrooms since the early '60s.

In 1963, there was a procession of top U.S. recording artistes — Brenda Lee, Hank Locklin, Chubby Checker, Jim Reeves and Johnny Cash. Locklin performed at the Arcadia in Cork on Saturday, April 20, and the bill also included the Bachelors and British singer Steve Perry. In September, it was the turn of Johnny Cash and, in November, Adam Faith paid his fifth visit to Ireland. In May '64, Little Richard paid a one-day visit to the North during his third British tour. He gave a thirty-minute performance at Belfast's Boom Boom Room. Backstage, he had encouraging words for the showbands. "From what I've heard, they sound terrific. In fact they sound better than the groups I've heard in England. I can see big things in store for the showbands." As The Sinners from Belfast played upstairs, their organ music could be heard in the star's dressing room. "I think that organ sounds just beautiful," he said.

In 1964, Irish fans greeted Ella Fitzgerald, Little Richard, Johnny Tillotson, the Rolling Stones, Cliff Richard, Marty Wilde, Mary Wells and Brenda Lee, otherwise known as Little Miss Dynamite. She first visited Ireland in April '63 and returned in '64 for four performances — two in Dublin's Adelphi Cinema on October 8th and two in Cork's Savoy next evening. Her supporting act was the Miami Showband who, a month later, played at the Empire Pool, Wembley, on a bill with the Animals and Rolling Stones.

Television compere Paul Russell drove Roy Orbison around the country during one tour. While en route from Dublin to Limerick, Russell increased speed to make the concert on time. He went into a corner fast, crossed the white line and was chased by a patrol car. The Garda lectured Russell before asking his name. "Your father was a decent man," said the garda. The travellers breathed a sigh of relief. Then, to their surprise, the agent of the law announced his intention to prosecute. Orbison said to Russell: "I thought he was a friend of yours." The garda snapped: "His father was. I don't know your name...you with the black tie and suit." Russell explained that his companion was Roy Orbison, the famous American singer. The garda began to write the name, but he couldn't spell it, and decided to wave them on their way.

Orbison was impressed by Eleanor Toner, of Newry's Hilton Showband, who was on stage when they arrived at the Royal Ballroom in Dundonald. Orbison said she packed a terrific punch, rather like Brenda Lee. The Big O had No. 1 hits in Ireland in '63 with *In Dreams* and *Blue Bayou*, and in '64 with *It's Over* and *Oh Pretty Woman*. Of the showbands, Orbison was most taken by the Victors; but he didn't share the view that the bands would be successful outside Ireland. "Playing for four or five hours at a time must hamper bands chances of originality," he noted, astutely.

In November 1964, the Bachelors — who came originally from Dublin — began a nationwide tour, playing to 80,000 dancers over thirty-nine dates. A month earlier, they achieved a No. 1 hit in Ireland with *I Wouldn't Trade You For The World*. In the Spring of 1964, the group reached the No. 1 slot in Britain with *Diane*, which sold a million copies and made them the first Irish group to reach the Top Ten in America. The record went to No. 2 in Ireland, quickly followed by *I Believe* which achieved the same chart ranking.

Ballrooms provided the bridge between touring acts and their Irish fans before the existence of major indoor and outdoor concert venues. Top draws like Reeves, Orbison or Cash could pull 3,000, or more, a night to a crossroads in the middle of nowhere. Conditions may have seemed primitive to such hot properties of the music world, but fat cheques helped to focus their minds on the financial reality. Equally, big showband attractions who supported them could expect their dance attendances to run into four-figures. More importantly, to support a big 'star' meant prestige and a boost to their own ballroom ratings.

The business was built on a foundation of ballroom networks. The chains, that started out with a couple of halls and then multiplied, developed their own dance markets and protected them. They brought the 'punters' and their showband heroes together under one roof and turned the experience into a money-spinner. The chains were powerful because they could fill bands' diaries for a year at the stroke of a pen — or else, wipe diaries clean with equal ease.

Associated Ballrooms was established in 1964. It was just a name to formalise the business relationships of three of the best known ballroom owners — Con Hynes, Jack O'Rourke and Donie Collins. The AB umbrella covered almost three dozen ballrooms from Drimoleague to Enniskillen. The chain linked Mallow, Listowel, Newcastlewest, Macroom, Cahir, Templemore, Galway, Castleblaney, Fermoy, Bray, Enniskillen, Drimoleague, Ballincollig, Sligo, Tuam, Ennis and Tullamore. The biggest ballrooms were: The Talk Of The Town, Galway; the Arcadia, Bray; the Majestic, Mallow; and Olympic, Newcastlewest. There were three Las Vegas ballrooms: Templemore, Listowel and Tuam. There were two Arcadias: Bray and Cahir.

Donie Collins, from Askeaton, had his own band on the road since the early '50s, and was highly rated. He became a partner of Jack O'Rourke in the Majestic. It was his first ballroom venture. The Majestic was opened by the eight-piece Collins Showband amid a blaze of publicity on August 10th, 1962, at Gouldshill, two miles on the Cork city side of Mallow. It could accommodate 3,000 with parking space for 800 to 1,000 cars. (O'Rourke bought Collins' stake some years later) At the same time, Collins also partnered Con Hynes, and they cast a wide net. The business relationships of all three would be intertwined.

Hynes' first ballroom was the Las Vegas in Templemore. It was built in '61. Plans for a Garda depot in the town gave him the idea. Hynes had been in the dance business since '51, erecting marquees at crossroads throughout the country. Dance committees and carnivals rented out his marquees. Two-week dance festivals attracted big numbers. Tiny villages like Abbey in east Galway became the focal point of social life for a radius of twenty miles. Upwards of 700 flocked nightly to a field in the middle of nowhere. "How many people would I get today if I went to Abbey and put up a marquee?" he wonders.

Collins teamed up with Hynes in '62 when the latter built his second ballroom, the Arcadia, Cahir. They cemented the partnership by building more ballrooms in Tuam, Sligo, Galway, Listowel, and so on. All came under the AB banner in '64. The new format gave Hynes, Collins and O'Rourke more power in making bookings, linking dates and getting bands at the best price. It improved efficiency and marketing. Newspaper advertisements where AB had ballrooms took the form of a large block of dance dates listed for each venue. An 'AB' logo headlined their dancing diaries in the entertainment pages every week. Ballrooms in the chain staged a combined total of forty-two bands a week.

O'Rourke ran the Majestic, Mallow. As a young man in the early '50s, he went into concrete block manufacture with his brother. O'Rourke started in the entertainment business by bringing a mobile cinema to country halls. In 1958, he was bitten by the dancing bug. As fundraiser for Pallaskenry soccer club, he booked two dates, at £60 each, for the upcoming Royal Showband. In 1960, he went into partnership with a friend, Paddy Linnane, and they built the Olympic, Newcastlewest. It could hold 2,500. Linnane ran a small ballroom in Kilmeedy, Co. Limerick. While a film was being shown one night, O'Rourke chatted with Linnane in his kitchen. They decided, over a cup of tea, to build a ballroom. O'Rourke's showbusiness career was born. Two years later, he built the Majestic with Collins. Prior to the opening, congratulatory messages included one from the Reynolds'.

By this stage, Albert and Jim had five ballrooms — Cloudland in Rooskey, Roseland in Moate, Dreamland in Athy, Rockland in Borris-in-Ossory and Fairyland in Roscommon. The Majestic became a major centre of social activity in North Cork. It was so successful that the devil came all the way from Mayo one night. "There was a terrible commotion. It was very serious at the time. Years later I used to laugh about it," says O'Rourke. Other visitors caused a more agreeable hysteria: among them Johnny Cash — a 'great character', — and Chubby Checker — a 'gas man'. One of O'Rourke's treasured pictures shows a youthful Checker with his arms wrapped around members of The Vanguard Six. It was taken at the Majestic on July 21st,

1963. Joe Loss was another frequent visitor. "I can recall opening my doors at 9pm on a fine summer's evening here in Mallow to find two queues outside my box offices," says O'Rourke.

Ballroom owners such as O'Rourke and Hynes maintained a finely balanced love-hate relationship with the bands. "One always had these problems when booking bands," recalls O'Rourke. "You never knew whether they were going to turn up or not, even though you had them on the dotted line. In effect, there wasn't much you could do about it. Okay, you adhered to the rules by having everything properly done. Take a top showband that didn't show up. If I sued them, I was literally suing myself. I was shooting myself in the foot. I'd want them again in a month's time. The most popular bands always had the upper hand."

Hynes felt that the bands always wanted it all their own way: "I would be no way popular with the bands. It wasn't easy doing business with some of them because they wanted every shilling you'd take in at the door. Some of them wouldn't — more of them would. They were trying to do the same thing that we were trying to do. You had no choice but to take them...take as many dates as you could get. They wouldn't give you too many anyway because they would only play one venue maybe three or four times a year. If they gave you a date, and later got better money somewhere else, they'd give you some excuse. You let them off, gave back the date, and let them play somewhere else. That left you in the lurch because you'd be booking those fellows ahead. Then you wouldn't be able to get a good band at short notice.

I blame the greed of the showbands for a lot of the things that happened, for the downfall. At the finish, all they wanted to do was come and take your cheque and hardly play at all. That's my summing up of them. They had 'relief' bands and then they'd come on for an hour. They killed it, in my opinion. It was like everything else: if you got away with it, why not? The majority of them weren't business people at all. They had a get-rich-quick attitude. We won't be here tomorrow and to hell with you. That kind of thing." Hynes sums up his business approach: "When the dancer is sweatin', the promoter is happy. But when the promoter is sweatin', he's in trouble." He admits to having done his share of sweating, but he rejects the perception that proprietors were lining their pockets with vast sums.

"If you were doing the business, that was alright. But if you weren't, you had some liability around your neck. If you had a ballroom doing badly that time, no matter what band you put in, it made no difference. You could put the same band into a ballroom that was doing well, and get 50% more people. If a ballroom was doing badly, drawing 300 or 400 on a Sunday night, sure, you might as well be closed by the time you had everybody paid. You'd be better off closed. You might be left with 40% of the door. You had to take staff and advertising and the cost of buildings into consideration. You couldn't do the same kind of thing today on the profit that we were working on then. People say that we'll get back to the old ballroom of romance days. That's rubbish. You're never going to see the day that you could build a ballroom in the middle of the country and get 1,000 people to a dance. Just look at the facilities people are looking for today compared to years ago. There's no comparison. You could spend £40,000 or £50,000 today doing up a nightclub."

Once the AB structure had been formed, it was a relatively easy business to run — so long as the crowds came. Hynes, Collins and O'Rourke toured the ballrooms every week to ensure that everything was operating smoothly. O'Rourke recalls: "I was flying around from pillar to post. Mary, my wife, used to say, 'my God, Jack, would you ever stay at home!' But it wasn't that I wanted to be out for the sake of it. It was the challenge. The goal was there. One of the reasons I lasted so long in the business is because I ploughed back a lot of the profit into it. A lot of people would say today that people like me made money the easy way. They would see me at night in the ballroom with packed houses and walking away with all the money. But they didn't see the hard work, the ground work, which lasted for as long as I was in it. People didn't know the background of Jack O'Rourke. They didn't see him getting up in the early hours of the morning doing round trips to the other side of the country."

Part-time managers were hired in each location where AB had halls. The biggest concern, according to Hynes, was "to get the bloody thing going. Then it was like any other business. The people came to you. If they didn't come, no matter what band you put in, you wouldn't do the business. We were really more dependent on the bands than on our management. All the manager had to do was make sure there were no rows. The whole thing was to get the right venue. A lot of guesswork went into that. We'd pop around once a week, or every second week, and have a look at the ballrooms."

During one such tour, O'Rourke got the first indication of the devastating effect that the troubles in Northern Ireland would have on the business. He was going over figures with the AB man in Enniskillen, Willie Gilleasy, when a bomb threat was telephoned. They were seated in a corner of Gilleasy's pub across the street from the Emerald Ballroom when an anonymous caller warned of an explosion that night. Bomb scares were ten a penny. Nevertheless, Gilleasy informed the RUC. He decided to go ahead with the dance. The ballroom filled with people. By 11pm, he got another call to say that a bomb had been planted under the stage. He ordered an evacuation. "The last man was going out the door when the bomb went off," says O'Rourke. "It blew half the Emerald Ballroom to bits. Luckily, nobody was hurt." By the mid '70s, the AB chain was being sold off piecemeal. The three kingpins set their sights on new ventures. O'Rourke sold his interests in the remaining ballrooms but retained the Majestic. In 1990, it became the studio of a local radio station.

Many independent ballroom owners around the country drifted into the business by accident and built mini-empires. They had to compete for bookings against the might of the Reynolds and AB chains. The only hope was to site a ballroom in a place where the tentacles of the chains had not yet reached. In Cork, builders Murt and Jerry Lucey diverted from their first major construction project into the dance business and went on to become ballroom moguls. They spotted an opportunity in '56 to build a mini-holiday camp at Redbarn, outside the seaside resort of Youghal, Co. Cork. They bought eight acres and began construction. In an effort to boost tourism, the government agreed to match pound-for-pound money spent by developers. However, the promises were never fulfilled and the brothers were unable to complete the holiday camp. The Luceys needed cash flow and decided to build a ballroom capable of holding between 1,500 and 2,000. But the crowds were flocking to the Showboat and Strand Palace ballrooms in the town. Mick Del drew dancers from all over east Cork every summer season.

Redbarn was opened on June 6th, 1957 by the Johnny Butler Band, with Joe Lynch as special guest. Bill Kenny, owner of the Olympia, Waterford, made an inspection of the place. "He said that if we gave him the hall for nothing, he'd bring the Clippers," recalls Jerry. "We agreed. We only had a bit of profit in the mineral bar. He brought the Clippers once every four weeks. We put in smaller bands in the meantime. That's how the crowds started to come. He also brought Bridie Gallagher between appearances by the Clippers. Eventually, he brought the Royal Showband." Initially, the Luceys rented out the hall to Kenny, but by late '58, they were running dances themselves every Sunday night. "From then on it was showbands all the way," says Jerry. "We took the crowds from the Showboat. Not intentionally; in our ignorance we did it. If any sane people looked at the scene properly and saw that Mick Del was filling the other places, nobody would build a ballroom in that area. We got the showbands because Mick Del was packing the Strand Palace and the Showboat. Then the young crowds started to follow the showbands. It all happened by accident." Bridie Gallagher could draw 2,000 to Redbarn. By 1960, it was one of the top dancing venues in the south. The Champions played relief there for £12 a night in the '60s. One Sunday night in '64, Jerry stood near the box office chatting to dancers on the way in. The 'relief' band had been on stage for half an hour. Everything was going well until another 'relief' showed up. They insisted that they had been booked. "I said that I couldn't do a bit about it. The 'relief' band was already on. I couldn't put two 'reliefs' on. This fellow in the band started to get saucy. I said, 'I'm sorry but you can't go on'. It got worse. I said he'd have to go away. That was Rory Gallagher."

Redbarn generated the seed money that helped the Lucey brothers build the Majorca in Crosshaven in '64. It was the second biggest ballroom in the country, after the Arcadia, Bray. Initially, they rented some of the nights at the Majorca — as had been done earlier at Redbarn. The ballroom name was suggested to the Luceys by T.J. Byrne. "T.J. had been travelling abroad and had these fancy names in his head," says Jerry. "He just said to me one day, 'why not call it the Majorca?' So that's what we did." It was another great success story.

In 1968, the brothers opened the Stardust Ballroom at Grand Parade, Cork. It quickly monopolised the dancing business in the city. Showbands liked the idea of linking three dates: they played Friday night at the Stardust, Saturday night at the Majorca and Sunday night at Redbarn. While the big chains had first call on dates, the Luceys were in a sound bargaining position by being able to offer three linked dates. "Associated were the big fellows," says Jerry. "We were big as far as Cork was concerned; but we were very vulnerable because if one of those fellows moved in, they'd have a monopoly of the bands. It would have been very difficult to compete against them if they moved into Cork. If they had a ballroom here we'd have to close up. There was always a danger of that. They might have been afraid perhaps, because our ballrooms were in pretty good places. We became personal friends of most of the managers and the band leaders. That's mostly how we got the top bands really." The Stardust appealed to a younger age group — more a Platter-men/Freshmen type venue. "We could put on Tiny Tim in the Stardust but you couldn't put him in Redbarn or Crosshaven. Tiny Tim was magic. I remember the place was jammed."

The Luceys divided responsibilities: Murt handled the financial affairs and Jerry dealt with the bands. Catherine Cogan, a member of their organisation, booked the bands and took care of administration. "Murt was the brains, and I was the brawn," says Jerry, with a giggle. "I can't add two and two, for God sake." Jerry looked after Redbarn while Murt kept an eye on the Stardust and Majorca. "There wasn't a lot to do really," explains Jerry. "Just have the place ready for the people and open the doors. Sure they were gone in a few hours." He scoffs at the suggestion that big money was made, and tells of bank pressures that caused sleepness nights.

"I had an aunt who was a nun in Drishane Convent. Like all nuns, she thought that money was the damnation of people. She used to pray constantly that we'd never have money to spare. She was right. Her prayers were granted. We were always on edge." He lists the top drawing performers as Bridie Gallagher, the Clippers, Royal and Dixies. "Bridie Gallagher was unbelievably big — easily as big as any of the showbands." The Stardust provided the Luceys with a bridge to young audiences of the '70s as the ballrooms began to wane. Murt died in 1971.

As top bands raised their percentage demands, Jerry became disillusioned with the business. "When they started looking for 80/20, I said 'this is ridiculous; we'll have to get out of this bloody thing'. That's why the showband scene died actually. There wasn't enough money to put back into the halls to do them up properly. When the percentages went from 60/40 to 70/30 to 80/20, I knew it was the end." By '73, Lucey was running a 'disco special' on Saturday nights at the Stardust, now billed as Cork's top 'night spot' — a clear, and final, shift from the 'ballroom' status of three years earlier.

Lucey's funniest memory of the Stardust days concerns one of his employees and Bjorn Ulvaeus of ABBA. With the press in pursuit of the world's biggest pop group, Ulvaeus slipped into Cork for a break in September '76. ABBA were blitzing the charts with *Dancing Queen*. He went out with a Corkman for a night on the town. They turned up at the door of the Stardust at 7pm — two hours before it was due to open. He knocked. An employee opened and asked what they wanted. The Corkman explained that Bjorn was from a famous pop group and wanted to go in. To the doorkeeper, ABBA was just a new four- letter word. Doors would not be opened till 9pm, they were told. Again,the local man stressed the importance of the celebrity. The doorkeeper had enough, shut it on Ulvaeus and said: "G'wan away, boy, and come back at nine 'o clock." He did.

The Dixies — Clown Princes

Cork Harbour, Monday April 10th, 1967.

The majestic *Queen Mary* slips into Cork Harbour and drops anchor one and a half miles from shore. A party of VIPs, led by the Lord Mayor, is taken out to greet the grand old lady of the seas. An SOS is sent to shore — not from the *Queen Mary*, but from the Dixies Showband. A twenty-foot cruiser manned by the Cork showmen, *The Dixie* has run into trouble nearby. Amateur sailors on board need to be rescued only a short distance from land. For once, the Dixies have struck all the wrong notes.

First, the steering comes away in the hands of bass guitarist Chris O'Mahony as the cruiser circles the giant liner. *The Dixie*, guided by a wrench clamped to the steering nut collides with a harbour tender, carrying the VIPs beneath the liner. Guitarist Steve Lynch bruises his face and hands slightly. The musicians abandon their pleasure cruise and decide to return home. Brendan O'Brien, the lead singer, is at the improvised helm. Murphy's Law rules: The cruiser runs aground on sand banks half-a-mile from shore. A launch is sent out to take them off, but meets the same fate at low tide. For another twenty minutes, the two small vessels are stranded with their passengers. Finally, another rescue launch from Cobh arrives and takes them all ashore. Later, at high tide, both craft are re-floated. The day that the Dixies went to see the *Queen Mary* had ended in near-disaster.

The showband had driven nearly 300 miles overnight from Derry to see the liner. They left at 3am, stopped for soup in Dublin and made straight for Carrigaloe to board their new cruiser. Joe McCarthy and O'Mahony had spent hundreds of pounds on the boat. The visit of the *Queen Mary* seemed an ideal opportunity to launch out as sailors. Back on terra firma after their misadventure, Dixies' leader Sean Lucey told reporters: "We're cold, tired and never more delighted to see land. What a day! That's the trouble with being amateurs." O'Brien said:

"It was a disastrous trip." There was some compensation. The rescue grabbed headlines: 'The Dixies Sail Into Trouble — Queen trip ends in chaos', screamed the Daily Mirror. The visit of luxury liners to Cork harbour traditionally meant colourful copy as journalists were welcomed on board and given the opportunity to mingle with a sprinkling of celebrities. Newsmen poked out the rich and famous in first class. But the dearth of stars on board the *Queen Mary* sent them sniffing elsewhere for a story. Reports of the Dixies' near disaster was enough to fill the vacuum, and the column inches. For days afterwards, the incident was exaggerated to the point where it was even suggested that the Dixies had 'rammed' the *Queen Mary*!

The Dixies were arguably the best news-makers in the halcyon days of the showbands. They had a flair for publicity; no other band was more talked about or got up to as much mischief. The Dixies broke all the rules, but they survived longer than any of their contemporaries. They defied the odds by re-launching in the '80s. They were different to the others. For a start, they never took themselves very seriously, and this was a major factor in their remarkable success. McCarthy was a brilliant drummer, and hilariously funny. There were high jinks, endless pranks, and encounters with the famous — the *Queen Mary*, the Pope, Jack Benny, Jimmy Durante and Arabian princes. When Durante was introduced to McCarthy in Vegas, he pinched the Corkman by the nose and said: "Hey, you've gotta superior weapon."

They were guests on the *Forest Duke TV Show* in Las Vegas with Bobbie Gentry and Jack Benny. They decided to test Benny's reputation for meanness. Finbarr O'Leary, the keyboard player, asked him if everything written about his 'tightness' was true. "Not at all," said Benny; "that's all just image." Benny then played a trick on the inquisitive Irishman. During their chat, he reached to a cigar machine on the wall, turned to O'Leary and asked for the loan of a quarter. Dumbfounded, O'Leary returned to McCarthy and Lynch: "It's true alright lads."

No prank was considered too outrageous. McCarthy discovered a pet rabbit in the early hours of the morning at the foot of the stairs in a Dublin hotel. He thought he was seeing things.

He said: "Hey, boys, I'm in the rats." They said: "No Joe; it's a rabbit." McCarthy knew that O'Leary, 'a quiet fella', had gone to bed. "We took the rabbit up to Finbarr's bedroom," recalls McCarthy. "He was asleep. "All the boys came into the room. We slipped the rabbit in at the bottom of the bed. We waited. You could see it moving, making its way up along Finbarr. He woke up...Wah!" The Dixies worked hard and played harder. Their madcap humour broke the boredom of hours spent travelling over narrow roads the length and breadth of the country. Rival bands were spattered with eggs and flour as the Corkmen overtook them in the dead of night. When band leader and ballroom proprietor Donie Collins showed off his luxury bus to the Dixies, they waited for an opportune moment to fill the hubcaps with tiny stones. The new bus rattled down the road to roars of laughter.

The Dixies often marched down boreens playing trumpet, trombone and sax for the cattle at four in the morning — or they flew model airplanes over the Curragh at daybreak. Lynch and Mac caused confusion at Cork railway station by playing a tape recording of the Angelus at 4.30 in the afternoon. A group of nuns waiting for a train were seen to bless themselves, then fumble for their watches. Bands regularly requested that a customs officer be on duty at 3am on cross-border journeys to certify that they had returned home with all their musical gear intact. It was a mere formality. Once, the request was refused, and the Dixies were stranded up north. McCarthy had a flash of inspiration. He phoned the customs office from a local hotel, and put on his sternest military accent.

"Major Featherstone" he declared. "Passing through at 4am...can you have someone there?" The Dixies were waved through while the customs officers waited for 'the Major'. McCarthy has an endless store of one-liners and wisecracks. Question: is image important Joe? Answer: "If image was important I'd have had a facelift years ago!" When McCarthy laughs, everybody laughs. He was once voted top comedian in Las Vegas. He appeared on a TV game show where contestants were given the chance to win big cash prizes if they kept a straight face while famous comedians tried to make them laugh. One contestant resisted the best efforts of Jerry Lewis — but collapsed when confronted by the rubber faced antics of the Corkman.

It wasn't all fun and games. There is a tragic side to the Dixies' story: the father who lost a son and daughter-in-law in a road accident; another father who also lost a son on the roads; the handsome singing idol who was seriously injured in a stage accident; whose career was wrecked; whose marriage broke down; who fought a battle against booze, who faced financial troubles, and did a two-week spell in prison. "You could say I've had a lot of tough breaks in my life," says Brendan O'Brien who rivalled his friend Brendan Bowyer as Ireland's greatest heart-throb. The two Brendans have similar tales to tell. Each fell to alcohol. The Dixies wore smiling public faces while the lives of some band members were torn apart by trauma and tragedy. As a band, the Dixies defied all odds by making a successful comeback in '82 — ten years after the original band split up and twenty-one years after they turned professional. The longevity is remarkable.

In the beginning, they were called the Dixielanders, but that mouthful was soon reduced to The Dixies. Their remarkable career can be traced back to 1954. Three pals who worked as tradesmen — Theo Cahill, McCarthy and Lucey — formed a jazz band. Cahill played trombone; Lucey, clarinet; and McCarthy, the drums. They needed trumpet and piano players to build a five piece. The spots were filled by Larry Neville on trumpet and Mick Murphy on piano. The first break came when they landed a residency at Shandon Boat Club, performing every Sunday night for two seasons.

"We just went down to play jazz, to do something we loved doing," says McCarthy. They played elsewhere in between the boat club dates. The name came later when posters were being prepared for a date at the university. "The students wanted to know the name of the band," recalls McCarthy. "We said, 'we don't have a name'. They advertised us as the Dixielanders on the paper." Band managers didn't really exist at the time. Lucey made the bookings and kept a diary. Music was a part-time interest: Lucey was a radio serviceman, Cahill an electrician in the ESB, McCarthy an apprentice upholsterer at Cashs, Neville and Murphy college students. They knew each other since schooldays. All except O'Mahony — who joined later — were educated at the North Monastery, a nursery of Irish culture run by the Christian Brothers. Lucey was in the same class as Lynch. Cahill was a class ahead, and Mac a class behind. O'Mahony attended Eason's Hill School.

Their first musical experiences were with the Butter Exchange Brass Band. The Dixies later learned their craft at the Arcadia where they imitated the Clippers' breezy style. McCarthy was a natural comedian: dancers laughed when he pulled faces and acted the eejit. "The Clippers were our first big influence," says the drummer. "I mean, they were the living end of entertainment. They looked great, were very clean-cut and very professional. They put on a terrific show: *Juke Box Saturday Night*. They dressed up and sang all the popular records of the day. This was long before TV, so you were listening to the music of artistes you'd never seen. You watched Hugo Quinn doing Frankie Lane, and he *became* him."

By the late '50s, Jimmy Mintern joined as an additional sax player/singer and O'Mahony joined on bass. Conveniently, Mintern had a car as well as a PA system...just a small set of amps. The Dixies took up residency at the Arcadia as the relief band every Saturday night. Other recruits soon followed: John Sheehan, instead of Neville on trumpet; Lynch, on electric guitar, joined in '59. The sound improved, bookings increased, and the future looked bright. The musical range extended from jazz to rock'n'roll to just about anything the "punters" wanted to hear. "We had enough instrumentation in the band to follow any trend," says Lucey. Murphy returned to college to complete his medical studies and he was replaced by O'Leary on piano. At the Arcadia, the aim was to "watch what the others did, do it better and blow them off the stage next time around," says former road manager Michael O'Riordan. He would years later become marketing and music publishing director of Ritz Records in Dublin, chairman of the Republic of Ireland Music Publishers Association and deputy chairman of the Irish Music Rights Organisation.

In 1960, the Dixies were ready to go fulltime. The break came when they were spotted at the Olympia Ballroom in Waterford by Northern dance promoter Jim Aiken. He heard about the sensational Cork showband and drove to Waterford to see them. He booked them for a tour of the North. They headed off in a van that broke down in Dundalk. A picture in one of Lynch's photo albums shows them sitting on their instrument cases by the roadside. The tour was a success.

"We took about a week or ten days off our jobs to try the circuit and see would we like it," says McCarthy. "We liked it, and they liked us. We decided we were going to pack up the jobs and have a go. We said we'd try it for a few years...all except one fellow, Jimmy Mintern, the other sax player and lead singer at the time. He had a good job." The others had trades to fall back on if the bubble burst. Says Lucey: "We knew that if we packed it in, we could all go back to jobs in about four or five years. We could make money and still go back to our trades. But Jimmy didn't have a trade, so he didn't want to take the gamble. Brendan O'Brien had sang one or two songs with us. We decided that if Jimmy packed it in, then we'd bring in Brendan."

Word spread nationwide about the exciting new band with the zany drummer. "Bands like the Royal, Johnny Quigley and Gay McIntyre were obviously telling promoters up the country that we were very good," explains Lucey. "In fact, a lot of top bands found it hard work to come down and play with us as the 'relief'. We'd blow them off the stage. The Cork crowd were very supportive. If they didn't like a band they'd let them know and they'd be screaming for the Dixies to come back on."

In 1961, at the age of twenty, O'Brien was offered a place in the band. Three years earlier, he got his first taste of showbusiness in London when he won a talent contest at the Finsbury Park Empire. He was working for the summer in London with a friend from Cork, Tony Halpin, who later became managing director of a local brewery. "We were like brothers," says Halpin. O'Brien left school and went to work as a junior architectural draughtsman in an office at Oxford Street. London was exciting, and he followed the latest trends. He had known The Dixies since schooldays and, in '61, jumped at the opportunity to join up. "We paid his fare over," recalls Lucey. "He sang a few songs with us and we said, 'okay, you've got the job'." The Dixielanders turned professional and went on the road in September 1961. O'Brien had joined as a rhythm guitarist: "In those days, it was just the three chord trick." Peter Prendergast, owner of the Arcadia, took over as manager and, typically, threw himself wholeheartedly into the job. Mintern left and joined another local band, The Music Makers.

The Dixies launched their professional career with a two-week tour of Britain. Cork immigrants in London, already familiar with the band from the Arcadia, flocked to dancehalls such as the Gresham, Galtimore, Blarney and Banba. The band packed halls in London, Birmingham, Manchester and Coventry. On their return home, the Dixies criss-crossed the country. In the early days, they hit the road for two week periods before settling into a six-night routine. Prendergast — nick-named 'Isaac Zubes' by McCarthy — was a gifted publicist. He pulled stunts that put the band on the front pages. He had done it before for the Clippers in the '50s: when the Strabane show-men made a triumphant return to the Arcadia fresh from an American tour, Prendergast assembled a huge cardboard cut-out of a plane on stage, complete with windows and markings. Using pictures of every member of the Clippers, he managed to put each smiling face behind a window, peering out to the dancehall audience. Prendergast made individual posters for all showbands who played at the 'Arc'. When the Dixies arrived back in Cork from dances at six in the morning, it wasn't unusual to see lights on upstairs in the 'Arc as Prendergast worked all night on his posters.

The first of Prendergast's many stunts for the Dixies was executed in October '63 when they became the first showband to make 'personal appearances' in Paris and Rome. By now, bands toured Britain and the U.S. annually, but trips to European capitals were new. The weekly schedule was: Sunday — The Oyster, Dromkeen; Monday — Gresham, Holloway Road, London; Tuesday — Paris; Wednesday — Rome; Thursday — Shanagolden, Co. Limerick. Prendergast knew that nobody would believe him — so he prepared the proof before the Dixies left Cork.

First, he bought postcards of Paris and Rome depicting typical scenes such as the Eiffel Tower and St. Peter's Square. The technique was to superimpose his own pictures of the Dixies on these cards. The band flew to both capitals and posted the

Send 'em Home Sweatin' 143

cards to DJs and showbusiness columnists immediately on arrival. The postmark confirmed it was no fiction. Prendergast displayed similar ingenuity when the Dixies toured Britain. Again, he made Dixies' postcards that featured them against the background of Big Ben and the Tower of London. Prendergast's PR handout for the European dash spoke of "possible" TV dates in Paris and Rome. An interested agent "wishes to introduce the Cork band to his Continental audiences." The handout was accompanied by a humorous shot of the Dixies, taken by 'famous photographer Dezo Hoffmann who photographs the Shadows, Beatles and all the stars'. A headline in the *Cork Evening Echo* read: 'First Irish Showband For Paris'.

While in Rome, the Dixies were granted an audience with Pope Paul VI — thanks to a Christian Brother who taught Lucey at the North Mon. "Bro. McConville," says Lucey, "was a friend of a man who happened to be in charge of the audiences. So I got onto him and he wrote to his friend. We all got invitations." O'Brien recalls: "We were sitting in the office at the Arcadia with Peter. We rang the Vatican. We got straight through. No problem."

The Dixies were treated as VIPs when they arrived for their audience with the Pope. Says Lucey: "We were taken inside to the top room, up in the front with all the cardinals and bishops, and there were the Dixies in between them. We couldn't believe it. The Pope passed by and I jumped up and shook hands with him." His Holiness was reported to have recognised McCarthy — or so McCarthy claims. The continental tour was a publicity victory for Prendergast. Another was convincing McCarthy to insure his legs for £50,000. "I used to do a lot of jumping around — the splits and all that," laughs McCarthy. "The legs were definitely part of the appeal. They were insured against breakage or damage. It got lots of publicity and headlines all over the place."

The Dixies were kings of the Arcadia. Officially, Jimmy Shand, the Scottish ceili master, held the attendance record for packing in 4,000. Unofficially, the local heroes claimed to have topped that figure by 300 on a St. Stephen's night. "We had the same crowd paid in, but people broke in the back doors — so we had a few hundred more. We had 4,000 plus the people who didn't pay. Shand still has the record and we're in second place," says Lucey. The Dixies' first appearance in Cork was in a concert at City Hall with Maureen Potter on Feb. 5, '63. That year also they made their recording debut with Decca. That first number, arranged by Cahill, was an instrumental called *Cyclone*. Cahill wrote it in March '63 in the hope that someone would provide lyrics for it. At the time, he was calling it *Teenage Heart*. During a tour in London, the band brought it to Mills Music Publishers who liked the tune, but not the title. They renamed it *Cyclone*. Cahill sold his tune to the sheet music publishers. Cahill came up with another number, *The Mardyke* which was to be the flipside of the single released by Decca. *Cyclone* was released on May 17th, 1963. Decca wanted the Dixies to change their name to avoid confusion with similarly named groups in Britain and the U.S. A suggest-a-name contest was organised by the embryonic *Spotlight* magazine.

In July 1963, the band appeared on Telefís Éireann's *Showband Show*. They went on another tour of Britain in September and recorded several numbers — this time for EMI. In October, they made that publicity-winning dash to Paris and Rome. The Dixies built up a considerable following in Waterford. In November, '63, they joined other top name bands like the Royal, Clippers and Black Aces at the Majestic Hotel in Tramore to celebrate the 25th anniversary of the Olympia Ballroom. The host was proprietor Bill Kenny. Guests were treated to an operatic performance by Brendan Bowyer's parents, Stanley and Maura. The Dixies next record, *It Depends On You*, came out in October. In December, they released *Christmas Time*, featuring O'Brien, and *Sticking Out A Mile From Blarney*, from Mac.

"It's difficult to understand today, but recording that time was very new to everyone," says O'Brien. "They found out that I had a good recording voice. We had no singer in particular. I wound up a singer and Joe wound up the funnyman. We were really a team. Joe was doing the comedy. I was doing the singing. Theo was the backbone of the music...so we had an ideal combination. We got on very well together."

That's the way it was from the beginning. "We've never had a punch up in all the time we've been on the road," said O'Brien years ago. "It's remarkable that when seven fellows are lumped together for twenty-four hours a day, five days a week, that they shouldn't get more than a little bored with each others' company. Of course, we don't always agree, and Joe tends to get a little irritating at times with his wisecracking — but there's never been a big row. We enjoy each others company, so much so that we tend to meet up on our nights off. Joe Mac, undoubtedly, is the most unusual one of us. He's never serious except on the rare occasion when he gets to talking about religion or some similar subject that doesn't bear joking about. He always finds a funny side to every situation and his stock of standard jokes seems to be just about limitless. I still find myself laughing at practically everything he says — except when he wakes us all up in the middle of the night to tell us a 'great one' he's just thought of. Then we fling whatever is handiest at him. I suppose the biggest joke of all — on us at the time — is that the girls seem to like him best. Perhaps it's his face. That's certainly unusual enough."

O'Brien's ambition then was to have a number one hit in Britain. EMI promised that if the band came up with the right number, they'd give it full promotion there. He told Spotlight of his hopes to go into real estate when he packed away his guitar. Whatever about his sex appeal, McCarthy agrees that the band was like a family. "We were a very close knit band. We were like brothers. We were closer to each other than a lot of us are to our brothers and sisters because we spent so much time together on the road."

The Dixies were clocking up high mileage every week. A typical Sunday night dance might be at the Royal Ballroom, Castlebar. After tea, sandwiches and a few drinks, they would load the wagon and be ready to leave about 3.15am. They would arrive in Cork about 7am. Monday would be a day off, and they would rise about 3pm. On Tuesday, they might have to go to Mullingar. They would leave Cork at 2pm and, by teatime, had set up the equipment and begun rehearsing in the empty hall. By 7.30pm, they would have shaved, put on fresh clothes and polished their shoes, for the 9pm show. They carried two or three band uniforms each as these became dirty quickly on the road. In later years, there would have been nothing to do until they went on at 11pm. By 2.30am, they were ready for the road again.

"The lads drank when they came off stage, had a good time and a bit of crack around town," says former road manager O'Riordan. "I can't say that they went mad with money. They were up to all kinds of devilment, though. A big egg war went on at one stage. You saw a new wagon on the road. You passed it out and waved. Just as you were about level, you pelted it with eggs. If the Hoedowners were coming down the road and saw Dickie Rock's new wagon, they pulled up level and threw eggs and tomatoes at it. Once you got a little bit ahead of the wagon, you threw out a bag of flour and it stuck to the eggs. A terrible mess.

There were mornings we'd arrive into Cork at 11.30am, having driven from Derry. We were cold, miserable and hungry. Some fellow was sure to say, 'God, ye've a great life all the same'. The wagons were very uncomfortable. In the summer they boiled you out of it and, in winter, they were very cold. You'd always be hoarse because the engine was so loud. You had to shout over the noise. Once you got up to fifty miles an hour you had to keep it at that. Everybody took turns driving so you got some sleep travelling through the night." Prendergast rarely travelled with the band, so O'Riordan became a kind of tour manager. Lynch — another good man for gimmicks — was their travelling PRO. O'Brien once said he'd sell refrigerators to the Eskimos.

The Dixies were hot favourites in Derry; at the Orpheus and Romanos in Belfast; the Flamingo in Ballymena; the Olympic in Dublin; Jetland in Limerick; Seapoint in Galway and Olympia in Waterford. As semi professionals, the money had been small, but that changed when they went fulltime and drew bigger crowds. They got 50% of the door takings and that increased as T.J. Byrne succeeded in getting a bigger slice for his band. "The Royal were the boys who stuck in for the money," says Lucey. "They got 60% and then 70% T.J. actually made the money for the showbands. The Royal were in a ballroom and they'd be on 60%. We'd play the same place and be nearly as big as them. We'd look for 60% next time, and we'd get it." On a 60/40 deal,

(Photo: Cork Examiner)

playing to a hall of 2,000 at 10 shillings a head, the Dixies took £600.

1964 opened with the Dixies in the charts with *Christmas Time*. A three-week British tour followed in Lent, and then came their first record success in May, *I'm Counting On You*, which went to No. 6 in the charts. This was followed in August with *It's Only Make Believe*. The record went to No. 4. The Dixies managed to keep Billy Fury's version lower in the charts. The band were now signed to Pye Records. In September, they were taken to the U.S. for two weeks by promoter Hugh Hardy, who had a radio programme in New York. They took the Irish-American ballroom circuit by storm, performing in New York, Boston, Chicago and San Francisco. They also did a few dates for Bill Fuller. McCarthy was repeatedly asked if he was a 'Beatle'. The tour brought one of the highlights of the Dixies' career — an appearance on a star-studded programme at Carnegie Hall. True to form, Prendergast came up with a special postcard to mark the occasion. It showed the Dixies as passengers in a spacecraft hovering over New York. The Dixies 'brought the house down' in Carnegie Hall, according to the *Irish Echo* on September 26. The newspaper reproduced Prendergast's card to accompany their review. The Corkmen's Association in New York presented the Dixies with a trophy to mark the Carnegie Hall triumph.

The band's welcome home from the citizens of Cork was of a kind usually saved for an All-Ireland winning team. They were taken through the streets on an open-top bus from which Lynch showed off the trophy. The celebration was organised by Prendergast. Thousands packed the railway station. It took the Dixies half an hour to reach the bus. Several people were hurt in the surge. "The word went to the press in Cork that the Dixies were given the Corkmens Association special award and that we'd be bringing it home on that night," recalls Lucey. "We flew into Dublin and came down by train. Other showbands came out to meet us as well. It was like the Cork team coming back from Croke Park. We had no idea it was going to be that big. It was as if Cork had won the cup."

By now, O'Brien was one of the elite group to have had two records in the Irish Top Ten in 1964. Although the early recordings were done for Decca and EMI, the majority of the Dixies' hits were with John Woods of Pye Records. Woods took a personal interest in their recording career and they achieved notable chart successes. O'Brien carried the music of Buddy Holly to a new generation of pop fans in Ireland. His versions of *Oh Boy, Peggy Sue, Rave On*, and *It Doesn't Matter Anymore* were all hits in Ireland. The former junior draughtsman was now a star in the same league as Bowyer, Rock and Moore. "There was a gang of us together...Dolan, Bowyer," says O'Brien. "We were inseparable. We'd meet up in New York, Chicago or Las Vegas. We could bump into each other anywhere. We still keep in touch."

The Dixies were rarely out of the charts during the golden years. They made twenty-seven records — among them *I'm Counting On You, It's Only Make Believe, Oh Boy, Dream Lover, Wooden Heart, Ebony Eyes, Katie's Kisses, I Love You More Today, I'm Gonna Love You Too, Together Again, In Person, Honky Tonk Girl, He's Got You, Peggy Sue, Little Arrows, It Was Only A Heart, It Doesn't Matter Anymore, Together Again, Love Made A Fool, Save The Last Dance For Me, Don't Let The Stars Get In Your Eyes, The Joys of Love, All Together Now,* and *Tomorrow's Love*. The majority of these were Top Ten hits from '65 to '70. Three reached No. 2: *I Love You More Today* ('65), *It Doesn't Matter Anymore* ('66), and *Katie's Kisses* ('68).

Their biggest hit was achieved with *Little Arrows* which went to No. 1 on September 7th, 1968, and stayed in the charts for twenty weeks. It was a huge seller. As a result of that success, the Dixies dominated the *Spotlight* Awards for '68: they were voted Band of the Year; *Little Arrows* was Record of the Year; Joe McCarthy, Showman of the Year; Steve Lynch, Instrumentalist of the Year; and Brendan O'Brien, Singer of the Year. The awards ceremony took place early in '69 at the National Stadium, Dublin. The compere was Terry Wogan, who told O'Brien of his plans to go to England to look for a job.

For the Dixies, it was Las Vegas that beckoned in 1969. That year, the band recorded The Joys of Love. Although this release failed to match the chart success of *Little Arrows* and *Katie's Kisses,* it reached No. 4 and remained in the charts for nineteen weeks. Fuller brought the Dixies to Las Vegas for an audition held by booking agent Rocky Sennes. They passed. It was a significant achievement because many other showbands were auditioned and rejected. The Royal and the Dixies were the only bands to win acceptance in Las Vegas. The Corkmen mixed with the jet set and became friendly with Perry Como, Andy Williams, Jack Benny and Jimmy Durante. The Dixies performed for eight weeks in 1969 at the Desert Inn and returned the following year for twelve weeks. Bowyer was at the Stardust nearby. The Dixies performed three shows a night, six nights a week, followed by parties into the early hours. They lived like kings and rubbed shoulders with famous showbusiness names. Home in Vegas was the Bali-Hai Motel. Lynch got to know a member of the cast of the TV show *Car 54,* another motel resident. Lynch told the actor of the show's popularity in Ireland. The actor liked to hear of his fame in the Emerald Isle and frequently asked Lynch to re-tell the story to friends by the swimming pool. "After a while, I started to embellish the story and they loved it," laughs Lynch. "I told them that when *Car 54* came on TV, farmers all over Ireland stopped milking the cows and ran in from the fields."

The meeting with Jimmy Durante was organised by a member of the cast of his show who stayed in the same motel as the Dixies. The comic marvelled at the size of McCarthy's nose. The Dixies appeared on the *Forest Duke TV Show* with Jack Benny and Bobbie Gentry. Gentry was No. 1 in the Irish charts with *I'll Never Fall In Love Again.* The Dixies' were up in lights at the Desert Inn, advertised on the same bill as Bob Newhart. A host of celebrities came to see them, including Connie Francis and the Everly Brothers. McCarthy loved Vegas. "I don't think we slept at all. You'd be afraid to go to sleep in Vegas in case you'd miss something. It goes on twenty-four hours a day. You'd finish work at 4am. Then you'd go to a party or go to another show. You might get to bed at seven or eight and be up again about eleven. It was mad." Their Las Vegas experience was "one big laugh," according to O'Brien. "Anything for the crack." The entertainment lounge at the Desert Inn was closed in '70. The Dixies completed their twelve weeks and returned home.

They closed the book on Las Vegas and never bothered to pursue any more work there. "We were making as much money in Ireland, so what did we want going over for," says McCarthy. The band needed to spend at least three months in Vegas to make it financially worthwhile. That meant being away from families and friends. "Bowyer stayed and we came home," McCarthy goes on. "We didn't think...maybe if we had stayed we could be like the Beach Boys now. When we toured America, people were coming up to book us for a month here and a month there. We could have had a year's work out of Vegas, no problem." As Lucey puts it: "We were playing in Vegas, the top place for entertainment in the world. We never realised it was so big. When we went elsewhere in the States and told people we'd played Vegas, they were knocked out... 'Gee... you've played Vegas?'...every artiste in America was trying to break into Vegas. The Royal came first and then we came. We were treated like stars in Vegas. We were great crowd-pullers. We were from Ireland and had something different to offer. We did a complete show with something for everybody. We played to audiences ranging in age from 21 to 70." When the Dixies returned from Vegas in '70, they couldn't have imagined that they were about to enter the twilight years for the showbands.

Within twelve months, the Royal flagship from Waterford was sinking. Bowyer, the original boy wonder, and his talented partner, Tom Dunphy, had jumped ship to form the Big 8; Butch Moore had quit the Capitol years earlier; Murty Quinn and four other members of the Miami moved out to form The Sands with Tony Kenny. Now it was to be the Dixies' turn. O'Brien and McCarthy quit the Dixies to form Stage Two in January '72. "We got an offer from an entrepreneur," says McCarthy. "Tom Dunphy and Brendan Bowyer had done the same thing a year before us. We had spent twelve years together on the road. We just felt like a change. It was a natural kind of progression."

The Dixies found a new drummer and brought in Sandie Jones to replace O'Brien as lead singer. She won the National Song Contest in 1972 with *Ceol an Ghrá* and represented Ireland in the Eurovision Contest. The song went to No. 1 on March 18th and stayed in the charts for five weeks. Jones and the Dixies followed up with another No. 1 on May 6th, *What Do I Do*, and it stayed in the charts for nine weeks. The reformed Dixies could not hope to maintain the same popularity following the loss of the two star attractions. The band gradually went downhill, although managed to achieve two hits: *Goodbye My Love Goodbye*, which went to No. 6 in '74, and *Una Paloma Blanca* at No. 11 in '75. "It was a completely young band," says Lynch, who remained on. "I pulled out about '76. I managed them for a while. They were still called the Dixies but were a different band. We did a few tours. They went to Canada. I arranged trips to Spain and different places. I went into another business then. I left them motor on by themselves, and they faded away."

Meantime, Stage Two had competed with the Dixies on the ballroom circuit, became hugely popular and rated among the top showbands in the country. They had a hit with *Beautiful Sunday* which went to No. 5 in the summer of '72. The new band returned to Las Vegas where Bowyer and the Big 8 were resident entertainers. O'Brien told later how he introduced himself and Stage Two to the manager of the biggest hotel in the world, the Union Plaza in downtown Las Vegas in March '74. The boss was impressed and offered O'Brien a contract, but without the band. He turned it down. O'Brien, McCarthy and Stage Two were booked solid at home, and had to refuse work.

Disaster struck for O'Brien on the evening of October 1st, '74, as he sang at a charity dance in aid of the Gurranabraher Handicapped Wheelchair Association at the Stardust Ballroom, Cork. O'Brien reached out to adjust the height of the microphone and grasped it with devastating results. The microphone was live. He suffered a severe electric shock. He described it later as feeling like a pneumatic drill in his hands, "but a thousand times worse". The force of the shock threw him backwards about six feet on the stage. He felt he was "dying." He suffered severe burns on both hands as well as severe thrombosis of the main veins of his body. The singer was rushed to St. Finbarr's Hospital, went home the following day, but returned within days because of severe pains in his stomach. He was admitted to hospital a week after the accident and remained until December 7th, 1974.

The injuries brought his showbusiness career, at home and abroad, to an abrupt halt. The accident marked the beginning of a chain of events that tore his life apart. Doctors said he could never go back to the stage singing as before. O'Brien said later that if the accident had not happened, he would still be on the road with Stage Two doing well. Giving evidence five years later in a court action taken by O'Brien against the owners of the Stardust, Michael O'Riordan of Release Records revealed that, around the time of the accident, he was discussing an album with the singer and negotiations were underway with studios. O'Riordan's intention was to promote O'Brien and record one long-playing album a year. He would have negotiated a five-year contract with O'Brien. O'Riordan envisaged that, with the right material and right producer, the singer would have had a couple of further hits. Impresario Oliver Barry, who also gave evidence, said that if O'Brien had continued his career, his potential earnings were £1,000 a week gross — and the star would nett 50% of that gross if he was the sole owner of the group on the cabaret circuit. Barry evaluated O'Brien as "first class by Irish standards." His popularity and personality would be "on a par with the best in Ireland."

Stage Two lost its lead singer and co-founder. McCarthy later told how he kept the band going as he waited for O'Brien to recover sufficiently to return. "We sort of cruised on our laurels in the hope that Brendan would be back." A year later, it was clear that O'Brien's showbusiness career was over. McCarthy made an agreement with him about his share of the band. He continued to run it as a functioning dance band until April 1979. The lack of success was due in part to O'Brien's absence. McCarthy got a job with Power Securities, a property company run by ex-dance promoter Robin Power, which developed the Savoy and Queens Old Castle shopping centres in Cork. At the end of the '70s, all former members of the Dixies had retired from showbusiness.

O'Brien had taken more than his share of knocks since his world fell apart in '74. He lost his High Court action against the Stardust in 1979, and succumbed to alcoholism. He appealed the High Court result to the Supreme Court where the case was settled.

"When I lost that court case, I lost a lot," he admits. "I lost everything. I had invested heavily in commercial property. The cash flow stopped after the accident. I had to sell off what I had invested in. The banks closed in." O'Brien told the High Court in '79 that, for the first twelve months after the '74 accident, he received £3,700 from Stage Two. Then, his earnings ceased. He was forced to sell his home at Leeside, Tivoli; he had to sell his cabin cruiser; he had to sell his wife's car and he could not afford to keep his son at a college he was attending. "From 1974 to 1980, the financial troubles were moving in on me all the time," he says.

"But what kept my head above water was that Sean Lucey and I started a coin-operated business. We supplied pool tables and video games. That was quite successful at the time because I'd say we were the first to bring pool to Cork. So, that kept me going for a while. But that faded as well. Then the banks moved in and I had to sell off my investments. I had quite a lot of property. It was a tremendous blow to lose the case...very, very big. Even by today's standards, my investments were quite big. I invested wisely. Everything was above board taxwise. I had to repay the banks. I'm still repaying them. Having the banks move in, I had to sell my home. I had to sell my cabin cruiser and different things."

Drink took control of the showband idol sometime between the accident and 1978. O'Brien speaks frankly about his battle against booze. "The problem really showed itself around '77/'78," he says. "It's a disease that a man or woman can have for three years before it will show, so you can't really put a day, or a month, or a year on it. It took over then; very, very bad. It has to be the worst drug addiction in the world. I wasn't a violent alcoholic. I just needed drink like a drug addict needed a fix. That came first and foremost. Nothing else mattered once you had your booze. The only thing you can do is stop. Arrest it. There is no cure. It wasn't so much the quantity I consumed each day. What matters is to get the effect of it. There are about three stages: primary, intermediate and chronic. As you get older, and this even applies to non-alcoholics, your tolerance goes. You can get pissed on very little. I went to dry out a few times. Today, I go to AA meetings. They ask you to stay off one drink for one day. I can't tell you directly how long I'm off it. But this is my longest ever. That's why AA is such a success. You have to be one to fully understand it yourself. Things are pretty good now. They could be worse. I'm in good form."

A car crash in Las Vegas jolted Bowyer into facing up to his alcoholism: but no there was no such dramatic moment to alert O'Brien. "That moment comes every morning," he says. "I tell myself, 'today I'm not going to booze'. It's a daily struggle, and sometimes an hourly struggle. That song *One Day at a Time* gives you the whole story. People say to me, 'you were an alcoholic'. I say, 'no, I *am*'. But they say, 'you're not drunk'. I say, 'no. *I don't intend to be either'*." The problems weren't helped by the failure of his marriage which, as he puts it, "crumbled over a period of years."

O'Brien returned to the Dixies when they reformed in '82. But his return to the stage was shortlived. The band "let him go" in '85: "I wasn't turning up for gigs and things like that. I don't blame them. I really don't." On Friday, March 7, 1986, a short news item on the front page of the *Cork Examiner* reported that O'Brien had been released from Cork Prison after serving two weeks of a two month sentence. The article said: "The pop idol of the '60s had the sentence imposed after failing to pay approximately £700 in fines resulting from contraventions of the Road Traffic Act. Mr O'Brien was released after outstanding amounts due to the State were paid by a man closely involved in the entertainment business." O'Brien was taken to jail from his home by gardai. He says of the circumstances that led to his imprisonment.

"It's quite simple. A friend of mine from New Zealand asked me one day if he could borrow my car. I asked if he was insured. He said, 'yes'. He returned the car that afternoon to me. Apparently, the cops had stopped him. I was charged for having a car uninsured and fined, unknown to me, somewhere in Co. Waterford — £700, or two months in jail. They arrived up to my house and said, 'pay the money now or you go to jail.' Just like that. I said, 'look, I can pay it tomorrow.' They said, 'no cheques, no bankers' cards'. They put me into the car and bunged me up to prison. Sean Lucey and a friend of mine paid the fine and took me out. I was there for nearly two weeks, actually. It's as simple as that. I know nothing whatsoever about it. I'm still thinking of taking some legal action. I got no summons, no prosecution, no notification of a court hearing. Nothing; except they arrived up to my house in Glounthaune in an unmarked car, took me out and threw me into jail.

I was very annoyed about it. I asked my kids about it later. No summons came to the house; no notification to appear in court...so I never turned up in court. The court hearing went ahead in a place called Kilmacthomas in July of some year. I don't remember the year. Apparently, this friend of mine from New Zealand was stopped and didn't have insurance. I owned the car. I didn't ask him where he was going. He was a friend of mine. I'm easy with cars. That comes from being with the Dixies because we all drove each others' cars once we were insured. I knew absolutely nothing until I woke up next morning in jail. The *Examiner* slapped it across the front page when I was released. Everyone assumed, knowing I'm an alcoholic, that I was slung in jail for drunken driving or something. I was totally wronged again for the umpteenth time. I got no notification until they came up to my house and physically took me out under my verbal protest, and put me into prison. They told me it was because of fines. I asked to see the prison warden. I was told that my car was not insured. They said that a court case came up in Kilmacthomas and I was notified. I said that I wasn't. They said, 'you were'. They said they gave it to an Aileen O'Brien. No such person exists. It's something I'm still talking to my lawyers about. It was very wrong. I had enough on my plate at that time without being thrown into prison as well. It wasn't very nice being 'inside' for nearly two weeks. You could say it was a tough break."

O'Brien spent the latter half of the '80s picking up the pieces of his life. O'Brien's achievements in the '60s are widely acknowledged. In his book of Irish charts hits, DJ Larry Gogan rates O'Brien among thirty-six artistes who achieved most hits in the Irish charts from '62 to '83. He had seventeen — one more than Bowyer. Despite his troubles, O'Brien has, at least, been spared the tragedy that struck the families of two other members of the Dixies, McCarthy and Lucey.

Behind the Dixies happy-go-lucky image lies a story of sorrow. McCarthy and Lucey both lost young sons in separate road accidents in 1981. Lucey lost eighteen-year-old James on the June Whit weekend. He died shortly after the motorbike on which he and another eighteen-year-old were travelling went out of control at Crosshaven. The other youth was also killed. On the night of Tuesday, November 24, McCarthy's son, Aidan, who was 20, and daughter-in-law, Linda, who was 19, were killed instantly in a crash on the main Cork-Dublin road near Twomileborris, Co. Tipperary. The couple left an infant daughter, Amy Michelle Ann, who is being raised by the McCarthy family. Both tragedies cast gloom over the band of Cork showmen who grieved with their two friends.

"You don't cope," says McCarthy of the loss. "You can't understand it. But you do come out of it, eventually. There's no magic tablet you can take. You just have to go through it. My mother died four months after my son. It didn't take a feather out of me. And my father died a few years later. And then Theo died. I don't think Sean and myself were as shocked as anybody else. We had already been through a lot together. Tragedy makes us human like everybody else. Life goes on. Anytime we read now of a tragedy where a young person is killed on the roads, we can feel straight away for the parents. That's because we've been there too." Lucey reaches similar conclusions. He says: "Everybody tells you that time will heal it. First, you don't believe them. But time does heal it. You just have to get over it...and that's it. A child to die on you is different to your mother and father. It's the end of the world, especially a grown up fellow about eighteen or nineteen. After that, any knock or hurt you get is only secondary."

On Tuesday, July 10th, 1990, the Dixies mourned the loss of Chris O'Mahony, one of their founder members, who died suddenly in a Cork hospital almost two years exactly after the death of another founder, Theo Cahill, who collapsed after playing in Achill. O'Mahony had played his last 'gig' with the band on the previous Sunday in Moate, Co. Westmeath.

Professionally, the last chapter in the Dixies story opened in the '80s when the showband veterans made an astonishing comeback. The book is not closed yet. The re-birth began with a few nostalgic dates followed by a helter-skelter ride back to commercial success including tours — again — of Britain, the U.S., and even the Middle East. Nobody was more surprised than the Dixies. McCarthy reflects, in his inimitable fashion: "Look, if some fella tried telling me back in '81, 'you're going to be back on the road with the Dixies; ye'll go to America and ye'll play in the Middle East, out in the Persian Gulf,' I'd say to him, 'you're mad.' I mean, who's to say next year we won't be playing in space?"

The idea was to get together for a once-off gig at the Arcadia on St. Stephen's night, '82. Prendergast, who still ran the 'Arc, was all for it. The seed was sown in Mac's mind when a friend came to see him at his coffee shop in the Queens Old Castle, Cork. McCarthy was told that Big Tom had played in Tralee on the previous night and had attracted a huge crowd.

He recalls: "I said to myself, 'that man is years older than me and he's still at it'. I rang Sean (Lucey) and said, 'what about getting together to do one night down in the Arc?' He said, 'no, it wouldn't work.' Then Sean rang me back and said, 'why don't we have a meeting?' The thought of having a go at the Arcadia sank in. Peter thought it was a good idea. So we had a meeting in Sean's office to thrash it out between us. We got together at the first rehearsal. We tried something that we used to play. When the noise came out we were going to pack it in straight away. On the second night, it got a bit better. Brendan was on the piss when we decided to reform. We straightened him. Then we went hard at it, rehearsing three and four nights a week. We got a programme together. As word went out that we were playing at the Arcadia, we got another few gigs. We did about two months' rehearsal. Everybody was back. We had one new-comer, though. Our original piano player, Finbarr O'Leary, had moved to Dublin, so we brought in Ted Moynihan on organ.

The line-up was: Brendan O'Brien, Steve Lynch, Chris O'Mahony, Joe McCarthy, Sean Lucey, Theo Cahill and Ted Moynihan. We did a week and we packed all the halls. It was like the old days all over again. We just kept going then and we're still at it. We're doing as well as ever now. Brendan stayed with us for about two years, on and off. He was low at times. About five years ago we brought in Terry McCarthy as lead singer."

In 1983, the reformed Dixies were back in the charts with *Ballroom Dancing*. They decided, initially, not to travel beyond

Munster. Then, offers came their way from all over the country, and there were offers of tours in Britain and the U.S. "We caught the bug again in a serious way," says Lucey. "We were affected all over again." McCarthy burst out laughing when a Corkman, based in Abu Dhabi, walked into his coffee shop in late '83 and asked if they would play in the Persian Gulf. "I thought he was a raving lunatic," laughs McCarthy. "I said, 'we would, yah...' I asked about money. He wanted to have some tapes, records and a few write-ups about the band. He gave me his address, and I told Sean. They all felt that he was a bit mad. We posted off these things anyway."

This out-of-the-blue proposal led to a ten-date tour in the United Arab Emirates around St. Patrick's Day, 1984. The tour included a three-night residency at the Sheraton Hotel, Abu Dhabi. The band have since returned annually to the Middle East. The Dixies also toured the U.S. annually with dates in New York, Boston, Chicago, Cleveland and Philadelphia. Since '84, the U.S. trips have included performances at the Leeds Irish Festival in the Catskills, north of New York, over Labor Day weekend. On the first visit, the Dixies were introduced to a bouncer at the entrance to a marquee that housed the festival of Irish song and dance. He was a black youth in his teens. An organiser told the Corkmen that he was a boxer who packed a mean punch. The bouncer was Mike Tyson. "It's crazy," says McCarthy. "Here we are out of retirement flying off to the Persian Gulf and to America. We came back to do one night and look what's happened eight years later." The Dixies began to record again.

A lot of water has passed under Brooklyn Bridge since the Dixielanders threw up their day jobs in '61. Like the other top showbands, they were spoiled by instant success at home. "We were once offered a big record deal in London with Decca Records," recalls McCarthy. "The company wanted to take us over. Phil Solomon would promote us. Solomon was connected with Decca. He managed the Bachelors at the time. We said, 'no'."

Lucey explains: "We were doing so well in Ireland, we'd have to go over and start afresh again. We said we're not interested at all. But it was a chance. We didn't see that we could have gone worldwide that time. We wouldn't leave Ireland. We were making good money, so why should we take a chance. Bands like U2 have done it since. We never realised there was such a market out there." McCarthy shares Lucey's recollections of the unease felt about a new challenge: "We didn't regret anything. But it's a pity we weren't more aware. We should have weighed it up a bit better. Remember, we made it big here and made it to the Irish community in Britain. But this offer would take us to a new market. We were going to be promoted to appeal to the English community. That seemed to mean coming down a peg in status and starting off again. So we didn't really want that."

As for the Dixies, the band plays on. The secret of their success is versatility, pure and simple: a real showband in the best sense of the word.

The National Aphrodisiac

Wexford, Thursday July 18, 1968.

A bombshell is dropped after a dance in Wexford. The members of one of Ireland's top showbands want to break up. It looks like the end of the road for the Drifters. Joe Dolan is stunned. As usual, he has just come off stage high as a kite, mopping those thickly-set brows and catching his breath. It usually takes Dolan about half an hour to calm down after a show. Now he is caught off guard at a vulnerable moment in the Talbot Hotel immediately after a dance at the local Dun Mhuire hall. The news doesn't sink in immediately: he can see no valid reason to spoil everything by splitting just when the band is making a strong impression on the dancehall circuit. Since *The Answer To Everything* broke into the Top Ten in '64, it was uphill all the way. Why end it all now?

Dolan decided to stay with the band in Wexford that night. His brother, Ben, and their manager, Seamus Casey, returned to Mullingar. They tried to make some sense of the rift in the band during the journey home. In Wexford next morning, Joe realised that the musicians meant what they said the night before. The next date was at the Majestic, Mallow, on Friday. Casey and the Dolan brothers agreed to meet at the Hibernian Hotel before it. Casey and Ben wanted a discussion with the band to identify their grievances and settle them. Joe disagreed: "We don't have to talk. It's all finished. The lads have made up their minds. If that's the way they want it, that's it." He then told Casey: "I want you to ring the papers now: tell them that the band is finished; tell them that we'll finish up on Sunday night in Castlerea." Joe Dolan says he didn't have a clue about the dissension. In hindsight, he believes there may have been resentment at his solo ventures: "I was doing a little bit more solo work than before. I was missing for quite some time. I'd be in Spain or Germany or some place doing television. I'd be gone for a week or two. There was no bread coming in for the lads, and they decided to split." Casey's conclusion: "There was a musical content: some fellows wanted to go one way, and we wanted to stay with the formula. They thought that we were slipping. From memory, I think there were 1,200 at the dance in Wexford that Thursday night. We should have had 1,600. As it happened, everything turned out for the best for everyone."

Joe felt he had the right to be informed of any grievances. "I was disappointed in some of the fellows because we were really friends. They never gave me any inclination as to what they were thinking, or talking about. They never discussed it once with us. We went out on a high. It wasn't traumatic for me. I was delighted. Genuinely, I was. I had a good band. They were good lads. But I knew that we could do better. I was always confident. Even when things were down, I was confident. I never felt that this is the end or it's not going to work. I reckoned that we should just keep at it."

Casey made those calls to Dublin that night in Mallow. A statement to the *Evening Press* and *Evening Herald* said precisely what Joe wanted it to say: the Drifters were breaking up. The story was told in big, bold type on Saturday afternoon. It sent shock waves through the entertainment business. Ironically, the publicity led to a bigger than usual turnout on Saturday night at the Arcadia, Bray — and again on Sunday night at their final appearance in Castlerea. There were emotional scenes at both 'farewell' shows. The floodgates opened as the last songs were sung and final notes played: women cried and boyfriends consoled them. Autograph hunters besieged the dressing rooms to get the last signatures. It was like a wake. However, it wasn't the end of the road for the Dolans — far from it.

The Dolan story began at the family home a mile outside Mullingar. It was a 'half-way' for school friends who got together with guitars on Sunday afternoons and imagined that they were musicians. "Nobody could play anything," says Joe. In 1958, he left school and became an apprentice printer on the local newspaper, the *Westmeath Examiner*. The practice sessions continued: Ben, Joe and a few friends started to learn how to play properly. Their first dates were at local weddings and charity functions. A band format evolved, and they went in search of work around the midlands. Fees started at £10 — and anything higher was considered a bonus. By 1960, the band was taking only one booking a week, but later they increased them to three or four. They played as semi-professionals in all kinds of venues, from tiny parish halls to small dancehalls. They weren't fussy. The band gradually built up a following and turned professional in Easter '62. Joe turned his back on the printing business. The band was soon doing six, and sometimes seven, nights a week.

Joe thanks supermarket supremo Pat Quinn for "really putting us on the road". Quinn promoted a beauty contest as a promotion for the supermarket; heats took place in ballrooms and marquees around the country; contestants were judged during each dance. Quinn booked bands for the tour. He offered the Drifters a supporting role to the Rhythm Boys from Buncrana. It was a significant break for the Mullingar band. The tour gave them access to audiences in Sligo, Moate, Roosky, Longford, Dublin and Galway. "We were actually playing to a crowd of people for the first time and were very grateful for that," says Dolan.

Still, the Drifters were eclipsed by bands such as the Royal, Capitol, Johnny Flynn, Johnny Quigley, the Clippers, Melody Aces and Rhythm Boys. Casey, whose allegiance to the Dolans remained constant over the years, was the Drifters' manager from the beginning. The former schoolteacher ran dances at a few venues in the midlands. The band played for Casey at Edenderry Town Hall, in Co. Offaly, on Thursday nights every six weeks. The Drifters wore red showband suits and became known as the "red devils of entertainment." Casey had been friendly with Ben Dolan for a number of years. He loved the "thrill" of showbusiness. He says that his transition into band management was "easy." One day, he went looking for dates and returned with a bookfull. "There was no signing up," recalls Joe. "He became the manager then and he's still there today."

Casey invented Driftermania with Joe as the central object of desire for fans. The concept was copied from 'Beatlemania'. The success of Casey and the Drifters paved the way for other bands in the region. Casey was the first professional band manager in the midlands. "They were the first big band to come out of the region," says Donie Cassidy, who once played support to The Drifters with The Firehouse Five. "Because Joe was successful, we all got enthusiastic."

The next break did not come so easily. Following considerable lobbying, the Drifters secured dates in the Reynolds' ballroom chain. Joe says that Albert refused, initially, to give them dates. He explains: "It wasn't that easy to get a date off Albert at that time. We weren't a known band then. He wanted somebody who would draw people into the hall. He already had people like Donie Collins, the Clipper Carlton, the Capitol, Brendan Bowyer and, of course, Johnny Flynn. A lot of bands were drawing crowds, and we weren't in that league. It took us a long time before we got a gig from Albert. Don't get me wrong: I like Albert; he's a great guy. But he didn't do us any favours in the beginning.

"Albert and Jim built the Roseland in Moate. We used to play a lot of gigs around that area. We played the Crescent in Athlone; the County Hall in Mullingar. We were playing a lot of smaller halls around the place a long time before Albert gave us a gig. The reason we got a gig at all was because we were hurting him...genuinely. He was bringing in big bands to the Roseland and we were playing at the Crescent in Athlone. Okay, we could have a thousand people at the Crescent while he'd have somebody on in the Roseland. That meant he'd be down a thousand people. Then Albert started giving us gigs. I don't blame him for that. He had to get you to prove your worth. He wasn't in business to do anyone a favour. He was in it to make bread."

The Drifters signed a contract with Pye Records, and it marked the start of a fruitful recording career. The majority of singles were released by Pye, although Dolan recorded also for Release Records in the late '70s, early '80s. The first hit was Burt Bacharach's *The Answer To Everything*. DJ and music journalist Ken Stewart found the song for them, says Casey. The Drifters' version climbed to No. 4 in the charts in September '64, and was voted the best showband record by the panel of Telefís Éireann's *Pickin' The Pops*. It was cut in June for Pye, but the Drifters had to wait until August before it was released. "The record came out and we sweated out the first fortnight of sales," said Ben. "On September 14th, we heard Des Keogh —

then *Ireland's Top Ten* compere — say... 'in at number nine we have, for the first time, Joe Dolan and the Drifters' *The Answer to Everything*'.

"In Mullingar, everyone was thrilled. We stayed in the Top Ten for seven weeks. The record itself made all the difference to us. Before it arrived on the scene, we had been doing good business. Then, suddenly, the crowds went up and up. The letters looking for dates shot up and our manager had an average of twenty phone calls a day. We got tremendous receptions for the record at every dance, and especially in the cities. Sometimes I used to pinch myself and say, 'is this all happening to our band?'" Casey puts the success into perspective: "We went from being an ordinary band to one of the top bands."

Trumpeter Tommy Swarbrigg, an eighteen-year-old former apprentice electrician, began song writing. His first published work, *When You Say I Love You*, was picked as the 'B' side of *The Answer To Everything*. The Drifters criss-crossed the country, like every other band, playing five and six nights a week. One of the Drifters best annual dates was Christmas night at the Ulster Hall, Belfast. "It was an occasion more than just a dance," says Casey. "Some people might think it terrible to be working Christmas night. You had your Christmas dinner, and then headed for Belfast. It was a magic show."

The line-up was: trombone Joey Gilheaney; trumpet Swarbrigg; saxophone Ben; bass guitar Jimmy Horan; Joe on lead guitar; keyboards Des Doherty; and drummer Donal 'Sid' Aughey. As they broke into the charts in '64, *Spotlight* raved that Joe was fast emerging as one of the most dynamic personalities in the business. They joined the showband exodus to Britain during Lent and played in Irish clubs like the Shamrock and Harp in Birmingham; in London at the Banba (Kilburn), the Blarney (Tottenham Court Road), the Gresham (Holloway Road) and the Irish 32 Social Club (Harlesden). Back home, the Drifters worked hard, and played hard.

"God, we had a lot of fun," says Joe. "We used to play golf and everything. When we came to any town, if there was a golf club, then we were there. Even though I put 100 per cent into a show, I don't take it that terribly seriously. It's not the be- all and end- all. It's just something I do. But when I go on to do it,

I give 100 per cent. It's not the end of the world if it doesn't work. A lot of the people in those days were taking themselves far too seriously. That's what made it harder work."

A string of other hits was achieved between the first chart success of 1964 and the break-up of 1968: *I love You More and More Every Day* ('65), *My Own Peculiar Way* ('65), *Aching Breaking Heart* ('65), *Two of a Kind* ('66), *Pretty Brown Eyes* ('66), *House With The White Washed Gable* ('67), *Tar and Cement* ('67), *Love of the Common People* ('68). The biggest hits were *Pretty Brown Eyes* and *House With The White Washed Gable*: both went to No. 1 and were in the charts for ten weeks. Two other releases went to No 2: *My Own Peculiar Way,* in the charts for twelve weeks, and *Aching Breaking Heart,* in the charts for nine. *Tar and Cement* reached No. 3 and was in the charts for twelve weeks.

When the Drifters split up in summer '68, the Dolans were isolated as the remainder of the band went off to form a new outfit, the Times. Jimmy Swarbrigg came home from London where he was singing with a semi-pro band. He did an audition in Mullingar and joined his brother in the new band. Jimmy became lead singer. Other new faces were Sean Kenny from Boyle, Co. Roscommon (lead guitar) and Gene Bannon from Cootehill, Co. Cavan (saxophone). The Times took to the road in August '68. The two Swarbrigg brothers maintained the song writing momentum — a feature that made them different to other showbands. The Times had a series of Top Ten hits: *Dozie* ('69), *Hitching to Miami* ('69), *Looking Through the Eyes of a Beautiful Girl* ('70), *The Entertainer* ('72), *It All Depends on You* ('73), *If Ma Could See Me Now* ('74) and *Hold On* ('76). Their biggest hit was *If Ma Could See Me Now.* It went to No. 1 on July 25th, '74 and was in the charts for eight weeks.

The Swarbriggs represented Ireland at the Eurovision Song Contest in '75 and '77. Their song for Europe in 1975, *That's What Friends Are For,* came sixth at Stockholm and, at home, reached No. 2 in the charts. Their Euro entry in 1977, *It's Nice To Be In Love Again,* came third in London and, at home, became a No. 1 hit and stayed in the charts for thirteen weeks. The Swarbriggs achieved two other No. 1 hits: *Joanne* ('76) and *Someone Else's Land* ('76), in the charts for thirteen and fourteen weeks respectively.

Meantime, as the Times took to the ballroom circuit back in '68, the Dolans sought replacement musicians. Interviews were conducted and the reformed Drifters were back on the road by late '68/early '69. The timing of the Drifters' break-up could not have been better: a new band meant a new start and a fresh outlook. Then came the blockbuster hit that charted across Europe in '69. John Woods of Pye Records recommended to Casey that Dolan and the Drifters record *Make Me An Island*. Casey travelled to Dublin to meet Joy Nichols and Geoffrey Everitt of Shaftsbury Music Publishing, London. "John suggested that they play this song for us," says Casey. "We liked it, but weren't over the moon about it. We decided to record it. We had to wait because there was a possibility that Tom Jones might record it as his next single. He had a hold on it." *Make Me An Island* was a new song, written by the Hammond and Hazelwood team in London. The duo, who later ended their partnership, also wrote *Teresa* and *Good Looking Woman* for Dolan. He had good reason to be thankful to them. *Make Me An Island* sold more than one million copies. The record became a 'power play' on Radio Luxembourg. "The whole band went off on holidays to Spain in May," recalls Casey. "I never bothered to ring to find out how the record was doing. When we came back, we discovered that the record had started to sell in England. We found this hard to believe. It kept picking up and broke into the charts. Suddenly, everything happened. Joe was on *Top of the Pops* with it."

Dolan flew to London on Wednesday evening to pre-record his first appearance on *Top of the Pops,* but was also booked to perform at the Ags dance in the Olympic Ballroom, Dublin, on the same night. So, he chartered a private aircraft to fly back to Dublin. Dolan had bought a trendy rust-coloured suit in London especially for his *Top of the Pops* debut. However, such was the hurry home that he didn't have time to change. Dolan got a taxi to Heathrow and flew to Dublin where a waiting car drove him to the Olympic. Over 2,000 packed the ballroom and screamed for Joe. He arrived at the Ags fifteen minutes after midnight. "I'll always remember it was a lovely suit," laughs Casey. "But within five minutes, the jacket was in ribbons. They pulled him from the stage and tore the sleeves off. That was the end of the suit. I think he threw the jacket out to the people. On the following night, Thursday, the suit made its one and only appearance on *Top of the Pops.*

Dolan broke into the charts in fourteen countries with *Make Me An Island.* The song was voted Record of the Year in three, and gave him access to markets in Germany, France, Spain, South Africa and Australia. Initially, *Make Me An Island* sold well in Ireland, and then suddenly disappeared. Eight weeks later, the record took off in Britain where it reached No. 3 in June and stayed in the charts for eighteen weeks. It re-appeared in the Irish charts and went to No. 2. The record was in the Irish charts for twenty-two weeks. It later re-entered the British charts in November '69 at No. 48 for one week.

1969 was Joe Dolan's year. The next hit, *Teresa,* went to No. 1 on November 7th and was in the Irish charts and reached No. 20 in Britain. Both hits made Dolan and the reformed Drifters more popular than ever on the ballroom circuit. Dolan became a sex symbol, and was regularly mobbed in the dancehalls. He was frequently lucky to escape injury at the fingernails of determined females. The ex-printer was a star. Success on this scale created a conflict between his potential earnings abroad and the more limited, if steady, business at home. In 1970, mid-week dancing was dying in Ireland. Dolan could make up to £2,000 a week in cabaret in Britain. He took off to wherever there was an audience, but the pace was gruelling.

Take November 1970: he sang for Ireland at a festival in Rio de Janiero, flew to Luxembourg to receive an award, appeared on a European TV concert, flew to London for a recording session, and returned home to perform at a small country ballroom in Cavan. In fact, Dolan arrived late for that Cavan dance, having touched down behind schedule at Dublin airport on a flight from London. He had no time to change and went straight on stage. Image was important: the band wore smart double-breasted suits. "If those people out there put on good clothes to see us, then they'll appreciate it if we do the same in return," said Ben. "I know there are some scruffy groups around, but dirt isn't modern. There's no fella making dirty suits with holes in them, although there's plenty wearing them."

During those hectic times, Joe sang between over thirty songs a night. At the end of each performance, he signed autographs, distributed photographs, kissed the girls and wrote his name on the arms of more dedicated worshippers. Dolan's next release, *You're Such A Good Looking Woman*, reached No. 4 at home in February, '70, and went to No. 17 in Britain where it was in the charts for thirteen weeks. Casey believes that if *Good Looking Woman* had followed *Make Me An Island*, it would have been a No. 1 hit. Dolan had fans waving back in Rio De Janeiro, although he didn't come close to winning that festival in 1970. It was a memorable trip for Dolan and his manager. They could have lost their lives on the long flight to Rio. Unknown to them, the plane was struck by lightning and had to make an emergency landing.

"We flew to London and then to Paris. It was a straight flight from Paris down to Rio. It was Joe's birthday," recalls Casey. "We got friendly with a group of English newspapermen on board. We all celebrated the birthday and started to drink. There was no drink left on the plane when we finished. We had great crack. We drank the plane dry. We all fell asleep. Suddenly, the plane landed in darkness in a place called Recife, a military air base about six hundred miles north of Rio. The pilot said he had to refuel. The real story was that the plane was hit by lightening while we were all asleep. The pilot's instruments were knocked out by an electrical storm. The pilot lost contact with the ground. He didn't know where he was. He literally had to find the air field by himself. Otherwise, that plane would have crashed. I only learned the truth ten years later. We could have crashed. That would have been the end of us. We didn't care... sure, we were happy at the time."

Dolan asserted his individuality with those hits of '69 and '70 at a time of reassessment in the business. By now, the showbands had seen their best days. During this period, only artistes with the ability to produce original material and develop a new act stood any chance of survival. Some bands — such as the Royal/Big 8 — had ensured survival by emigrating for part of the year. Others hid away in a '60s time-capsule and fooled themselves into believing that cover versions would fill ball-rooms forever. That blinkered view persisted until, eventually, they played to near-empty halls. For this reason, it was fortuitous that Dolan achieved international hits at the end of the '60s and dawn of the '70s.

Dolan's career went into a lull from '71 to '74, and then Italian songwriter Roberto Denova wrote *Sweet Little Rock'n'Roller*, which sold well in Germany, France and Spain. Next from Denova's pen came *Crazy Woman* which, says Dolan, was 'monstrous' in France, Germany, Holland, Belgium and South America. The new material provided a bridge to the continental market. *Lady In Blue* was No. 1 in France where Dolan sold 700,000 copies. Denova wrote *Goodbye Venice*, "a standard with us now." Dolan also worked with Kim Wilde's famous father, Marty. "He was never my scene. I couldn't gell with him. He was too bossy... and I don't like that."

At home, *Sister Mary* was Dolan's biggest hit in the mid '70s. The song went to No. 1 on July 15th, 1976. Dolan did TV shows all over Europe during these years, and Casey usually accompanied him on these trips. The Mullingar singer once worked in Berlin for two days in the shadow of the Wall. Dolan returned to the No. 1 slot in Ireland on September 1, '77 with *I Need You*. The record reached No. 43 in Britain, and was in the charts there for one week. It's progress in the charts was halted when twelve of Elvis Presley's records were released after his death in August. The next Irish hit was *Silent Night* which reached No. 2 over Christmas '79. Then, '81 brought two big hits: *More and More*, at No. 1, which was in the charts for 15 weeks; and *It's You, It's You, It's You*, at No. 3, in the charts for six.

Dolan had the rare achievement of straddling markets at home and abroad: people sang *More and More* and *It's You, It's You, It's You* in Johannesburg and Capetown like they did in Mullingar and Athlone. Dolan had nineteen number one hits in South Africa. He can list hits also in Germany, France and Spain. In 1981, he performed for a total of 99,000 people during an eleven-day tour of the Soviet Union. The Russians waved their arms like they did in Mullingar, he remarked later. A keen ear for an original song separated Dolan from other showband stars. He believed that even a mediocre original was far better than a good copy. Dolan achieved twenty-four Irish chart hits from '64 to '83 — topped by Rock with twenty-five.

A quarter of a century after Dolan achieved his first chart success, the adulation is more restrained. Yet, his popularity still overshadows other Irish entertainers of his generation. Dolan is playing at a cabaret/dance complex called Maudie Mac's near Mallow. As the show goes on, his road manager, Tommy Begley, stands outside the door next to the box office. Begley is a strapping Mullingar man with a sharp wit. He has been with Dolan for twenty years, "on and off." He knows every road in Ireland, and almost every dancehall proprietor — the mean and decent. He tells me of one owner up the country whose meanness is legendary. "He won't turn on the heating till the dance starts. Freezin'! He wouldn't change a light bulb if he could get away with it. I was there one night with the lads. We were all starving. He gave us tickets to hand in at the bar for half a ham sandwich each. Half a ham sandwich! Put that in the buke!"

Inside Maudie Mac's, Dolan is romping through the tried and tested material that keeps him in a job. The voice soars up to the roof again; his shirt is soaked and the buttons are ready to pop. Buckets of sweat are lost on stage. Dolan gives great value for money. People call up requests, and he obliges. After it's over, he takes a shower.

Meantime, the boys in the band read the latest article written about him, published in that morning's North Cork supplement of the *Cork Examiner*. It's illustrated with a picture of Dolan in full flight. "Joe hasn't worn that tie for years," says one of the lads with a chuckle. The story, written tongue-in-cheek, is laid out under a headline spread across the centre pages in huge type: "Jose Dolano!" It begins: "If you had paid over your life's savings, to say nothing of an advance on your next month's salary, children's allowance, confirmation money and the contents of the gas meter, to finance a couple of weeks on a Spanish beach surrounded by suntanned pulchritude, sipping the local distillation and relaxing to the sound of guitar and castanet, who would you least like to hear warbling from a nearby transistor and indeed every disco on the Costa de Sol? The Fureys would have had me committing hari-kiri in the paella; Big Tom would have sent me threshing Corkwards across the Med on the pedalo;

and even Joe Dolan — for it was he who shattered my illusions of a brief escape to paradise — tore from my soul an anguished oath, in pure Castilian, of course. That was all of ten years ago and it proved to me in a dramatic manner that the man from Mullingar had indeed become an international star."

Dolan gets a kick out of the article, and wants the band to keep a copy for him. Then, he agrees to do an interview. Was he really the wild man that's been so often suggested? "No, I wasn't, really. Newspapers have been very good to me over the years. I've always had a nice deal with newspapers and reporters. But some of this wild man stuff came from somebody's imagination. I was never a wild man." He pauses for about ten seconds, and smiles..."well, I was probably — but maybe didn't realise it. There are things you can be that you don't always know about."

Dolan doesn't worry about money...so long as he has enough to buy what he likes and entertain his friends. Ben takes care of investments. The brothers own a pub in Dominick Street, Mullingar, and celebrated their 13th year as publicans in 1990. Joe is known as a generous host. His tastes are simple enough: he drives a good car, a turbo Saab, and plays a lot of golf. The professional and social parts of Dolan's life have always been intertwined, and he takes great pleasure out of both. Joe argues that fortunes were not made in the '60s. "Look, you're talking about 10 shillings-a-head in, and three thousand people at a gig. That's only £1,500. Yes, you'd probably be on a percentage. In those days hotels were expensive as well. Food was the same price. No matter what you get paid on the road, you're not making any money: you're staying around in different places, running two cars here tonight, a van and a truck, and carrying all that equipment. That all has to be paid for. Everybody has to be paid. The cars have to be fuelled and maintained. You know what it's like if anything goes wrong with a car...how expensive it is."

He describes the '60s as "my apprenticeship to what I'm doing now. I learned an awful lot over those years...not just about music but about everything else. Showbusiness isn't just about getting up on stage and singing a few songs. There's more to it than that. I can't explain it." Did he still feel like a sex symbol? "What ? I'm not into that sort of stuff at all, " he says with characteristic self-mockery. "I had a huge female following, and it's still there. But I don't think that I'm a sex symbol. Good God, no!" Then, he mocks again: "Jose Dolano, right...a sex symbol?"

Dolan has been no stranger to controversies over the years. In one, he was barred by Aer Lingus from their planes for three months. "We were flying to Greece. I followed the instructions on board. The seat belt sign comes on — so you fasten the belt. The no-smoking sign comes on — you don't smoke. The seat belt sign is switched off; so is the no-smoking sign. You're advised not to smoke if walking around the cabin. I was walking around the cabin. I was chatting to a couple of friends a few seats up. This hostess claimed that I was in her way. I wasn't in her way. There was a girl seated and her boyfriend was next to her. I was sitting almost on the girl's knee inside the seat. This hostess claimed that I was causing an obstruction. She made a complaint. I'm sure they were all very sorry for doing it because they got the raw end of the stick, really and truly. At the time, they had a spokesman commenting on everything that happened when it was all over. I never made a comment. I never spoke to a newspaperman. I didn't speak to anyone about it. They were doing all the commenting. Every evening there was a story in the *Press* or *Herald*. 'An Aer Lingus spokesman said...' or whatever. But there was never a comment from me. It just died away after that. I was banned from Aer Lingus planes. Very harsh, in fact. But I got at least £100,000 worth of free publicity from Aer Lingus, which I have since thanked them for."

Today, Dolan and Aer Lingus are the best of friends, and he cannot sing their praises enough. During the ban period, he switched to British Airways. "I was making a fuss of BA at the time. Aer Lingus didn't like it, so they asked me to come back and fly with them. I said, 'okay, I don't hold any grudges'. It is a fantastic airline. They treat me beautifully, and I treat them beautifully."

South Africa has been another controversial issue for Dolan. His popularity there is amazing. Despite the success, he operates a self-imposed ban on playing there because of his moral objections to apartheid. There is also the possibility that any links with South Africa could prevent him from touring other countries. During his visits there in the '70s, Dolan played to anyone who bought a ticket on the door, regardless of colour. The trips angered the anti- apartheid movement. To Dolan, these were just 'gigs', plain and simple, and he sang his heart out for those who paid to see him. He remarked later: "We usually brought the night porter at the hotel where we stayed to the shows. He was a black fellow, but a great character. I didn't give a damn about the whites or anybody else who minded." Casey says that Dolan was the only foreign selling act, in terms of records and live performance, to cross the racial divide. "We worked incredibly hard down there," he recalls. "We were doing twelve shows per week on a six-week run. The only day off was Sunday. We did two shows a night in most places. We worked everywhere in South Africa. It was great."

Dolan goes on: "We started playing South Africa in 1971. We went back about three times up to 1980. Then we pulled the plug. You see, we're unbelievably huge in South Africa. But we don't go. We just put a block on it, and that's it. End of story. We get letters every week asking us to come and tour. We just say, 'no; we can't'. We're not going and that's it. But there's a great chance that South Africa will straighten itself out. I'll have the ticket booked as soon as they do. *Make Me An Island* was huge over there. A song called *Hush, Hush, Maria* was number one for seventeen weeks. We've had nineteen number ones there. It's impossible to remember them all. I've no regrets about having played South Africa. A lot of people who spout about it have never been there. I saw South Africa at first hand, so I know now why I'm not going." Dolan's other chart hits in South Africa included *Lady In Blue, I Need You, My Love*, and *More and More*.

Dolan does not like comparisons with Demis Roussos — the Greek chanteur who sounds as if he got his vocal coaching in the Roseland. He had Top Ten hits in Ireland in the mid '70s with *My Friend the Wind, Happy to be on an Island*, and *The Roussos Phenomenon*. "Look, I was around a long time before Roussos," says Joe. "Where is he now? I'm still here. I never heard of Demis Roussos until he did one TV show here that made him. I've met him several times. He's a nice chap. He remarked on the similarity. But he gets it as well. It's one of those things."

Dolan doesn't regret his failure to achieve global success on the same scale as some major Irish acts of the '80s. "I've had plenty of international success. I still have it. There's only one U2; there's only one Beatles; only one Rolling Stones. I wouldn't want to be like any of them. I've fantastic time for U2. I saw them in Croke Park, and they were brilliant. But those guys must miss the road a lot. Remember, they were working six and seven nights a week before they hit the top. They're basically a working band. I'm sure they'd like to be doing a gig here and there. They'd prefer to be working rather than sitting back for six months or a year. They can't just tour like anybody else. When you're in that calibre, you play the big venue: you must get 60,000 people in. That's why I'm sure they miss the road."

What motivates Dolan today? "The same thing that did twenty years ago. You're just striving to be better...to do better songs and perform better." He never tires of the stage — "as long as I get plenty of time to play golf. If we do six weeks away, the moment I love is when we're finished and I'm going home." Dolan remains, as always, a homebird. He took a conscious decision to stay in Ireland, despite the temptations to concentrate exclusively on a career abroad. "However bad this country is," he once said, "I'd hate to leave it." It's not easy to explain Dolan's staying power. Originality certainly plays a part. "People didn't look for original songs in the sixties," he reflects. "Bands were quite content to do covers of this, covers of that and the Top Twenty chart. As soon as we got *Make Me An Island* and a few other original songs, we stayed with our own stuff. Regardless of how bad or how good an original song is, at least it's original. It doesn't have to be the best song in the world. That's what I attribute to my longevity. We go on stage and play our own songs."

Dolan has the common touch and an innate sense of what the public wants to hear. His fans are fiercely loyal: a group in Maynooth, who call themselves the Dolanettes, follow him to every show within a fifty mile radius. For them, and many others, he will always be the king. A new generation of Dolans is now carrying on the tradition. Joe's niece, Sandra Dolan, is lead vocalist with In Too Deep, a five-member rock and blues band under the management of her brother, Ray. They have the same hopes and dreams of their father, Ben, and uncle, Joe, who worked hard for recognition in the early '60s. Ray, who also plays percussion with the Drifters, fell into conversation with a '60s veteran early one morning after a dance in Westmeath. The man remarked: "I'd know you were a Dolan a mile off." Ray asked: "How would you know?" The stranger replied: "You've got that faraway look in your eyes..."

Fixers, Fortunes And False Hopes

Strokers, chancers and rip-off merchants were endemic in showband-land. They discovered ways to translate glamour into profit. They took short cuts at the expense of gullible young musicians and singers who chased dreams and who either neglected, or else didn't know how, to take care of business. Many bands were blinded by fame and adulation, caught like dazed rabbits in the glare of a headlamp. They were too busy lapping up the propaganda to see that somebody else had their fingers in the till. It was years before some bands realised they'd been ripped off all the time.

This was the great injustice of the showband era. These bands were conned on several levels. For example: some shrewd managers sold the act according to the band for one price, and according to the ballroom owner for another. The band thought they were earning £100 while, in fact, the true income was £300. Or else, the manager returned a false count of dancers to the band, claimed a percentage of door takings from the ballroom proprietor based on the higher, accurate numbers, and he pocketed the difference.

"You can't mention names, but there is no question about it, bands were ripped off," says Fr. Brian D'Arcy. "Young fellows in some bands were going around playing for peanuts. It took them a long time before they copped on. Basically, the money was going to some managers, promoters or the owners of bands."

Some ballroom owners were taking short cuts as well. The numbers racket was the oldest of all. Proprietors gave a false number of dancers to the band, paid them for a figure well below the actual attendance and kept the rest. Dishonest managers and ballroom owners could make a financial killing but, if caught, could never be trusted again. Credibility, once lost, was impossible to recover. Bands never worried about the big ballroom proprietors. It was some hall owners, and committees, who had to be watched. The risk of being ripped off was great when bands were paid on a percentage basis.   The proprietor returned, say, a count of 800 dancers instead of 1,000 and, if the box office wasn't monitored, the band couldn't prove otherwise. Some proprietors evaded the band's road manager — whose job it was to watch the box. That evasion took various forms: tickets were sold on the sly to dancers at a back door, in the car park, or coming off buses. A band who were ripped off, or simply not paid by a proprietor, could report the culprit to the 'Fed' — the Federation of Irish Musicians. As an extreme measure, the Federation could blacklist a hall until a dispute was resolved.

Top band managers argued over percentages with proprietors, but their dealings, in the main, were straight, if only because they had to be. Business could not be conducted efficiently if a manager had to spend the night looking over the shoulder of a proprietor, and vice versa. There had to be some trust. The ballroom business was a small goldfish bowl in which everybody knew each other. Managers were aware of ballrooms where extra vigilance was required. On safer ground, many reputable owners were pleased to greet experienced managers to the box office because fiddles were sometimes perpetrated against the interests of both parties. Box office and door staff hired for the night might have made their own 'arrangements': tickets taken at the door might be slipped back to the box for re-circulation. In this way, extra monies were not accounted for on the roll.

Road managers generally followed ticket rolls throughout the night. Some managers went into the box and helped to sell the tickets. Nothing was left to chance. Bands worried most about dance committees. Some of these were notorious and invariably included individuals who took money from everybody — band and committee.

Some ballroom owners also indulged in business practices that were perfectly legitimate, but not exactly admirable. For instance, a proprietor staged, say, the Dixies on a Sunday night, and they drew 2,000. On the following Sunday, it was the Royal who drew 2,500. Both bands were paid 60% of the door takings. On the third Sunday, however, he put on the Arrivals, a smaller band, for a fairly modest fee — perhaps £200. As a result of the impetus built up from the previous two Sunday nights, the attendance reached 1,500. The door takings were his own.

In the late '60s, some owners financed the formation of their own bands to create even further windfalls. Again, they would have had top bands on the first and third Sundays. On the intervening Sunday, they played their own bands who didn't have to be paid nearly as much. The combinations would vary: three good bands followed by their own, and so on. Then, proprietors who owned bands took it a stage further. They exchanged their bands among themselves and, by sharing dates, had greater control and more profit. The bigger showbands on percentages militated against this practice, but could do little to stop it.

Ballroom owners hated handing over 60%, 70% — or even 80% — of door takings. After all, they claimed it was they who had made the capital investment and carried the overheads. However, showbands argued it was they who drew the crowds. Bands felt that they were going to have a few good years and, like professional footballers, wanted to make as much money as possible before being relegated to oblivion. A top band who could draw 2,000 or more dancers was in a strong position to take on a proprietor. When the boss saw that the numbers added up — especially on a big night like March 17th — he reluctantly agreed to raise the percentage for the band. He had little choice because no proprietor wanted to lose a top band on a busy night to a rival ballroom. In the end, he had to pay.

Some bands insisted on a guaranteed fee as well as a percentage. The big boys flexed their muscles, told ballroom owner what to charge at the door and took up to 70% of the take. Generally, their percentage demands started at 50% in the early years, settled generally at 60% and, occasionally, went to 70%. Top managers were the most powerful figures in the business. Most bands 'tolerated' managers. Musicians felt it was they who pulled crowds and worked hard on stage while the managers sat back and counted heads. Bands considered that managers and ballroom owners were living off their earnings. But the backroom boys never worried about being sneered at: they were laughing all the way to the bank.

The most cunning managers built up a stable of three or four bands. They never had a problem getting dates for any of their lesser-known acts. The ultimate threat was to take the big draw to another ballroom unless the proprietor booked the others as well. It was blackmail.

Second and third division bands were in no position to dictate terms to proprietors. Instead of high percentages, they were paid guaranteed fees, agreed in advance. But some proprietors broke agreements at the end of the dance by claiming that the crowd was down. So, instead of handing over an agreed guarantee of, say £400, they only gave £100. The band had to be satisfied with crumbs because to argue would jeopardise any future dates. The proprietor had the power to scratch out 50 or 100 dates: lesser-known bands who depended on his goodwill were all too aware of that fact.

The taxman didn't always get his pound of flesh. Two words were enough to send shivers down the spines of many in the business — Revenue Commissioners. In ballrooms, government tax was based on the number of tickets sold. Some crafty proprietors evaded by not tearing all tickets upon purchase at the door. These were slipped back to the box office and re-sold by an employee or member of his family. So, while 1,000 people may have paid in, the official record showed that only 700 tickets were sold. The Revenue Commissioners soon wised up. Taxmen made spot checks in ballrooms but, generally, found evasion difficult to prove. It was a game of 'cat and mouse'. There were other practices: some proprietors handled cash only, and dodged the taxman. Others paid bands' fees by cash and cheque. So, if a proprietor handed over £1,000, he only declared £600 by cheque to the taxman. Tax returns by certain bands and dancehall owners reflected only a fraction of their real income. The Revenue Commissioners even set up a crack team of inspectors to hunt the dodgers.

Showbands were soon at the centre of a shrewdly-run business with cut- throat competition, buoyed up by the media and stroke-pullers. Rumours were rife about strong-arm tactics by a minority of band owners and managers. One musician who reneged on an agreement with the management reportedly had his legs broken and, then, he was left in the middle of O'Connell Street, Dublin, as a public warning to other dissenters in the 'stable'. The story was never proven. In fairness, violent threats against musicians were not a widespread feature of the business.

Showbands were a unique breed who shared a 'twilight-zone' existence. Ronnie Reynolds, leader of the Kings, once listed the requirements for survival as a showband musician: the skills of a diplomat; mechanic; map reader; businessman; the stamina of a horse; the health of Hercules, and the fortitude of a lion. "Whether you win or lose depends first of all on the lads themselves," said Reynolds. Musicians, he said, must be first-class; dancers were quick to distinguish between the good and the mediocre, and they had no hesitation in telling you what they thought. "Nowadays a band is often launched with the care and preparation given to the introduction of a new make of car or a new style in TV sets. Players, managers and promoters alike study the market with all the devotion of advertising executives."

The average band could earn enough to pay its members three times what they'd earn as clerks, shop assistants or junior salesmen. They earned from £15 to £20 a week starting off, but raked in up to £100 a week at the peak of popularity. Bands were mostly of two types: the employer-employee band and the cooperative band. In the case of the former, the band was owned by the leader who paid the members a weekly wage. In the latter, members shared the spoils equally. As a general rule, each owned a share, including the manager who was treated as another member of the band. The take was split after travelling expenses were taken out. Other managers were on 10% of earnings, or even more. A band may have been owned by an independent businessman: the frontman, who made the act popular in the first place, was paid the same wage as everyone else. Musicians who felt they were worth more than a relatively modest wage frequently went off to form a cooperative band where everybody got a decent slice of the action. Money was the most common cause of friction that broke up bands. For example, when the lead singer got two shares or two-and-a-half shares of the band's earnings, and the rest only one, jealousies set in. A big feature of the Dublin scene in the second half of the '60s was the practice of moneymen who coaxed 'stars' away from bands to front new manufactured outfits that made money for them. Other causes of band disputes were drunkenness, womanising and, of course, clashing egos.

It was a business that revolved around the box office. The showband boom raised the admission from five shillings at the end of the '50s to ten shillings at the end of the '60s. Bigger bands charged most. Ticket prices started at 4/- (20p) in 1955, just before the explosion, and settled at an average of 10/- in 1968, but it wasn't uncommon for the biggest bands to command 12/6 (62.5p)

The money was enormous for the elite. For example, 2,000 dancers at 7/6 in 1965, a big year for showbands, yielded £750, of which a band on 70/30 took home £525. The equivalent figures in 1990 would be **£5,163.36.**

First division bands played to an average of 8,000-a-week in the glory days. On this basis in '67, with admission at ten bob, and a 60% take, that gave a weekly income of £2,400 (**£22,224.70** in Feb '90) and a monthly income of £9,600 (**£88,898.80** in Feb '90). This amounted to an annual income of £120,000 — a staggering **£1,111,235.06** in '90.

It's a reasonable assumption that some top earning bands were, at one time or another, in the millionaire league, solely on the basis of annual income. Other factors to be considered in the projections are: big nights during the year that drew 3,000, or more, to major ballrooms like the Arcadias in Bray and Cork, Majorca in Crosshaven, Jetland in Limerick; a jacked-up percentage to 70/30 or 80/20 by the top bands on certain nights in specific areas; seasonal variations in business; earnings from record sales; fees for personal appearances; overseas tours. Bands had high running costs, advertising and publicity bills and expensive insurance.

The truth is that only a small handful made large sums on a steady basis. A number of them made good for fleeting periods, and the majority earned a comfortable living. Some of the big-earners invested and set themselves up for life. Others squandered money foolishly. Some, at least, had the good sense to invest in property. They paid in cash. "These were the wise ones," says an insider. "At the end, they had bricks and mortar...something to show for it all." Houses converted into flats were popular investment vehicles.

High earnings were used to support artificial standards of living. Inflated incomes meant they could surround themselves with the trappings of success and indulge in a hedonistic way of life. The chief temptations were sex and drink. Some fell — others didn't. The lifestyle imposed strains on marriages and families. Bandmen missed out on their children growing up, and that remains a big regret. They slept during the day; the kids went out to school, and they were gone for the next dance before the kids returned home in the afternoon. The routine made it difficult to maintain normal relationships with wives who were getting up when their husbands went to bed during daylight hours.

Bandmen lived a schizophrenic existence, explains Fr. Brian D'Arcy. "They were doing a thousand miles a week. You had a crowd of people cheering last night. When you went home, you didn't want to hear about problems with the children. You were going to hotels, drinking and eating steak. You had all these fans following you. It was an unreal world. Then, all of a sudden, you came home to a small house. The kids were shouting. The wife didn't look half as well as the bird did last night who was screaming at you."

The lifestyle revolved around alcohol. Outsiders, who held down regular day jobs, had enough money to go to the pub once or twice a week. By contrast, bands earned far more and had daily access to alcohol in hotels around the country, before and after dances. Drink became a physical rather than psychological habit. They drank to go on stage. They drank to go to sleep. They drank to wake up. For some, it proved to be a psychological habit, and they became alcoholics.

Sexual exploits were a feature of some showbands. Glamour boys, both married and unmarried, could use their magnetism to get 'one night stands'. Certain musicians never considered the night complete unless they had 'banged' the opposite sex. The pick-up process began during a dance when the men on the bandstand excited the swooning girls at their feet. It was a nightly ritual. A musician spotted the girl of his fancy. No words were exchanged. He established eye contact, sent out the 'vibes', and she responded.

The next moves were made when she waited back at the end of the night. Then, the pair slipped away discretely to find a love nest behind the ballroom, in the back seat of a car or on the floor of the wagon. It was an unwritten rule that no musician disturbed a colleague 'busy' in the wagon. 'Hangers-on', women who chased their heroes around the country, were always available after dances. These were the women who hung around dressing rooms and waited to be summoned. They were known only by nickname. The names were always appropriate. This was the unpublicised part of the showband story.

Some bands had a ready supply of contraceptives, bought abroad and smuggled home. A tale is told of one musician who imported a stock of Durex by hiding them in the back of an amplifier. However, he forgot to remove them before his first ballroom appearance on arrival back in Ireland. A smell of burning rubber pervaded the stage mid-way through the dance. The fire brigade was called and the amplifier had to be taken apart.

"Of course, there was a lot of sex," says one insider; "remember it was the swinging sixties. It went on more in the cities than in the country. Country girls were still nervous of pregnancy, nervous of everything. But, in the cities, it was no different than today. If you wanted sex and 'one night stands', you didn't have to look far." Some musicians, married or unmarried, also maintained steady relationships with girlfriends in villages and towns from Cork to Derry. Married men and their girlfriends kept in touch through fan clubs which were usually run from the manager's office. Letters marked 'personal' were passed on by the office. Home telephone numbers were never given to girlfriends. Their sexual exploits were known to all in the business — everyone, that is, except their wives.

In Ireland, girlfriends or 'hangers-on' rarely accompanied musicians back to their hotels. The risk of being seen was too great, for both parties. He didn't want to be recognised by hotel staff as a 'womaniser'; she didn't want to be branded a 'slut' in her home town. Abroad, it was a different story. Anonymity, thousands of miles away, gave those who sought sexual adventure a field day...and night. Again, the rule was that no musician interrupted another who displayed the 'Do Not Disturb' tag on his hotel bedroom door. Sexual exploits on foreign soil were open secrets. In London, the majority stayed at the Atlantic Hotel — and in New York at the Woodward Hotel.

These showband 'haunts' became the scene of casual late-night encounters with girlfriends or prostitutes. There were also voyeurs among the bands: some pooled their money to hire strippers for private shows behind closed doors at their hotels. Live sex shows were expensive to stage, but the bands could afford to pay. Some were dazzled by the 'red' lights on tour and became regular customers of the strip clubs. A well-known Irish band once brought the house down with roars of laughter. The guitarist mocked a stripper who removed her bra: "Jeez, my mother has bigger tits than that". A colleague delivered a punchline from the back rows: "Then bring on your mother!"

Bands obeyed a code of silence upon their return home. No tales were told, so wives or girlfriends never knew about their mens' dark side. It was a sensible pact because anyone who talked risked their own secrets being revealed.

A combination of womanising and drink put pressure on marriages, and some broke down. Fr. D'Arcy says: "I don't think they were any worse than politicians or businessmen or anybody else. They just got a name. The people who keep saying that about them never know them. The only time they know them is when they want them to do a charity gig to raise money so that they can look holier than thou. I always felt there was an unnecessary judgmental attitude towards the bands. They were ordinary guys who worked hard for a living. People envied their instant money and instant success. I always found them very decent honest-to-God fellows. There was the same proportion of rogues and good people as I found in the priesthood."

There was a level of hypocrisy in attitudes to showbands in rural Ireland: conservative community leaders and the Church frowned upon their excessive lifestyles and nocturnal antics. Yet, it was the bands who frequently swelled Church coffers by

playing at parish-organised carnivals and marquees. Many churches and parish halls were built on the backs of the bands.

Fr. D'Arcy, a pop journalist since 1965, ordained in 1969,
was the bands' chaplain during the '70s to whom many turned
for spiritual guidance. He was once described in a newspaper
profile as an intermediary between the bucklepping community
and their Maker. He heard the sins of showband-land. Fr.
D'Arcy gave day retreats for the bands in the '70s. He says:
"They wanted it themselves in order to get their act together.
They were married young fellows, having difficulties. Some
weren't able to go to Mass on Sundays, and it was a problem for
them. They weren't able to live up to the high moral and
religious standards they were brought up to respect and felt
guilty. The temptation of women was there...getting drunk too
often...going over to London and all that sort of thing. Their lives
got into a bit of a mess. The idea of a retreat was so they could
get back to the straight and narrow." Fr. D'Arcy, who broke into
journalism by writing for *Spotlight* and the *Musical Gazette*, was
privy to the showband secrets. He was trusted and gladly offered
his advice.

He had followed his showband heroes in the late '50s and
'60s, and went on to become one of the best known personalities
in showbusiness. The memory of his final moments as a layman
is indelibly etched in his mind. The farewell to the outside world
took place at the Astoria Ballroom, Bundoran, two nights before
he entered the priesthood at Enniskillen in late August, '62. It
was a two-band session: the Melody Aces played support to
Butch Moore and The Capitol. "It was my goodbye," he recalls.
"We had a car that night. I thought I would never see a dance
again. That was me finished. I was leaving all this behind. We
went up to the Devenish Cafe for fish and chips on the way
home." That year marked the birth of many showbands. Fr.
D'Arcy, a student priest, watched the business become more
organised. His favourites were the Plattermen... "but I will
always love Bowyer. I have a soft spot for the Royal Showband.
I don't think anybody had the entire range that they had. Many
others had bits of them. Joe Dolan is a wonderful man, too. He's
a super guy. He's a king.

A plethora of new acts took to the road each year. All had one thing in common, regardless of musical differences. They needed money to start off. Hugo Quinn of the Clippers wrote a witty article on the requirements of a 'DIY' showband in the '65 Golden Annual of Irish Showbands and Ballrooms. Sum needed: £5,000. "This must be chiselled from somewhere, or someone; then cut, planed or chopped into small and large pieces," he advised. "The largest must go towards the purchase of a means of transport. This is usually referred to as 'the wagon'. Now you need three guitars — one, called a bass guitar, does the boom-boom-boom; a rhythm guitar plays the chink-chink-chink; a lead guitar plays the plink-plonks. This, with a kit of drums, completes what is known as a 'rhythm section'.

You then have a choice of either a piano or organ. I recommend the organ as it works out cheaper in the event of a wedding involving a member of the group. Now you need a trumpet and trombone — that's the one that slides in and out. To complete the ensemble: a tenor sax, a clarinet and flute. All you need then is an amplifier, some mikes and speakers. The next stage is to get nine men, or boys, to play them. The ninth is to play the amplifier. As well as playing these instruments, they must be able to sing, look well, have a good personality, jump six feet, never get sick or tired and can laugh, even when they have a headache, a hangover, toothache and wet feet. Now all you need is a publicity agent to tell everybody how good you are and a manager to collect all the dough you're going to earn. Final stage: sit back and you won't have to work for the rest of your natural life."

Every band followed the same formula: astute manager + a couple of lucky breaks + a disc contract + suitable material + some musical ability = stardom. Managers had the task of running the business operation and keeping bands booked five and six nights a week on the dancehall circuit. It wasn't an easy job: some musicians were unreliable and failed to turn up for work on time, either because of drink, women or gambling. Managers also had to settle internal rows that blew up unexpectedly. "They were the toughest people to manage," says one former manager. "Frank Sinatra wouldn't be hard to manage compared to seven or eight Irish musicians on the road. You were sending them out to gigs every week. In the early days, you had unreliable musicians, unreliable transport and, sometimes, unreliable promoters at the other end. You had unreliable amplification, unreliable instruments and, in some places, uncertain power supply." Life on the road made bands bad insurance risks: some were notorious for 'writing off' cars and wagons.

The showband calendar began on Easter Sunday after the long weeks of Lent when musicians and singers toured Britain and the U.S. They returned with money in their pockets and gave a boost to the home economy. Indeed, the showbands' impact on the economy has never really been fully estimated. The formation of a band brought a direct financial spin-off to a city or town. A new band had to buy a wagon, instruments, get suits made and advertise. In 1965, a Commer twelve- seat light bus cost £1,025 from Buckley's Motors of Whitehall, Dublin; Murphy and Gunn Ltd of Rathgar, Dublin, supplied coaches and cars to the leading showbands; coaches cost up to £5,000 and £6,000; Pigotts of Dublin and Cork specialised in showband instruments, amplification and equipment; a saxophone, for example, cost around 200 guineas.

Fennessys of Dublin specialised in shoes, while tailors such as Hughes and Louis Copeland of Capel Street, Dublin, emulated Saville Row in the quality of showband suits. Band members bought about twelve suits a year. Automobile engineers competed with each other to produce the most streamlined wagons, and photographers kept busy taking promotional pictures, with bands giving away about ten thousand photographs a week.

Printers got lucrative orders for brochures, posters and cards; newspapers raked in valuable advertising revenue, and ballroom construction sparked off a country-wide building boom. When Jack O'Rourke and Donie Collins built the Majestic, Mallow, the ballroom gave work to twenty-five people between the mineral bar, cloakroom and car park. Mineral suppliers such as Crystal Spring of Walkinstown Road, Dublin, were contracted by ballroom owners. Inside the ballrooms, between 50 and 100 dozen minerals were sold in one night. When a top band came to town, hundreds of cars pulled in for petrol. Some filling stations opened all night to facilitate the bands, and a few even sold take-away meals and snacks to them.

By 1965, it's estimated that there were 5,000 young musicians criss-crossing the country. Five hours on stage made arms ache and legs feel like jelly. In the early days before 'relief' bands shared the workload, bands sweated for their money. A full programme from 9 till 2 demanded stamina, and so did the routine of endless hours on the road. A flashy custom-built wagon was a status symbol. More importantly, it alleviated at least some of the travel discomforts. Aspiring bands chased fame and fortune in cold, shoddy wagons. It was a gruelling apprenticeship. "In the old dancebands at the beginning, we travelled in Bedford trucks with no heater," recalls Sonny Knowles. "By the time you got to the hall, your legs were numb. Sometimes, we used to wear pyjamas under our trousers. After the dance, it was back into this meat wagon. You'd be ice-cold by the time you arrived home." Bands had different ways of keeping up their strength. The Victors, from Cork, worked out in a gym a couple of times a week. *Spotlight* asked the leader of another band how the lads kept fit. He replied: "Simple, we stay in bed all day." Comradeship existed in all bands. "You slept and ate with these guys every night," says one musician. "They were more like brothers." On a night off, usually Monday, Dublin bands flocked to the TV Club, Harcourt Street, where they compared notes and swopped stories.

For singers and musicians, image was everything. A catchy name was crucial. It had to sound different, and reflect the style of the band. Some called themselves after the founder or leader; however, the majority searched relentlessly for exotic names. Imaginations were stretched in order to create the most sensational identity. On stage, no bandman drank alcohol in those pioneer-pin days. Musicians who liked a few jars beforehand used 'Gold Spot' to kill the smell of drink. Their motto: 'Clean-cut and half-cut!'

Accessories were used to maintain the best possible stage appearance: cosmetic toothpaste for a sparkling smile; lacquer to hold hair-styles in place; and stage makeup to create a tanned continental look. In the heat of the night, it wasn't unusual to see streaks of sweat running down their faces. The glamour boys, whose sex appeal lured a female following, kept their image right by removing wedding rings before going on. In the public mind, none was married. Female adulation of bands was at fever pitch. Lead singers were pulled off stage by ecstatic fans and, occasionally, injured. "You fell head first to the ground," recalls one band member. "The blokes all envied us when the girls grabbed and rushed forward like bees around honey. But, I can tell you it was a frightening experience." The bands' M.C., who announced the dances and talked to the 'punters', helped to get the image across: he was the 'spoofer'. The showband steps were coordinated, and everyone in the frontline swayed in time to the music.

Showbands indulged their surrealism on stage. They invented gimmicks that became trademarks. For example, the 'mysterious' Silhouettes, a Belfast band, dressed up like space aliens, complete with masks to hide their faces. The gimmick: nobody could tell who was in the band. Typically, the 'image' frontman or woman could be utilised as a gimmick. Another band, The Derek Joys, hired the coloured singer, Earl Jordan. He was an immediate crowd-puller. Gene Chetty, lead singer with Gene and The Gents, was Asian, and so the band hyped his image. Similarly, 'punters' flocked to see a good looking girl fronting a band, such as Kelley of the Nevada or Eileen Reid of the Cadets. Gimmicks depended on the element of surprise. When Art O'Hagan of the Clippers was seen sitting during August '64, *Spotlight* asked why. Apparently, he had broken his leg in an accident. A special chair was installed for him on stage. Said Art: "The fans were so used to seeing us jump and move about the stage that at first they thought it was another gimmick." Later on, the gimmicks became more bizarre. 'Magic' — a young man who literally lit up via a battery pack and suit of tailored bulbs — illuminated the stage in the '70s. He was born of that great showband tradition of gimmickry. Images, publicity and gimmicks were tools of the trade. Poor musicians compensated by becoming funnymen.

It was a world that nurtured terrific 'characters' like Eddie Masterson who never held a microphone or went near a stage, but was known by all in the business. Masterson, a solicitor, carried his office around in his overcoat pocket. He was outside the business, but yet at the centre of it. He wrote Larry Cunningham's 1965 hit *Tribute To Jim Reeves,* and, say friends, tributes to nearly every county in Ireland. Masterson followed the Mighty Avons and loved to hear Cunningham Reeves' songs. Cunningham told later, in a *Sunday World* interview, how Masterson approached him after a dance one night with verses of *Tribute To Jim Reeves* written on the back of a cigarette box. Masterson said: "I know nothing about music. Can you put anything to them?" Cunningham added the music and tried the song at rehearsals in Cavan. The band didn't think much of it. A week later, they went public with the song at the Astoria Ballroom in Bundoran. Cunningham recalls: "I didn't know the words, so I stuck them on the top key of the sax where I could read them. I looked down in the middle of it to discover that 3,000 people were standing still. We had to do it three times that night." Masterson was a showbusiness 'insider' who always had the latest gossip. Promoters rang him to find out what band was 'hot' on the scene. They trusted his judgment. He told them who was good and bad. He followed bands the length and breadth of the country. A typical pose for Masterson was hunched over a public phone, cigarette suspended from his mouth with ash dripping on his shoulder, dialling contacts in the business in order to get the 'read' or news. He never married and lived for seventeen years at Barry's Hotel, Dublin.

Showbands and those who worked with them spoke in code...a rhyming slang called the 'Ben-Lang'. It came in useful when they didn't want others to understand a conversation. Some typical examples: 'Duke of Kent' (rent); 'chicken's neck' (cheque); 'dog and bone' (phone); 'the apples and pears' (stairs); 'tin of fruit' (suit), 'brown bread' (dead), 'uncle Ned' (bed); 'Franz Liszt' (pissed), 'bo-peep' (sleep); 'jo-maxi' (taxi); 'mother goose' (juice, as in petrol), and 'bengal lancer' (chancer).

New phrases were invented regularly. A 'Jekyll and Hyde', for instance, rhymed with the slang word 'ride', a word describing sex. Everybody in the business was called a 'head'. Almost thirty years later, the eighty-two-year-old mother of one showband veteran still refers to her middle-aged son as 'the head'.

This description of business colleagues once mystified Tom Jones during an Irish tour. When Jim Hand brought him to see the head of Blessed Oliver Plunkett at a church in Drogheda, the promoter was reported to have told Jones: "There's the *original* head."

As the business became more organised, the Federation of Irish Musicians tried to assert authority. Musicians had to be paid 'Fed' rates for playing and extra for travelling. The meal was specified. Only card-carrying members could go on. The 'Fed' stipulated the minimum number of musicians required on stage, and anything less broke their rules. Union officials inspected ballrooms to count heads. Dancehall owners became accustomed to the average eight-piece showband format. Many of them even booked bands on the strength of numbers. Bands that turned up with four or five musicians weren't allowed on stage. Some small outfits even carried two or three 'passengers': they couldn't play a note, but stood on stage, held saxophones or trumpets and were paid a few bob at the end of the dance.

The 'Fed' did not gain real control over showbands because the structure was controlled by older musicians drawn from the orchestras of the '40s and '50s. They looked down their noses at these young 'stars', who weren't always as good as them musically, but were making much more money. The AGM was usually held on Sunday mornings in Dublin. However, all the top bands played on Saturday nights and travelled into the early hours. It was impossible for many to attend — and so they failed to get elected to the committees. Curiously, the AGM was never held on a Monday or Tuesday night when most showbands were able to attend. The 'Fed' never adapted to the young bands or recruited the youth to its committees. A more liberal attitude might have stopped the exploitation that came five or six years later when naive aspiring bands and groups actually had to pay promoters to play. Showbands, in common with all other musicians, were required to join the 'Fed'...otherwise they wouldn't get near a stage. A compulsory test paved the way for union membership. The 'Fed' protected all within the fold by insisting that union rates be paid. However, teenagers who joined groups in the mid '60s were outside the 'Fed' and had, therefore, no protection against exploitation. Non-union musicians were abused by ruthless dancehall owners who seized upon another opportunity to cut corners and make more money for themselves. The level of exploitation was so bad that, eventually, some kids had to grease the palms of proprietors. It wasn't uncommon for upcoming Dublin beat groups to buy their way onto a bill with a big star.

The 'Fed' had the opportunity to make a considerable contribution to the business, but failed to avail of it. The greatest mistake, since acknowledged by many former members, was not to draft the youth to its ranks and nurture the talent of the future. For example, a scholarship scheme for young musicians would have promoted the development of the business. The 'Fed' could have achieved a higher profile and enhanced its image by organising a National Awards Show. But the musicians' union lacked foresight, and never moved with the times. Successful showbands never worried about what the Fed' thought of them... they called their own shots, and were too busy making money to bother with union affairs. This, of course, is no criticism of the paid staff and officials of the Federation.

Hype In Type

Publicity was the lifeblood of showbands. Unknown acts struggled to find work because ballroom owners only booked bands that pulled crowds and made them money. Media exposure was vital for bands to stir the interest of fans, maintain a steady stream of bookings and support their manager's claim for hefty fees. The object of the exercise was to achieve a high public profile and keep the band name permanently before the 'punters'. To appear on the cover of *Spotlight* meant as much to showbands as a *Time Magazine* cover meant to U2.

Bands concentrated their energies, initially, on the print media: the evening newspapers, *Spotlight* and, to a lesser extent, the *Musical Gazette*. Advertising was the obvious vehicle: bands were never short on superlatives, and all claimed to be the best. But advertising was costly, so managers invented publicity strokes that put their bands in the headlines for free. The print medium woke up to the rapidly increasing interest in showbands and saw the enormous potential for advertising revenue. Showbusiness pages became standard sections of the evening newspapers.

Sponsored radio gave bands a valuable platform: they made recordings in order to get air plays and spread their music to audiences throughout the thirty-two counties. Bands curried favour with the DJs who had the power to spin their discs. Indeed, broadcasters and showbusiness journalists were treated like gods. A hit record was a bands' 'calling card' at the ballrooms — their passport to the financial 'action'.

Next, bands sought TV exposure in the mid '60s, and RTE broadcast speciality pop programmes to every living room in the country. By the end of the '60s, a coterie of sophisticated media handlers emerged from showband-land: they knew precisely how to keep their acts in the headlines or else on the air.

Spotlight was the 'bible'. It first ran off the presses in Cork in April 1963 as an experimental monthly with a small local circulation. It grew to become one of the top selling weekly magazines in Ireland. *Spotlight* set the beat for the showband phenomenon. It represented a thread that ran through the business and cut across all boundaries: a common denominator that united all who kept the band wagons on the road; read by moneyed promoters at one end of the business and by legions of dancers at the other. The pulse of Ireland moved irregularly, beating in time to the brass and rhythm sounds of the showbands, and *Spotlight* helped in no small way to maintain the momentum.

A smaller publication, *The Musical Gazette*, also known as *The Dancing News*, catered for the country'n'Irish fans. It was published monthly from Lower Main Street, Longford. Early contributors included Colin McClelland, now editor of *The Sunday World*, and Fr. Brian D'Arcy, a columnist with the same newspaper. According to Fr. D'Arcy, the *Musical Gazette* was the only publication that "took the mickey out of the business. If you wanted to find the humorous history and the punters' history, that's where you would look." Editor Jimmy Molloy frequently sent up the showband stars by featuring caricatures: for example, Joe Dolan's head on Dolly Parton's body.

But *The Musical Gazette* was completely overshadowed by *Spotlight*. The showband 'bible' was as important to the youth culture of the '60s as *Hot Press* was to the contemporary rock culture of the '80s. It glamourised the bands and their good-looking frontmen, and fleshed out a fantasy in an age of innocence. It brought a dash of colour to the relatively mundane lives of young people in rural Ireland who saved all week to go dancing on Sunday night. They looked up to the bands and envied their high lifestyles, anxiously awaiting reports in *Spotlight* about their heroes. Girls wanted to see pictures of the glamour boys... Bowyer, O'Brien, Dolan, Moore and Fagan. Devoted fans collected copies of *Spotlight*, and made their own bedroom picture galleries.

Spotlight assembled a world of excitement and adventure between its covers, providing part escapism for self-conscious young people in search of a collective identity in the '60s. It used the Royal as primary raw material, dutifully reporting their every move and celebrating their triumphs. Bowyer was all but canonised by *Spotlight*. His words were gospel. A Royal Showband 'special', published in June '64, honoured the young ballroom princes. The band's rise was chronicled in detail — no highlight omitted. That 'special' was spread across six pages, including the cover, and framed by adverts from ballroom owners all over the country who wished them well. Promoters were always happy to be associated with the Royal's success: after all, they were good for business.

Spotlight thrived on the showband explosion of the early '60s, but never achieved the same success later during the glam rock excesses of the early '70s. It benefited directly as money flooded into the business: bands, managers and ballroom owners had plenty of cash to spend on advertising. It gave a rose-tinted view of showbands. Fans in parishes all over Ireland — many of whom didn't even read daily papers — waited for the latest copy to arrive at the newsagents. Those who lived in isolated country areas, who had to wait months for their favourite band to come around, followed their fortunes by subscribing to *Spotlight*. In that way, the bands seemed more accessible: readers monitored their progress in the charts, noted forthcoming dance dates and lapped up the gossip.

Bands and their handsome frontmen played to the gallery: they said what everybody wanted to read and lived up to the popular perceptions of them. Band leaders invariably reviewed the triumphs of the year in bumper Christmas editions. The magazine was never short on superlatives. Every new record release was 'the biggest break yet'. Profiles were predictable. Offstage, every singer and musician enjoyed hunting, fishing, shooting, golf and tennis... but nobody asked where they found the time. Not all hobbies followed the same pattern though. One 'star' identified his likes in life as...'a good game of poker, steaks, dogs, golf, tennis and buttermilk'. For the benefit of female readers, Bowyer, O'Brien, Moore, Dolan and Rock were always asked what they thought of girls. And every showband man dreamed of buying a farm or opening his own business one day.

Spotlight set the right moral tone at a time when no self-respecting suitor ever left home on Sunday night without his pioneer pin. It cherished the image of seven-nice-boys-next-door who made good on the bandstand, wore smart suits and peered from its pages with broad smiles frozen on their faces. Pictures of top-earning bands lining up beside flashy wagons and cars, escape vulgarity by the innocence of the time. Women were glamourised too: when Eileen Reid of the Cadets appeared on the cover wearing a white wedding dress and holding a single red rose, to mark her release of the Kitty Wells song, female readers imagined they'd hear wedding bells one day.

Spotlight embraced the legions of fans who 'adopted' different bands and fought off any attacks from rival supporters in the letters page. Not surprisingly, the postbag was dominated by champions of the Royal. But many letters came from fans of lesser acts such as Dave Glover, the Witnesses, Hilton, Gaylords, Black Aces, Skyrockets and Billy McFarland band. Letters even came from Britain and the U.S. because copies were frequently posted by friends and relatives to emigrants abroad. Readers pleaded for features on their heroes.

Spotlight ran quizzes and competitions that offered 'fab' transistors and record releases as prizes. Fans clubs used the magazine columns as a recruiting ground. The circulation figures rocketed. In 1964, *Spotlight* formed a 'promoters' club. Readers were encouraged to tell their friends, neighbours, workmates or classmates about the magazine. Launched by Bowyer, it boosted sales: by cutting out a coupon and ordering six or more copies, readers automatically became club members. They received monthly newsletters and qualified for competitions to win discs and autographed photographs of the stars.

The annual *Spotlight* poll gave readers the chance to vote for their favourite bands and singers. The much sought-after awards recognised the top draws of the year, and best individual talent. The poll was conducted by filling out coupons available in the magazine at the end of the year. There were categories for: best Irish showband; best male Irish vocalist; best female Irish vocalist; best Irish showband instrumentalist; best Irish recording artiste or group; best Irish showband, group or artiste record; best British group; best American group; best British or American male vocalist; best British or American female vocalist. The Royal were consistently voted the best showband, and

Bowyer the best male vocalist. They dominated the awards for many of the glory years.

As the semi-official publication of the business, it helped to bring record companies into direct contact with the record-buying public. Latest showband releases by Pye, EMI and other companies were hyped with large block advertisements. It wasn't uncommon for the Royal to herald their new release with a full-page advert. *Spotlight* was used to reach the marketplace. Advertising space was booked by recording studios; record shops; musical instrument shops; manufacturers of bass amplifiers, echo units, electric guitars, drums etc; showband tailors; shoe shops; printers; publicity agencies; mineral suppliers; and even late-night restaurants that catered for touring bands.

Spotlight may appear amateurish and gawky to a generation today raised knee-deep in slick, glossy, pop and fashion magazines. But it broke new ground when the first issue was published in Cork by the Lee Press on April 19th, 1963. *Spotlight* was the first indigenous pop magazine. It was the brainchild of ballroom owner Murt Lucey of Cork and a local journalist, John Coughlan. Lucey part-financed the magazine. Coughlan — who compiled the showbusiness page of the *Cork Evening Echo* and had extensive contacts in the music scene — became the editor. It was an experimental project, a gamble. The first adverts were booked by local ballrooms and record shops where copies of *Spotlight* were available. Initially, it was published erratically, but soon became a monthly publication. By the end of '63, printing switched to the *Limerick Weekly Echo* at McKerns Printing Works, Glentworth Street. As circulation increased, extra pages and columns were added. A special twenty-page Christmas edition with Presley on the cover sold for a shilling. The Cork offices were located at Exchange Buildings, Princes Street. The magazine was distributed to newsagents. Sales increased significantly, and so did advertising revenue.

In 1964, *Spotlight* was firmly established as Ireland's showband monthly. A national perspective replaced the early Cork bias. Ballrooms advertised dance diaries, and bands recognised the promotional potential of *Spotlight*. It listed the top selling chart singles in Cork, Dublin, Belfast and Ireland generally.

Although entrenched primarily in a showband constituency, north and south, it accommodated the growing beat scene and looked to the pop scene of Britain and America.

Technically, *Spotlight* improved with each issue: spot colour was used on the cover for the first time in November '64 when advertising manager cum artist/cartoonist, Kevin Sanquest, produced a drawing of Roy Orbison; the '64 Christmas edition published a colour picture on the cover of six leading showband idols holding aloft a giant cracker. Inevitably, as nationwide sales and advertising continued to increase, *Spotlight* Productions Ltd moved to Dublin where the monthly magazine was edited and printed. The headquarters were first located at Pearse Street, and then transferred to Grafton Street. The '64 edition had been printed by the Brunswick Press at 179 Pearse Street, with full use of the latest colour technology.

It seemed logical that Coughlan and Sanquest should move operations to the capital. The transfer was completed in January 1965, with an accounts office retained in Cork. "We just gave up our jobs and took off," recalls Sanquest. "It was an awful gamble to take." The move was timed to coincide with the transfer in printing from Limerick to Dublin. '65 marked a name change to *New Spotlight*. A year later, it went full colour and became one of the biggest selling magazines. Some of the best known names in broadcasting, journalism and showbusiness contributed to *Spotlight* in the '60s — among them Ken Stewart, Larry Gogan, Eanna Brophy, Shay Healy, B.P. Fallon, Michael Hand, Fr. Brian D'Arcy, Pat Billings and, later on, Pat Egan.

Editor Coughlan was a highly influential figure. He was on first-name terms with all the top managers and members of the leading bands. "John was like a god to the bands at that particular stage," recalls Sanquest. "He had a lot of power." Coughlan wasn't blind to *Spotlight*'s pivotal role. "You see, everybody went dancing in those days, and everybody followed these bands," he says. "The whole social life of the country revolved around dancehalls. The bands certainly did think that *Spotlight* could influence their careers. A big break would have been a write-up in *Spotlight* and the release of a record. They'd be nearly equally as important. *Spotlight* was important because of the fact that the people who went dancing read it. Those bands were the heroes of the time, even more so than sportsmen."

Coughlan saw many hopefuls come and go — only a small handful reached the top. "An awful lot of them never made it at all," he says of the casualties. "They invested money in equipment, advertising, hype and promotion and just disappeared without trace. I'd have to say that very few of the bands invested their money wisely. They lived well, drank a lot, and fornicated at a great rate."

It wasn't unheard of for some determined bands to try and buy their way into newspaper and magazine headlines. Those tactics didn't sway Coughlan. "There was little point in trying to bribe me because, as a major shareholder, one of my main aims was to ensure that *Spotlight* made money," he recalls. "So, if offered personal bribes, I wasn't interested. What it really boiled down to was that I wanted to get in advertising, and I wanted to sell the publication. The more we did of both those things, then the more lucrative in theory it would have been for me."

Using words and pictures, *Spotlight* compiled what could be regarded now as a social history of a breathtaking decade. Showbusiness photographers such as Roy Esmonde captured the atmosphere of ballrooms and beat clubs on film. His 35mm lens recorded the weird and wacky world of showbands. Kilkenny-born Esmonde, now a producer/director with RTE, processed the pictures and Coughlan edited them into *Spotlight*. Esmonde had to overcome practical problems. "I used to look at photographs in the UK magazines of three and four-piece groups," he recalls. "But when a session happened for me, six, seven, eight, nine and sometimes ten musicians would squeeze into my little studio up against a backdrop. They were fantastic times. Great sessions." Some memorable shots were described three decades later as nothing less than 'painting with light'. The major breakthrough in the development of *New Spotlight* happened in 1967 when it went weekly, printed and part- published by the Creation group. Sales and advertising revenue justified an assault on the market. The expansion was fast and furious. The Creation deal elevated the magazine to a new plateau, even though it remained tied essentially to the showbands. "That's when things really took off," says Coughlan. "We made a printing and publishing agreement with Creation. We thought that the potential was there for a weekly and, encouraged by Creation, we made the changes. They had the facilities, and already had a stable of magazines."

New Spotlight was the biggest selling magazine in its field, and ranked with the other top-sellers, most notably *Woman's Way* and *Ireland's Own*. The circulation peaked at 44,000 in 1969. The magazine accommodated other musical tastes: first the growth of beat groups like The Creatures and Granny's Intentions; the folk boom with Danny Doyle and Johnny McEvoy; the Country'n'Irish assault championed by Larry Cunningham and Big Tom who led a posse of bands such as The Smokey Mountain Ramblers, the Cotton Mill Boys and the Hillbillies; a traditional music revival led by Planxty; and, in the early '70s, Celtic rock with Horslips and a new breed of Irish rockers.

New Spotlight had to come to grips with a constantly changing market of music fans. The once steady flow of advertising revenue from the showbands dwindled as it entered the '70s. "Financially, it had a couple of good years, and several bad years," says Coughlan. "On balance, I'd say there was very little out of it except a lot of fun and satisfaction at a time when I really believed in all this sort of thing. When beat groups came along, we incorporated them. When the folk era started, we included folk pages. We tried to stay on top of the scene. But then, of course, the Irish aspect faded out, other than the groups that went on and made it abroad. Very few achieved that: Rory Gallagher, Thin Lizzy and later U2.

Spotlight was kaput by then. It finished in 1974. As the showbands declined, so the advertising revenue declined. The new rock groups that came along were absolutely penniless. The showbands had made a good living because they did a dance circuit around Ireland. The rock groups had a few clubs in Ireland, but had to go off to England to try and make a name for themselves. Most of them didn't. They didn't have the money to spend on advertising, so sustaining *Spotlight* as a weekly publication proved impossible. There wasn't enough revenue to support it. *Spotlight* had been supported by the record companies too. But it was too highly geared for the showbands. As the showbands declined, the readership dropped as well."

Faded copies of *Spotlight*, the magazine that once sent young hearts racing, are stored in library archives. For the '90s generation, the images reflect nothing more than people from another age in funny clothes and odd hairstyles. For the '60s generation, now middle-aged, *Spotlight* was more than just a magazine... much more.

Showbands gained access to a vast audience who read the dance diaries and gossip published in the *Evening Press*, *Evening Herald* and *Cork Evening Echo*. Managers astutely targeted the columnists. In the beginning, there were fairly standard 'good' stories: a trip to America was novel, as was the first disc. But by the mid-'60s, everybody went abroad and most of the top bands made records. Therefore, stunts were contrived to steal bigger headlines. 'Tempo' of the *Evening Herald* once wrote about the columnists' dilemma: "The 'sensations' in the industry have become so commonplace that one must be an oracle of wisdom to separate the truth from the fables. In any one week, I could be confronted with six different stories. A showband travels to Japan to play for the Emperor... a new record scores in three different countries at the one time... a band leader breaks both legs but the show still goes on — with him included of course... a manager negotiates a world tour. I know that in two of the stories at least, there is only a particle of truth. I must play these only for what they are worth. It makes for a rather intricate situation."

Radio played an enormous part in the development of showbands. At home, sponsored radio programmes carried the sounds beyond the ballrooms into the home, office and factory floor. Abroad, the better showbands got plays on Radio Luxembourg, and some were even given their own series. Sponsored radio programmes were hugely important to the showbands before the advent of TV in Ireland. Apart from band recordings, the Eamonn Andrews Studios produced about twenty-five sponsored radio programmes a week in the late '50s and early '60s. Showbands got valuable air play on the sponsored shows, and ballrooms also took a keen interest in them. The Astoria in

Bundoran, owned by Phil O'Connell, sponsored Larry Gogan's first show as a DJ. Associated Ballrooms sponsored their own show later on. Bands were particularly keen to have their records played on the night-time sponsored shows. At one time, Gogan presented fourteen sponsored programmes a week. He became well-known later for the Television Club Show on Saturday afternoons. In 1965 Gogan said of the craze: "Without the showbands, the pop scene in this country would today be dominated by British artistes like America. No artistes — except perhaps the Beatles, the Rolling Stones and Cliff Richard — can create anything like the stir our top showbands do in halls around the country." Showbands were featured on the sponsored radio programmes presented by Jimmy Magee and Harry Thuillier.

Gay Byrne — who worked for the Guardian Insurance Company and 'nibbled' at the edges of radio for a long time — also cut his teeth on the sponsored shows, and he too observed the rise of the showbands. Byrne first broke into sponsored radio by reading commercials in the mid-'50s. He'd been applying "to everybody under the sun, including Radio Éireann proper, and I was on to every advertising agency in town over a long period." He applied to O'Kennedy Brindley who were doing a programme for Urney's chocolates in Tallaght. It was presented by Joe Lynch, with Norman Metcalfe on organ. Metcalfe played tunes and people had to identify them. The programme was recorded in the CIE Hall, Marlborough Street, Dublin. Pat Layde, the Abbey actor, was reading commercials on it.

Byrne had done all the auditions for O'Kennedy Brindley, and "persecuted them with letters and telephone calls." Layde wasn't available one week because of acting commmitments, so Byrne was asked to step in. Layde couldn't turn up the following week, and Byrne was called again — he was still doing it ten or twelve years later.

Byrne presented a programme at 1.15pm on Thursdays in '58, '59 and '60 for Prescott's cleaners and dyers. It ran for a long time and featured new releases hot off the presses, including a lot of showband material as well as American and English records. Joe Linnane and himself frequently toured the eighty shops in the chain. Byrne returned to Dublin with tape and edited it down for the fifteen-minute programme slot. Imco Cleaners also sponsored radio shows, compered by Terry O'Sullivan who later became the *Evening Press* diarist.

The early showband records were of poor quality. "They were all considered to be awful because the quality was so awful," Byrne recalls. "Everybody complained about them. We all wanted to play Frank Sinatra, Sammy Davis Jnr, Gene Pitney and so on instead. The early records were pretty gruesome. But the sponsored programmes certainly featured a lot of show-bands. Ninety per cent of the sponsored programmes featured the bands. Then, Radio Éireann realised that they were missing out and better start doing something. They started doing pro-grammes as well featuring the better showbands. But, some of them were close to unbroadcastable because they weren't very good musicians. The best ones were okay. The Capitol were always good. They were slick. But the rest were pretty mundane musicians. The general attitude about showbands was that the recordings were pretty pathetic in the early days."

In 1965, the peak of the boom, Byrne produced and presented a major four-week Radio Éireann documentary series, titled *This Showband Thing*, on the phenomenon sweeping the music scene. It was an hour- long programme, broadcast each Sunday. Bowyer's hit, *The Hucklebuck*, was the signature tune. "It was a very big series at the time," says Byrne. "It was after I came back from London. I interviewed just about everybody there was to be interviewed. I played their music. They told me the history of the thing, how much they were earning, how many people were in the band and where they thought it was going. You're talking about Dickie and the Miami, the Drifters, Joe McCarthy and the Dixies, the Capitol. It was a well put-together documen-tary. It was a great deal of trouble. There was a great deal of editing on it. But I covered just about everybody. I covered the managers like Tom Costello and T.J. Byrne, as well as John Woods of Pye."

On reflection, Byrne says that the best showbands, in his opinion, were the Capitol, the Clippers and Dickie Rock and the Miami. He presented a programme for Radio Éireann called *The 17 Club*, recorded in a hall at O'Connell Street near Nelson Pillar. The format included a live showband or two each week, records and an audience of teenagers. This programme was 'wildly popular'. He also compered a half-hour TV show on Saturdays, *Pickin' The Pops*, and was succeeded as it's presenter by Larry Gogan, who also introduced Radio Éireann's Top Ten each Monday night. *Pickin' The Pops* aired new releases and had a juke-box-jury element with a panel of invited guests. A familiar face on the panel was BP Fallon.

Byrne recalls his routine during these years: "I was in Granada Television in Manchester at the time. I used to come home on Thursday night or Friday morning. I would record sponsored programmes on Friday afternoon. I would do *The 17 Club* live on Saturday afternoon. I would do an hour of records then from six to seven on Radio Éireann on Saturday, and then go out and do *The Late Late Show.*"

Telefís Éireann's *Showband Show*, compered by Paul Russell and produced by Adrian Cronin, had a great influence. It was first screened in June, '63, and played a big role in the growth of the business. It hit the peak of the TAM ratings. Musical instrument sales increased dramatically after the programme went on the air. Cronin also produced *Pickin' The Pops* and *The Go-2 Show*. However, bands faced considerable difficulties in adapting to television. The lack of studio experience made many of them look clumsy and amateurish — despite the best efforts of floor manager Michael Lindsay-Hogg to put them at ease. TV demanded discipline and bands had to be note perfect. Some who didn't fare well blamed the producer; others stayed away altogether.

As Byrne puts it: "Some of them went on and were seen to be as bad as they actually were. In a ballroom, banging it out on the amplifier, they could cloak a lot of what they were doing. But, in the stark reality of a radio or television studio, every mistake in those conditions is multiplied and amplified. A lot of them went on television and suddenly discovered they were shown up for what they were. The imperfections were all magnified. A few of them got scared of going on television or radio. Remember, our recording techniques were pretty basic as well. Radio Éireann was certainly not in the forefront of developing new recording techniques and new equipment. So you really had to be good to get across." By contrast, the top performers, such as Bowyer and Rock, came across extremely well.

Byrne did not feature showbands on *The Late Late Show*: "We only had a resident pianist. If anybody decided to sing a song or whatever he was there to do his thing. But we didn't have bands as we do now. We didn't have set-up musical interludes. The music then on the *Late Late Show* was really an interruption of the talk."

For country'n'western fans, Telefís Éireann broadcast *Jamboree* on Tuesday nights at 7.15pm. This programme gave a platform to Dermot O'Brien and the Clubmen and Maisie McDaniel.

Amid the big media hype, fans were treated to *The Golden Annual of Irish Showbands* and *Ballrooms* — a glossy book, priced at 7/6, that combined a diary with a series of articles on the world of showbands. This included band profiles, interviews, as well as observations by managers, band leaders, journalists, DJs and TV producers. It published, in alphabetical order, a comprehensive directory of ballrooms and bands. It was packed with adverts and band publicity photographs. The showband annual — a perfect handbook for fans and for those who made a living from the business — opens a window to an unreal world.

B.P. Fallon concocted an 'exclusive' story based on an interview he conducted 'somewhere in the midlands' with a visiting Martian, called *Gonk*, who wanted to learn about the bands. The Martian Talent Scout (MTS) greeted B.P.: "Oh Great Hairy One, I wish very much to be enlightened about these Irish Showband records we have been hearing on our interplanetary radio. I have been told you are the foremost authority on records in Ireland." B.P.: "You flatter me, although what you say is true. What do you want to know?" *Gonk* asked B.P. how he thought Irish records would fare in Britain. B.P. replied: "They would have to improve considerably and get widespread coverage over there. I think the only group capable of achieving this in 1965 is the Greenbeats, who are not a showband at all." (In fact, B.P. had taken John Keogh's Greenbeats to play at the Cavern in

Liverpool a year earlier. B.P.'s confidence was shared by Dickie Rock who described the four-man beat outfit in November '64 as the best of the groups).

Adrian Cronin wrote in '65 that the potential of the showband was limitless: "Where do we go from here? Already in Britain the pundits are asking — have the Beatles and the other groups run their course; have they reached the peak of their popularity, and are they likely to go on the wane? There is no such nervousness about the future of the showband business. The beat and pop groups might conceivably be caught in a teenage swing away from the *Twist* and its successors. But, because the showband is based on adaptability to anything new that comes along, not only is it unlikely to be affected by a sudden swing in teenage taste, but its future could be enhanced. The appeal of the showband is to a much wider age range. Even after sixteen years it does not appear to have reached the peak of its potential development. To me the showband is unique." A similarly optimistic forecast came from Larry Gogan who predicted an invasion of the British charts. He was sure it would not be long before the 'Blarney Sound' replaced the 'Liverpool Sound'. And 'Paul Jones' of the *Evening Press* agreed: "It looks like being a big takeover in England by Irish Showbands."

The only dissenting words came from Ken Stewart. He quoted Tommy Scott, an arranger/producer/composer, who was asked what he thought of the Irish showbands. "I could lavish plenty of praise on Irish bands for their musicianship. But their recordings are quite undistinguished. Where is the originality that would give them some chance in England and America? They simply aren't trend-setters. That's why I can't envisage a showband boom in Britain." Stewart himself concluded: "Even the most ardent showband supporter must concede that is food for thought..."

Walking The Streets With Butch Moore

Naples, Saturday March 20th, 1965.

It's all over. Butch Moore disappears backstage to his dressing room and pours a large brandy. Juries in eighteen countries across Europe cast their votes. A TV audience of 100 million is entertained by Italian tenor Mario del Monaco. But few in Ireland care one whit for Mario and his repertoire of Neapolitan songs. Prayers are said that the rest of Europe will vote for Butch's entry, *I'm Walking The Streets In The Rain*. Luxembourg wins for the first time since the Eurovision Song Contest began in '56. The winner, eighteen-year-old France Gall, can't believe her luck. She says: "I came down here expecting to get nothing but a plate of spaghetti." Britain comes second; France is third. Ireland is sixth — a satisfactory result for our debut in the contest.

Moore, a twenty-two-year-old former printer, is congratulated by Telefís Éireann producer Tom McGrath, Capitol Showband manager Jim Doherty and band leader Des Kelly. The relief is palpable. The trio are whisked off to a party, thrown by the Italians. A great weight is lifted. Doherty and Kelly were bundles of nerves backstage earlier as the countdown to Moore's performance began. "We were terrified that he'd forget words or that something would go wrong," recalls Kelly. "Jim and myself were in bits beforehand. We couldn't relax. Tom was doing his best to calm us down. He said not to worry, everything will be fine."

The man of the moment had looked extraordinarily composed under the circumstances. He wasn't. "I had that habit of appearing sort of cool. Inside I was shaking," says Moore. "I'll never forget the feeling walking on stage. It was like the whole world was watching me. There wasn't much time to think about everyone at home. I had rehearsed the song with the orchestra and planned to do it a certain way. That was foremost in my mind. Nothing else. When I finished I started thinking about home and then I really got nervous. I nearly collapsed. I couldn't believe it was over. There was a huge build-up since I won the National Song Contest. We rehearsed for a week before Eurovision in Naples. We were like athletes: you had to be fit with no late nights. Tom was great to work with — so cool and calm." The performance went smoothly. "Butch floated through it beautifully," recalls Kelly. "Everything went well. It was terrific to come sixth. When we went back to his dressing room afterwards, Butch was sitting down with a bottle of brandy and a big smile on his face."

1965 was good to Butch Moore and the Capitol: *Walking The Streets In The Rain* rocketed to No. 1; *Born To Be With You* also went to No. 1 and then settled at No. 9 while the Eurosong topped the chart; the band appeared on Sunday Night at the London Palladium; the Naples performance made Moore the hottest showband property and the focus of hysterical attention.

But the glamour of Eurovision had a sting in the tail: the Irish delegation flew home to newspaper revelations that Moore was married with a family. He and Kelly insisted that this was never 'hidden' from the public. Kelly phoned home from London airport, en route to Dublin from Italy. "Be prepared," said his wife, "you're going to have a rough time when you get back." On arrival at Dublin airport, the Eurovision entrant was besieged by newsmen who wanted to know about his marriage.

"The headlines in the evening papers said Butch was married, as if it was a big expose," recalls Kelly. "We assumed it was known all along. There was never any question of hiding it. Butch got so much publicity around that time...I suppose you did play down the family part of it because you felt that your professional life belonged to the customers. You obviously didn't show pictures of Butch with his wife and children because...who wants to know about that? But nobody ever denied the fact that he was married. There were cameramen ducking around Butch's house that afternoon on our return. They were taking pictures of his wife, Nora, hanging washing out on the line. Butch was asked about the story at the airport. He said he was looking forward to going home to see his wife and kids and couldn't understand what all the fuss was about."

Privately, Moore was annoyed: he expected a big press turnout at Dublin airport and anticipated questions about his Eurovision appearance. Instead, he found himself on the defensive about his marriage. "It was a big front page thing. I honestly don't know why it was so surprising to everybody that I was married with a family," he says of the controversy. "It was no secret. The fans were interested in the music and the singing. You're on the road the whole time and it's something you don't really publicise. Nowadays, things are different: everybody knows everything about the music stars. But, in those days, most publicity was about what you did on stage and what your hobbies were. I got married in 1962 and had three children."

Eurovision '65 caught the imagination of the Irish public, and so did the young man who carried Irish hopes to Naples. Fame brought hysteria, and Moore became public property for the rest of the year. His career took on new momentum during those post-Eurovision months: he was the biggest draw in the ballrooms, and a sighting of him was enough to draw a crowd onto any street in Ireland. He frequently needed garda protection to leave big ballrooms like the Arcadias in Bray and Cork. A picture that hung on the wall of his former pub in Milbury, a suburb of Worcester, Massachusetts, many years later, showed him being escorted from a ballroom by two policemen. It was a talking point for American customers. Irish visitors to the pub already knew the story: even to get from the stage to his dressing room required the presence of gardai and bouncers in some places during those hectic days.

Moore narrowly escaped injury at the hands of frenzied fans in July 1965 when pulled off stage by a crowd of girls in the Arcadia, Bray. "To tell you the truth, I nearly broke my shoulder that night," he recalls. "Girls used to reach up, and you'd shake hands with them. I was distracted and looked behind me. At that moment, four girls grabbed my arm and I came flying off the stage. They'd pull you down and rip off your tie for a souvenir. It was all a bit of fun, but you could get hurt. I mean, all those feet were tramping about, and I fell about five feet or so from the stage. I hit the ground with my shoulder. I was okay. Paddy Cole and some of the boys helped me up. There were many incidents like that for the rest of '65. We were serious about our music and did a lot of rehearsing and arranging. But when we went on stage, the girls began shouting and screaming and you couldn't hear the first few songs."

Butch and the Capitol were spotted dining at Cruise's Hotel, Limerick, one summer's night at the height of his Eurovision lap of honour in the ballrooms. Fans converged outside on O'Connell Street and blocked the entrance to the hotel. The band was smuggled out another door for their own safety. Similarly, when the band stayed at either the Imperial or Metropole Hotels in Cork, their exit was always made through the kitchens to waiting cars at the back door. It wasn't unusual to find two hundred fans outside the Imperial on Sunday mornings in the hope of catching a glimpse of Butch and the band.

"It was like Beatlemania that year because Eurovision had been publicised so much. It got to the point where I couldn't even go out for a beer. I suppose you could say I was on top of the world. My big memory is of the hysteria. It wasn't a laid back kind of success with people calmly enjoying the music and singing. It was crazy. My interpretation is that the hysteria was a throwback from the Beatles visit sixteen months earlier. People wanted to have their own heroes in Ireland. Brendan Bowyer had it, too."

Two girls worked fulltime in their fan club replying to letters. The club was run from Cabra Road, Dublin. A twenty-page souvenir booklet of band pictures went on sale for 2/- at dances. Moore was in demand...and not just by legions of female fans — celebrity status raised his value and extended his constituency beyond the ballrooms, TV and recording studios.

Moore now made personal appearances. Limerick businessman Vincent Power enlisted his services to open a new toy shop in Patrick Street. He installed the showband star on a platform overlooking the street at an upstairs window ledge. Moore sang his Euro song, and amplifiers carried the voice to adjoining streets. The star brought the city-centre to a standstill: traffic diversions were put in place and gardai were on duty to control

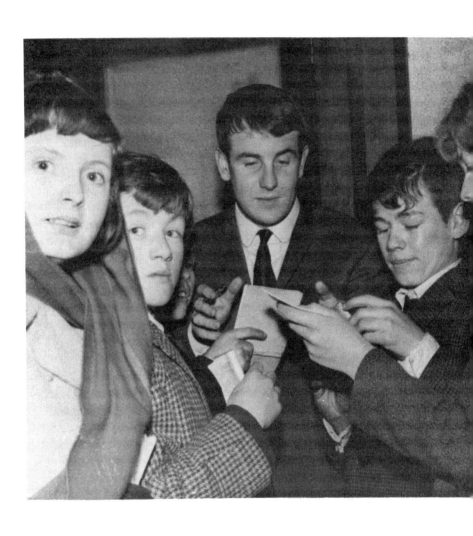

(Photo: Cork Examiner)

crowds. "He was so good-looking," says Mrs. Margaret Power, wife of the shop owner. "I'll never forget the screams of the girls when Butch first appeared at the window."

Fame and fortune can be transient though, as the Eurovision hero discovered by the end of the '60s. Moore's marriage collapsed, and his career nosedived after he quit the Capitol. A fallen star left Ireland broke and disillusioned. He picked up the pieces in America where he made a new life with Maeve Mulvany, later to become his second wife.

Nobody knows for sure precisely when the name Butch first stuck. It came from an American movie popular during his early schooldays in the late '40s. He can't remember the title. He looked like a kid in the movie called *Butch*. Pals christened him thus. "I never got rid of it going through school." His real name was James, but his mum, who never recognised 'Butch', called him Seamus. Interviewed by a TV reporter in Dublin airport at the Eurovision homecoming, she insisted: "His name isn't Butch. It's Seamus." He heard about her comment to the nation later and thought it hilarious. That reluctance was shared by Radio Éireann. At 18, he got the chance to sing with the Light Orchestra. The powers-that-were found 'Butch' objectionable. "I had quite a time trying to persuade them otherwise."

Moore was one of a family of four sons and one daughter who lived at North Circular Road, Dublin. The family later moved to Glasnevin. His father, Tommy, worked in Dail Éireann where he went on to become the chief usher.

At twelve, Moore was recruited into the choir at O'Connell School, near his home on North Circular Road. He sang as a boy soprano. He also tap danced. The school choir gave performances on Radio Éireann. At fifteen, he joined Jomac Productions, a Dublin group of artistes who perform free for hospitals and charitable institutions. The Bachelors began their career with Jomac. He spent about three years with them while completing his schooling. "I learned a lot. We did sketches and just about everything."

From Jomac sprang The Melochords, formed by Moore and four friends in the mid '50s. The band played in tennis clubs and small venues around Dublin. They became reasonably popular but didn't make much money.

By '57/'58, he left school and got a job as an apprentice printer with the Powell Press in Parliament Street. A secure trade was important in Dublin of the '50s. His family wanted to see him settled in a steady job. However, Moore wanted the stage. By night, he had switched to the Blue Clavons, one of the most popular Dublin bands. Jimmy Hogan, their guitar player, later joined him in the Capitol. The Blue Clavons once broke the record for crowds at the Olympic Ballroom. It was an unusual band: plenty of rhythm, no trumpet or sax.

Moore and Hogan first met Des Kelly when the band played at the Seapoint in Galway during '59. Kelly was about to move to Dublin to continue his college studies. Their paths would soon cross when Kelly, as leader of the new Capitol Showband, went scouting for musicians. As Moore acquired experience in the ballrooms of Dublin during the late '50s, he was enlisted into the membership of the Federation of Musicians. He had to obey union rules. "Joining the Fed then, you had to be able to read and write music," he says. "It was a great thing because vocalists had to learn how to play an instrument. I got guitar lessons from a great guy called Jack Gregory for about two years. I went into the guitar a lot...not the three chord stuff. I was into jazz. I had to know the guitar because of the union push and their programme. That stood to me later on when I came to America in the '70s because, otherwise, I'd have had to pay people to back me in small clubs. I was able to carry it all."

The first significant break came in '60 when Jack Flahive, President of the 'Fed,' recommended Moore as a vocalist to Billy Carter who had a resident band at the National Ballroom. "Jack was a good believer in me. He introduced me to Billy. Up to then, I had been doing all pop stuff and singing in tennis clubs. I really wanted to get into a big band at the time because I liked that type of music. Jack said it would give me good experience. I learned a lot about music with Billy Carter. Billy wasn't too impressed the first week, but I had worked up a whole repertoire within a month. One reason they brought me in was to popularise the band. It was always big band stuff: Frank Sinatra, the standards. I brought some of the pop stuff, plus the standards. It was a mix of everything."

Moore worked as a printer by day and performed seven nights a week for a year with Carter at the National. "It was tough keeping it all going, but in those days I was very fit, even though the hours were horrendous," he recalls. "I'd get home from the National at one or two in the morning. I'd be up again at seven. I didn't smoke or drink. I was a big swimmer: in fact, I had a Leinster championship medal. When you're young and fit, you have the stamina to do everything."

The Billy Carter band was his springboard to the Capitol towards the end of '60. He joined at the invitation of Kelly, and so began a dazzling career. Both men became life-long friends. Kelly, the guiding light behind the Capitol, had also experimented in local groups as a schoolboy with his brother, Johnny, in Co. Galway. The Kelly brothers were music-makers long before the Capitol became a showband sensation. Their roots in showbusiness went back to the early '50s when a group of schoolpals played music one night around a bonfire near the Kelly home at Turloughmore. The Quicksilver band was born. They played semi-professional in dancehalls around the west: on October 4th, 1954, they earned the sum of £12 for a gig at the Cummer Ballroom, outside Tuam. Des, a band leader while still in his teens, was paid for his services for the first time. It was a fortune to schoolboys studying for the Inter Cert at St. Joseph's College, Nun's Island, Galway, popularly known as 'The Bish'.

The Quicksilver was a family affair: Des played piano accordion; Johnny was the drummer; their sister, Bernie, played bass, and sang. The line-up also included Bridie Carrick, Joe Morris, Joe Killarney, Michael Costello and Christy Dooley. It was a semi-ceili outfit, steeped in traditional Irish music. The band played three nights a week: Thursday, Friday and Sunday. "There were only small venues available; the real ballroom of romance situation," recalls Des. "There was no electricity in the majority of them: you took the battery out of the car and hooked it up and that's how you got your PA. They were nicknamed Paraffin Oil sheds because candle grease and paraffin oil were used to make the floor slippery. Can you imagine that as a fire hazard today? We played waltzes, quick steps, foxtrots, siege of Ennis...everything."

The Clippers had the biggest musical influence on the Kelly brothers. Des first saw the Strabane showmen in action at the Hanger Ballroom, Salthill, in '58. "I remember having to queue for ages to get in. I couldn't believe it when I heard them because they sounded exactly like the records. They were doing a gospel number called *Rain, Rain, Rain*. As soon as I saw the Clippers, I knew that was the way I wanted to play music professionally. The Clippers made fortunes for people who followed later. We learned our trade from them." The Quicksilver continued to play the dancehalls — even as the Kelly brothers studied for college exams. Des, an agricultural science student, was the envy of his classmates. He earned anything between £30 and £40 a week from the band and could afford to drive a Wolsey 450 to lectures at UCG. He took a four-year course in agricultural science: the first two at UCG and the final years at UCD. When Des moved to Dublin in '59 after passing his first two exams, the Quicksilver was disbanded.

The music scene in Dublin was dominated by orchestras. The bigger ballrooms such as the Olympic, National and Metropole had resident bands. Familiar names were Billy Carter, Jimmy Honeyman, Jimmy Wiley, Johnny Butler, Joe Coughlan and Jack Flahive. The heavyweights of the touring circuit were Mick Delahunty, Maurice Mulcahy, Johnny Quigley, Johnny Flynn, Gay McIntyre and the Clipper Carlton. Kelly played relief spots with dancebands. He met pianist Eamonn Monahan, another agricultural science student, at one of the Ags dances in the Olympic. Monahan, in turn, introduced him to trumpet player Paul Sweeney.

The trio played together at student hops. They were joined by a drummer, Tommy McNamara. They played at dances run by Tom Doherty for student teachers at a hall in Parnell Square. "We were getting good reaction," says Kelly. "After playing there a few times, Tom put the idea into my head of forming a professional band. He saw that the Royal were successful. He was a canny man. He knew there was something happening, so he came up with the notion of forming a band and calling it the

Capitol, bringing in his brother, Jim, to manage us. I took it seriously and started to shop around for musicians. I was doing my third Ag in college at the time."

The Capitol emerged from a university environment, and gave an early outlet to the songwriting talents of another college student, Phil Coulter, of Queens, Belfast. Kelly first recruited Jimmy Hogan and Butch Moore, both of whom he had known since their days with the Blue Clavons. Moore had now moved on to the Billy Carter orchestra, making a name for himself as a vocalist. Hogan, an accomplished guitarist, was still with the Clavons. Moore listened to Kelly's proposal and agreed to "give it a shot." So did Hogan. The band decided to work on a semi-pro basis in '60: they wanted to test the waters and judge whether the Capitol had a future. Everybody held on to their day jobs. Des Kelly continued his college studies and passed the third Ag exams. Johnny, who was studying medicine at UCG, followed his brother to Dublin and joined the band. Given the all-pervasive influence of the Clippers, Des wanted brass — and so recruited Pat Loughman on trombone and Eddie Ryan on sax.

The Capitol went on the road five nights a week. Des did the driving. It was a hard slog around the country: dances were from 9 till 2. After a solid five-hour show, the band squeezed into their van and returned to Dublin. Kelly regularly turned up bleary-eyed for first lectures at UCD. "I often came from a gig and went straight to college. I'd then try to skip a lecture in the evening to get out and start all over again. I'm sure I held the record for sleeping through lectures, even though I did get my third Ag." Johnny gave up his medical studies.

Although still semi-professional, the Capitol had all the trappings of a professional band: manager/publicist, instrumentation, uniforms, handout photographs. The line-up was: Johnny Kelly, drums; Eamonn Monahan, piano; Jimmy Hogan, lead guitar and banjo; Butch Moore, lead singer and rhythm guitar; Paul Sweeney, trumpet; Pat Loughman, trombone; Eddie Ryan, sax; Des Kelly, bass, vocals and musical arrangements. The Capitol went professional in early '61 with Jim Doherty as manager. They bought a custom-built wagon, made by coach builder George Duffy of Dundalk. Two members, Loughman and Ryan, decided not to go full-time. Loughman was replaced on trombone by Don Long, of Cork, who had played with Donie Collins. "We saw him with Donie at the Olympic," says Kelly. "He was doing the Bobby Darin number, *Clementine*. We realised immediately there was nobody else in his class around. Then Don came to have a look at us in the Crystal. He asked how much we were willing to pay him. I told him what we had in mind. He said, 'great, see you in two weeks'. That was it. No messing."

Ryan was replaced on sax/clarinet by Paddy Cole. Kelly and Sweeney had seen him in action with Maurice Lynch at the Olympic. They liked his sound. It took several trips to Castleblaney before Cole signed up. His father, also Paddy, was in favour of the proposal, but not his mother. He reluctantly refused the offer. Father and son had played together in Lynch's band when the line-up had four saxes and two trumpets. Cole senior was the lead alto and clarinet player. He knew of the big push behind the Capitol. He felt that their prospects were good. However, Mrs. Mary Cole didn't want to see her only son taking flight for the big city. "She heard about me going to stay in a flat in Dublin. To her flats meant living in poor areas of the city. She was worried. But the boys in the band thought I was looking for more money or something. They came back to negotiate again. Eventually, somebody spoke to my mother and I went off with the band. Don Long joined at the same time as me."

Recruits were guaranteed a minimum of £30 a week, plus a share in the band. The money nearly always exceeded the guaranteed wage. As founder, Des Kelly retained two shares. The musicians and manager had one share each. Like the Royal, the Capitol commanded percentages in ballrooms. These spiralled as their popularity increased. The Capitol went on their first U.S. tour in Lent, '61. The deal was straight-forward: they played exclusively for Bill Fuller at the Crystal, in Dublin, and he arranged a trip to the States once a year. The band toured his ballrooms in New York, Boston, Chicago and Philadelphia. They were amazed by New York. "It was very exciting for a crowd of young fellows," says Kelly. "Going down Broadway and 42nd Street for the first time in your life was marvellous." Trips to the U.S. were pencilled in the diary every year: on one occasion, they were flown out to New York just for St. Patrick's night. They played Castlebar, Dublin, London and Queens in New York on consecutive nights. A U.S. tour usually meant a Fuller operation, but they also went for two other promoters, Jimmy Barter and Harry McGurk.

The Capitol brought together some of the best musicians in the business. The frontline comprised lead men in their own right. It was a musical band in the best showband sense. Inevitably, the programme was chart-orientated, but each member did feature spots: for instance, Don Long did *Angelina*, a Louis Prima number; Des Kelly and Jimmy Hogan specialised in country material. "If you had a gap, you did a country song as a filler," says Kelly. The band played a lot of dixieland jazz. Their stage style was adopted from the Clippers: smile, look happy and move around in flamboyant suits. Moore had a good voice and a strong stage presence.

In 1963, the Capitol became the first showband to appear on Telefís Éireann — and the first to land a twelve-week series on Radio Luxembourg. The TV debut was made with Sligo balladeer, Maisie McDaniel, in a half-hour show. "We know that it could have been better," said Kelly later. "We're content in the knowledge that the show was a yardstick for other bands to go by and possibly a yardstick for Telefís Éireann to have a showband series on." The Radio Luxembourg spots brought an encouraging reaction from Britain and mainland Europe. Fan letters increased to 400 a week.

1963 also marked their second U.S. trip. They met great jazz musicians such as Woody Herman, Duke Ellington and Dizzy Gillespie in New York's Metropole Bar. Des Kelly was introduced to country star George Jones at the interval of his show in Newark, New Jersey. "I managed to struggle through *I Dreamed Of An Old Love Affair*. I was never so nervous in my whole life." The Capitol also had the distinction of being the first showband to release an LP at this time, titled *Presenting the Capitol Showband*. It featured their special numbers like *Angelina, My Lagan Love* and *You'll Never Walk Alone*. Paul Sweeney quit to resume studies in architecture. He was replaced on trumpet by Bram McCarthy, who was recommended to the

Butch Moore and the Capitol

(Photo: Sunday World)

band by fellow Corkonian Don Long. The introduction was deliberately staged for fans one night at the Crystal, Dublin, in early '63. Kelly was worried about how their followers would react to a new face. Sweeney handed over to the latest recruit half way through the dance. When McCarthy finished *The Lonely Bull*, the ballroom erupted in applause. "Everybody made him feel welcome," recalls Kelly. "I was always proud of the way that was done."

The Royal had recorded the first showband single and pressure mounted on the Capitol to follow suit. They began recording with John Woods of Pye. They recorded a song written by Phil Coulter, *Foolin' Time*. It went to No. 3 in the charts in February '64. "Phil helped us a lot during those early days with arrangements and things like that," recalls Kelly. "He was a student at the time in Belfast. He used to come down to Dublin and stay with me. He'd go to rehearsals with us. He'd help us over stuff that we found musically difficult. He was only a kid. He was brilliant."

Coulter was good for the Capitol — and the Capitol were good for Coulter. "The songs he wrote were great," says Cole. "Nobody knew Phil Coulter at that time, but everybody knew the Capitol. Phil became known because he wrote for the Capitol. I remember once we told him about the popular TV show, Get Smart. He sat down at the piano and wrote a song for Don Long there and then. We went to London and recorded it. I remember coming out in the taxi to the airport. We thought it would be a No. 1 hit because everybody in England and Ireland watched this programme. But it just didn't click." Moore sang Coulter's praises in a '64 interview: "He's the most talented fellow I've ever met. To me, he's even above the level of the best English composers. I'd go as far as to say that he's capable of writing a standard, an evergreen." *Foolin' Time* an up-tempo number, was followed in the same year by another Coulter original, *I Missed You*. While recording a session in Pye's London studios, the band found themselves short one number. A call was made to Belfast and Coulter caught the next plane to London. He wrote the song on the flight. It had a big brassy beat, but didn't make any impact on the charts when released on

March 31st. However, it got air plays and led to an appearance by the Capitol at the London Palladium in '64.

While on a promotional trip to London, Phil Solomon, their British agent, negotiated a spot at the Palladium. Two of his other acts, The Bachelors and The Big Four, were also booked to perform. Roy Orbison topped the bill. It was a glittering charity night: tickets were twenty-five guineas each with proceeds going to the Freedom From Hunger Campaign. "We went down a bomb because we were so different," recalls Kelly. "We were an eight-piece band. We played traditional jazz, our own numbers, country orientated stuff and even some Clancy Brothers. We got a standing ovation. Few people realise what it's like to appear in a place like the Palladium. I'd never seen the boys in the band so close to tears as when the final curtain came down."

The Palladium appearance was followed by a showcase night for the band at the Lyceum Ballroom on the Strand, organised by Phil Solomon. The 2,500-strong attendance included top booking agents who were brought along to see the band. They were impressed. Lucrative offers of work in Britain were made to the Capitol — among them a six month contract at the Palladium. But the band were already making big money on the Irish ballroom circuit, and so rejected the offers. "It was probably a missed opportunity," recalls Cole. "We could have broken the British scene then. If we had gone to the Palladium, we could have used it to go anywhere we wanted. But we were already booked solid at home and making more money. We didn't see any reason to change things at the time."

Next the Capitol made a dash to Cologne to perform in concert — again with The Bachelors — for the British forces there. In the run-up to Christmas '64, the Capitol got valuable TV exposure on *The Showband Show*. Moore did a TV special with St. Mary's of the Blind. He sang four songs which were later recorded as an EP. Sales of the band's latest single, *Down Came The Rain*, were boosted by the TV appearances. It entered the charts on November 30th, 1964 and became their first No. 1 on December 11th. Their next chart-topper, *Born To Be With You*, arranged by Coulter, went to No. 1 three months later, on

March 8th, '65. "It was an oldie, like a folk song, and Phil jazzed it up," says Kelly.

The Capitol's greatest triumph came when they performed on *Sunday Night At The London Palladium* on January 24th, 1965. It was the night that Britain mourned the death of Winston Churchill. The show was normally televised live to a viewing audience of millions. It was considered an achievement for an Irish showband to be invited on. "That was something we really wanted to do. It was on a par with any show in the world. Frank Sinatra used to do it," says Kelly. But the death of Churchill caused panic at the rehearsals. The show was on-off. Eventually, the TV bosses decided against a live broadcast as a mark of respect. It was recorded for transmission on a later Sunday. In a last-minute change of schedule, the Capitol were asked to do two spots instead of one. The change heightened their anxiety. Moore got so nervous he lost his voice, but recovered later.

When the band walked on stage at rehearsals, they peered below into the orchestra pit and saw musicians they'd admired for years: Kenny Baker on trumpet and Don Lusher on trombone. Bram McCarthy was overcome by nerves while playing an awkward piece on trumpet. He missed it a couple of times. Baker and other trumpet players came to the band's dressing room afterwards. Baker told McCarthy: "We heard you blowing and we know you're a good player. We know it's not easy. You're up there on stage doing what we couldn't do. We can sit down below and play. Relax, we just want to see you doing it right." Cole was impressed by their support: "They compared trumpets and blew a little bit among themselves. They relaxed Bram so much that he went out and got straight through it fine. I thought it was a marvellous thing to do." The band performed *Granada, Born To Be With You* and *Down Came The Rain*. "When it was over, the lads started crying," recalls Kelly. "It was very emotional. It was a release of tension when we knew we got a good result."

1965 was Eurovision year. *Walking The Streets In The Rain* became his third consecutive No. 1 on April 5th while, at the same time, the previous hit, *Born To Be With You*, was still in the charts, having slipped back to No. 9. The Capitol cashed in on the Eurovision glory: ballrooms were bursting at the seams. "We were bigger than the Royal in some parts of the country," says Cole. "We were both huge draws. I remember when we played at the Ags dance in Dublin, Paul Sweeney had to leave the stage and go out for air because the ballroom was so packed. The Capitol had a name of being a very musical band which the Royal hadn't. The Royal had a name of being a very exciting band. On reflection, I suppose the excitement was a better tag to have than the musical tag. We got the name because we were handpicked musicians. In that sense, Johnny Quigley had a kind of classier Royal Showband. They did *The Hucklebuck* before the Royal." However, the Royal were consistently voted tops. *Spotlight* readers voted the Capitol Ireland's No. 2 showband in 1964, followed by the Miami.

At the height of his Eurovision fame, Moore declared: "It's about time this country, from the government down, dropped the snobbishness and began to realise that the biggest industry in Ireland at the moment is showbands." Moore always spoke his mind in press interviews, but not everybody agreed with him. For example, Henry McCullough, lead guitarist with Gene and the Gents, took him to task in November '64 for having made a judgment on rhythm'n'blues. In a letter to *Spotlight*, McCullough — who years later played with Paul McCartney's Wings — hit back: "After reading Butch Moore's comment about rhythm'n'blues, I had to laugh when he said they didn't really like the 'stuff,' but had changed in the last six months. They even thought it was monotonous. The Capitol are a good band, but let them stick to the country'n'western trad jazz, because I'd hate to hear them play what they might call rhythm'n'blues."

No expense was spared to keep the image right: the Capitol fashion was blue jackets, white slacks and white shoes. It was copied from the Rudy Ventura band whom Des Kelly saw perform while on holiday in Sitges, Spain. The Capitol had their stage clothes made in London by Dougie Millings, the Beatles' tailor. Money rolled in. In an interview with Moore, Ken Stewart suggested that the salaries of doctors and politicians were relatively modest compared with bands' astronomical fees. Moore replied: "A politician is only a showman anyway. A good entertainer will get more than a good politician. And why not?

A doctor is a qualified man, and so are we. We've studied this business closely." The Capitol were big spenders. On trips to London, they stayed at The Cumberland Hotel. "No doubt about it, we lived well," says Cole. "We had all the trimmings that were expected of us. We drove expensive cars; we wore sheepskin jackets; we ate steak in every hotel: all the usual ould bull that goes with showbiz. We thought this thing would never end."

They were practical jokers, and Moore was frequently the target. "We used to play holy hell with him," laughs Des Kelly. "Eamonn Monahan and I were agricultural students. We were once discussing a new breed of pigs. Butch came over and asked what we were talking about. Eamonn said we were talking about a new breed...racing pigs. Butch believed him. Sometime later Butch got talking to these two farmers in a ballroom in Waterford. He asked them if they kept racing pigs. When Butch came back to the dressing room, he was absolutely livid." Moore was the victim of another prank in a New York recording studio. Cole slipped into the singer's cubicle before the session and scratched an old date on the wall with the message... "Elvis Presley — hope I make it." Butch did a voice check in the cubicle and returned to the band. He said: "You know, the engineer in there told me all the top stars use this studio. As a matter of fact, Elvis started off here doing his recordings." Says Cole: "Eventually, when somebody told him I had written it, there was a terrible row in the band. He blamed Eamonn Monahan for it."

In-fighting was a feature of showbands, and the Capitol were no exception. The burden of keeping the band together fell to the leader, Des Kelly. "The hardest thing was to keep them motivated. I had to get everybody on stage smiling, even when some row was going on between two or three of them. That was the toughest part of the game for me. There were guys with egos. I had to keep those egos regularly massaged. If a new number came out, three or four fellows might want to do it. But I had to make a decision to give it to one, and that left the other two sulking. Trying to keep everybody happy was very difficult. It involved lying to one guy and calming another guy down by massaging his ego, or doing whatever it took."

Moore and the Capitol achieved three other Top Ten hits in 1965: *Our Love Will Go On*, at No. 10 in August; *So Many Ways* at No. 5 in November; and *Christmas* at No. 5 in December. Their peak in '65/'66 coincided with a proliferation of so-called showbands and managers. Traditionally, bands had worked on an employer-employee or co-operative basis. The structure of the business changed in the mid '60s when managers moved in and took most of the profits. Their approach was to pay a big wage to the lead singer, an 'image man', and back him with poorly-paid musicians. "From that day on, the business was never the same," says Kelly.

Like other lead singers, Moore, became a target for businessmen. A carrot was dangled and he took it. The Capitol never recovered from his departure in '66. The move backfired on Moore. Des Kelly was shocked by his resignation. "He just came and told me the truth," recalls Des. "He didn't know how to tell me because he was such a gentle fellow. He couldn't turn down the offer. It wasn't so much the money he was interested in: he was interested in what they were going to do for him. He'd have his own show here and there and be brought to Las Vegas. The Capitol were just 'an anchor around his neck'. I knew he was making a mistake; I knew he wasn't doing it out of badness or anything. I didn't resent him: I resented the situation. I knew Butch's strengths and weaknesses. He'd have been protected within the Capitol. He got a phenomenal offer to leave the band. We advised him, but couldn't stop him. He was offered a colossal weekly wage plus the world at his feet. The whole thing fell flat. It was terrible for us when he left about a year after Eurovision."

Moore was sad quitting the Capitol... "we were all like brothers." His main reason for going was a desire to do something different. In the resultant upheaval, Phil Coulter found his loyalties divided between both sides. Coulter recalls: "I remember there was a big rupture in the camp. I was torn very much between my friendship for Butch and my loyalty to the band." News that Ireland's Eurovision entrant was leaving the Capitol Showband made the front pages, and was the top story on Radio Éireann bulletins. His fans were shocked. Moore claims it was an amicable parting. "Butch felt that if he didn't do it then, for years after he'd have thought he should have given it a try," says Cole.

In 1967, Moore turned to cabaret. It was a mistake. He was backed by a trio — his brother Des, guitar; Fergie Gibson, bass; Gary Quigley, drummer. The cabaret circuit was still in its infancy, and far too limited. The concept was predictable: the trio did a few numbers and then Moore came on stage to complete the show. He had always been associated in the public mind with the big sound of the Capitol. "People went along expecting to hear the brass and the whole effect," says Cole. "They found just a trio and himself. It wasn't the same thing at all." The new act opened at the Television Club in Dublin. Moore got an enthusiastic reception from his showbusiness friends, who went along. "They thought the show was excellent," he recalls. "But there was nowhere to go with it. We had three great musicians. We sounded great. There was no market then. We couldn't make a living fifty weeks a year at it. Ten years later, there would have been no problem. The ballrooms were still going big. There weren't enough cabaret venues. We ended up going more to England. We were ahead of our time."

Moore made a return to showbands. The handlers made him a guest star with the Kings: the band played for about an hour, and he joined them on stage for the rest of the dance. It was a far cry from the magic of the Capitol Showband. "Butch told me afterwards that he had the most miserable two years of his life in Ireland," recalls Kelly. "They hawked him all over the country. The quality of the musicians wasn't the same. He came way down in level. That was sad because we had always lived well, and stayed in the best hotels. Butch was broke when he emigrated. Fair play, he worked his way up again through his own talent and ability." The Capitol kept the show on the road. Moore was replaced as lead singer — first by Noel McNeill, and then by John Drummond, who was a "brilliant musician as well," according to Kelly. In 1967, country'n'western became a huge force in rural Ireland. Sniffing a commercial opportunity, Des Kelly recorded a country number, The *Streets of Baltimore*. To his great surprise, it shot to No. 3 in February '67 and was in the charts for fifteen weeks. "I was quietly delighted with myself. In my position as band leader, you never got a chance to fly your own flag. I felt my job was to get the best out of other people. My own end of it suffered as a result. Johnny (Kelly) had heard *The Streets of Baltimore*. It was a song recorded by Bobby Bare, a well- known American country singer. Johnny suggested that I record it. I hummed and hawed a bit, but eventually decided to do it."

In summer 1967, Johnny topped the charts with *The Black Velvet Band*. It became one of the biggest sellers in the history of the Irish music industry. It entered the charts on May 25th and went to No. 1 on June 15th. It was No. 1 for eight weeks, and in the charts for a staggering 23. The idea of making the recording was the brainchild of Eddie Masterson, who recommended it to Des. "I met Eddie one day and he said that Johnny should record *The Black Velvet Band*," says Des. "Eddie was ubiquitous. There wasn't a dance or a dog fight he missed. The hit was great for Johnny, particularly since he was the drummer and wasn't usually out front much."

While such notable successes helped the Capitol to maintain popularity in the absence of their star attraction, Moore's own professional career had run into trouble. There were tensions too in his private life: his marriage collapsed. "It's sad when a relationship breaks up," he says. "I'd have to say that the lifestyle impinged on my marriage. When I was with the Capitol we'd be away all the time. I was away. We didn't carouse, or that type of thing; but, on the other hand, you're away, and it's tough. It was different when Maeve and I came to America. We were away all the time, too — but together. That might have been the reason for the break-up, or else things just grew apart. I don't know." Moore worked with Phil Coulter during this low period in his career. "Phil got a grant to produce some albums with singers of his choice. I did a session of six songs. One of them, *I Will Love You Till Then My Love*, a beautiful ballad, went well in Ireland. In fact, we still do it today in the States. Phil didn't forget me. He's a super guy."

Moore had met Maeve Mulvany briefly during his last days with the Capitol. Ronnie Drew of The Dubliners introduced him to her at a reception in O'Donoghue's pub. Says Moore: "I was on my way to London with Jim Doherty to promote one of the records. We were fogged in at Dublin. There was a big bash at O'Donoghue's for The Dubliners. I'd known Maeve to see in the business, but Ronnie formally introduced us. Then we got a flight and were gone. I didn't meet her for perhaps a year after that. Johnny Kelly was Maeve's biggest fan, but it wasn't my type of music. It was Johnny who made the second introduction when the Capitol opened a ballroom in Tralee during the Rose Festival. He invited her to the bandroom where we met again." Butch and Maeve did some TV and charity work together.

In late '69, Bill Fuller, proprietor of The Old Sheiling in the Bronx, New York, invited them over for cabaret performances during the first three weeks of '70. They were spotted singing in New York by Matt Kane, a Washington bar and club owner. He invited them to his premises. They had a few weeks of their work permit left, so they decided to go to Washington. "When Maeve and I came to America for that three weeks, I was pretty broke. I wasn't in good shape at all."

In Washington, Kane persuaded Butch and Maeve to sing together. Moore thought it was a ridiculous idea because they had such different musical backgrounds. He didn't think that the partnership would work. "Maeve was really authentic in what she did. However, she taught me a lot of the Irish stuff. We got away from her rebel songs and even ended up singing some pop songs together. That was a big deviation for her. It worked. We had some dates in Ireland, but it looked like it would be worth cancelling out and trying this. It was the best thing we ever did because, in about a year, we were going from South Texas right up to New Hampshire and booked all the time. That's how the Butch and Maeve thing started. We'd be booked two years ahead of time. We toured around the country. We never had a home until 1976 because we were that busy."

As Moore's career took a new direction in the U.S., the Capitol entered their last phase with a new line-up. The two Kelly brothers had left the band by '70. Des suffered a bad attack of pneumonia in '69 and returned to the stage before a proper recovery. "On our last trip to the States it was horrific." says

Des. "I was in bed for the whole trip, except to get up and play. I made a decision to come home and pack it up." Johnny quit six months later. Paddy Cole and Bram McCarthy were the last remaining members of the original showband. The new faces were Frankie Murray, lead guitarist; Mike Dalton, bass; Mickey O'Neill, drums; Stan Byrne, sax; Tony O'Leary, lead vocalist. The recruits had once admired the Capitol for their professionalism, but the old dynamism was missing. The void created by the loss of Moore and the Kelly brothers was never filled. Like other bands, the new Capitol were at the mercy of circumstances that ultimately defeated the showbands and the ballrooms. When the Capitol set up their equipment on stage at the Swan, Monaghan, on a cold and wet Sunday night in November '70, there were only five people in the hall by 10pm. The pubs were packed: it was 11pm before the hall filled up. The band surveyed an empty hall. Behind them on stage was a backdrop painting of a South Sea scene with palm trees and blue sea. But the winter wind that howled through the open doorway of the ballroom cut like a knife. It was a dying business.

"They were all good lads," recalls Cole. "But word was out that it wasn't the same Capitol. The boys had left one at a time until eventually there was just Bram and myself left. Jim Hand was managing the band at the time. He took more of an interest in young rock bands like the Dreams. We worked the circuit and could have been doing a lot better. We didn't record enough. In the last stages of the Capitol, the band went on a tour of Canada for seven weeks. Bram went on the tour. I stayed home rehearsing with the Big 8. The writing was on the wall for the Capitol. It was a little bit unfair at the time because Bram could possibly have been into the Big 8 on trumpet. The country bands were really big, and Des was managing the Smokey Mountain Ramblers and other bands."

Kelly, founder of the Capitol, went into management. He began with electric folk band Sweeney's Men who had a hit in '67 with *Old Maid in the Garret*, a ballad sung by Andy Irvine. Later, he went on to manage the Smokey Mountain Ramblers, the Virginians and Margo. Kelly, a friend of Irvine since the days of Sweeney's Men, became involved in the affairs of

Planxty until a car accident cut short his management career. Then, he went into the hotel and pub business.

Meantime, in the U.S., Butch and Maeve worked mainly around Massachusetts and Conneticutt by '76 and bought a condominium as a base. The travel was hectic: home for a month and off on tour for three more. They were married in '77. "Then the kids came along," says Moore. "Rory was born. It wasn't bad because we were still able to travel, but it was harder to get a babysitter to come with us. Then we bought a house. Tara came along. It became more difficult to travel because Rory started going to school. When we came back to America after the Capitol re-union in Ireland in '84, Maeve was expecting with Thomas. That was the end of the travelling, so we went into the pub trade in Massachusetts." They also presented a local radio show for two hours every Saturday morning for eight years.

The original Capitol reunited in '84 for a nostalgic month-long tour. "We opened in the Braemor Rooms and that was a magic night," says Moore. "I had a ball being with all the lads again. I had no friction with any of them because I'm three thousand miles away." He regards the highlights of his career to have been the Eurovision Song Contest, and appearances at the London Palladium and with Maeve at the Kennedy Centre.

Regrets? "No. There were some things that could have worked out better. But I'm glad I made the steps along the way because that's what I wanted to do. I think I learned by every-thing that happened — even by leaving the Capitol that time because I was really becoming very stagnant. I didn't regret going, even though it didn't work out. That's showbiz: there are ups and downs. I learned a lot by moving on. I was able to do other types of work instead of being always just a showband guy. Everything worked out for me in the end. I don't think I'd have led my life any differently..."

Phil Coulter
The Call Comes Through

Derry, Saturday, January 18th, 1964:

A college student gets a surprise phone call from the leader of one of Ireland's top showbands. The Capitol's Des Kelly has a proposition for Phil Coulter, who is home for the weekend from Queen's University, Belfast. The band want to record his song, *Foolin' Time,* as their first single. Coulter agrees. He puts down the phone in the hallway at Abercorn Terrace, and only then does reality sink in. "I couldn't believe that this was actually happening," he says of the call that changed his life. "It was a day I'll never forget. That call ranks alongside selling out Carnegie Hall, winning the Eurovision Song Contest, having a hit with Elvis Presley or a number one in America. It started a whole chain of events that led me to where I am right now. Make no mistake about that. In this business, there is no standard laid-down procedure for becoming a songwriter, a record producer, an arranger or whatever. You see a gap in the hedge and you go through it like a ferret. Des Kelly gave me the gap in the hedge."

Next came an invitation to attend the record launch at Portmarnock in February 1964. He loved the publicity and the praise for the song. "Nothing would have kept me away from the launch... hanging out with Butch Moore, Paddy Cole and Don Long. All these guys had been heroes of mine - and here I was in the middle of them. I got my picture taken with Butch and Des. My head was spinning." Kelly asked him along to rehearsals next day, and so began an enduring relationship with the Capitol. He was smitten with the showbusiness bug. He wrote songs, did arrangements and worked out medleys for the band. "Des had me down in Dublin and I just went missing from Queens," he recalls. "It was very irresponsible, but this was it. I emerged from Queen's on a Friday and started work in the music business on a Monday."

Foolin' Time climbed to number three in the charts. The Capitol broke new ground by recording original material, courtesy of Coulter's prolific pen. *"Foolin' Time* was a big deal then," he says. "To have a hit record in Ireland in those days probably meant that you sold four hundred copies. But it didn't matter because this was glamour, glamour." Coulter wrote the song at Queen's with one of his own bands, the Gleemen. They recorded it as a stunt for Rag Week. Somebody on the committee proposed that a student record be made. The task was given to Coulter: he was 'Mr. Fix-it' of the college music scene who had his own band, and booked others for student dances. Coulter founded a 'glee club' that ran late night concerts with visiting acts.

He says of the recording: "We went into one of the university common rooms. A guy who studied electronics had a tape recorder and a set of mikes. We threw things over the windows and...bang, bang, bang, recorded the whole thing right there on a domestic tape recorder. We pressed up a couple of thousand records on an independent label. We knew that we wouldn't have a prayer going to EMI or Phillips. The whole idea of an independent label was quite visionary then, although it became the norm in the seventies."

Coulter was a showband fan. The Capitol captured his imagination as he dabbled in bands while studying music and French at Queen's in the early '60s. His empathy with them was real — they also had been to university where they experimented musically. The fateful phone call followed Coulter's first meeting with the showband in Bundoran. He and the Capitol were playing at separate venues on the same night. Coulter had just finished a set with his quartet at the Great Southern Hotel at 1am when he got a call from a friend, another showband follower, who worked as a chef there. "Phil, you've got to get down here quick," he said. "I'm in the Allingham Hotel for a late drink. The Capitol have just arrived, and they're bringing in their instruments. There's going to be a blow." Coulter wasted no time. "If he had been calling me from Sligo," he jokes, "I'd have started running. I'd have crawled over broken glass to be part of this: just to see and hear the Capitol."

The jam session continued into the early hours. When pianist Eamon Monahan took a break, Coulter asked Kelly for permission to sit in. He replied: "Fire away." The budding songwriter picked his moment and played *Foolin' Time*. It was an up-tempo number similar to those of Bobby Darin whom he admired. Butch Moore was impressed. He asked: "Did you write that?" Coulter said, "yes." Then Moore added: "I'd love to hear it again." Coulter sensed an opportunity. When the Capitol arrived at the Great Southern's golf course next morning, he was there to greet them with a copy of the record.

"That was the start of our relationship," says Coulter. "I still count Des Kelly as one of my close friends. He spotted that I had something to offer. He was the man who gave me my first shot. I think he was the one who prevailed on the rest of the band in the ensuing months. The Royal had made a hit record, *Come Down The Mountain Katie Daly*. The pressure was on the Capitol to do the same. All showbands were making records. It was the thing to be at. But they were doing covers of country and western songs and things like that. Des said, 'we should do an original.' That's where I came in. In subsequent years, I recorded and worked with a lot of other showbands. But I always had a soft spot for the Capitol. They were a special breed: very bright and classy guys. I admired them so much."

Showbands gave Ireland's future king of the ivories a springboard. His early experience with the Capitol is the basis of a career marked by what he describes as a "series of different manoeuvres." Coulter, the musical chameleon, first began to write and arrange for showbands and quickly learned the importance of commercial success.

"You might be tempted to give me credit for being more clever than I really am, because a lot of things just had a knock-on effect," he says. "I mean, working with the Capitol led me to getting a job with Phil Solomon. Various things have happened by some sort of happy accident along the way." Coulter has over one hundred platinum, silver and gold discs, but he never lost regard for his showband roots. He lights up when recalling Johnny Quigley or the Capitol in full flight: the sounds, the excitement and, above all, the glamour. He says there were more showbands per head of population in Derry than anywhere else. Quigley and Gay McIntyre were the big names, but most were second-string bands who still managed to get work five nights a week. There were frequent rows and changes in personnel. Promoters who gave an ordinary band a date in January, and a return booking in March, invariably met new faces: the only familiar person being the one who filled the diary, the key operator.

Three factors contributed to the showband boom in Derry. Firstly, a strong musical tradition already existed: there was a proliferation of brass and reed bands; boys learned to play the trumpet as early as fifteen or sixteen. Secondly, unemployment was rampant: the notion of converting music into money, even while on the dole, was widespread. Men were out of work; women were the breadwinners, and many got jobs in the shirt factories. By night, unemployed men dabbled in bands. Thirdly, danceband musicians were always in demand in Derry because of the British and American bases whose presence fuelled the growth of bands and orchestras. Sit-down bands played Jimmy Lally orchestrations - or 'orcs' as they were popularly known.

The business was non-sectarian: if a band needed a trumpeter, nobody asked whether the applicant was a Catholic or Protestant. Every Derry youngster with any musical ability wanted to play in a showband. "To me there was never a problem utilising my music to make money," Coulter explains. "Looking at my long-term goals, I was aware that music could be a means to a livelihood." To this day, he makes no apologies for his strong sense of commercialism. Critics try to dismiss him by saying he's trivial and geared to trying to be too popular. He retorts: "Well, if it was that easy to appeal to such a wide audience consistently, then everybody would be doing it."

Coulter's father was a sergeant in the RUC. He was a bobby on the beat who cycled to work. Phil was one of a family of five children who lived in relative comfort in the Abercorn district. The Coulters' were neither poor nor well-off. "I grew up just across the bridge into the city side, not a very exclusive area by any means. It was just an ordinary working class area." He developed a love of music early on and his mid-teens coincided with the rise of the Royal Showband.

But it was Johnny Quigley, the local hero, who first captivated Coulter one Friday night at the Borderland Ballroom in Muff, Co. Donegal. "I was just a kid. I checked in my coat and then came into the main concourse. Quigley was playing. I was transfixed by the whole sound and glamour of it all. I can even remember to this day what they were wearing. The band had brownish jackets and yellowy cream slacks. Quigley was in a separate coloured suit to the others. It was all happening. There must have been about nine or ten in the band. They were standing up playing the instruments. They looked the business. It was just so slick, slicker than anything I had ever seen produced by local musicians. It was Hollywood. They were doing a bit of jazz at the time. It astounded me how good the dixieland was. Their pops were so much like the records. I was totally infatuated by pop music at that period.

"They took a break. When they came back on stage, they had changed: now they wore yellow coloured blazers and brown slacks. This was showbusiness with a capital S. They went into a medley of Coasters numbers that they did so well. I was just astounded. I became hooked right there and then. I was fascinated. I'd have volunteered on the spot. Nobody could do the Coasters like the Johnny Quigley band — hits like *Yakety Yak* and *Charlie Brown*. The Quigley band was different in as much as they didn't have the stock trumpet, trombone and sax. They had two or three saxes, a couple of trumpets and a trombone at full peak. They were really heavyweights. That's like what somebody would have dreamed up if he wanted to get a proper brass sound together, a brass section. The Quigley band were quite superb in that era. Musically, you couldn't say that about a lot of the showbands."

In his early teens, Coulter recalls the excitement generated in the locality by the impending arrival of the Clipper Carlton 'bandshow'. His older sister went dancing to them. They had a summer residency in Portrush, and people flocked from miles away to see them.

"The idea of getting rid of music stands, standing up and playing, sounds like a simple thing today, but it was a big step at the time," says Coulter. Gradually, a formula was developed. It was an unlikely musical combination: trumpet, trombone and sax, allied to rhythm sections of various sizes. Many youngsters had already learned their craft playing in brass bands. Now they superimposed brass licks on pop songs. Bands were expected to pump out a good beat for dancing and jiving. Coulter remembers when jiving was frowned on in some ballrooms. "It was seen to be in some way decadent. Other ballrooms that were less rigid allowed one jiving session per night: three tunes were played and that was a good session. If you dared to jive any other time, a bouncer tapped you on the shoulder and said, 'no jiving'." As showbands mushroomed, the specialty set established by the Clippers became a standard routine. The Capitol, for example, played *In A Monastery Garden* while Eamonn Monahan whistled and made bird noises; Don Long sang Louis Prima numbers; Bowyer sang *The Holy City*.

In 1960, Coulter, aged eighteen, packed his bags and left Derry for Queen's University. He studied music and French, and played by night in jazz bands. He took music seriously. Fellow Derryman and journalist Eamonn McCann once recalled: "It was always clear that he was going to have a career in music. He was aiming high and full of confidence. He thought about music as a serious matter, to be understood as you would understand chemistry or geography."

In the first few months at Queen's, Coulter set up his own band. He began with a small three or four-piece outfit, but at one stage expanded to form a showband called The Quartermasters. It did not last because there were too many musicians to pay. Coulter stayed mostly with a four-piece format. He took whatever work was available. He was primarily a keyboard player, but also experimented on guitar. He was given a secondhand guitar as a Christmas present by his brother, who studied at Maynooth. He taught himself to play. While at university, Coulter founded a club that enticed any pop artistes visiting Belfast, such as Emile Forde or Helen Shapiro, to perform informally after their city concerts. He earned summer money playing piano as a Butlin's holiday camp 'red coat'. It was 'wallpaper' music, but people paid to listen.

While still a student, he got a part-time job with the Gay McIntyre band. The offer was given to him at a music shop in Derry run by Johnny Peel, a singer with the Johnny Quigley band. "On holidays up from university, that store would be the Mecca," recalls Coulter. "You'd go there for a chat, and talk to the other musicians. I loved it. Johnny would tell you stories about being in the Quigley band, among other things. I was sitting there one day playing an electric guitar, which I didn't possess. I only had a cheap little acoustic one. Gay, a famous band leader and great musician, came into the shop. He was looking for some reeds for his sax. There had been some altercation in the band. His guitar player left after a fight, something that was quite normal in showbands. McIntyre was minus a guitar in the band at that point."

When the band leader saw the student strumming on the guitar, he offered him the job on the spot. McIntyre said: "Coulter, I thought you played the piano." Then, he asked: "Do you play the guitar?" Coulter nodded. The band leader told him: "Right, be at the end of the bridge tonight. I think you'll fit into the jacket as well." When McIntyre left the shop, Peel remarked: "There you are, kid, you're in business." Coulter didn't have a guitar or amp, so Peel allowed him to take out the equipment on 'appro'.

This chance encounter, while on Christmas holidays from Queen's, gave Coulter his introduction to showbands. He laughs at the memory: "I got a job in a showband with a guitar and amp that I didn't own. They were supposedly out on appro, but I had no intention of buying them because I couldn't afford to. And I wasn't even a guitar player, for Goodness sake! Listen, I wasn't about to say, 'no, I'm not that good'. I was there at the end of the bridge, as agreed."

McIntyre adopted a showband line-up, complete with rocker Jim Fontane. Every band in Derry had a rock'n'roller who jumped up and down and threw himself around the stage. The three McGonigle brothers were known the length and breadth of the city: Jim, the eldest, sang with the McIntyre band and used the stage name, 'Jim Fontane'; Sean's professional name was 'Johnny Rivers' and the youngest, Martin, was billed as 'Martin Manners, the Boy Wonder.' In the showband fraternity, all three were nicknamed 'Spasms, Yackums and Gackums.' Other Derry leapers were: John Patterson — 'Jumpin' Johnny Lee,' and Richard Duffy — 'Rockin' Rickie Steevens.' Says Coulter: "They were coming out of the woodwork in Derry."

After that first experience with McIntyre, he spent his free time from college with other bands in Derry, among them the Imperial All-Stars, with whom he played bass. Piano players weren't being hired by showbands. There were a lot of good guitar players on the circuit, but Coulter wasn't one of them. Then, bands started to replace double basses with bass guitar. At university, the music department required him to take up a second instrument. "I volunteered craftily to take up the double bass in the university orchestra," he reflects. "I said to myself, 'this could be useful.' They had a double bass that I could learn on."

When bass guitars became standard, Coulter bought one on the 'never- never' from Johnny Peel. He now played bass guitar with his own bands at college, and with others while home in Derry. "At the time, I didn't care whether I was making any money," he says. "It really didn't matter at all. I played music for the hell of it. On a number of occasions after the gig, I actually went home without lining up to get my 'box' because I was just so fired up on the whole thing. I remember bumming lifts many times from guys I knew at university to go and meet up with a band from Derry that was playing somewhere around the country."

The chance to work with the Capitol was a dream-come-true. Des Kelly's confidence in Coulter's *Foolin' Time* was justified when the record climbed to number three in the charts in early 1964. The Derryman graduated and went to work with the Capitol, writing and arranging. On reflection, Coulter says if he had been asked to join the band as a musician on leaving university, he would have jumped at the chance. He regarded the Capitol as the best showband. "Maybe it's just historical loyalty, but I would still say that." After the first chart showing, courtesy of Coulter's prolific pen, he wrote the follow-up, *I Missed You*. It failed to repeat the chart success. "It didn't really happen at all," he says. "I thought it was a great record. I still think it was a great record. Paddy Cole did a great baritone sax solo on it." While recording *I Missed You*, and other tracks, with the Capitol at the Pye studios in London, Coulter was spotted by Phil Solomon, who promoted the band in Britain. A shrewd and influential operator, he had a publishing company and managed a stable of acts including the Bachelors as well as Van Morrison and his rhythm and blues band, Them. "In fairness, he must have recognised some kind of talent," says Coulter. "I worked my ass off for him. I said to myself, 'well, this is the way I get into the music business.' You can't turn up at a music publishers with a diploma and say, 'look, I'm qualified.' It doesn't happen that way. You just hang around until you get an opportunity. I was convinced it would only be a matter of weeks before I'd be arranging scores for superstars. In point of fact, I was arranging sandwiches for the office girls during the first six months or so."

Solomon set out to exploit the showbands' recording potential. He was an independent producer, a link between the bands and major record companies. He had the right connections to get record releases and TV exposure in Britain. He worked on an ad-hoc basis with the bands who paid him for deals to make records and get them released. He offered an all-in package. Few bands were good enough to make the grade. In due course, Coulter was put to work on arrangements for the Bachelors and keyboard backing for Van Morrison. He also worked with the better showbands: his job was to either write or 'find' songs, do the arrangements and go into studio with the band.

He scouted Irish dancehalls in London for recording potential. He regularly checked out places like the Galtimore, the Hibernian and the Banba to see whether various Irish bands were worth recording. He maintained contact with the Capitol, and also extended his range to other top showbands such as the Cadets and Pacific. Coulter had two notable successes during this period with Solomon. He made a record with the Capitol called *Born To Be With You*. It had been a hit for the Cordettes in the '50s. The new version was released in the U.S. under the group name, Butch Moore and the Capitols. The name change was necessary because the Capitol 'Showband' would have been meaningless in the States. The record entered the singles charts and rose to No. 60 in the Top 100.

Coulter did a version of another existing standard, *Jealous Heart*, with Eileen Reid and the Cadets. It reached No. 42 in the British Top 75. "Any kind of international success like this was enough for showbands to make mileage out of at home," he says. "That's what it was all about... a point-scoring exercise over the other bands." Coulter was travelling back and forth to Ireland on scouting missions. "I remember once going to Cork to listen to a band called Art Supple and The Victors. I never worked with the Royal or the Miami. But I worked with a hell of a lot of others. I worked closest with the Capitol. The Freshmen did one of my songs, an album track. I liked the Freshmen and was very happy to have a song recorded by them. I wasn't disappointed not to have worked with the Royal. Because of my connections with the Capitol, I would have regarded the Royal as opposition. I would have regarded it as being disloyal to the Capitol to work with them. I could see that the most successful bands were those that worked hardest and reinvested. It's something I have believed in ever since. If you want to be the best, you have to be prepared to work hard, invest and slog it out." Coulter's involvement with the recording of Butch Moore's '65 Eurovision entry, *Walking The Streets In The Rain*, sowed the seed for his later song contest endeavours with Bill Martin.

"Being so close to the Capitol, and seeing the excitement and glamour of it all, turned me on to the Eurovision," he recalls. I thought to myself, 'this Eurovision is definitely something'." Soon, the showband links were being broken as he scanned the market for other opportunities. He quit his job with Solomon.

Coulter teamed up with Martin and wrote hits for the likes of Dave Dee, Dozy, Beaky, Mick and Tich, Ken Dodd and the Troggs. In '67, they wrote *Puppet On A String* for Sandie Shaw. It was a snappy, happy novelty number - the result of careful research into previous Eurovision winners. The formula worked and Britain swept to victory in Vienna that year. They wrote

Cliff Richard's Eurovision entry, *Congratulations*, in '68. As juries cast their votes, the song was in the lead and looked like being the winner. They lost by a point. Coulter said of that experience years later: "The total devastation of that stayed with us, despite the fact that people remember the song as a winner - it has since become a standard. I learned from the experience that any creative person's life is a series of highs and lows. While we trumpet our successes, we jealously guard our failures. We draw a protective cloak over them. That hurt - but I discovered it was an emotion that I could not afford."

Two years after being pipped at the post, he came across Dana and *All Kinds Of Everything*. He re-arranged the song and it won the Eurovision Contest in 1970. By now, Coulter was becoming an international commodity. One of his songs, *My Boy*, was featured by Elvis Presley in his Las Vegas repertoire. Presley decided to record the song in 1974, and it was a hit on both sides of the Atlantic.

The '70s marked Coulter's assault on the lucrative teenybop market with the tartan-bedecked Scottish group, The Bay City Rollers. Coulter and Martin manufactured the five-piece Scottish group into a chart sensation with a string a catchy hits from '74 to '77: among them *Shangalang* ('74), *Summer Love Sensation* ('74), *All of Me Loves All of You* ('74), *Bye Bye Baby* ('75), *Give a Little Love* ('75), *Money Money* ('75), *Love Me Like I Love You* ('76), *I Only Want To Be With You* ('76), and *It's a Game* ('77). During one three year period around this time, there wasn't a month when Coulter and Martin didn't have a record in the Top 75. The songwriting partnership with Martin ended in '80. Coulter switched from disposable hit singles to adapting Irish traditional tunes. Coulter, the performing star, tinkled piano melodies with his orchestra and received standing ovations from the Grosvenor Hall in Belfast to Carnegie Hall in New York. Having composed, conducted, arranged and produced in studios for twenty years, Coulter, ever versatile, concentrated on Irish tunes. Leaping from the Rollers' *Shangalang* to *My Lagan Love* presented no difficulties. His first three albums — Classic Tranquillity, Sea of Tranquillity, and Peace and Tranquillity — outsold the combined forces of U2, Bruce

Springsteen and Michael Jackson in Ireland during '85. *The Sea of Tranquillity* album alone sold a quarter of a million copies.

Coulter returned to the road fronting a full orchestra and launched mammoth annual tours, clocking up mileage from Shinrone to Boston's Symphony Hall and New York's Lincoln Center. He has done three tours of the U.S. with a full orchestra. He celebrated his 48th birthday in February '90 while doing a series of one-night stands in Ireland with a travelling troupe of thirty musicians and stage crew. The ebony and ivory gave him a big lease of middle life. He never plans far ahead and says that, six years ago, he had no idea he'd be doing concerts now.

Coulter's curriculum vitae is as varied as it is comprehensive. Since the Capitol's Des Kelly gave him the first 'gap in the hedge' over a quarter of a century ago, he has tasted success at performing, producing, recording and songwriting. He enjoyed each level and "gave it my best shot." He brought England's World Cup soccer squad to No. 1 in the charts in '70 with *Back Home*. He wrote musical scores in Hollywood, and produced albums by the Dubliners and Planxty. He was also musical director on the Irish production of *Jesus Christ Superstar;* worked on the Continent writing hits for Mirelle Mathieu and Sylvie Vartan and maintained a chart presence in London with Cilla Black. All this was managed in between his work with the Bay City Rollers.

His life has been etched also by personal tragedy. He says he's not alone in having had a lot of tragedies — no more than other people. The song, *Scorn Not His Simplicity*, sung definitively by the late Luke Kelly, is about Coulter's little son, who was born with Downes Syndrome. The child died at the age of three.

The list of professional achievements is staggering. He's a household name who, according to legend, once had to go to an Indian restaurant in Dublin to escape from hearing his own works! The CV that began with an early apprenticeship in the showbands continues to expand in the '90s. He scoffs at suggestions of retirement. In his own words, he's a "doer rather than a watcher"...and adds that there's a lot of things he hasn't done yet.

Spit On Me, Dickie

Dublin Airport, Monday, March 7, 1966.

Hundreds jostle for position on the balconies. They're packed five and six deep against the barriers. Necks are craned. All eyes scan the night sky for the first twinkle of approaching aircraft lights. Twenty buses have taken teenagers to the airport. Ambulances run a shuttle service between the airport and Dublin hospitals. Twenty are treated for shock and minor injuries in the crush. Gardai link arms in front of the arrival and departure terminals to prevent 1,000 fans from smashing through the glass doors. Suddenly, a huge cheer rises from the terminal balconies. Dickie is home.

When the aircraft comes to a halt, hundreds of teenagers chant: "We Want Dickie." As he steps onto the tarmac, the Ballyfermot Boys Band strikes up *Come Back To Stay*, which came joint fourth in the contest. Rock waves to his fans in a flashbulb blaze created by press photographers. The crush on the balconies intensifies, and many fans faint. Rock is shouldered by members of the Miami Showband into the VIP lounge. He is hugged, kissed, patted on the back. The moment is captured in a picture published in the following morning's papers. Rock is perched on the shoulders of two Miami musicians. He looks up to the balconies with the right arm raised. His face beams with delight. It was a night that made news in Dublin. Rock's triumphant return was a big story — for a few hours. It was scrubbed from the front pages to make way for the blowing up of Nelson's Pillar at 1.32am next morning.

Eurovision '66 was, of course, compulsive viewing. Ireland held its breath as Rock sang *Come Back To Stay* to a hundred million TV viewers. At home, his romantic song for Europe was No. 1 in the charts. Families from Cabra to Youghal were glued to the telly as national juries cast their votes. Eurovision was the TV highlight of the year. It was more than just a song contest: national pride was at stake. There was an immense psychological uplift to watch an Irishman singing with the best of them and indeed, better than most. Rock almost had ambassadorial status, and achieved more to enhance Ireland's image abroad than an embassy of diplomats. The euphoria generated by Rock's top ranking in the contest was enormous. His was the golden voice of Irish showbusiness.

Rock was different from other big showband names. Professionally, he was fulfilled at home. Bowyer and the Royal had already conquered the ballrooms, taken the highest pop award in Britain and would look to Las Vegas to supplement their earnings at home. Rock simply wanted to consolidate his position as Ireland's superstar, and never lose the title. So, he became an unchallenged king, a counterpart to the British pop stars of the day. Rock was seen as the nice lad next door who didn't smoke or drink. The excitement of those heady days in '66 was captured in the RTE documentary, *'Dickie — Portrait of an Artiste'*. Producer Adrian Cronin and a TV crew followed Rock to ballrooms from Cork to Galway, home to Cabra West and even to the church when he wed Judy Murray, a shorthand typist. The documentary painted a picture of the homegrown hero untainted by fame's corrupting influences: perfectly creased suits; tie straight; pioneer pin; a kiss for mother and a friendly chat with his family around the breakfast table. Cronin updated the remarkable story eighteen years later and, on that occasion, followed Rock from the stage at the Grand Hotel, Malahide, all the way to his villa on the Spanish coast between Marbella and Fuengirola.

Unlike Bowyer, O'Brien, Dolan and Moore, Rock wasn't good-looking. Yet, he attracted a huge female following. He sang romantic slushy songs because he loved romance. The most dedicated fans thumbed lifts to Kerry and Donegal to see him taking off from Dublin on Friday evenings and returning on Sundays. Girls cried at his feet and gave him handkerchiefs to wipe the sweat from his brow. He inspired one of the great mating calls of the '60s: 'Spit on me Dickie'. He says of the adulation: "I could never understand it. I loved it, but I could never understand it. What am I doing? I mean, if I look like Elvis, okay. But I didn't. Was it in the voice? Was it in the presentation? It's undetectable."

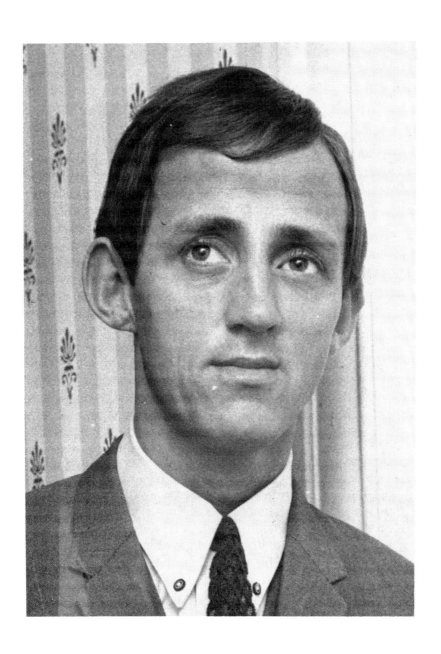

(Photo: Sunday World)

Thousands of women envied his bride, Judy, when they walked up the aisle of the Church of Our Lady Queen of Heaven at Dublin Airport, on Monday, June 20th, 1966. It was the showbusiness wedding of the year that followed a whirlwind ten-month romance. They met at the Ierne Ballroom in Dublin. It was love at first sight. The wedding took place in Rock's year of Eurovision glory. The church was besieged by fans. The ceremony was performed by his cousin, Rev. Tom Walton, who travelled from the U.S. Hundreds pushed forward as the groom entered the church, accompanied by his best man. Gardai had to clear a path for the bride into the forecourt of the tiny church. The crowds had swelled by the time that the couple emerged to pose for photographs. Twenty gardai and a dozen airport security men kept fans at bay as the newlyweds tried to reach their car. The happy couple celebrated at a reception in the Country Club, Portmarnock, and then flew off to Majorca for their honeymoon. "When we came back," recalls Rock, "Judy hardly saw me at all because I was working five, six or seven nights a week." Rock remembers '66 for other reasons: six months after the Eurovision honours, his young brother, Joseph, died in a road accident at the age of eleven. The little lad was knocked down while playing on a bicycle. He had been with his family at the airport months earlier to welcome home his famous big brother.

The mass hysteria caused by an Irish entry to the Eurovision Song Contest has long since faded, but Rock — one of the greatest survivors in showbusiness — is still regarded as a VIP at Dublin Airport. "Rainier fan of Dickie Rock," read the headline over a story in the *Irish Independent* on Saturday, September 30th, 1989. It told how Rock and other selected Irish entertainers were taken to a privately chartered jet at Dublin Airport and flown to the Hotel de Paris in Monaco for an official dinner hosted by Dr. Michael Smurfit in his capacity as Ireland's honorary consul. The function was attended by Prince Rainier, who listened to Rock and others croon the night away. Most of Rock's showband contemporaries are long since settled back into day jobs; yet he sings to princes and commands four-figure sums for an appearance anywhere in Ireland.

His career spans three decades. It's a tough business, but he — unlike so many others — kept his head. He was a thrifty pragmatist whose flamboyance confined itself to stagecraft. Today, he's still a consummate professional who adores performing. He's also a canny businessman. The perspiration-soaked ballrooms have long since been replaced by TV studios, theatres, dinner shows and cabaret venues. Yet, even in the most formal settings, such as the Gaiety Theatre or Clontarf Castle, that familiar cry may sometimes be heard from the gods...'Spit on me Dickie'. It gives new generations a clue to his amazing appeal back in the '60s.

The Hotel de Paris is, of course, world's away from the Olympia Ballroom in Waterford where Rock and the Miami got one of their important breaks in 1963. The band left the stage in a lather of sweat, and the crowd screamed for more. It was a bold strike by the young Dubs in a land where only one showband reigned supreme: the Royal. What's more, it was done in a ballroom that played such a pivotal role in the early success of the Royal. Suddenly, a Cabra lad with a matchstick body and beautiful tenor voice competed for the allegiance of the ladies...in Bowyer's backyard. The pretender sang powerfully, tenderly, emotionally. There was a natural rhythm in his lithe frame. There were early signs, too, of a professional's sense of stage timing — but that still needed to be perfected. As the rising star passed through the crowd on his way to the dressing room, he overheard the remark: "That fella Rock... he's a good singer, but too slick. He's too big-headed." Begrudgery, that most tenacious of Irish characteristics, had found a new target. Bowyer was the Main Man — and not just in Waterford. Comparisons were inevitable. Rock had a standard reply: "No, I don't jump around the stage as well. Brendan Bowyer jumps around the stage; Joe Dolan jumps around the stage: but I *move around* the stage."

By Christmas 1963, Rock's first record with the Miami, *There's Always Me*, entered the charts. It reached No. 1 on January 3rd, 1964, dominated for six weeks and stayed in the charts for twelve. Rock had come a long way since, as a working-class kid, he first raised his voice in the choir of the Church of the Most Precious Blood, Cabra West.

Loyalty to Cabra stems from the fact that he was born there himself, one of five children. "It was the people of Cabra West who made me," he said years later. "I will never forget them or sacrifice them for any other class." Dickie's father, Josie, was a blacksmith at the Board of Works. All his father's family, who can be traced back to Germany, were in steelwork — welders, fitters, riveters and shipyard workers in the Liffey dockyard. His mother, Julia, was musical and often sang *Only God Can Make A Tree* at family gatherings. The Rock children were taught basic values: hard work, honesty and respect for others. Those deep-rooted family values were passed on to Dickie's own six children. Dickie was picked as a tenor for the church choir and became involved also in charity choirs that visited the hospitals.

At the age of thirteen, he joined an amateur variety group, the Casino Players. He left school before taking any formal exams, and says he educated himself later by travelling and meeting different people over the years...and by listening. "That's real education." He worked for a time in Edward's Jewellers, Talbot Street. By night, he experimented in various little-known bands. When he entered one talent contest, 'Search for a TV Star', at the Theatre Royal, friends and neighbours from Cabra West turned out in force to support him. A School of Irish dancers came first, Limerick comedians Tom and Pascal second, and Rock in third place. He persisted and entered other talent contests in halls around Dublin.

By sixteen, he joined a popular Dublin band, the Melochords, that later formed the basis of the Cadets. He started his own rock group, Dickie Rock and the Echoes. As a teenager, he was interested in the 'quality' singers like Frank Sinatra and Tony Bennett. Rock joined the Miami in 1962. The band had already been on the road for a year. It was launched by Tom Doherty whose brother, Jim, managed the Capitol. The brothers ran Topline Promotions. Tom selected the cream of musicians for 'the greatest band in Ireland' — among them Murty Quinn, the trombonist with the Chris Lamb band. Rock's opportunity came along when the Miami's lead singer, Jimmy Harte, left for America. Rock auditioned for the position in '62 at the Palm Beach, Portmarnock. "We were impressed with Dickie," recalls Tom. "He got the job." Rock says he had some misgivings about joining a showband: "At first, I wasn't too keen on the idea. A showband was a showband to me at the time. You know the way kids think about showbands. I was more into rock and roll. I decided to join anyway and we had good success immediately."

Pop music was going through a counter revolution, led by the Beatles and Rolling Stones, as Dickie and the Miami began an assault on the charts in '63 and '64. Bowyer struck No. 1 first, in September '63, with *Kiss Me Quick*. Rock competed with him for the top chart ratings, and achieved three consecutive No. 1 hits: *There's Always Me* on January 3, '64; *I'm Yours* on May 29, '64; and *From the Candy Store on the Corner* on October 30, '64. These records sold hugely, opened up the country for the Miami and catapulted Rock into the big league of showband stars. Bowyer was already the epitome of rock'n'roll, and Rock was fast becoming the epitome of romance. He sang big romantic ballads, and this helped to assert his individuality. Dickie and the Miami experienced one of their highlights in '64 when they played at the London Palladium with Petula Clark top of the bill. She was high in the charts with *Downtown*.

The Miami criss-crossed the country like other showbands, playing in small dancehalls and big ballrooms. The line-up: Joe Tyrrell, organ and band leader; Tony Bogan, drums; Murty Quinn, trombone; Clem Quinn, lead guitar; Dickie Rock, lead singer; Martin Phelan, sax; Tommy O'Rourke, trumpet; and Denis Murray, bass guitar. Like their rival bands, they suffered their share at the hands of gombeen ballroom proprietors, playing in cold dirty halls. "Four walls in a plot of land and they called it a ballroom." It was, apparently, a pleasure to perform in the chain of 'Land' ballrooms owned by Albert and Jim Reynolds. The Reynolds' had decent changing rooms and gave bands a good meal. "I look at Albert Reynolds' success in politics and in business," said Dickie years later, "and I can see why he is successful. He was honest and straightforward with the bands and treated us great."

Dickie resumed his assault on the charts in 1965 with a string of Top Ten hits — *Just for Old Times Sake, Round and Round, Every Step of the Way, I Left My Heart in San Francisco,* and *Wishing It Was You.* Two of them reached the top: *Every Step of the Way* came straight in at No. 1 on May 24th, and *Wishing It Was You* reached No. 1 on November 22nd. The former record was a phenomenal success, and sold over 100,000 copies. Clem Quinn released *Bucks Polka* at Christmas '65, and the record reached No. 8. Another band member, trombonist Murty Quinn, achieved a Top Ten hit in January '66 with *One Kiss for Old Times Sake.* Next came Dickie's song for Europe, *Come Back To Stay,* followed later in '66 by his next release, *Darling I Love You,* which reached No. 4.

Rock specialised in the big ballad: "For example, *Every Step of the Way* is a good ballad, with strings. I was doing it before anybody else. I was only interested in doing good songs. That way I felt you won respect and were treated seriously as a performer. Anybody can be a pop star; they come and go. But to be treated seriously as a singer and performer, that's the important thing to me. I consider my success at that time was due to singing and performing well. It's what carried me through all the way while many others have come and gone." The chart hits made the Miami a huge draw in ballrooms all over the country. Rock was hugely popular in Belfast among Protestants and Catholics alike. "I became very popular in Belfast, and still am," he says. "Again, it was a city. I did the kind of material that they wanted...the same as in Cork or Dublin. People like to hear you sing a good song and perform well. In the country, it all happened for the likes of Margo."

Rock's favourite ballrooms were Caproni's in Bangor, Romanos in Belfast, Arcadia in Cork, Majorca in Crosshaven, Jetland in Limerick, the Arcadia in Bray and Palm Beach in Portmarnock. The Miami were the biggest draw at the Arcadia in Bray, and they frequently played to between 3,000 and 4,000 on Saturday nights. "Imagine 4,000 people paying today's prices," he reflects. "Six pounds a head... that's a lot of bread..."

Tensions began to surface in the Miami during the post-Eurovision days in '66. Dickie broke ranks with the other musicians and, Oliver Twist style, asked for more money. He argued that he was the one being besieged for autographs in O'Connell Street. It was his voice that sold the records. "We were each getting £50 a week when my father was earning £9. It was huge to us," he says. "But we should have been — and I should have been — on double that. We were all thick. Really it was my own fault."

Rock says he didn't make anything like the money made by Bowyer. That remains a regret to this day. He explains: "The biggest crowds of all time came to Dublin Airport after Eurovision. Thousands of people from Cork and Belfast and everywhere. That's when I started looking for more money with the Miami. I was on the same money as the rest of the lads in the band, but I had five number one hit records. It's no good being stopped in the streets, having big crowds come after you, if you're not getting the returns. I was stupid. I am not saying that I was ripped off in that anything was stolen from me. The money was nothing compared to what we should have been getting...what I should have been getting apart from members of the bad. You could replace a sax or trombone player, although they had become an integral part and identity of the Miami. But it would be more difficult to replace the likes of Dickie Rock, Brendan Bowyer or Joe Dolan. During my time with the Miami — from 1963 to 1972 — I didn't make anything like the kind of money that I should have made...nothing compared to what Bowyer was making.

"I became so big and invaluable to the Miami that I could write my own ticket and I didn't. I didn't take advantage of it. I had the power but didn't use it. They were short-sighted because they lost me. I blame myself for being stupid for allowing it to happen. They didn't see that, in me, they had something of value as a performer. They didn't do it right until I left the Miami in 1972 and formed my own band with the same management. The money should have been made at the beginning of the Miami during the height of the showband thing in the '60s when the crowds were huge. It would have made things much easier for me later on; set me up better. Not that I want to be grabbing: I just want to get the value of what I think I'm worth."

Rock claims that the manager, Tom Doherty, should have demanded bigger fees for the Miami. He says: "Tom is basically a very nice, honourable and honest man. Although he was one of the top managers and was well respected, he didn't get the money for the Miami that he should have been getting. Look, you can work seven nights a week if you work for nothing. We'd be packing out a place and, instead of being on sixty per cent of it, we'd be only in for fifty per cent. But we should have been on sixty per cent like every other top band. He wasn't demanding the fees. It might have been different if I came from a business background. My father might say, 'you're very popular, but you're not bringing home the money that you should be bringing home for all your popularity.' If you have power and something that's drawing crowds, then you've got to get the maximum money while you can. If your popularity drops in four years time, the ballroom proprietor isn't going to pay you any more than you're worth at the time just because you were nice a few years ago. Tom had a very foolish philosophy: you treat the promoters and proprietors right; treat them fairly, and they'll look after you. Mick Quinn (his next manager) was the opposite. His philosophy was: you get as much off them while you can demand it. That's because when you can't demand it, they're not going to give it to you, and you don't blame them."

Doherty counters Rock's claims by stating that 50% was adequate, and the band would not have been able to claim any more. He says that 10% of the Miami's weekly revenue went to finance recording, posters and publicity — much of which featured Rock, even though other band members wanted to record too. Doherty says he established a first class rapport with ballroom owners. This won considerable respect for the Miami, as well as consistent bookings. "A promoter came to me with an empty diary," says Doherty. "We'd pick the dates for the year, and he knew that they'd be honoured. We agreed a price and stuck to it. Whereas, other bands thought nothing of breaking their agreements and jacking up the price later on. I believed in being honourable, and it worked for us."

When Rock got more money in 1966, this bred discontent in the band. "The others were jealous, which was stupid," says Rock. The Miami broke up in 1967. Murty Quinn and four of the band — Clem Quinn, Denis Murray, Martin Phelan and Tommy O'Rourke — quit to form the Sands. "It was an amicable parting," says Murty. "There was no ill-feeling. We just felt that we could more successful than the Miami, and we were right." The Sands, which featured Tony Kenny, became one of the best known showbands. They began recording in '68 with three Top Ten hits that year — *Help Me Rhonda, Yummy Yummy Yummy*, and *Dance Dance Dance*. Other hits, in later years, were *Candida, Knock Three Times* and *Lend a Helpin' Hand*.

Meantime, the Miami reformed and Doherty brought in replacements — among them Fran O'Toole, Paul Ashford and Des McAlea. Rock achieved his seventh No. 1 hit, *Simon Says*, on May 11, '68, and returned with another Top Ten hit for December, *Christmas Time and You*. Rock was still unhappy, and decided to quit the Miami to start his own band in '72. He remained under Doherty's management. "I stayed with the same office, but I had more control," he says. "I left the Miami to be able to make more money within the context of a new set-up. I left the Miami because I was too long in it. The only way I could see myself making more money was to leave and form a new band. I stayed with Tom Doherty...safe, you see. Then I left him in 1975 and went to new management under Mick Quinn. He originally managed the Pacific Showband."

Upon Rock's departure from the Miami, Fran O'Toole took over as lead singer. Rock continued to achieve Top Ten hits during the first half of the '70s. His next No. 1 came on June 23rd, 1977, *Back Home*. In all, Rock had twenty-five Irish hits from '63 to '83 — surpassed only by Cliff Richard, Elvis Presley, the Beatles, David Bowie, Rolling Stones and Brendan Shine.

Rock took care of business in the '70s and, as soon as he began to make money himself, invested in property. Rock has always been upwardly mobile. He frequently changed residences, ever conscious of the resale price of his homes. "I saved a lot and invested as much as I could," he admits. "I didn't spend money. Not because I was mean. I had a good holiday with my wife. I made sure that we had everything for our family and were comfortable. I made sure we had a nice home. Judy doesn't drink or smoke. We didn't socialise to that degree because when you don't drink, you're not into that area of socialising. That way I could save more money than others who probably made more money than me, but spent it: booze and whatever. I invested my money in a bit of property. Nothing spectacular; just a little bit here and there. I have a place in Spain for holidays. That's because my wife has rheumatoid arthritis and she needs the dry climate — not the sun so much. I didn't need to drink or smoke to enjoy my life. Some people need the flash, the staying out late and all that. That doesn't do anything for me. I get my kicks from performing. Some people get their kicks from being in the pub atmosphere, having a drink with all the fellows and being one of the lads. I don't seem to need that, and I'm glad."

Unlike many of his contemporaries, Rock's career did not collapse with the demise of the ballrooms. The growing cabaret circuit, and the trend towards pubs and hotels, opened up a new market. Recording copper-fastened the success and made him accessible to a generation who never knew the old ballrooms. He moved with the times. The term 'serious performer' pops up frequently in conversation with Rock. It is a description he uses to judge himself, and others. For example, Elvis Presley did not, in his view, fall into that category. Sinatra did. He explains his thinking: "You have the guys who start off as pop stars. They have something and develop then into serious performers. Then you have guys who are pop stars, and that's all they are. Elvis was one of them. What John Lennon said was true, in my opinion. Elvis died when he went into the army.

"He was a pop rock and roller; a fabulous looking guy. But that's all he was. He was nothing else. That's what killed him. I don't think that Elvis could come to grips with the fact that he was getting old. He couldn't handle it. He wasn't a legitimate serious performer. Can you imagine Elvis in a dress suit like Sinatra? You can't. Although he started as a pop star, he didn't have the machinery to carry through to develop into a serious concert/cabaret performer. He was what he was — a super pop star. He was a great rock and roller in the early years. That was great. Unfortunately, that's as far as it went. People forget that before he died, you couldn't give away Elvis records. Sinatra was also a pop star — twenty years before Elvis shot to fame.

The difference is that this guy had the magic. He had a voice. He developed from being a pop star into a serious performer, a serious actor, everything. That's why, even at his age today, Sinatra is still the king. Who else has lasted so long? Nobody. He's the greatest popular singer who ever lived."

This brings Rock to a pet subject: the lack of serious performers in Ireland. "Anybody can have a hit record nowadays," he complains. "If I wanted to spend four or five grand with you, we could go into a studio, get a song and make a hit record. That's possible in Ireland today with all these people coming out of the woodwork. You see some fabulous looking fellows and girls on stage. Some are very popular; huge draws. They can't sing a decent song. It's an amazing thing; they can't perform, but it's whatever way they're coached."

Rock sees red when mediocrity succeeds: "That really drives me around the bend, because I know how hard I worked and how hard I do work to perfect my art...to try and be a good singer...not just sing a song, but to interpret a song. To perform properly on stage. To learn everything about my profession in the same way that an accountant or doctor learns about his and studies for years. I try to do the same with my business."

Rock has been less than generous in his appraisal of certain other Irish entertainers, particularly country and western singers. His belief is that the goods must be delivered live with no artificial aids. He applies strict standards to himself. It's all about performance, and Rock continues to practise his stagecraft after twenty-eight years in the business. He wants to give each individual a good night out and, indeed, feels a sense of duty to do so. "I'm very conscious that this could be a special night. They don't want to know if I have a cold or if I've had a row with my wife or if I'm depressed. They're there to watch me perform. It might be my 15th night...but it's their first night. I'm aware of the importance of the night to them. Sometimes it might be a woman who has followed me for twenty-five years. She'll have her daughter with her. The daughter didn't want to come but she came anyway. And the mother can point to me and say, 'there now, that's Dickie Rock, that's the fellow I've been telling you about'. The daughter has got to say, 'you were right

Mam. I see what you mean'. If the daughter doesn't say that, I'm letting the mother down. What I'm working for when I'm out there is the applause. The money doesn't come into it. I love seeing people who supported me from the time I began. It justifies their faith in me. I've tried to develop my art over the years. I look intensely out into the audience. Look at me...I'm singing this song for you. When I sing these words, these words are for you. When I sing...*I'll Never Stop Wanting You*...and I look briefly into a woman's eyes, I'm singing for her. That's the feeling I try to create. That's why I'm still here today."

Rock is evasive about his wealth. Is he a millionaire? He describes himself as 'comfortable' — which could mean he's not stuck for a few bob, or he's a millionaire. The general belief in showbusiness circles is that he leans more towards the latter category. "Rich is a very indefinable word," he muses. "I'm rich in the fact that I have a beautiful wife and six beautiful children. We're very happy. I don't have to worry financially. It's the working class people who have made me that. I appreciate it more than if I was born with a silver spoon in my mouth. My whole world revolves around my family. I'm very lucky. I'm doing a job that I love. I get great pleasure from it. My big interest is looking after my family. They're going to school: helping and guiding them. But, at the same time, looking after ourselves. We have rights, too, as well as the children. I try to guide the children to respect people and be respectful. You can't demand respect. You have to earn it."

One son, Jason, has his own rock band. If any of his children should choose showbusiness, he considers it important that they have another string to their bows. "It's very important in the music business to rehearse seriously and take the whole thing seriously, but it's more important to set yourself up for life in something else. You think when you get a recording contract it's great — it's not great. There's only one U2 — one Beatles. Look at all the big groups who have fallen by the wayside. Without a safety net, the unsuccessful performer is lost. Unless you make it big, you're always on the fringes...mickey mouse venues, mickey mouse money, mickey mouse status."

It's a measure of Rock's professionalism that he still receives accolades. In 1986, he was named Showman of the Year by his peers in the Variety Club of Ireland, recognising his work for handicapped children. (One of his own children was born handicapped). No one in showbusiness disputes his talent, although some feel he is a victim of the limited success he achieved in Ireland. He once mused that he might have gone to Las Vegas like Red Hurley and Brendan Bowyer if he had been single. It's unlikely now that he'll make it internationally.

Rock had opportunities to try his hand in an international marketplace, but refused to leave Ireland. "Maybe if I was born in England or America, I could have done it," he reflects. "But I would have to go abroad. It's a price I'm not prepared to pay. I wasn't prepared to pay it seventeen years ago, when I had a wife and only two children and I got the offer of going with United Artists in Britain, to base myself over there, to be available for TV shows and all that. Now I have six children. I'd love to have an international hit. The way the charts are now with some of the songs that get in, anyone can have a hit record. You never know. I can still work in my own country without having to go away to make a living. Let's face it, it would be great to be a huge international star. But what price do I have to pay? I was offered that years and years ago — to go to England. I'm happy with my family and to be able to work and make a good living in Ireland. The price for international fame — go away from home, be away from my kids, maybe breaking up the family — is too high. I'm not prepared to pay it."

Rock still makes the headlines, whether singing for Prince Rainier or attempting to get a driving ban revoked. On October 24th, 1989, he failed at the Dublin Circuit Court to win his licence back — just four months after escaping a jail sentence for having no tax or insurance on his Rolls Royce. The judge rejected an application to restore his licence. The eight-month ban was imposed in June, '89, when the judge quashed a three-month prison term imposed by the District Court. The initial jail sentence was a source of serious embarrassment to Rock and his family. On reflection, Rock regrets the incident: "If it never happened, I would be pleased. I was stupid. However, that the press played on it so much has to be a compliment; that they even bothered has to be a compliment to me." He lifts his right arm and squeezes a thumb and index finger together — to emphasise that a few lines of newspaper space would have been less than flattering. "If they reported it in a little column down in the corner that singer Dickie Rock had been fined, I'd feel that I was in trouble. But when they spread it across the papers and on the 6 o'clock news, who merits that? It was a compliment. If they're going to do it, let's do it right. Seriously, it's a thing that should never have happened. You should never take a car out without insurance, even if you're just running around the block. I took a chance. I was driving it down to the garage. I like a nice car, purely for comfort. It's one of the trappings that I indulge in."

Retirement is not on the cards for Dickie Rock, the Irish institution. He scoffs at the notion: "Look, you could ask a solicitor or an accountant, 'how long are you going to continue'? This is my life; this is my profession. I'll go on as long as I can." He has no insecurity about the future, "because I know I can continue making a good living for some time to come. But, in another sense, I'd love to know I've made enough for the rest of my life, to live in comfort and to provide for my children and to help them when I can." His ambitions are modest: to develop his performer's role, and to make good recordings. His heart would probably stop without the thrill of the stage. Age is irrelevant.

Dickie's lepping is more restrained, and he doesn't tear through a rock'n'roll set with the same energy as twenty-five years ago. Yet, the magic of this seemingly ageless entertainer continues to have a potent effect. The long road taught him how to play an audience and make them his. Young and old still sway to his songs of sweet romance, as I discovered one night during September '89 at a cabaret lounge in the Cork suburb of Togher.

The atmosphere was rich with nostalgia. All Rock's old Cork fans, who danced to the Miami in the Arcadia many moons ago, were there — and some brought their teenage daughters along. The audience was predominantly female, and many had middle-age spread. Rock sang big numbers from the '60s. Requests were handed up and the recipient was almost the only lean, middle-aged man in the house. Rock's body measurements are more or less what they were a quarter of a century ago. He introduced *Every Step of the Way*...'one of my biggest hits'. He came off stage at the end, and returned again to loud cheers. The audience sang with him. The look of delight on the face of a blonde in her late teens said everything about Rock's perennial appeal. She could just as easily have been a fan of Milli Vanilli or Paula Abdul. He stared deep into her eyes and delivered a plaintive cry from a broken heart...

Massacred On The Road

Co. Down, Thursday July 31st, 1975, 2.08am.

A torch flashes. Men in military uniforms flag down the Miami Showband on the road between Banbridge and Newry. While the band were playing in the Castle Ballroom, Banbridge, an Ulster Volunteer Force (UVF) gang set a death trap for them seven miles south in the dark of night. Ballroom manager Cecil Thompson was pleased with the turnout for the dance. Next it would be the turn of the Mighty Avons, on Friday night. The Miami left a little earlier than usual to get home to their wives and families. Other bands usually stayed on after gigs to relax before setting off. The Miami's journey from Banbridge to Newry, a distance of about twelve miles, is brought to a halt by a figure waving a police-type torch. The Volkswagen van pulls to the side of the road.

It looks like a UDR checkpoint; the musicians are ordered out of the van which, they assume, will be searched. Soon danger becomes apparent: this is no legitimate UDR road check. The driver, Brian McCoy, and his four band colleagues, are lined up at gunpoint by a ditch. Two of the UVF men carry a 10lb. bomb into the van and begin to put it into place. The other gang members point weapons at the five men and check their identification. Suddenly, the bomb explodes. It rips through the van and blasts two of the terrorists to pieces. The hostages make a run for it. The remaining gunmen open fire — four of the five musicians are shot at point blank range in the back and head. Desmond McAlea — stage name Des Lee — is thrown by the force of the blast into the hedge as the shooting begins. He flees across a field and emerges on the roadway some distance from the ambush site. He flags down a lorry and car and gets a lift to Newry police station, five miles away. McAlea is in a state of deep shock.

Dead are lead singer Fran O'Toole (29); trumpeter Brian McCoy (30), and instrumentalist, Tony Geraghty (23). A fourth band member, Stephen Travers, is found in the field beside the carriageway. He is critically injured with bullet wounds in the chest and abdomen. The sixth band member, Ray Millar (23), escaped the ambush: after the dance ended in Banbridge, he drove in his own car to his home in Antrim town. Road manager Brian Maguire also had a lucky escape. He left the Castle Ballroom in his car and was driving about a quarter of a mile ahead of the van. The terrorists who died in the explosion were Horace Boyle, a UVF 'major' from Portadown, and Wesley Somerville, a UVF 'lieutenant' from Caledon, Co. Tyrone. Both were well known to the British army, the RUC and the intelligence services.

Dawn breaks to reveal a scene of carnage and devastation. Bits of bodies are strewn with the van wreckage along the roadway and into the adjoining field. An arm with the tattoo mark, 'UVF', lies among the twisted metal. Personal belongings of the dead musicians are scattered on the road: photographs, playing cards, a pair of high-heeled brown boots, a torn map, a record, a book, 'The Who' by Garry Hermann. The fly leaf of the book is marked 'Tony, Des, Ray, Fran and Dave', where they had been keeping the score of a card game.

At seven that morning, a chamber maid knocks on a bedroom door at the Galway Bay Hotel, Salthill. Dickie Rock is awakened. The hotel employee is distressed. She cannot find the right words to convey the news reported on the morning radio bulletins. "The Miami Showband has been in an accident... a crash... they've been held- up." Rock dresses quickly. He rushes downstairs and listens to the news reports. The scale of the horror does not sink in. It will be four days before Rock fully realises what has happened. If fate had dictated otherwise, the victims could have been Rock and his new band — or indeed any of the top Irish showbands who played frequently in the North. Traditionally, both bands performed at Seapoint during the Galway Races Festival in July. On this occasion, the Miami, with Fran O'Toole, played at Seapoint on Monday and Tuesday nights. Rock was booked to play on Wednesday and Thursday nights. The New Miami played their two nights at Seapoint, and went home. Rock drove to Galway on Wednesday. He sang that night while the Miami were giving their last performance in Banbridge. The founder and original manager of the Miami Showband, Tom Doherty, who is stunned by the murders, drives from Dublin to Newry. Des McAlea, from Andersonstown, Belfast, spends much of the morning briefing detectives at Newry police station. By midday, he is brought to Daisy Hill Hospital for treatment for a slight leg wound: a fragment of metal is removed. The RUC escort him to the border where he is met by the gardai who accompany his car until it is well clear of the area.

Families are stricken with grief at the homes of the dead bandsmen. Mrs. Pat Lenihan, mother-in-law of Fran O'Toole, breaks the news to his wife, Valerie. She is heavily sedated at their home in Bray, Co. Wicklow. Relatives comfort their two children. Tony Geraghty's father, a manager at Irish Biscuits Ltd., in Dublin, tells newsmen: "Tony has been music mad since he was a boy. That's all he was really interested in. What harm could that do anyone?"

McAlea is reunited with his Cork-born wife, Brenda, at their home in Swords, Co. Dublin. Looking tired and dishevelled, he jumps from the car and runs into the house. A friend describes him as 'a very frightened man'. News of Brian McCoy's murder is kept, for the moment, from his elderly parents in Caledon, Co. Tyrone. His wife, Helen, hears confirmation of the atrocity on radio news bulletins. Drummer Ray Millar, who escaped, is too shocked to talk. A friend comments: "It was always the custom of the boys to return to their homes if they were playing nearby. Ray drove from Banbridge to Antrim because the band had no engagement tonight (Thursday). He was to have linked up with them again on Friday."

In early afternoon, Daisy Hill Hospital issues a bulletin on Stephen Travers. He was admitted at 2.30am with high-velocity bullet wounds to his abdomen and chest. He underwent three hours of surgery, and was still critically ill.

Ballrooms throughout the country are silent: dances cancelled as a mark of respect to the murdered bandsmen. "This is an appalling thing," says Patrick Malone of the Irish Federation of Musicians. "So much has been said about this mindless psychopathic killing. But I am shocked beyond belief that this sort of thing should come into our business." The outrage opens the eyes of southerners to the fact that the troubles affect all on this island. Nobody can understand why a showband comprising Protestants and Catholics should be singled out. The attack made no sense on sectarian grounds: the UVF would hardly have wished to kill Protestants. "Of the band, seven of us travelled all the time," said road manager Brian Maguire. "Four of us were from the North — two were Catholic and two were Protestant. For that reason, there was no sense in it then, and there's even less sense in it now." The showband business was long past its glory days. Showbands faced extinction: the massacre helped to put the final nails in the coffin. 1975, a black year for the business, would be remembered for Tom Dunphy's death in a road accident and the Miami murders. Both events had a profound psychological effect. Dunphy's death left a void that would never be filled; the career of O'Toole and the Miami was just beginning to blossom.

The Miami outrage was different because the North's showband and ballroom scene seemed to transcend sectarian hatred. Bands drew their members from both sides of the border. In the words expressed by one Northern danceband promoter at the time: "If you can play the guitar and swing, you've got it made no matter where you come from, or what religion you are." The best of the northern bands were respected in the south — and vice versa. The Miami attracted large crowds of Catholics and Protestants to all the leading halls in the north. Within days of the massacre, cross-border links seemed set to snap. The Federation of Musicians said it was up to bands to decide about engagements in the north. At the same time, northern promoters reported that some southern bands had cancelled bookings. The outrage even hit bookings from the UK: the young Scottish singer, Lena Zavarone, who had a hit in 1974 with *Ma He's Making Eyes At Me*, cancelled a booking at the Ritz Cinema in Belfast.

Rock grieved the loss of his friends. "It was four or five days before the full impact of the disaster hit me," he recalls. "Then I felt very sad. I didn't feel so sad at the beginning. Afterwards, like a delayed action, it hit me. These guys whom I had worked with for years...I wasn't going to see them again. Brian McCoy, a Protestant from Co. Tyrone, was the most beautiful human being you could ever meet. A lovely fellow, he wouldn't harm a fly. Killed. What made them do a thing like that? I don't think that they meant to kill the guys. There was panic all around. The bomb exploded. The fellows ran. The shooting started. I stopped going up north for two years. Apart from the terrible loss of life, the tragedy led to a great financial loss for bands. I said that I'd never go up again. It was a rash statement at the time. Obviously things change."

Rock had left the Miami three years before the atrocity. The New Miami was fronted by Fran O'Toole as lead singer. O'Toole had joined when the original Miami broke up in 1967. Promoter Mervyn Solomon said that O'Toole had just finished a record, about to be released in America, Germany, France and Holland. Solomon described him as a "brilliant songwriter and dynamic personality." O'Toole had been making a name for himself as a songwriter. He was chosen as one of a select few to be featured on the Me and My Music series on Telefís Éireann. His show was to have been televised on Monday, August 25th, 1975. As well as lead vocalist with the band, O'Toole played the organ. He had a Top Ten hit with the Miami in October, '74 — *Clap Your Hands Stamp Your Feet.* Two months after his death, O'Toole's Love Is went to No. 3 and was in the charts for ten weeks. He was 29, married with two children, and lived in Bray. Anthony Geraghty (23) of Stanaway Road, Kimmage, Dublin, was engaged to be married. He had just joined the band. Brian McCoy (30), a native of Co. Tyrone, lived at Woodbine Park, Raheny, Dublin, with his wife and two children. He played the trumpet and sang. He joined the Miami in '67. Stephen Travers was aged twenty-six, and married. He was the bass guitarist and joined only six weeks earlier. He was a native of Carrick-on-Suir, Co. Tipperary. Des McAlea, from Belfast, a vocalist and sax player, joined in 1967. Before joining the Miami, he played for a time in Cork with Declan Ryan and The Arrivals, a popular local band.

Three men received life terms for their role in the massacre — two in 1976 and a third in 1981. On October 15th, 1976, at the High Court in Belfast, two former members of the Ulster Defence Regiment (UDR), Thomas Raymond Crozier (25) and James Roderick McDowell (29), both of Lurgan, were sentenced to life imprisonment. At the end of a seven-day trial, Lord Justice Jones recommended that they serve not less than thirty-five years. Five years later, a third man, John James Somerville (37), of Dungannon, Co. Tyrone, was also jailed for a minimum of thirty-five years for the murders. The full truth about the Miami murders was not uncovered by the trials.

The Northern Lights

Paradise Island Hotel, Bahamas,
Saturday, December 20th, 1969.

It's showtime at the Trade Winds Lounge. Guests spill from hotel casinos and take their places for the nightly floor show presented by an Irish showband. A lavishly-decorated table is set up in front of the stage for a VIP and his entourage. All eyes are on the party singled out for special attention. Waiters flit about them, and a few autograph hunters seize one of the most famous signatures in America. Lights dim. The Witnesses, a Belfast band, is the big attraction of the night. The leader, Harry 'Trixie' Hamilton, stands in the spotlight glare, clutches a microphone and welcomes Elvis Presley. "We're very honoured, ladies and gentlemen, to have the king himself with us," says Hamilton, with a slight quiver of nervousness in his voice. "Let's hear it for Elvis." The audience erupts in applause. Presley stands to take a bow, then rejoins his wife, Priscilla and bodyguard Mike Stone.

The Witnesses, all top musicians, live up to their reputation for professionalism, excitement and glamour. Presley is impressed, and he says so later when invited on stage by the Belfast showmen. He congratulates Colm Wilkinson on his singing. He holds a guitar and poses for photographs with the Witnesses. "Everybody thinks Elvis came up and sang a number with us, but he didn't," recalls Hamilton. "Elvis was on holiday, so we didn't push it. Afterwards, in the elevator going upstairs, Elvis said he thought we were limeys, meaning British like the Beatles. When he realised we were Irish, he said that the only Irish songs he knew were *I'll Take You Home Again Kathleen* and *Danny Boy.*"

Their paths first crossed a week earlier. The Witnesses had a five- week residency at the Paradise Island Hotel, Bahamas, as part of a grand six-month tour of the Americano hotel chain in the United States and Caribbean. The tour was negotiated by a London agent, Sidney Rose. While other bands at home prepared for Christmas, the Witnesses flew to a sun-drenched resort of the super-rich. The culture shock was enormous. "The hotel was on a private island," says Hamilton. "You had to pay a dollar to get across the bridge. It was like Lurgan with a roof. There was a concert hall, casinos with thousands of slot machines, black jack tables, roulette and crap tables. We played in the Trade Winds Lounge twice a night for five weeks. We were the floor show."

Presley and his wife arrived on vacation during their residency. The Witnesses were waiting for showtime one evening, seated in the hotel foyer with their instruments. When the support band struck up a certain tune, that would be their cue to slip backstage and set up behind the curtains. Suddenly, Presley breezed past them on his way to a casino. Hamilton turned to the bell boy and said: "Yer man's a dead ringer for Elvis." The kid replied: "But sir, that *is* Elvis." Hamilton jumped from his seat and followed him. He recalls: "Elvis took over a whole black jack table. He had fifty dollars in each hand. He was smoking a cigar and drinking bourbon. I'd always read that this all-American boy didn't smoke, drink or gamble. The first time I saw Elvis he was doing all three."

While Presley concentrated on the tables, Priscilla and Stone went to watch the floor show staged by the Witnesses. This became a nightly routine: Elvis gambled and Priscilla sat through a total of nine shows. "Elvis always stood in the doorway as we played the last number," says Hamilton. "Then, he sat down beside Priscilla at the end. He bought drinks for the band every night." Eventually, Presley invited the Witnesses to join him at his table and remarked: "Priscilla says it's a great show. I'm coming down on Saturday." It was the highlight of the week's performances: queues formed outside the lounge. As usual, the Witnesses sat around the foyer. Presley was surprised at the crowds and said to one of the musicians: "I didn't know there would be so many people. Do you think I'll get in?" Guitarist Alex Burns replied: "Just mention my name, Elvis, and they'll let you in." Presley and his wife became friends of the band. The Presleys' two-week vacation was cut short because bad weather halted their plans to go deep sea fishing. The most famous couple in America checked out after ten days. The Witnesses accomplished their mission and moved on to the next hotel. The tour ended early in the New Year at the Drake Hotel, Fifth Avenue, New York.

Although the majority of showbands supplemented slack periods at home by brief overseas tours, the Witnesses, a breakaway from the Dave Glover band, were the first to take on prolonged world tours. Apart from doing the usual British and American circuits, the Witnesses became Belfast's travelling showband ambassadors: to the U.S. and Caribbean for six months; to Sydney for almost five months; to the American bases in Germany on a regular basis; to Canada, and even Mexico pencilled in the diary at one stage.

The band were bigger abroad than at home. While performing in Germany, top brass from the Pentagon attended one of their shows at an American base near Frankfurt. It led to an invitation to play at Richard Nixon's inauguration ball in January 1965... which the Witnesses turned down! Hamilton recalls the night: "There was a group on before us called The Korean Kittens. They were going down a stormer. How were we going to follow this? So we did our act and said 'good night', and the audience cheered and gave us a standing ovation. After the fourth encore, we had a routine whereby I told a few jokes, dashed off stage and we came marching up the aisle doing the Saints. The Americans thought this was the last word. I remember one of the guys from the Pentagon was called John Ryan. They wanted to book us for Nixon's ball. But we were already booked for an eighteen week engagement in Sydney. We couldn't do a one-nighter in the middle of that tour. We turned down the offer because we were contracted to go to Sydney. In hindsight, I suppose we couldn't have paid for that amount of publicity." During their Sydney tour that lasted nearly five months, the Witnesses took part in four TV shows as well as thirty TV commercials.

The Witnesses, rated as one of the best musical bands to emerge from Belfast, 'destroyed' the English cabaret scene, and were supported in the clubs there by entertainers who later became household names...among them Engelbert Humperdinck and Freddie Starr. Journalist John Trew, showbusiness columnist for City Week magazine in Belfast, who covered one of their British tours, recalls: "The Witnesses were brilliant musicians. They were masterly. Their show was brilliantly conceived, orchestrated from start to finish. It was extremely professional. Every single one of them had a speciality. They were consummate musicians. They were going to be the first thrust of a big showband invasion on the mainland.

"English managements were fed up paying literally telephone numbers for big names like Shirley Bassey and Tom Jones. They discovered that Irish showbands could not only do an hour and a half, but could do five hours, and entertain the crowds hugely. The Witnesses were brought over to spearhead a campaign by the northern club owners association. I went over when they got a residency at The Talk of the North in Manchester. They were terrific."

Ironically, although the Witnesses were a successful showband export, they failed to make the bigtime south of the border. "We could never figure it out," reflects Hamilton, now general secretary of the Northern Ireland Musicians Association. "At the odd place in the south, we got needle from people who said, 'they're from the black north.' We were popular in Dublin. People queued outside the Crystal to see us. But, we didn't crack it outside Dublin. We weren't heavy into country music at the time. Maybe we didn't make it because we didn't play enough old time waltzes and country. In Dublin, people loved our dixieland stuff. But, in places like Galway, people wanted old time waltzes and a lot of country. We didn't do that too well. Some of the boys in the band had a wee attitude about it: they wanted to play jazz, big band and Tom Jones hits."

The Witnesses, a good trad jazz band, had their roots in the Dave Glover Band that ruled the music scene in Belfast and commanded respect throughout the North. Glover began his career in '47 playing trumpet with the Bob Robinson orchestra, in residence at the Floral Hall, Belfast. Glover earned seven pounds ten shillings a week. A year later, he formed his own four-piece for Saturday night dinner dances at the Midland Hotel, Belfast. Glover played summer seasons in '48 and '49 at the Palais de Dance, Portstewart. He had built a dixieland line up — trumpet, trombone, sax, bass, drums and vocalist. Next came seasonal work at the Palladium Ballroom, Portrush, in '50 and '51. Glover opened the Arcadia Ballroom, Portrush, with a fourteen piece orchestra in 1952, and played summer seasons there for fifteen years. In 1953, Glover trimmed the line-up to a seven-piece and brought in a female vocalist, Lynn Shaw.

In '55/'56, Glover called his act a showband, and staged a twenty minute show. There were comedy routines and speciality numbers. A singer, 'Big' Joe Clarke, did all the rock'n'rolling, jiving, twisting on the floor and somersaults. The band was on the road between the summer seasons in Portrush. The line-up: Glover, trumpet; Gerry Rice, sax and clarinet; Andy Wilson, trombone; Harry Mitchel, keyboards; Harry 'Trixie' Hamilton, bass; Davy Martin, drums, Alex Burns, guitar; and Clarke, vocals.

The band broke up in '63 and the majority left to form the Witnesses — Hamilton, Mitchel, Rice, Burns, Clarke and Wilson. The new outfit recruited a trumpet player, George Mullen, and hired a manager, Jimmy Adgey. When Mitchel left afterwards to manage Bill Fuller's ballroom in San Francisco, he was replaced by Tony Morelli. Mitchel later rejoined the Witnesses, and then left again to go solo in '68, to be replaced by Colm Wilkinson. Hamilton says of Wilkinson: "He was in a class of his own. He had this soulful voice, a mixture of Tom Jones and Ray Charles. He saved our bacon many a time in American bases where the audiences were mostly black. Colm used to sit on a bar stool, get his guitar and pick a tune off his head. The black soldiers applauded him, patted him on the back and said, 'man, you got soul'. It was beautiful." Wilkinson later launched a successful solo career in the '70s with such hits as *There Was A Dream* and *Born To Sing*. He turned to stage musicals — from Jesus Christ Superstar and Evita to his Broadway triumph in the smash hit musical, Les Miserables. (In 1990, he played to record-breaking audiences in Canada as the lead in the Phantom of the Opera).

Meantime, Glover had regrouped with a new line-up: Jim McDermot, sax; Johnny Anderson, trombone; Jim Gunner, guitar; Jackie Flavelle, bass; Dessie McCarthy, drums; and Muriel

Day and Mike Munroe, vocals."That's when the showband really took off," says Glover. "The double boy/girl vocals went down a bomb. They did all the big pop ballads and stuff like that...singing to each other and holding hands. That band cleaned up for us all over the States and Canada. It really clicked."

Muriel Day won the National Song Contest in 1969 with *Wages of Love*. Her song went to No. 1 in the charts on March 29, and was in the charts for seven weeks. Her first stage performance after the song contest took place at the Stardust in Cork. Glover recalls the excitement: "The gardai had to meet us three miles outside Cork to escort us through the crowds. Traffic in the city-centre came to a standstill. I'll never forget it. The reaction was so good that there was a lump in my throat and tears in my eyes. We couldn't get into the place because of the crowds. The bouncers helped us inside. The Capitol Showband was playing on stage. It was so emotional that when Muriel got up to sing *The Wages of Love*, she just dried up. She couldn't sing and was crying. I went up to her on the stand and held her hand. I remember saying, 'for God sake, Muriel, don't let me down now of all times'. She eventually sang. The cheers were ear- splitting. It was the most fantastic night of my life." Muriel Day represented Ireland at the Eurovision Song Contest in Madrid. Glover later emigrated to Canada, and returned home subsequently to start an agency booking bands.

The Witnesses, meanwhile, had undergone further changes. Hamilton and Burns left the band in 1970. The band was due to travel on a nine- month tour of Canada, the U.S. and Mexico. But the tour collapsed because, unlike Hamilton and Burns, their replacements were not members of the American Federation of Musicians.

The North traditionally spawned top class musicians, and many of them emerged in Derry. Technically, some were of an international standard. Bands wanted to be regarded as good musicians first, and showmen second. They found it difficult to make a breakthrough south of the border — mainly because most avoided country'n'western and concentrated on the pops. Up north, bands had to work hard for recognition. Young people there were more impressed by British pop stars, due to the influence of the media. The showband explosion was housed primarily in Belfast and Derry.

Some of the finest ballrooms in the country sprouted across the north, and the business gradually became more organised during the first half of the '60s. Graham McKenzie, show page columnist of *The Belfast Telegraph*, wrote in '65: "All over Ulster, ballrooms have been built at a fantastic rate. There is not a single town of any size in the province which does not have a hall of its own. Fast disappearing are the days of the small man who hired a local hall to promote the odd dance. Nowadays, the showbands perform in well-appointed luxurious halls built specifically for the purpose. And they deal with professional promoters who know what they want and what their audiences want. The Northern Lights will be shining for a long time to come." In 1965, there were sixty established showband venues — and eighty bands to play in them.

The best known bands in the North were the Clippers, Dave Glover, Johnny Quigley, Gay McIntyre, the Plattermen, Freshmen, Witnesses and Melotones. The North readily accepted the cream of southern showbands for whom there was no border. Even bands from the second division — such as the Regal from Cork — played to packed houses at Romanos in Belfast on Friday nights and at the Flamingo in Ballymena on Saturday nights.

Derry became the main launching pad for showbands. They appeared at conveyor-belt pace. Their progress was marked by rows and frequent re- shuffles in personnel. The Magnificent Seven, for example, never carried the same line-up for more than six months. Due to high unemployment in the north West, youngsters turned to music for a means of livelihood. But there was a surfeit of bands, and a constant supply of musicians. "There were just too many," says George Jones of the BBC who played bass with the Glover band. "It was like having a football manager who had too many players to pick from. They arranged a line-up, went out and became popular. They discovered a slight flaw. The sax player wasn't that great, but somebody's aunt around the corner knew a better one. These regular line-up changes rocked the boat and made them unstable."

Jackie Flavelle, who played with Glover and Quigley, remembers a time when there were twenty-six touring bands in the Derry union...all on the road fulltime. Another notable band were the Esquires. "Derry was a musical city," explains Flavelle. "There was never any work for males there, and all the women worked in the shirt factories. The men either went to England or America or else played in bands." There were geographical factors as well: Derry provided a spin-off into Donegal, and then a direct route to the south. It was home to the Johnny Quigley All Stars. The nucleus comprised four brothers: Johnny, leader, sax and clarinet; Mickey, sax; Edmund, sax and bass; Joe, trumpet.

"With the four brothers and the rest of us, we were able to get a big band sound," recalls Flavelle who joined Quigley from the Glover band in '60. "The dances were from 9 to 1, or 9 to 2. For the first half, we'd play big band dance music... Glenn Miller tunes and a little bit of jazz. At the interval, we'd change into yellow jackets and come out and do rock'n'roll. Mickey Quigley had worked in America, and he came back with all these rock'n'roll ideas. We were famous for the Coasters numbers. It was probably one of the finest bands in the country. We had an English trumpet player called Roy Adinell. He had been playing in Belfast with a big English resident band at the Mecca Ballroom, the Plaza. The wages were a lot better for Irish showbands than English resident bands. Roy moved up to Derry and he did all the arrangements. The band was quite famous in parts of the country. We used to play Waterford and, what became the Royal Showband, often played at the interval."

Flavelle, now a producer with Downtown Radio, quit with drummer Tommy McMenamin to form their own band in Derry, the Jokers. Musically, it was a good band... "but we couldn't get any work." Flavelle moved to Birmingham where he led a resident band in an Irish club. He became friendly with a visiting band, the Swingtime Aces from Co. Galway. He joined them as bass player in '62/'63 and set up home in Athenry. "It was hilarious," he recalls. "We had an absolute ball." Flavelle and another band member, Jim Gunner, returned to the north and joined Glover after his band broke up in '63. When Flavelle quit the Glover band, for the second time, to join the Chris Barber band in '66, he was replaced by George Jones.

Glover argues that some of the most talented musicians in Ireland came from Derry: for example, saxophone player Jim McDermot and Johnny Anderson, "a fabulous trombone player." And, of course, there was Gay McIntyre, a brilliant jazz sax player who, say observers of his career, would have been good enough to headline jazz festivals anywhere in Europe. The Platters, from Omagh, later to be known as the Plattermen, were led by Pat Chesters and included a superb lead guitarist, Arty McGlinn.

Belfast had a strong tradition of orchestras and ballrooms. It was on the Mecca circuit and housed the Plaza Ballroom. The Floral Hall always had a resident orchestra. The Melotones, a popular Belfast band, were resident first at Maxim's Ballroom, and then at Romano's. "I think Belfast was more influenced by the English scene, whereas Derry was influenced by the American scene," says Jones. "Belfast was more prosperous than Derry on the employment front. So, therefore, more people were going to the dancehalls. The showband scene took off to a certain extent in Belfast, but was very quickly overtaken by the group scene, early beat groups. Buddy Holly, Eddie Cochran and Gene Vincent came straight in here because we got a direct feed from Britain. Then, with the emergence of the Beatles, groups superseded the showbands. From that moment, everyone wanted to be like the Shadows or Beatles, and certainly no more than a four or five- piece group. Funnily enough, those type of groups found it very hard to get work. Even though they loved it, there was never a scene for them, simply because when they went outside the outer perimeter of Belfast, the place was totally inundated with showbands. People outside Belfast who went to dancehalls expected to see a full seven- piece line-up on stage. Otherwise, the band was no good."

Showbands never thrived in Belfast to the same extent as Derry. There was a lack of brass players: sax and trumpet players were difficult to find. But there were plenty of guitarists searching for outlets. Jones explains: "The easy way out for them was to play a lot of instrumentals. Hence, guitar instrumental groups based themselves on Johnny and The Hurricanes, The Shadows, The Ventures. Their material was easy to pick up and copy. At the outbreak of Beatlemania, the tunes were again easier to play, as distinct from having to play material that required a full line-up with saxes, trumpets and trombones. Belfast groups turned from the Beatles songs to blues." The city had a livelier beat scene than Dublin. The blues provided a bridge from the dixieland jazz of showbands: young people who were weaned on jazz warmed to blues and rhythm'n'blues. Traditional jazz venues which once catered for a minority of fans became haunts for musicians who played the blues.

R&B groups couldn't hope to fill big ballrooms like Romano's or the Plaza, so they created their own venues on Friday and Saturday nights. The Maritime Hotel, where Van Morrison and Them made their name, housed the best known club. Jazz and R&B groups played in dance studios such as Sammy Houston's at Great Victoria Street. A venue that played a central role in the growth of 'rock' was known as The Pound Club at Oxford Street. It was simply a function room at the rear of a pub, situated on a site once used as the city pound for stray animals. This club nurtured notable musicians... among them Jim Armstrong who was recruited to the line-up of Van Morrison's Them. Armstrong was rated as the best rock guitarist to emerge from Belfast.

The showband phenomenon was eroded in Belfast before it died in Derry. At one time, there were more ballrooms than showbands in Belfast. Glover was up to date with the latest pop releases in the hit parade, established his own following, and says he was never threatened by the groups. "We had nothing to fear," he claims. "I never worried about pop groups. It might have been different for the likes of the Melody Aces and some of the other country bands. The groups might have had the big guitar sounds, but we still had the numbers and the vocalists." The decades may have slipped by, but Glover still commands respect across the North where he's regarded as a survivor.

The Freshmen — Good Vibrations

London, March, 1964.

The Freshmen, from Ballymena, invade the dancehalls of Britain. On the Top Rank circuit, most dancers have never seen a showband. The Freshmen pass the test: they play two dates in most ballrooms on a six-week tour, and, as word spreads, the crowds double second time around. Gary Brown, music controller of the Rank circuit, says: "Never have I heard such remarkable comments from my managers. They report that there hasn't been such talk about even some of the top English groups." He wants to come to Ireland to book more showbands. Freshmen manager Peter Dempsey says their success is an eye opener for the British promoters. "It was amazing," recalls Freshmen founder, Billy Brown. "There were no paddies in these places at all. They loved us. It was the equivalent of *Top of the Pops* live, every night. It was super."

The Freshmen were not an ordinary showband — and Brown was no ordinary showman. For a start, they were musicians in the true sense, born of a tradition in Northern Ireland that demanded a firm grasp of musicianship — unlike the '60s acceptance in the South of bands who mastered the three-chord-trick and called themselves musicians. The Freshmen could play... and play well. Rory Gallagher, no fan of showbands, regarded them as the best. The showband tag did not fit the Freshmen because they never set out to be one. "Inevitably, we became known as a showband. You couldn't escape it," says Brown. "It was being tacked onto our name by promoters. We'd come along to ballrooms and see The Freshmen Showband on the posters. We hated that because we didn't want to be classed as a showband at all."

By December 1964, almost the height of the craze, one poll placed the Freshmen as Ireland's fourth most popular showband after the Royal, Miami and Cadets. The Freshmen were different: musically, they kept the fans happy with the required showband mix, but they also dared to experiment at a time when originality was frowned on. They were without the inhibitions of the southern showband image-men who played their roles exactly as expected. The Freshmen were free spirits: only Billy Brown would try to get away with wearing jeans on stage. It was no coincidence that they first made an impact in Cork. Traditionally, the Arcadia was receptive to something different. Robin Power knew he could pack it by booking the Freshmen, even on Wednesday nights, before the band made it in the rest of the country. The Freshmen established a cult following. Many independent observers say they were the best thing to happen musically in Ireland during the '60s, despite being eclipsed by the Royal during the boom years.

Brown, who could play any instrument, except the accordion, was hailed as a musical genius. "If there is music in hell," he once said, "it will be played on an accordion." An outstanding pianist, he was rated too as one of the country's top sax players and a fine clarinettist. He also played bass and rhythm guitars, drums, trumpet, trombone and flute. He was a gifted songwriter, and arranged the music that gave the Freshmen their distinctive sound. Brown aspired to the high professional standards set by Derry bandleader Johnny Quigley. At the same time, he didn't turn a blind eye to the rewards of the showband business. The Freshmen made pots of money. They prided themselves on doing cover versions better than anyone else.

They specialised in the Beach Boys whose surf'n'fun harmonies became their trademark. The golden era of the Beach Boys — '63 to '69 — coincided with that of the Freshmen. Finally, they became stereotyped. "We became too much identified with them," says Brown. "Nobody else could do the Beach Boys songs. We put flesh on the sounds that the punters wanted to hear to such an extent it became a race to see who could get the chart hits off first. If the Beach Boys had a new single pending, there would be near frenzy on its release. We'd be obliged to have the thing off. We were able to get an audience into the like of the Television Club in Dublin to hear the rendition of this wonderful new piece of music. It was a dawdle half the time. Dead simple. Having said that, this guy Brian Wilson (the head Beach Boy) was thirty years ahead of his time. They're still trying to get the sounds he got. That's the pity of the thing. The *Good Vibrations* one was the acid test. Another band came to the Television Club one Monday night, saying to themselves...'no chance of getting this off'. We appeared on stage and did the thing to perfection.

"The Beach Boys thing was to our detriment because, at that time, we were thinking of writing our own stuff. It happened because we had a lot of singers in the band — so when the Beach Boys came out with that surfin' thing, we were able to do what nobody else could do. They hadn't enough singers. That's because the format of other bands was decided by the managerial types. The moguls said... 'right, you need a singer, trumpet, trombone, saxophone, guitar, bass and drums, That's it, a band. You're on the road, boys. Make us money...' We were a different kettle of fish because — rather than having two singers, or three at best — we had six good singers. So it seemed a sin not to utilise them when the vocalisations came out — not only the Beach Boys for which we became famous, probably more to our harm than our good, but other outfits as well like the Swingle Singers. This was a higher intellectual plane of operation. It would stage us a wee bit above the punters' heads. At the same time, nobody else could do it because they didn't have the raw materials."

The Freshmen were different from the plethora of southern showbands. The influences on them were broader. Firstly, the showband concept originated in Northern Ireland; secondly, the UK connection exposed people in the North to British musical trends. Communications were more advanced: the media offered a better choice in pop programmes. Dancehalls there were generally of a higher standard. Finally, the Derry influence was very strong in the mid-'50s: it encouraged youngsters to practice and become competent musicians. The presence of an American naval base in the Waterside area brought the contemporary sounds of the U.S. directly to the young people of Northern Ireland. It brought a touch of American culture to the city. Indeed, some Derry youngsters joined the U.S. Navy. "There were guys going around with the Benny Goodman-type glasses without any rims, and with short hair cuts," says Brown. "We used to call them Derry Americans. Whether they were actually Derrymen or Americans, or a product of both, nobody could ever figure. But it was from those guys that a lot of the talent came from. Most of them were musicians. A lot of them were war babies. There was a lot of sneaking about done in those days. There were great players — world class players — in Derry when there were no great players anywhere else in the country."

As Brown entered his teens in the late '50s, he was influenced by Johnny Quigley, whom he still rates as the best; Gay McIntyre, "a world class saxophone player," and, to an extent, by the Clipper Carlton. Brown came from a musical family: his father and uncle were musicians, playing in their own band around Larne. The sounds of his childhood were those of Glenn Miller. By his early teens, he was fascinated by Quigley, who performed a revolutionary "band show" in dancehalls across the North. The Clippers were doing it, too, around the country. Quigley had been a huge force on the dancing scene since '54. Other bands looked up to the Derryman. "It was the Johnny Quigley band show — it actually was a show," says Brown. "Musicians stood up and played. The rock'n'roll thing had just begun. The Clippers weren't so much into the rock'n'roll. They were a calypso band. It was more slapstick. They had good singers, too. But Quigley put the glamour into it. His band was superb. It was really exciting. They did all the rock'n'roll that was popular, right up to Fats Domino. At that time, bands were the substitute for the live act. They were able to present what people heard on the wireless. The only radio programmes you heard were on Radio Luxembourg. You had to stay up half the night to hear it. I think that's what made it so exciting. Quigley was the first I saw doing it. When the Royal appeared in my horizons later, they were doing the songs and had the coloured suits. But Quigley's band was the first I'd seen with all this glamour on stage and a bit of presentation.

"In the early days, most guys in bands were interested in music for its own sake. In fact, you could say that they were musicians. When showbands became what they're now known for, you didn't need to be able to play well. If you were able to play at all, you could manage. But back then you had to be good because the bands had brass players. There were instrumentalists in most of the bands. The Royal cut it down to the bare minimum — trumpet, saxophone and trombone. But in Quigley's band they had two trumpets, four saxes and a trombone player. So you had the kind of band that in America, for example, eventually became Earth, Wind and Fire. They had features that the Royal never had. The Royal were just loud and exciting because yer man was such a good singer and such an attractive guy. His forte was to sing 'hymns' on the stage. I used to wonder about that. I used to ask myself, 'what the hell is going on?' The Holy City! There was certainly substance to Quigley, and a hell of a lot of it. But there was always a tradition of that in the North anyway, mainly because of the Derry influence."

It was a big occasion when Quigley played in any town or village in the North. When Brown was old enough to get into dancehalls, he was amazed by the quality of Quigley's sound: "It was exactly as could be heard on the wireless... rock'n'roll. Initially, they were a sit- down band. They played for the first hour or hour and a half. Then there would be an interval. They appeared back on stage wearing multi- coloured suits. That was unheard of because everybody wore grey suits in those days. But these guys came on dressed in strange yellow suits and pink shirts. They'd lambaste the place... they'd be so good."

Brown first saw the Royal at Ballymena Town Hall in '59/'60. He enjoyed their performance, but couldn't understand why Bowyer sang what seemed to be hymns. "I didn't approve of the hymns. I discovered these were the pop songs of the Irish Free State. They were obviously highly acceptable to what was a mainly Catholic audience." Brown was once supposed to play with a 'relief' band in Ballymena as warm-up for the Royal. "T.J. Byrne wouldn't let us play because we had become so popular in the area he was wisely afraid that we might steal the show."

Brown played his first gigs at twelve years of age. He hung around a dancehall in Larne while still at primary school. It was an Orange Hall — later used commercially as the Plaza Ballroom. It held up to 1,000 people. A Belfast band, the Avonaires, played swing for the Saturday night dancers. The piano player was hurt in an accident and, consequently, didn't turn up one night. The band knew that young Brown could handle the job, and they offered him his first paid gig. "I got the gig over

Christmas," he says. "I was on holidays, which suited. They gave me enormous amounts of money for doing it."

By the dawn of the '60s, every youngster wanted to be in a band. Inspired by Chuck Berry, Fats Domino and Little Richard, small rock'n'roll groups mushroomed. "It was easy... so approachable. I now realise that it's very hard to play that kind of rock'n'roll right. You've got to have talent," says Brown. "But the country'n'western rockabilly thing was easily approached by any young fellow. Anybody who could lift a guitar had learned the three chords. He was able to play it well enough to keep himself happy, and probably his mates as well. Whereas, previous to that, you had to be a musician to be in a band. You had to be able to play in order to get a seat as a saxophone player. Everybody was into rock'n'roll. Kids who couldn't play quite as well formed skiffle groups. All they had to do was bash the instruments. We never heard the term showband. It was alien to us. I never heard showband mentioned until I came to the Free State. The Royal Showband was the first one I saw."

Jobs in new industries, as well as greater educational opportunities, caused a shift in the young population in the late '50s. Larne, a sea port town, became one such industrial base. Jobs were available at Associated Electrical Industries (AEI), formerly BTH, as well as at the Northern Ireland Paper Mill and Larne harbour company. Larne was the nearest industrial centre to Belfast, where jobs were not so plentiful. Brown was fifteen at the time, attending the local technical college. It would have been socially unacceptable for him to go to grammar school. There was an influx of teenagers into Larne, and a thriving music scene developed. In a similar way, Derry attracted a young population from a big rural hinterland to its Catholic secondary schools.

"That's basically how it all started," reflects Brown. "There was a population of motivated young fellows, all busting their ass to play, but not really knowing anybody in their new environment. They were brought to Larne because of the industrial opportunities and to Belfast because of the teacher training. At the same time, there were guys in Derry already able to play. The sit- down bands had been playing in Larne. There was nothing like this happening in the country areas. So that's where we met each other...in this social scene. I got interested in music by listening to the radio and being in a musical family anyway. All my mates were musically inclined as well. Birds of a feather flock together. Small dances were held in the yacht club on Friday nights. Eventually, you'd find out who were the best players. These guys were all there trying to jam. You'd pick all the good ones. Through a process of natural selection, you ended up with what should be the cream in one band. That was the nucleus of our band. Then we picked up another few guys here and there that we heard about. We had all joined other bands at different stages before the Freshmen. If you showed any glimmer of talent at all, some guy asked you to join his band. We all did that. That's how we got together eventually...because there would be one or two friends in the same band."

Brown played with semi-pro bands. The first was run by the Mitchell brothers from Ballymena, John and Bobby, nicknamed The Bisto Kids. Brown played piano; he also played sax because of a dixieland influence. He had experimented in other bands during his schooldays. He formed a dixieland group at fourteen. The Mitchell band gave him his first real 'gigs'.

Everybody wanted to be an engineer — and Brown was no exception. However, artistic talents surfaced at the tech. He won a medal in a British art competition. "A decision was taken... to hell with the engineering." He moved to Belfast where he studied to become a stained glass artist. The course was run by the art college. The practical part was done at the stained glass firm of Harry Clokey. By night, he played in the Billy McFarland band.

"I suddenly discovered that I was earning as much in the band as I was as an apprentice stained glass artist," he says. "That wouldn't be hard. The course was stopped. We were offered a dress designer course, or some shit like that. To add insult to injury, at the back of Clokeys where the stained glass studio was located, they built a new technical college. It cut off the light. Amid all this despondency, the Beatles were beginning to make waves. The music scene looked good. There were gigs in every field. I was earning about 30 bob in Clokeys. One of the senior men there was on 30 or 32 quid a week. That was good money in those days when guys filling holes in the road for the council were getting about a fiver. But I was earning more money than him at the weekends...and he had worked in this place for twenty-five years."

Brown commuted to Belfast where he was collected and taken to 'gigs'. He decided to take up music fulltime. Brown and a friend, Terry McGahey, bass player in the McFarland band, became bohemians. McGahey was "a great character, great wit and a good bass player." They led lives of leisure by day. Their behaviour irritated the other band members. "In fact, I think we may have been the catalyst in the eventual demise of the band," says Brown. "We didn't do very much during the day. That appalled a lot of people because in those days the be-all and end-all of life was a secure job: get an apprenticeship, serve your time, keep your head down, and the Unionist gentry will look after you. Those were the days when there was an industrialised proletariat. McGahey was at Methodist College and had been earmarked for a career in education, which he eventually reverted to. He's a smart guy. After a while at that, we met these other guys with whom we liked to play and with whom we had played previously. We got together for a few nights, maybe a Tuesday night gig somewhere, a local hop or something. We'd be playing for nothing. We enjoyed it so much that we started a band called the Freshmen in early '62."

The south was still virgin territory to Brown and his mates. He did, however, cross the border for a tour with McFarland as support to British singer Mike Preston who had a hit with *Mr Blue*. Preston was the archetypal pop star who looked the part. A former boxer, he went into showbusiness in 1958 with his first record — *A House, a Car, and a Wedding Ring*. The other big names in Britain were Cliff Richard and Adam Faith. Faith, who visited Ireland frequently, appeared at some gigs with Preston on that tour.

"Preston was the headliner, but the punters had only barely heard of him. I remember we played in Tooreen during the tour, Mgr Horan's operation.... we better not go into that. We also played in Drumshanbo."

The South was a 'strange' place then — as it was when the Freshmen took to the road later in the early '60s.   There was a culture shock to be overcome.   "Here was a completely alien race of people. It was a foreign country," says Brown. "Driving down through the midlands on a Sunday afternoon was just unbelievable. It was a time warp. Backward as the North may seem to be, it was fifteen or twenty years ahead of the south as far as fashion and international communications were concerned. On our first trips down, there was no mid-teenage to early twenties age group around, certainly not in the west. They'd all buggered off to England. So we were playing to a crowd of thirty-year-olds whose musical tastes were formed in the late '40s. But along came Sean Lemass who saved the day by conjuring up all this imaginary wealth and prosperity. A crowd of the heads from England came home and started families. That's why there was a music scene at all in the '70s. Galway and Roscommon were once deserts. All the young people emigrated. By the late '60s and early '70s, a whole generation of young people were able to be educated and stay at home. Begod, it was like California there for that period."

The Freshmen were a big draw in the North, but they found it difficult to crack the south. The breakthrough did not happen easily. Bands were expected to play what the country people wanted to hear. "I had nothing in common with country people, not even in the north, " says Brown. "We had a lot more in common with Cork than Dublin. The population of Dublin are from the country. It's a blow-in operation. The big dances there were run by agricultural students and boys like that. So you were really playing to a country audience all the time. Unlike Cork, Dublin didn't seem to have any indigenous city population."

The Freshmen had the pick of the best musicians: Barney McKeon, vocals; Maurice Henry, sax, "the only serious sensible man;" McGahey, bass guitar; Damien McIlroy, lead guitar; Sean Mahon, trombone; Davy McKnight, drums; Brown, sax and piano. McKeon — "the poor man's Sam Cook" — was a good singer. However, he only stayed in the band for a short period. By '62/'63 Beatlemania was beginning to break out in Britain: *Love Me Do* went into the charts, followed by their three chart toppers — *From Me To You*, *She Loves You*, and *I Want To Hold Your Hand*. "I remember standing in Damien McIlroy's kitchen one day at lunchtime having gotten up late from a gig the previous night," recalls Brown. *Love Me Do* came on the radio. I remember being interested and listening to it."

Things were happening for the Freshmen too. They found a manager, or rather a manager found them. It was a fortuitous development that led to their breakthrough in the south. Previously, sax player Maurice Henry made the bookings. It was too much to handle, as well as playing gigs by night. Along came Peter Dempsey from Andersonstown...with all the right connections across the border. Dempsey was in the motor trade. By night, he ran dances in Andersonstown. He came from a middle class Catholic background. His father was a publican, "one of the few things that enabled Catholics to rise to any sort of prominence and become middle class." He ran dances in the local church hall where he met Johnny Flynn from Tuam. His life would never be the same again. Flynn was the biggest draw in the west. His drummer, Frankie 'Flash' Hannon, was a wonder. "He was the magic in that band whether anyone realised it or not," recalls Brown. "He had this strange gift for tempos that you only hear now on the really good American country outfits. He had the same lovely feel for the thing."

Flynn took Dempsey to Tuam and taught him everything he knew about the dancing business. "You wouldn't be too long going around with Flynn before you learned the ropes. He was a great operator, a great character. Dempsey became enamoured of this lifestyle. That was the whole thing. Then he found a band of his own, which was us. I think he may have introduced himself to us rather than the other way around. But he was the best thing that ever happened to our band because he knew the Free State, which we didn't. He knew the way a Catholic population worked in an emerging society. We didn't. We were an urban society in an already developing industrial situation. We were linked to the UK, had better communications and, of course, had the Derry influence. We had a lot more in common with the UK than with a rural society in the south. But Dempsey knew the score. He had relatives in Cootehill, Co Cavan, a bit of a backwater. Being upper middle class, he also had access to good motor cars. He knew something about them which we didn't.

"We'd be driving about in 1932 Rileys which would be worth hundreds of thousands of pounds today. We were picking them up for fifteen quid among four or five of us. We once went about in a hearse actually. The father of a drummer in one of the early bands was the local undertaker. He has a pub in Larne and still laughs at the memory. They had a big Rolls Royce hearse which was scrapped as far as funerals were concerned. We eventually got a Morris J2 van, an old battered second-hand one. The trick was: we used to take off the silencer so that the exhaust would roast the floor and keep it warm inside. These were the heating arrangements. You'd be obliged to sit five, and sometimes six, in the back. One guy sat in the front. You had to sit spoon-fashion. You played cards with your feet on this lovely hot floor. Dempsey's father used to have big cars because he was an upper middle class man. At one stage he actually had a Jaguar. You couldn't get much better than that. We used to swan about in the Jaguar. At that time we were making enough money to afford good overcoats which you were obliged to swathe around your shoulders as famous men do. We hadn't quite reached the dark glasses stage."

In 1963, the Freshmen began making an impact down south. Their latest recruit was an outstanding young Limerick singer, Tommy Drennan. He had natural talent. At twelve, as a boy soprano, he trained in the choir at Mount St. Alphonsus, Limerick, under Fr. Jim Torney, "who did more for my voice than any teacher had." At thirteen, he did a broadcast for Radio Éireann and sang for Mayor Robert Wagner of New York when he visited Limerick that year.

By 1960, Drennan was entering talent contests. He studied music at the Irish Academy and sang with the Radio Eireann Orchestra in the Gaiety. He considered becoming a professional concert artiste. But, he really wanted to sing to a younger audience. Paul Russell suggested that he write to the Freshmen. Drennan had already been spotted by the Freshmen on UTV's *Teatime with Tommy* show, and they offered him a place in the band. Spotlight declared that the Freshmen were definitely "in the '63 big beat groove." Wrote a columnist: "It's a long time since I've seen a band get such a reception as the Freshmen got in Redbarn (Co. Cork) recently. The clapping finished with

(Photo: Sunday World)

the national anthem. Like the Cadets, they've got a bright '63 sound — the beatiest I've heard in fact...the wonderful, very different voice of Tommy Drennan, the striking personality of Billy Brown. I like the idea of putting drummer Davy McKnight out there in the front line. Perhaps that's why the beat is so lively."

But Drennan got homesick and returned to Limerick in '64. He joined the local Monarchs Showband, and his career blossomed. Drennan had a string of hits — among them *Boolavogue*, *Molly*, *Connemara Cradle Song*, *Come Home Rolling Stone*, *Little Boy Lost*, *Love Is A Beautiful Song*, and *O Holy Night*.

Brown desperately needed a lead singer. He filled in for a while, but his heart wasn't in the job. He wanted to remain a musician. The idea was to recruit a good-looking front man who looked like Bowyer. Word reached them of Derek McMenamin, a handsome young Catholic training to be a teacher in Belfast. Brown and Damien McIlroy interviewed him at St. Joseph's, the training college. His personality captivated them. "He had it all," recalls Brown. "He had the good looks and even looked a bit like Bowyer. He could have been a candidate for the priesthood. Women fell at his feet. He could sing well enough. In fact, he turned out to be the best bass singer I've ever heard anywhere, and I've heard a hell of a lot of them. He was ideal for the job."

The new recruit continued his studies and did not turn professional for the moment. "His parents, and indeed his whole tradition, would have been against showbiz," recalls Brown. "The reaction would have been... 'what, a Catholic emerging from Strabane in north west Ulster, the land of the white negroes, with the chance of becoming a schoolteacher, decides he wants to be a musician!...'"

The Freshmen began recording in February 1964, with little early success. They cut their first record in London: *The One You Love*, backed by *I Love My Little Girl*. It was a revival of an old hit. By June, it was released to slow handclaps. "With the music scene as it is now," said *Spotlight*, "this could have been a wrong choice for the current British market, featuring as it does a dominant sax sound. Very clever instrumental and vocal work with the voice of Billy Brown is well to the fore." The flip,

I Love My Little Girl, was composed by Brown and lead guitarist McIlroy. The Freshmen recorded, on that first outing, under the name Six of One for the Mercury label. The record flopped. Many fans, puzzled by the recording name, never realised they had a single on the market at all. "It didn't mean a light," laughs Brown.

Derek had been burning the candle at both ends, singing with the Freshmen at night and studying during the day. He eventually left the band to take his final exams. "He stayed at the teacher training college," explains Brown. "He graduated. I don't think he ever taught a child. My heart used to go out to him. We used to drop him off him outside St. Joseph's after driving up from Cork or Youghal." By summer '64, Derek had finished his finals and returned to the band. Their popularity increased enormously following appearances on Telefís Éireann's *Showband Show* and UTV's *Pop Scene*. The Freshmen announced at Christmas '64 that the tongue- twisting surname, McMenamin, had been changed to Dean. The name, Derek and The Freshmen, was used for the band's next record, made in London in January '65. Called *I Stand Alone*, it was a slow romantic ballad written by Dean. The flipside — which was the 'A' side in Britain — was a beaty number titled *Gone Away*.

The band's first chart success was *Yenka*, a Top Ten hit in November, 1965. This copperfastened their popularity in the south, particularly Cork. Brown didn't take the charts seriously: "I don't think we ever had any hit records. I had no interest in that end of thing at all once I discovered the real story about the charts. We just took it for granted that we were successful in Ireland. We were trying to crack the UK which was nearly impossible to do in those days coming from this country. For a start, the UK acts were busting their ass to get over here to make a few quid."

In '65/'66, the cult of the Freshmen was well established. Fan letters multiplied. All the girls loved Derek. "Getting down to basics," he said years later, "the object of a showband's performance was to excite the girls. Where the girls were hottest, the guys would follow, and that's how you got your crowds. So I'd get up there and do it as best I could. The best and only way I knew to 'sell' a song was to sing it and thrust my hips at the girls. I could do that as well as Elvis, whatever about the singing and the looks, so I reckoned I was on to a winner."

The Freshmen were one of few Northern bands to break into the southern ballroom circuit. Dempsey was succeeded later as manager by Oliver Barry. It took time to succeed in the south because they wanted to be regarded as a group in the American/British sense. "We weren't innovators," said Dean; "but we attained a better musical standard than most of the southern bands. When we played Cork city or county, there were queues from 9.30pm and packed houses. One night we played two gigs in the city, the Arcadia at 10pm and the City Hall at 12.30am, each to 2,500. We had to get a garda escort through the crowds of girls." The Freshmen managed to bridge the cultural and ethnic differences south of the border — thanks to Dempsey's contacts, intuition and apprenticeship in the ballrooms with Johnny Flynn. The band's best business was done at the Arcadia, in Cork; the Adelphi, Dundalk and Abbey, Drogheda.

The Freshmen tried to be different, and they came to loathe the showband tag. "This rural Irish thing was beginning to rear its ugly head," recalls Brown. "There were all sorts of bands shaping about. Most were manufactured. Look, you had 500 bands with seven or eight guys in each. They couldn't all have been good...not with a population of three and a half million souls. We detested what happened to the business because we worked so hard from a musical point of view. We believed in our music. The majority of these guys were cashing in...and they freely admitted it. The heads were there for the glamour and the readies, or else they came along with some notion of having a love of music and ended up being manipulated by their managements. We always worked as a team with our manager. He was like another member of the band. Businessmen were now building empires for themselves. They started agencies and found a clatter of bands. The musicians were faceless people. Businessmen took over. We had been going long before that explosion took place in the mid-'60s. We had a history of dedication to music and professionalism. In our time, you had to be a musician first and foremost. But later on, people got the idea that if you could hold a guitar, and had the knack, you could be in a band.

That explains why no real success came out of the showbands. The business was swamped.

"Any talent that existed was fragmented. There might have been the odd guy in some of the better bands who knew what he was talking about. The talented guy who could handle the gig — the equivalent of today's Stevie Winwood — would be put to the back of the pack. He was made a faceless man who one week played for 'X and the All Stars' and, in eight months' time, was transferred to 'Somebody Else and the All Stars'. Nobody was the wiser.

At the same time, there were a lot of good journeymen players, perhaps in the same position with maybe no aspirations of international stardom. We were doing different material as well. We had men in the band of great insight. Derek had a genius for discovering what the punters wanted. He used to hatch these plots. He was a bit cynical about it actually a lot of the time. Much of it was tongue in cheek. At the same time, the bass player, McGahey, had an ear to what was going on in the U.S. He'd be listening to what the avant garde was doing there as far as popular music was concerned — or rock as it became."

The Freshmen made big money — and spent it. The Royal had turned the business into a bonanza — for the top bands, at least. The Waterford band made the financial ground rules. Brown once spotted the Royal driving through the streets of Larne. He was on the way to a 'gig' of his own. He knew they were earning a lot more money than him, and he tried to imagine what their income meant in real terms. The biggest Ford car on the market, a Zephyr, cost roughly £1,100 new. He figured that the Royal were taking in about £100 a week each. Therefore, it would take them only ten weeks to be able to afford that car. But the Freshmen soon graduated to the exclusive club of top earners. Not all earnings were spent on the good life.

"We also invested in equipment, which nobody else really did to much extent," says Brown. "In fairness, I must say that Jim Conlon of the Royal had the first Fender electric guitar, a red one. I don't know how we discovered about Fender. We must have been reading American music publications. McGahey got the first Fender bass guitar ever to appear on this side of the pond. It was a big white one, a superb instrument. That's the way we were thinking. We were looking seriously into the thing, wrongly perhaps. We were spending money on PA and stuff which nobody ever dreamt of doing." The Freshmen's *Papa-oo-Mow-Mow* reached No. 7 over Christmas '67 and stayed in the charts for eight weeks. The next releases were: *Go Granny Go*, at No. 12 in August '68; *Just To See You Smile*, No. 9 in March '69; and *Halfway To Where*, No. 10 in April 1970.

Offstage, the Freshmen lived like princes. Brown moved into the Great Southern Hotel in Galway during its heyday, permanently... "shelves up, pictures on the wall." Every luxury was at his command. In the same breath, he says it's easy to exaggerate the lifestyle: to stay in a hotel of such standard may still be regarded as a privilege today. Brown once bought a Porsche — as a second car. "We used to think nothing of that kind of thing." Brown liked the high lifestyle and makes no apologies for having indulged himself: "There are two ways of looking at it, and this still goes for all high-success pop bands. It's such a hard routine that you have two choices: either you live like a rat, save money and have a life of utter misery or else you enjoy it. The non-smokers and non-drinkers, who never spent a bob, live in misery to this day. While they may be comfortably off, they're still miserable."

The Freshmen toured the ballrooms of Britain and the U.S. when Lent brought the shutters down on the business in Ireland. America was something else: a vast playground waiting to be explored. The band was obliged to play to Irish Americans but, luckily, avoided being sucked into what Brown calls the 'Paddy trap'. Leading members of the Irish community waited for them to arrive at airports. They wanted to whisk the band off on a 'green' tour of Irish pubs, restaurants and halls. They wanted to reinforce their own perception of the 'ould sod,' and a visiting Irish showband gave them the opportunity. "Paddies would try to usher you off and show you Ireland as if nothing had changed," says Brown in disgust. "I didn't want to see that at all. I wanted to see the States. So we did our own thing really. We had great crack."

They played at the London Palladium, which became virtually an established venue for Irish bands in the mid-'60s... "so you wouldn't want to get carried away by that." The band set their sights on breaking into the British market as the glitter of the showbands began to fade. They took recording more seriously and landed a deal with CBS. That marked their return to the charts with *Halfway to Where*, a Top Ten hit in April 1970. "We were beginning to get things together," says Brown. "We'd done a big album for CBS. We'd written some of the stuff on that. It would have been one of the first of the major deals. The album got as far as being recorded and released. Fame at last: when you get to London airport, a man appears in a limousine with a cap on... and all this carry on. We were lucky to get out of that actually. The strategy was that if you were big abroad, then you could really clean up here."

In April 1971, Brown formed his own band and resumed the dancehall circuit. The line-up: Billy Brown, piano, vocals; Dessie Reynolds, drums; John Brown, bass; Keith Donald, sax; Pascal Haverty, sax; Tiger Taylor, lead guitar; Mick Nolan, trumpet. "Technically, it was a good band," says Donald who, a decade later, joined Christy Moore's Moving Hearts. "However, we lacked originality. We were still doing covers and not enough of our own material. We were still essentially a showband." The band lasted less than a year. The Freshmen continued to play on into the '70s. They climbed to No. 3 in the charts at Christmas '76 with *And God Created Woman*. Brown had two other Top Ten hits: *Leaving of Liverpool*, which went to No. 5 in March '74 and *Cinderella*, No. 3 in March '77.

By the late '70s, the Freshmen were a perishable commodity against the background of rapid change in the music business. They were world-weary and tired. Boredom set in. Still, the band outlived most showbands and survived well into the new decade. "The Freshmen just died a natural death really," concludes Brown. "It's a young man's game, regardless of how many wrinklies and grey beards are still staggering about. We were bored: the same ould gig; the same punters, bless them; playing other people's music not very well. At that stage, there were so many bands on the road there weren't any punters left who had any interest in music. That's because anybody in the country with the slightest interest in music had joined a band. There were no punters."

The wild days of youth have now given way to middle-age stability and contentment. Brown and Dean, like other symbols of the swinging sixties in Ireland, have seen and done enough in one decade to fill a lifetime for most mortals. Brown's talents are now channelled into art: he paints, mostly landscapes and wildlife. It's a far cry from the ballrooms: "I enjoyed it. There was no room for cynicism. That didn't appear until showbands became what we now know them as. Previously, the business was full of... not naivete but sheer enthusiasm. Nothing like it had ever been tried before by anybody. Anything that happened to us felt like a breakthrough..."

The Head Hunters

Jury's Hotel, Cork, Friday, July 29th, 1988.

Frank Dileo, flamboyant manager of Michael Jackson, is holding court at a table in the bar of Jury's Hotel. The superstar is elsewhere — behind locked doors in his suite of rooms, numbers 274 and 275. Dileo, surrounded by his entourage and CBS executives, takes deep gulps from a pint of Murphy's. The drink reminds him of beer brewed in his native Pittsburgh — except for the weird colour. The larger-than-life manager wisecracks with six middle-aged men who run the Jackson show and who look about as menacing as a convention of greengrocers. The exception is Dileo's portly bodyguard who could probably last a couple of rounds with any top boxer. Upstairs, their eccentric paymaster with a surgically restructured face practises dance routines on a specially-fitted floor in his suite.

Dileo — fired by Jackson seven months later — lives up to his Hollywood image: short, with a figure that makes Buddha look slimline; hair scraped back in a short ponytail; a sawn-off cigar; and the abrasive bonhomie. A vegetarian dish is being prepared for Jackson by his personal chef in the kitchen. Dileo is hungry, too, but doesn't share the same tastes: he orders a large tray of deep-fried chicken pieces and then promptly tells the waiter to bring 'hot sauce'. He showers half the bottle over the chicken, turns to me, and says: 'Eat, kid'. Sandwiched between Dileo and his minder, I'm in no position to refuse. Enter Oliver Barry, the quintessential Corkman who once promoted Sean Dunphy and the Hoedowners, and the Freshmen. Today, it's Michael Jackson.

'Ollie' — as Dileo calls him — joins the tour handlers. He has the confidence of the man who, for the moment, controls Jackson's four billion dollar empire. It's a strange partnership: the elder statesman of Irish showbands and a small fat man from the Bronx who was once described as a pocket battleship, well equipped to shake you by the hand or tear off your entire arm. Dileo's golden boy — the singing, dancing friend of animals, children and music business accounting departments — will 'moonwalk' within twenty hours at Pairc Ui Chaoimh, a bastion of GAA culture. Barry orders a soft drink, runs over a few last-minute details with Dileo and tour co-ordinator Sal Bonafede, and then slips away to set the stage for the two Jackson 'gigs'...just like the old days. It may seem worlds removed from running dances at the Crystal Ballroom in Dublin, but Barry sees a connection. The picture is bigger, and the stakes higher. Barry uses the same skills learned in the ballrooms of romance in order to hook a big 'draw', make money at the box office and send the 'punters' home sweatin'. "It's the same thing really," he reflects. "I'm still dealing with people. The same rules apply. The risk element always attracted me — except that the risks are much greater now." The glamour attractions of the '60s in Ireland — the Royal, Capitol, Miami and Drifters — are replaced by world names like Jackson, Prince, Madonna and U2.

Equally, it seems a monumental journey from the Crystal to a seat at Frank Sinatra's table in Reno, Nevada. When Barry and a travelling companion from Fermoy, John McCarthy, were feted there by Ol' Blue Eyes in July 1989, in the aftermath of his Dublin concert, a few mysterious phrases in conversation offered clues to the Corkmens' showband roots. Barry and McCarthy still use the Ben-Lang...whether on board Jumbo jets or in the fanciest hotels of Los Angeles, Las Vegas, Reno, New York and Atlantic City. While Barry promoted bands, McCarthy played in one, Michael O'Callaghan's big band from Buttevant. He went on to become a wealthy motor dealer.

Barry, like northerner Jim Aiken, was infected with a virulent form of the '60s entrepreneurial spirit. They are products of an environment in which those who dared frequently won. The Corkman served his apprenticeship in the dancehalls of Dublin while working as a laboratory technician at the Agricultural Institute. Aiken served his time in the halls of Belfast while working as a schoolteacher, and he used that early experience in dance promotion to earn a place for Ireland, years later, on the international circuit for the mega stars — a port of call as lucrative as any other during the '80s. Both men gave up steady jobs to translate the glamour of showbands into profit. Their business acumen and vaulting ambition pushed them ever onward long after the bands had ground to a halt.

Both are opportunists and risk-takers to varying degrees. A gambling instinct motivates them; the rewards are great... the pitfalls, treacherous. Today, the stakes are infinitely higher, but the business remains essentially the same: the box office is still the final test. Big league concert promotion is not for the faint-hearted. Aiken and Barry are masters of the calculated risk: set up the deal, trust your judgment and keep your cool. Both promoters have basked in glorious successes and suffered spectacular failures.

Barry was the youngest of a family of seven whose parents ran a fruit and veg business in Banteer. He was a keen sportsman. A Harty Cup player with St. Colman's College, Fermoy, he's proud of the college's hurling tradition and never misses the PPU's annual dinner. After five years at St. Colman's, he worked for a further year in the family business with his brother, Jim, who now runs a multi-million pound cash and carry business in Mallow. They had a fleet of vans. Oliver was in charge of deliveries to Killarney. It wasn't unusual for him to sell a load of fruit and vegetables to one customer. He was a good salesman. Then, like many another Corkman, he got a job in the civil service in Dublin where he worked in the Agricultural Institute for £13 a week. The country boy saw opportunity in the crowds flocking to ballrooms around the city.

By day, he worked as a lab technician; by night as a dance promoter booking bands for the Crystal, the CIE club and the Kingsway. Barry first promoted dances with Mick Nolan, a work colleague; then Jim Hand became involved. These ventures were 'mickey mouse'. Says Barry: "It was very exciting. The crack was good. Remember, the 'crack' was more important than anything else at the time."

Barry's next move was into showband management. In the Shelbourne Hotel, he noticed Earl Gill and his orchestra doing a regular spot. He seized them, and they went full-time as the Hoedowners, with whom Gill was trumpeter-in-chief. Barry responded to the showband craze by transforming the act, with Sean Dunphy as the frontman. He arranged a TV show for them in 1965. It was a success. Dunphy went on to win the National

Song in 1967 with *If I Could Choose*, and he was second at the Eurovision final in Vienna. Two years later, Dunphy had two No. 1 hits that became huge sellers — *Lonely Woods of Upton*, in the charts for twenty-four weeks, and *When The Fields Are White With Daisies*, in the charts for fourteen.

Barry's ability to spot the right act re-surfaced in 1966 when he saw the potential of the Wolfe Tones. It was to become an association that lasted for twenty-three years. Barry gave up the day job to concentrate on band management. His style was intensely personal. The strategy was to keep the number of acts in his stable to a handful: first the Wolfe Tones...then the Champions, Stockton's Wing and, for a while, Bagatelle. The Tones gave him a bridge from the dying showband to the cabaret boom of the early '70s.

Meantime, Barry's close friend, Jim Hand, began his career as a 'band follower, as distinct from being involved in it'. He says: "I just drifted into it. I started running a few dances with some of the bands. From then it just snowballed. I was a groupie, basically. I followed the bands from the Clippers to the Royal. I got involved in public relations. I saw a way, I thought, to make money and not get up in the morning. I was lazy. I still don't get up in the morning, and I've no money. I got involved with Associated Ballrooms about 1964/65. They used to bring in acts from England to their ballrooms around the country. The Arcadia in Bray held over 3,000 people. I used to act as tour manager for groups like the Tremeloes, the Marmalade, Status Quo, Tom Jones and Engelbert Humperdinck. I was in the PR end of things, making sure they got publicity and record plays. I ended up fixing and selling dates, particularly in the North."

Hand became friendly with Tom Jones on his Irish tours. He recalls one funny incident: "I remember bringing Tom to Omagh. That was on a Friday night. On the Saturday night we were coming back through my home town, Drogheda. I decided to take Tom in to see Blessed Oliver's head in a local church. It's just a skull. I met Tom years later in Belfast when Brendan Grace was doing support for him. We met backstage. The first thing he said to me was, 'how's Blessed Oliver Plunkett'? I said, 'Tom, would you believe, he's a saint'. He knelt down and blessed himself and said, 'I'm delighted'."

After a two year spell with Associated Ballrooms, Hand went to work for George O'Reilly whose office managed a string of bands. "I was more or less managing Dermot O'Brien, selling dates and organising tours," he recalls. In 1968/69, Hand and Barry formed a company called International Artistes Limited with offices in Burgh Quay. Hand managed Paddy Reilly; Barry looked after the Hoedowners and the Freshmen, having succeeded Peter Dempsey as manager of the latter. "Peter made an enormous contribution to the business. Then Oliver took us on after that," recalls Derek Dean. "It was a well- orchestrated attack on the dancing public."

At the height of Beatlemania, Barry and Hand turned up at Apple headquarters in London and presented themselves to the renowned singer/songwriter team with the words: "Hello John, hello Paul: I'm Jim, he's Oliver. We're in the dancing game ourselves." They were trying to interest Apple in the Freshmen, who had recorded a cover version of *Yesterday*. "We were involved in a company called Dolphin Records then," says Hand. "We started that company with Jim Aiken and Vincent Nolan. Dolphin Records had the Wolfe Tones, Sean Dunphy, and the Freshmen. We tried to get a deal for the label with Apple. That's why we were in Apple that day."

Hand saw the writing on the wall for showbands in 1970/71: "I knew it was a phenomenon. It was the only country in the world where, in the pop end of things, you had bands just doing cover versions. That couldn't last. The major record companies were coming in here. The whole record thing had just started. There had been a time when showbands could do a cover version of a hit and actually sell it here. That couldn't last. I saw the ballad scene as the only thing that was definitively Irish, and could travel. The Dubliners were an international act before I had them. Paddy Reilly is a huge attraction with immigrants in the UK, and in America. Then I had the Fureys. I managed them very successfully for eight years. I broke into the English and Australian charts with *Sweet Sixteen*. I didn't create the Dubliners. I took them over on the year of their twenty- fifth anniversary. I organised the *Late Late Show* special. I felt that they had a cult following among young people who didn't know them twenty years ago. I really went for the idea of a single with the

Pogues. *The Irish Rover* was a huge hit and gave the Dubliners a new lease of life, and a new audience. The Dubliners haven't cracked the American market, but maybe Bono and Ronnie will get together on a single or album. It would be great for both of them. They have a lot of respect for one another. Bono did one for B.B. King... why not Ronnie too?"

Unlike Barry, Hand was never tempted by big-time concert promotions: "That's not my bag. I'm not even a booker. I'm a personal manager. I have to be personally involved with the group... decide what type of records they record. You've got to have the gambling instinct for concert promotion. Both Oliver Barry and Jim Aiken are known gamblers. They would back their judgment. There are ups and downs in that game. I wouldn't trust my judgment. I wouldn't have a clue about the organisation of staff, security and staging."

Hand survived the demise of the showbands: "I survived because of thinking right, obviously. Luck has a certain amount to do with it... the Dubliners walking in to me on their twenty-fifth anniversary. I grabbed it with both hands, and it worked... Brendan Grace the same. I stuck with Paddy Reilly. My belief is that the hit single is almighty. I've made the English charts three times from Dublin with the Fureys, the Dubliners and, I *still* claim, Johnny Logan."

Meantime, Barry concentrated on promoting his own acts in the early '70s — the Wolfe Tones were his biggest seller. In 1975, he went to Hamburg to lure James Last to Ireland. The orchestra's regular visits attracted full houses, and there were memorable open-air concerts in Dublin and Tralee in '85. When Siamsa Cois Laoi first began in 1977, it was inevitable that Barry, a passionate GAA man, would be the impresario to give the festival a much-needed impetus. It began as a folksy, homely alternative to the mega acts presented by Jim Aiken at Slane Castle. The GAA had a huge debt hanging over Pairc Ui Chaoimh. Siamsa was later superseded at the end of the '80s by Barry's big star promotions — first U2 in '87, jointly promoted with Aiken; then Jackson for two concerts in '88, and Prince, who only sold one concert amid World Cup fever in 1990.

The Jackson contract was pursued with characteristic single-mindedness. A story relevant to that campaign illustrates the cute Corkman at work. Barry was summoned by world tour co-ordinator Bonafede to attend a meeting in Los Angeles during January '88 to finalise the dates. There also were other big European promoters present, including Barry Clayman from Britain and Marcel Avram from Germany. Although Bonafede was fairly familiar with the Cork stadium since his promotion of John Denver there in '86, he sought detailed plans. Barry gave a commitment to have the plan within twenty-four hours. The problem: he didn't have it. Barry was staying with McCarthy at the Beverly Wiltshire Hotel. Barry put on his thinking cap. He had installed fax machines in his Dublin office, and he instructed his staff by phone to get a plan of Pairc Ui Chaoimh from the GAA. He then told them to split it into twenty sections, number them individually, and run them through the fax machines direct to the Beverly Wiltshire. When Barry and McCarthy came down for breakfast next morning, the faxed pieces of paper were waiting for them. They spread out the numbered pages on the floor of Barry's bedroom, got down on their knees and taped them together. He honoured his commitment.

As Barry and Aiken ran dances in Dublin and Belfast during the first half of the '60s, another budding entrepreneur cut his teeth at the Arcadia Ballroom in Cork. Robin Power, a dental student, promoted dances there with three friends — John Barry, Jack Cantillon and Eddie Kenneally. They called themselves the 'Dinosaurs'. They gave discounts to students and booked the cream of the showbands. "Robin turned out to be a top-class negotiator," recalled UCC President Michael Mortell when he awarded the dentist-turned-property tycoon an honorary law degree a quarter of a century later. "He cut deals with the likes of Oliver Barry and Noel Pearson," said Mortell. "Not unconnected is the fact that he was also a very good poker player and had a great ability to read people and know when to call a bluff. If William Trevor is the author of *The Ballroom of Romance,* then Robin was probably the proprietor."

Power made quite a bit of money out of the showbands. He spotted a gap in the dance market, and the 'Dinosaurs' were born. "The big bands had some free dates mid-week," he explains. "There was no mid-week dance in Cork. The UCC students didn't go to Saturday night dances. There was a market opportunity. We had the biggest and most profitable mid-week dance in the country." Power did business with the majority of showband managers — mainly Barry, Pearson, Tom Costello, Tommy Hayden and Mick Quinn. Two of his biggest drawing bands were the Freshmen and Chessmen who enjoyed enormous support in Cork. A quarter of a century after the Chessmen played their first date in Co. Cork, at the Majorca in Crosshaven, they reunited for a performance at the Cork Summer Festival in the City Hall on July 30th, 1990.

Power also ran a beat club, known as The Crypt, during summertime at the seaside resort of Youghal. He was assisted by Rory Gallagher's brother, Donal. The club gave a platform to Cork-based groups. Power's favourite showbands were the Dixies and Freshmen. He learned valuable off-campus lessons that stood to him later in his career as a property developer. He says: "It's the same thing really. You try to look for all the risks and then eliminate as many of them as possible to increase your chances of success. The same basic rules apply to any business. You look to get value for money and to give value so that there will be repeat business."

Power graduated with a BDS degree in 1966. After a year spent chasing his fortune in England, he returned to Cork and set up a dental practice with a friend, John Barry, at MacCurtain Street. He opened a small restaurant in Paul Street and later split the property into boutiques. Power and some friends acquired a site at Marino Point which was sold afterwards to NET. It was to be his first major deal. Power abandoned a career pulling teeth. Motivated by the wheeling-and- dealing of big business, he set up a property company in 1973 that went public in 1987. Power Corporation, of which he is chairman and chief executive, became the largest listed public Irish property company in terms of market capitalisation. The empire stretched from Cork to London and further afield to Los Angeles. In the '60s, Power kept the students entertained by booking bands at the Arcadia. In the '80s, he drew on at least some of the lessons learned in the dancehalls to keep the banks and shareholders happy and his corporation ahead of the rest.

Another Corkman, Denis Desmond, watched the 'hip' bands, whose repertoire was far more 'daring' than the others, at the

Arcadia and Majorca Ballrooms. His favourites were Granny's Intentions, the Plattermen, Real McCoy, Chessmen, Tweed and the Billy Brown band. Granny's Intentions had a Top Ten hit in December '68 with their pop single, *Never an Everyday Thing*. Desmond, a civil engineering student at UCC, recalls that they were an unorthodox group who managed to invade the ballrooms and achieve success. "I got the buzz watching these groups," he says. Desmond served his apprenticeship as a "trainee manager" with a local rock group, Sleepy Hollow, during 1970/71. He soldiered alongside Joe O'Herlihy, later to become U2's sound engineer. Sleepy Hollow frequently played on the same bill as Rory Gallagher's Taste. Desmond made the bookings and learned how to cut a deal. Those early experiences proved a useful grounding for his career as one of Ireland's biggest concert promoters in the '80s.

"The lessons were basically in striking deals," he reflects. "I learned the business first from a management side and then, later on, from the promotions side. There's no great mystery or no great master plan. Promoting is simply a form of gambling. Nothing is a sure thing — otherwise everyone would be doing it. At the end of the day, the deal itself is all important. My rule of thumb in selecting artistes is their album sales. I'm not interested in hit singles because they're usually a flash in the pan. A good way of checking an artiste's popularity is to look at their back catalogue."

Desmond, boss of MCD Promotions, achieved one of his greatest successes over the August bank holiday weekend in 1990 when he promoted the first Feile at the GAA capital of Thurles. The three-day music extravaganza at Semple Stadium became the latest addition to the rock music calendar. It enticed a 'who's who' of Ireland's top acts to help lower a debt on the stadium: among them Van Morrison, Hothouse Flowers, Christy Moore, An Emotional Fish, Mary Black, Something Happens and The 4 of Us. As a promoter, Desmond is highly rated by Jim Aiken.

While Desmond was a 'punter' in Cork, up north, Aiken, a science teacher, made the equivalent of a year's salary out of one dance on Shrove Tuesday, 1964, at the Ulster Hall in Belfast. He counted the profits of that extra-curricular activity at the back of the school laboratory next day. The notes piled up on a desk and made a grand total of £650. It was a small fortune. Aiken found it impossible to set his achievement in any meaningful context, and comparison with his reward for hours of toil in the classrooms was pointless. That tot convinced him that his future was outside the sombre classrooms of the Christian Brothers.

Aiken, who today deals in millions, still recalls the elation at having made his annual salary as a teacher in one night as a promoter. "Those kind of earnings have never been replaced — that level of profit relative to everything else," he says. His other indelible memory is an appearance by the Royal Showband at the Ulster Hall on New Year's Eve, 1960. It was their first visit to Belfast — courtesy of Aiken — and word spread like wildfire about the hot act from the south. People queued for hours, and 4,000 rocked into the new decade with Brendan Bowyer. It was a state-of-the-art production, the likes of which had never been seen in Belfast. This was Aiken's first flirtation with the big-time, and he liked the feeling. "It was something that nobody had ever before perceived could happen. That set the tempo for the whole decade of the showbands."

Aiken first met T.J. Byrne in September 1959. His assessment of the Royal's hustler-in-chief merits some respect. It comes, after all, from a promoter who has since brought the biggest acts in the world to Ireland, and who has done business with the craftiest managers everywhere. He says: "T.J. was as talented a manager as I have ever met in any field. He possibly did not fulfil his full capabilities. He would be fully capable of managing a major worldwide act today. What made him so special was his courage in asking outrageous fees, convincing you that the band would do the business and then the band promptly doing that business."

Aiken was brought up in Jonesboro, Co. Armagh. He was a keen footballer as a teenager, and retained his interest in sport when he became a student at Maynooth Seminary. He played county football for Armagh. "I set out in life to go to Maynooth, and that was the first thing I did," he recalls. "I was going to be the best organiser that ever went through it; I was going to build, and I was going to win county championships and All-Ireland finals. Organising is the one skill that I like using. The reward does not have to be good." Aiken didn't continue his studies as a clerical student and decided instead to pursue a career in teaching. He taught at Hardinge Street CBS. He established a reputation as a tough but fair teacher.

Bands that he danced to did not play in Belfast. He wanted to change that; one way was to run your own dance. Initially, he promoted dances at St. Mary's Hall in Smithfield. He also ran dances in marquees across the north when showbands played for huge crowds at parish carnivals at summertime. The Freshmen, for instance, were popular at a marquee in Andersonstown. Aiken soon enticed cross-channel groups to the north.

Aiken took the first significant step when he moved operations to the Orpheus Ballroom on the top floor of the Co-op building in downtown Belfast. It became one of the most successful venues on the showband circuit in the north. Aiken ran dances there, under the title 'Big Band Date', every Tuesday night. The top draws were the Royal, Dixies, Capitol, Miami, Drifters, Cadets, Clippers, Pacific and Johnny Quigley. After he launched himself into the Orpheus, his business began to take off. "Jim took it over on Tuesday, a ridiculously 'off' night," recalls Jackie Flavelle. "He brought in the big showbands and I remember it was stuffed with people. He also brought in the English pop groups. He was the first proper impresario in Belfast doing this kind of thing. He was the first one to have a proper office and to run the business on a professional level."

But, before Aiken turned to promotions fulltime, he taught by day and made money in the dancehalls by night. His flair for organisation lay dormant in the strictly-ordered teaching routine. Once classes were over, Aiken metamorphosed into a creature of the night. The first band he booked was the Melody Aces. He liked the organisational demands of drawing all the strands together — tickets, advertising, posters, promotion, venue — for a project that started and finished within a few hours. His next target was a Cork band fast making a name for themselves: the Dixies. One Sunday, he drove down to the Olympia in Waterford to find out what made them so special. He liked what he saw, and became the first promoter to take the Dixies to Belfast.

As the '60s progressed, the Royal epitomised the new spirit of freedom. Their success at the Ulster Hall boosted Aiken as a promoter. He booked them for regular 'gigs' in Belfast: the Orpheus on Tuesday nights, the Floral Hall on Saturdays and the Ulster Hall on big nights. When the Starlight opened later on, there was a country jamboree on the bill every Thursday night, featuring performers such as Big Tom and Philomena Begley. Weekends were devoted entirely to showbands. By 1964, Aiken had carved his own niche in the business.

Nevertheless, he was a little anxious about throwing up a secure teaching job. Finally, that year, he quit the academic world — a decision that would have profound effects on the future of Irish showbusiness. In August 1964, he put on two concerts by the Clancy Brothers and Tommy Makem in the Ulster Hall. Both sold out. Within three years, he was setting the stage for the world's biggest names, including Tom Jones and Engelbert Humperdinck.

Side-by-side with those early dance promotions, Jim and his brother, Michael, sold insurance. Aiken Insurance did business with the showband fraternity. As a promoter, Aiken regards the success of the Royal at the Ulster Hall as a highlight of his showband years —in the same way that Bruce Springsteen at Slane proved to be the highlight of his career mounting large scale rock concerts two decades later. In terms of profit and numbers, the Royal came top of his list in the '60s and, by the same criteria, his running order for the '80s was Springsteen followed by Neil Diamond, U2, Chris de Burgh and Queen.

The 'troubles' destroyed the ballroom business in the north years before it faded away in the south. "Everything was going well until 1970," says Aiken. "Then many ballrooms closed. Dancing transferred to hotels. The ballrooms never recovered. The business moved to licensed function rooms in hotels. The smaller type of disco event started. The era of having 2,000 people at a dance ended. It became viable to put 400 or 500 into a hotel ballroom for a disco. That became the norm, which still exists. In 1972, I couldn't get back into dancing. I'd missed all the dancing thing. It had transferred to hotels. Then I started to do international acts in 1974."

It was a monumental task in those days to convince the big names to appear in a city that was a by-word for violence all over the world. Access to the handlers wasn't easy. Aiken was unknown outside Ireland. He quickly discovered the futility of ringing an agent in New York or Los Angeles and saying: "I'm Jim Aiken. I'm a promoter from Belfast." Ready access came only years later after extensive contact-building. Initially, it was a hard-sell. He would take a flight to Los Angeles, announce that he'd come specially from Ireland to see a particular agent and cross his fingers that the agent would be sufficiently impressed to respond. Next came the deal. First, he tried to find out the dates on which the artiste was free; produced the right venue; agreed on money, and in the currency they wanted to be paid. For instance, ABBA insisted on Swiss francs; other acts wanted German marks. If a deal was on, anything from the full fee to 50% had to be paid in advance. Artistes who demanded the full amount up front were those who had not done business with him before. Finally, there was the event itself: meeting the requirements of the artiste, organising accommodation for the visiting party, travel arrangements, promotions, advertising and making sure that every wish of the star, no matter how bizarre, was fulfilled.

One story illustrates the kind of unpredictable business Aiken is locked into. Legal agreements frequently stipulate that a performer be taken to the nearest airport at a specific time in order to fulfil touring schedules elsewhere. A rock'n'roll singer once refused to comply on the morning after a performance on stage at the Carlton Cinema in O'Connell Street, Dublin. He wouldn't get out of bed at the nearby Gresham Hotel to catch a flight at 11.30am...until he had polished off a bottle of brandy.

Another story gives an insight into the high-risk business. On May 16th, 1982, Aiken brought the re-united Simon and Garfunkel to Ireland for an open-air concert in Dublin. It was to be an evening he wouldn't forget in a hurry. At 7pm — an hour before the duo and their band were due on stage before 25,000 fans — the roof over the special stage was lifted off by a sudden gust of wind. Rain-filled clouds threatened disaster. Aiken could have cancelled the concert and subsequently collected insurance, but he decided to carry on. Simon and Garfunkel's management warned that if it started to rain, their stars would walk off. The clouds hovered ominously throughout the two hours of music, but never released a drop of rain. "My gamble paid off," he said later. "It was the biggest risk I had ever taken. I still tremble when I think of what was at risk that evening."

Since rising to the top of his trade in 1982, he has staged the biggest acts in the world here — among them Bob Dylan, the Rolling Stones, David Bowie, Neil Diamond, Queen, Springsteen, and U2. He teamed up with Lord Henry Mount Charles of Slane Castle, and that gave him access to the largest open-air venue in Ireland throughout the '80s. The fact is that — despite the ups and downs and misgivings of local residents — a succession of the world's major acts played there. This gained international status for Ireland as a stage for rock'n'roll. Aiken always believed that Slane was the world's best open-air venue. Before he paved the way, major artistes by-passed Ireland. The attitude of tour managers was that the 'crack' would be great, but the organisation a shambles. Aiken set out to prove them wrong. If somebody decided to include, for posterity, a brief history of the Irish entertainment industry in a time capsule, a reference to him might simply read: "Jim Aiken, promoter, Belfast — showed that Ireland could mount large scale rock concerts on a par with anywhere in Europe or America."

Aiken's knowledge of concert promotion is enormous. He can hold his own in the company of the best promoters. No more than thirty promoters worldwide are regarded as the real professionals in that they have the funds, connections and expertise to set the stage for the most sought-after performers. In his own words: "It's nice to know that if there was a meeting of promoters tomorrow, I could hold my head high and say I've handled most of the biggest acts and few promoters have done any better than me. I would put myself and my operation up there with the best of them. We can do it as well here as anywhere else in the world. Not second best; not taking fellows in from England to help. Just that we can do it as well as anywhere in the world. When acts leave, they say you did a fabulous job. There are no narks about payment; no narks about performance. You sign a contract and you keep every point. Your word is your bond."

At the end of the '80s, nearly all the biggest names in entertainment had performed in Ireland — promoted by Aiken, Barry and Desmond. Competition between them is inevitable in the hunt for world class acts like Sinatra, Jackson or Prince. The media hypes their rivalry as a million pound shoot-out, but they say that's exaggerated. Aiken describes Barry as 'a game one'. He says: "If I pick up the paper and read that I've lost an act, I don't blame the promoter who's got it. I'd be more inclined to blame the person who gave the act away because of our relationship over the years." Barry says that there's no war, and that the competition comes from all European promoters.

In making a play for an act, Barry concentrates his energies on the best offer and the best venue. He'll 'sweeten' a deal or increase the money if need arises. For example, while on the verge of realising a lifelong ambition to stage Sinatra in Dublin in 1989, a last-minute hitch almost wrecked the plan. During his tour in the U.S. Sinatra was 'pissed off' after spending three days in Michigan. Tour boss Elliot Wiseman asked him: "If you're pissed off now, how are you going to feel in Europe when you're away for maybe six weeks?" Sinatra replied: "Cut it." That meant if the European tour was to be pruned, then Dublin would get the chop. Wiseman told Barry the bad news.

"It was a bit of a knock," says the Corkman. "I thought the thing was lost then." Barry slept on it overnight and phoned Wiseman next day. He offered to fly out to the U.S. to iron out any difficulties. That wasn't necessary, he was told. In exasperation, Barry asked: "Is there anything we can do to make sure he makes it. What would attract him?" Wiseman replied: "Money." Barry increased his offer. The deal was back on. The Ultimate Event was a success.

In his campaigns, Aiken places store on his record and he tends to be more cautious on money matters. He says: "With certain acts, your performance is more important than your offer. With others the most important thing is the offer. Where it's performance, I'll have a reasonable chance. Where it's on money, I will not be foolish. If it's the money, I won't be afraid to spend. But I would be afraid to be foolish."

Although often in the headlines, most of Aiken's work is routine and unexciting. He shies away from the limelight and prefers the simple things in life. He's conservative by nature, an unlikely candidate for the glitzy world of showbusiness. Like Barry, he's more comfortable attending a football match than a cocktail party. Aiken and Barry are conventional businessmen who prefer to get on with the job. Before any of his concerts, the big northerner can be seen out front, talking to security men and checking for forged tickets.

Aiken rarely attends his own post-concert parties and, instead, supervises the dismantling of the stage and loading of equipment. Typically, following U2's spectacular New Year's Eve concert at Dublin's Point Depot, broadcast live to Europe, it was business as usual for Aiken during the first hours of 1990. He breezed through a party upstairs and headed for the empty concert arena where he directed dismantling operations. As I stood with him on the balcony and watched crews at work, Aiken stared below at the frenetic activity and said: "This is what my business is all about. My life is down there."

Although now sufficiently established to conduct his affairs by phone or fax, Aiken, like Barry, will not hesitate to catch the next flight to the U.S. if personal contact is required. That's what he did in July 1989 while arranging dates for Neil Diamond at the RDS. His routine that week displayed the kind of stamina needed to be a top promoter: "I was in Dublin on a Tuesday. I decided that I was getting nowhere on the phone. So I flew to L.A. on Wednesday via Paris. I was in L.A. on Thursday. The entire week went like this: I did Belfast on Monday, Dublin on Tuesday, Dublin and Paris on Wednesday, Paris to L.A. on Wednesday, L.A. on Thursday, L.A. to London to Dublin to Belfast on the Saturday. I was home on Sunday."

Aiken draws parallels between jetting off to L.A. to negotiate the Diamond concerts and driving from one end of Ireland to the other to book a showband back in the '60s. "It was exactly the same in the old days, but in a smaller way. Look, it's the equivalent of going to see the Dixies in Waterford. It took me two nights away to go and get them. You'd spot who'd be popular. If showbands were popular in Cork, then their popularity would spread to Dublin and then to Belfast. If the Freshmen or Plattermen were popular in Belfast, they eventually became popular in Cork. In the sixties, I was tied up in the biggest thing you could be doing in the entertainment world. There's really not that much difference with what I'm doing now. On a worldwide scale, if Bruce Springsteen is enormous in America and he hasn't been to Ireland, then you know he's going to be big here.

"Today, the world is a village. So, instead of ringing up the fellow who manages the Dixies or the Freshmen or the Royal, you now ring up whoever manages Billy Joel or Paul McCartney or U2. These managers are doing the same thing that showband managers did on a smaller scale. The world has become so much smaller because of communications. I read an American magazine called *Performance*. It's the equivalent of *Spotlight*. It lists the top grossing acts for the week. My work today is all about worldwide contacts. It all started with carrying in the equipment for the Royal or Dixies. Now, the business is about carrying in the equipment for Neil Diamond or U2. The business has just become more sophisticated, and a lot bigger..."

Getting Into The Groove

As Ireland went showband crazy, bands discovered the importance of records as promotional tools. Few bands took recording seriously: records simply provided the vehicle to enter the charts, get air plays and maintain their profile on the ballroom circuit. The motivation was more profit — not a desire to be immortalised on vinyl. A successful record made, or renewed, a band's status and gave it the power to talk terms with ballroom proprietors. Chart hits helped to pull bigger crowds. Records weren't big money-spinners for Irish bands unless they broke into the British market. Yet, they were useful 'calling cards' on the circuit. One showband manager summed up their approach to recording in a Radio Éireann interview with Gay Byrne for his documentary series, *This Showband Thing*, in October 1965.

"We calculated that we lost £1,000 on a gramophone record. We spent £500 advertising it in the national papers. It is a loss in one way. However, as regards publicity, it is not a loss. It increases your crowd and makes you more popular."

Chart-fixing was attempted by some bands. They could boost their placings by buying large quantities of their own records. Every band wanted a chart hit because it guaranteed regular bookings. It helped the case for a greater percentage of the door takings. A Top Ten hit was trumpeted by bands in their dance adverts. The effect of block- buying hundreds of records by some bands was considerable on a tiny market. Stocks were bought in loads, given away free to fans, or dumped. The first step was to figure out which shops were being monitored by those who prepared the charts. Then came the spending spree: about £400 was enough to put a number in the charts. For bands, this was a mere drop in their financial ocean. Disposal was easy: the Liffey became a favourite resting place in Dublin.

Chart-fixing did not exist in the early development of the business, but became common in the mid '60s when every two-bit band made records. What they lacked in talent they made up by sharp practice. Top performers like Bowyer, Dolan and

Rock didn't need to go on spending sprees: records like *The Hucklebuck* and *Candy Store* sold well anyway. Rock first became aware of chart-fixing when fans shouted for free records at the end of one dance. "At first," he says, "I didn't know what they meant. It turned out that some bands used to arrive at ballrooms with car loads of records and give them out to people." Records were even dished out to the bouncers, mineral bar and cloakroom attendants.

"We never did it," says Rock. "We didn't have to because our records sold. I could see no point in it anyway. Okay, so you got yourself into the charts. It doesn't last. If you've got it, you've got it. If you haven't, no matter what you do, you'll get away with it for a while — but it won't last." The general attitude of fixer bands was that their records needed "a little push."

Another way to forge popularity was to influence the poll conducted by *Spotlight*. In order to sample the record preferences of readers, the magazine incorporated voting slips which were cut out and returned. Some bands bought large quantities of *Spotlight* and returned the slips en masse. Bands competed to be first to 'cover' the latest American hits — even beating British pop stars in the race. Managers had 'spies' in the U.S. who got their hands on new discs and rushed them to Ireland before they'd been released in Britain. Irish showband stars received the first copies, rehearsed them immediately and delivered near-perfect 'covers' in the ballrooms. These were accepted in the Irish charts before, or even at the same time, as the British releases. Indeed, British stars could never understand, or come to terms with, the 'magic' of Irish showbands in this copycat procedure. The first chart was broadcast on Radio Éireann on October 2nd, 1962. It was compiled by Jimmy Magee, compered by Harry Thuillier and produced by Roisin Lorigan. A national chart has since been produced every week, presented by Larry Gogan, who was voted Ireland's Top DJ for sixteen successive years from '70 to '85 inclusive and who received a Jacobs' Award for his contribution to radio.

The recording industry developed slowly because the facilities did not exist. Most early showband recordings were made at the Eamonn Andrews Studios, Henry Street, Dublin, where sponsored radio programmes were also recorded. The first showband star to record is generally acknowledged to have been Tom Dunphy of the Royal with *Come Down The Mountain Katie Daly*, for EMI, in 1962. The flipside was a duet between Dunphy and Jim Conlon, *I Heard The Bluebird Sing*. Gerry Cronin of The Ohio later claimed to have recorded first, in America, but Dunphy was recognised as the pioneer of the Irish scene.

The first Irish showband to record an LP was the Capitol, led by Des Kelly, in 1963. Two key figures in the first showband recordings in Dublin were the O'Donovan brothers, Fred and Bill. Fred, with long experience in radio production, had his own production company, Broadcast and Theatrical Productions, at 40 Henry Street. The first recordings were made at these studios which later became the Eamonn Andrews Studios with Fred as managing director. He was also in charge of the Gaiety Theatre. Bill produced the sponsored radio programmes for Eamonn Andrews Studios on behalf of their clients, and these were broadcast on Radio Éireann. He also produced the showband records.

Bill produced the first records under what would be considered primitive conditions today. "They were done on one tape machine," he recalls. "You did everything at the one time. It was in a room no bigger than your parlour. The first showband record we did that had strings on it was Sean Dunphy and the Hoedowners' *Oh How I Miss You Tonight*. We were working on a single-track tape machine. There was no such thing as eight-track or sixteen-track or twenty-four-track. You recorded the backing track on the tape machine. You took the backing track off and put it on another tape machine. Then you dubbed it back on to the master tape machine with the fellow singing over it. That was the record. To stop the sound bouncing all around the room we put egg boxes on the ceiling. They were very effective actually. We started recording with the showbands and moved to 4 Henry Street where we had a four-track machine. Then we moved to the Television Club where there was an eight-track and sixteen-track machine. But, all the early recordings were done at 40 Henry Street in a tiny room.

"I remember once when Dickie Rock recorded there. It was summertime and we had the windows open. The street outside was crowded with people listening to him. He was waving back to them. We were making these recordings in what was essentially a studio for producing radio programmes. Then we built this other studio, which had four- tracks. It was a major step forward because four-track was unheard of in this country at that stage. That was at 4 Henry Street."

A tale is told of Bing Crosby once being turned away from the Eamonn Andrews Studios. The crooner arrived at 40 Henry Street, but the band recordings were made at 4 Henry Street. A young man at the reception desk told Crosby he wasn't booked in, and pointed him to the other studios at Henry Street. As the story did the rounds, the receptionist was reported to have told his boss: "There was an oul' fella in alright, but I fecked him out."

The Eamonn Andrews Studios operated twenty-four hours a day as bands queued to book studio time. Bands had no experience of recording and, in many cases, didn't bother to rehearse. They were up all night travelling and went straight to the studios bleary-eyed next morning. They were accustomed to playing in ballrooms, but now had to achieve studio perfection. A recording exposed flaws in a band that weren't easily detectable in a crowded ballroom. Bill O'Donovan decided to compensate for their lack of professionalism. "I got Noel Kelehan, and we auditioned session musicians," he recalls. "It meant that we could lay down a track and the band wouldn't even be there — just the lead singer. Then, they'd come in and the band would over-dub stuff on it. That's the way it worked. It was time-saving for everybody."

The most successful recording artistes were Brendan Bowyer and the Royal, Brendan O'Brien and the Dixies, Butch Moore and the Capitol, Dickie Rock and the Miami, Joe Dolan and the Drifters, Larry Cunningham and the Mighty Avons, Dermot O'Brien and the Clubmen and Big Tom and the Mainliners. Hit material was impossible to predict. Cunningham's *Lovely Leitrim*, a No. 1 hit in January '66 and a huge seller, was originally meant as the 'B' side. "We spent two and a half hours getting the 'A' side done," says O'Donovan. "Then, we spent the final half hour of the three-hour session recording *Lovely Leitrim*."

In fact, some of the greatest hits were first recorded as 'B' sides: Bowyer's *Hucklebuck* ('65), Dermot O'Brien's *Merry Ploughboy* ('66), and Big Tom's *Gentle Mother* ('67). This indicated that showband stars didn't know themselves what was commercial. O'Brien's *Merry Ploughboy* went straight into the Irish charts at No. 1 on September 26th, 1966. The record even managed to break into the British charts on two occasions — October 20th, at No. 46 for one week, and on November 3rd, at No. 50 for one week.

Showbands recorded songs that they liked, but the fans sometimes wanted something different. This was the great education of the showband era: the 'punters' became all important, and the philosophy was to please them. Bands who understood this fundamental lesson were the ones who survived. Recording was new and mysterious — especially to bands from rural areas. Country singers like Cunningham drove straight from the farm to recording sessions in Dublin.

Pye was the first record company to take showbands seriously. The market potential was recognised by John Woods, who was appointed general manager of Pye Record Sales Ltd in June, 1963. His first record was with Dickie Rock. Woods had an immediate hit with Rock's blockbuster, *There's Always Me*, which hit No. 1 in January '64 and sold almost 100,000. "That record took us off our feet," says Woods. "Then *The Candy Store* came along — and it was huge. Everybody was singing it." The record was so successful that it knocked Roy Orbison's classic, *Oh Pretty Woman*, from No. 1 in October '64.

"A lot of showbands were doing well then," according to Woods. "The showband was everything. You couldn't get in to see them at night because the halls were so full. Most recorded at the Eamonn Andrews Studios. They booked studio time and made a recording. The bands usually recorded and leased it to me to promote, present and make records. Other bands went to recording studios in England. In many cases, I'd be out in the ballroom listening to, and chatting with, bands. I'd know what they wanted. We'd agree beforehand. In some cases, they were very definite that they wanted to do something special. Once I got interested after Dickie's first record, and went out looking for bands. I realised that there was a market out there that hadn't been touched, so I signed bands to Pye. After a recording was made in the Andrews Studios, it went for processing to Pye headquarters in Mitcham, Surrey. The parts would come back to us and we'd pass them either to the HMV plant in Waterford or the Carlton plant in Dublin and call pressings off. At the same time, we'd print labels. These were printed in London until we got Irish printers capable of doing them. Then we had the record. We generally put sleeves on as well. It was up to us to distribute the singles to shops and ensure air play and press reviews. In the beginning we were only selling singles. By '67, we had a few EPs. Remember, an LP was almost unknown here then. Carlton Productions started in '67 and made a lot of records for many bands because the showband craze had escalated at that stage."

Eurovision gave the recording industry a big boost. Pye sold 80,000 copies of Butch Moore's *Walking The Streets In The Rain* in 1965. Next came Rock's *Come Back To Stay* in 1966. Pye also had Sean Dunphy's Eurovision entry in April '67, *If I Could Choose*, at No. 2, as well as Eurovision winner Sandie Shaw's *Puppet On A String*, at No. 1 in Ireland later that month. The company signed many of the top showbands including the Miami, Capitol, Cadets, Dixies, Hoedowners and Drifters. The recordings lacked the professional touches of later years. "We didn't have the techniques, the technical expertise or the studios capable of giving fully commercial recordings," says Woods. "But, remember, when people want something, they want what they like to hear — not necessarily what is perfect to hear. Anytime a record came out from Dickie, Butch or the Hoedowners, or whoever, it got us promotion and was usually accepted by punters all around the country and sold very well."

The charts were a barometer, whether accurate or not, of what was happening in the market place. Woods, who became managing director of Polygram Records in Dublin in later years, wasn't blind to the fact that bands indulged in chart-fixing. "That sort of thing went on alright," he confirms. "It will always go on. No matter what rules you apply, they'll always find a way around them." Shortly after his appointment as general manager of Pye Record Sales in '63, Woods hosted a reception at the Gresham Hotel, Dublin, for Chubby Checker who had a big hit with *Limbo Rock*. Phil Solomon brought him on tour to Ireland. "That was my first ever venture," recalls Woods. "Since I represented him here in Ireland, I had to look after him. It was quite an experience. He was the almighty then — like bringing in Neil Diamond today. He was a lively character. That experience gave me a lot of expertise in promotion and in handling other stars who came in like Lonnie Donegan, Kenny Ball, Petula Clark and other stars who recorded for Pye in Britain. I had hits with them which I realised could sell very well here. Up to then, there had been relatively no sales. The reason was that Pye Radio here were interested in radiograms and record players which were selling for £50 or £70 a piece. Pye Radio was an Irish company manufacturing radios. Because a record was selling for 7/6 in those days, the company didn't want to know about them. Later, however, Pye started recording Irish artistes. Dickie came to me. Then, I started scouting. I went to hear him sing and see the excitement he created in the 4 Provinces Ballroom in Dublin which later became the Television Club and also the Eamonn Andrews Studios."

One of Pye's biggest sellers was *The Black Velvet Band* by Johnny Kelly and the Capitol in 1967. It sold over 100,000. After the initial successes with Rock, bands came to Woods. He chose songs for Joe Dolan: "I used to spend days and days in the music publishers in London looking for songs for different artistes. I found *My Own Peculiar Way* in '65. I was able to ring Joe in Mullingar from London and say, 'I've got one.' They'd be waiting for me at the airport to hear the demo. I often whistled songs into the phone to Joe or Seamus Casey from London. After people signed, they'd come to me with all sorts of songs. We'd spend hours listening and shooting one another down. Many of the showbands weren't interested in recording as such. They were interested in the promotion that came from recording. In other words, coming up to September every year, I'd get an influx of people wanting to record. I'd realise that their diaries were being filled within the next month. They wanted to have a record out in two weeks to help them get the dates. We had to steer clear of that kind of thing. A lot of fellows went into showbands because it was better than a day job. They tried to make a go of it, didn't have what it takes and, in many cases, fell by the wayside. There was no way they could have done much better." Pye had number one hits in May '64 with the Cadets' *Fallen Star*, a revival by Eileen Reid of the old Jim Reeves favourite, and with Rock's *I'm Yours*. In September '64, *Spotlight* reported that Pye had the biggest showband stable, including the Miami, Capitol, Drifters, Pacific and Cadets. Pye had another hit with *She Wears My Ring* by Sean Fagan and the Pacific which went to No. 3 that month. This was followed by Fagan's *Distant Drums* which reached No. 5 in December. Woods decided to release Dominic Behan's *Liverpool Lou* in May 1964. It broke into the Top Ten and also became a huge seller.

"I liked the thing and released it even though I knew he couldn't sing well," he recalls. "I remember staying in Cork at that time at the Metropole Hotel after the record was released. Thompsons Bakery was just across on MacCurtain Street. I woke up on the third floor of the hotel one morning. I heard a baker coming out of Thompsons whistling it. I knew straight away it was a winner."

On another occasion, Woods was about to leave a London hotel to catch a flight to Dublin when Phil Coulter phoned. The Derry maestro, also in London, had made a recording of himself, and he wanted Woods to hear it. "I was on my way to Heathrow and hadn't time to wait for him," says Woods. "So, he said he'd meet me at the airport. He brought a tape machine out with him — in those days a bigger thing to what we're used to nowadays. He played himself singing *The Town I Loved So Well* for the first time to anybody. We agreed on the spot to release it. It was a hit for him in those days, even though he might cringe a bit now."

Contracts were fixed to a minimum of three years. "I liked a five- year contract; but if they weren't agreeing with me, or I wasn't agreeing with them, there was no harmony anyway, so it didn't matter about a contract," says Woods. "A contract was just something to keep them there if they were having success. If they weren't, then I wasn't interested. I'd let them go, even though there was a contract. It would be a mutual agreement." Once Woods had 'stars' on his hands, it wasn't unusual for competitors to try to poach them. "Obviously, others would try to steer them away from me," he says. "That's where you needed your contract. Competitors would promise them the sun, moon and stars and contracts in England. That's why, in 1972, I moved from Pye into Polygram/Polydor. It was an international company with thirty-seven markets around the world. I wanted to develop the Irish product outside. That's exactly what I did." Woods, now retired as managing director of Polygram Records, had over 1,500 Irish releases — singles, EP, album and CD — between '63 and '88.

Showbands were also signed by other companies, including Decca and EMI. Mervyn Solomon became synonymous with the record business during the '60s. He was a director of Solomon & Peres of Belfast and Dublin, distributors for Decca, as well as managing director of Emerald Records, an Irish label specialising in folk music. He gave recording breaks to Van Morrison's Them, Rory Gallagher, Bridie Gallagher, Patrick O'Hagan and Austin Gaffney. Solomon worked closely with his London-based brother, Phil, one of the best known promoters, who managed the Bachelors and the Big Four. Inevitably, there was sharp competition between the companies for the growing market for showband discs.

In November 1964, Pye launched a drive to stir interest in showbands in Britain by hosting a lavish reception for the Capitol and Pacific at London's ATV House. This marked the release of new singles by both bands. In terms of promotion, it was the full treatment: record plays on Radio Luxembourg, adverts in *The Musical Express* and TV appearances. EMI had the top showband — the Royal — on their books. The company arranged a publicity splash in May '64 for the recording in Belfast of the Royal's first LP, *One Nighters*, and their latest single, *Bless You/Californian Sun*. Rather than cancel an important date in Waterford, the Royal chartered two private planes to fly to the recording sessions in Belfast. They were greeted on arrival in Belfast by Harry Christmas, EMI's man in Ireland. The company flew in over £100,000 worth of equipment, and a temporary studio was set up in the heart of the city. The LP was released in August.

As bands released more and more singles, critics such as Ken Stewart of the *Evening Press* became important people to please. On one week alone, in '65, eight new discs were released. That year, Stewart wrote that he had in his possession every showband record produced to date. They were, with a few notable exceptions, in mint condition. That was because the vast majority were too dull to rate more than a couple of spins. Why? "To my ears, they lack the basic ingredients of an ultra-commercial disc: suitable material and a clever arrangement. Some singles defy description. They appear to have been issued without any thought on the part of the bands concerned." Irish bands found it difficult to make progress in the recording field. International companies with offices in Ireland placed most emphasis on distribution here of their overseas albums and singles. Mick Clerkin, who worked for one of these companies, decided to establish a recording company wholly owned by Irish business people and producing and promoting Irish music. Larry Cunningham became the first 'name' artiste to sign a recording contract. Dermot Hegarty was a major investor and director. The big names: among them Cunningham, Dermot O'Brien, Joe Dolan, Hegarty, the Nevada, Brian Coll, Red Hurley and Roly Daniels.

As the showband business died, Release Records closed the Irish organisation and Clerkin moved to a new base in London where he formed the successful Ritz Record Company — responsible for the British success of such artistes as Foster and Allen, Joe Dolan, the Fureys with Davy Arthur and Daniel O'Donnell.

The Wedding Dress Queen

Dublin, Thursday, November 7th, 1963.

Three fire engines are called from Tara Street to help gardai control rioting crowds in O'Connell Street. It's a last resort. Gardai hope that blaring sirens will help them break up teenage mobs. The trouble erupts when the first of the Beatles' two shows ends at the Adelphi Cinema at 8.30pm. Three thousand people leaving the theatre lock with those trying to get in for the second performance. Gardai form cordons in a bid to clear Middle Abbey Street, and the less patient start to scuffle with them. Screaming girls are pulled away; the cordons break and the crowd surges forward. Fights break out at the junction of O'Connell Street and Middle Abbey Street when youngsters try to force their way through the Garda ranks. More fighting starts in O'Connell Street as gardai move on groups throwing fireworks.

The forces of law and order eventually battle the mobs back and seal off Middle Abbey Street. But fighting again breaks out and Garda reinforcements are called. By the time the second show ends shortly before 11pm, gardai have taken a number of young men off in squad cars and a 'Black Maria'. More scuffles break out when they try to divert the crowds from the Adelphi into the laneway leading to Bachelor's Walk. Yet again, youths are dragged away as they attempt to get through the Garda lines. At the same time, the cordon holding back thousands in O'Connell Street gives way. Reinforcements close the gap, but this results in a number of men and women having to be treated by ambulance men. Amid the hysteria, the four young musicians ultimately responsible for it all are whisked away in the back of a newspaper van to the Gresham Hotel.

Beatlemania struck Dublin with a vengeance: over a dozen men arrested; cars over-turned in Abbey Street and O'Connell Street; fifty treated for minor injuries; three taken to hospital with limb fractures; a youth stabbed in the head in O'Connell Street; traffic in the city- centre disrupted while 200 gardai try to control over 3,000 people. The Beatles came to Ireland on the crest of a wave following the release of their first chart hits: *Love Me Do*; *Please, Please Me*; *From Me To You*; and *She Loves You*. One of those to get closest to them was the queen of Irish showbands, Eileen Reid of the Cadets. The legions of teenage girls who screamed their lungs out would have killed to be in her shoes. An old photograph frayed at the edges captured the moment. A meeting was arranged by Costello through Paul Russell, who interviewed The Beatles on *The Showband Show* on Telefís Éireann. A path was formed through the fans so that Eileen could get into the Gresham without being mobbed. She was accompanied by Costello and Pat Murphy, leader of the Cadets.

Her heart raced as she waited outside a bedroom door. Paul McCartney and John Lennon came out and shook hands; George Harrison and Ringo Starr remained inside. Lennon stood back and let McCartney do most of the talking. He wanted to know all about the Cadets' uniforms, which had impressed Mick Jagger when the band appeared with The Rolling Stones on the *Thank Your Lucky Stars* show on British TV.

"I didn't like John Lennon at all," says Eileen. "He was very cold. A very stand-off-ish kind of person. Paul was completely different. He was very nice. He seemed to have a very Irish kind of approach to their success. But Lennon was very snidey. The boys in my band used to do the Beatles stuff and were very good at it. They thought of recording some of it. Lennon told us not to record any of their stuff. I mean, the Beatles didn't have to worry about the Cadets for God sake. I suppose he was afraid that someone might record one of their songs and it might click. I was a very shy kind of person, despite being extrovert on stage. Paul was so nice. He asked us to get into the photograph. He came over and put his arms around us. That type of thing. Real friendly. I don't know what was wrong with Lennon... maybe the pressures were getting to him. He didn't wear us at all. I thought he felt that we were nobodies. Like... what am I doing standing here... that kind of attitude. He may not have been like that but that's the impression I got. The boys even thought that he was very cold."

The TV breakthrough in the UK achieved by Reid and the Cadets happened some months before Beatlemania brought Dublin to a standstill. The appearance on *Thank Your Lucky Stars*, a kind of forerunner to *Top of the Pops*, boosted their popularity enormously in Northern Ireland. The embryonic Rolling Stones and Helen Shapiro also appeared on the show. Eileen giggles at the memory of Mick Jagger eyeing up their classy uniforms. The Stones were a fairly amateur group at that stage. They drank tea with the Cadets and asked their advice about the business.

"I remember Mick couldn't get over the uniforms. He thought it was a great idea. He said why didn't they think of something like that. It would have gone a storm. When you think about it, we were probably before our time with uniforms. The likes of Michael Jackson discovered many years later how important uniforms can be. He's all into them. The Rolling Stones looked great. Mick was very nice. But I was very shy. I was afraid to talk to them. The boys got on great with them. They had tea together up in the canteen. Can you believe it? Tea. It would be a drink nowadays." Eileen again posed for photographs.

In Ireland, the Cadets were image trend-setters. Eileen's "wedding dress," for instance, was a stroke of marketing genius — a stage prop that made her name in every ballroom in the country. She first wore it in the Arcadia in Bray. She looked sensational walking on stage to sing her hit song, *I Gave My Wedding Dress Away*. Three thousand people shouted for more. She had to sing it six times. Her hairstyle became a trademark, too. When she appeared in country ballrooms, local girls thought she wore a wig. Style like that had been seen before only in the movies or glossy magazines.

The former Jacobs factory girl enjoyed a remarkable career throughout the '60s during which time she achieved a number one hit with *Fallen Star* and entered the British charts with *Jealous Heart*. The schedule was long and punishing, but there are no scars and few, if any, bad memories. Unlike some other women survivors of that time, she speaks affectionately of the showbands and doesn't like to hear people running them down.

Eileen Reid entered showbusiness via a ladies football team. At Jacobs, she took to the soccer pitch, playing for the stock department side in a factory league. They won. A victory dance was held in the recreation hall. The Blue Clavons, a popular city band, provided the entertainment. Team mates approached the stage and asked the band to allow Eileen to sing. She did, and five songs later, the factory girls were still shouting for more. The next taste of the stage came when she joined the Melody Makers in 1960. They frequently played in Finglas, occasionally teaming up in a two-band show with the Blue Crystals.

In 1961, word reached her that a big band was being formed by Tom Costello. Auditions were held at the Town and Country Club in Parnell Square. Eileen went along and gave it her best shot. Musicians were drawn from the Melochords to form the new line-up. The Melochords were a respected city band who were popular at the Olympic Ballroom where they sometimes took part in a two-band session with Jack Flahive and his Olympic Showband. The idea was that the Melochords would form the basis of the new showband. "They picked the Melochords. I was delighted when I was told it was them," says Eileen. "They were a great band. They were well liked on the Dublin scene. We had a ready-made band. I was the only female at the auditions. They told me a week later that I'd be the lead singer. I was thrilled."

There was opposition from members of the new band who didn't want a woman as lead singer. "When the boys found out, they nearly had a fit. I didn't regard myself as any big, gorgeous sex symbol. I regarded myself as being plain. The boys wanted to go for Dickie Rock. Everything worked out best in the end. He joined the Miami, and was a huge success. We were huge, too. The boys felt uneasy about having a female in the band. Pat Murphy, the leader, told them that the ballroom promoters wanted me and, if they wanted to go, then they could go. He'd get a new band. Then they backed down. I ended up marrying one of them, Jimmy Day — the one who definitely didn't want me in the beginning. He said he had nothing against me. He just didn't want me in the band." Murphy spent months scouting ballrooms before he was satisfied that he had recruited his ideal group. He regarded Eileen as his greatest discovery and staunchly defended her against criticism.

Tom Costello's concept was simply to respond to the growing public demand for good dance bands, strong musically and vocally. The Cadets had to develop a broad musical repertoire, from dixieland, comedy, American country music to the pops. The Melochords had not played country, but the Cadets did. In January '62, Eileen was on the road with the Cadets. After spending a hard first year on the road, the Cadets launched into radio, TV and records in '63. Eileen was transformed from a poorly paid seventeen-year-old factory worker to a glamour girl of the showbands. She giggles when asked about the glamorous image.

"I don't know about sexiness... you could have fooled me... I suppose I looked different to all the other girls." Her hairstyle was created by a "terrific" English hairdresser who suggested trying out an idea taken from a magazine. Back-combing wasn't fashionable at the time. She put Eileen's hair up in curls. It looked great. "Doing the hair in curls after that was an ordeal," she recalls. "The Beehive took an hour and a half every day... it was worse than the five hours on stage." She was the showband girl with the piled mop of blonde hair, who set trends in fashion. Eileen was the first to wear hot pants: when she wore white velvet pants one Christmas at the Arcadia in Bray, dancers thought she was wearing knickers on stage. During the Cadets' heyday, Eileen attracted ardent male followers: she once received a hundred marriage proposals over a three week period from places as far apart as England, Germany and even the Aran Islands. "I'd certainly have had my choice of places to live," she jokes. The band travelled about 2,000 miles a week. As a singer, she had a range and depth that enabled her to tackle anything from the most complex ballad to easy-going country'n'western material. She spent a third of her life in ballrooms, and enjoyed swimming during her time off.

Eileen liked the glamour and excitement of life in the band, but it was no job for the faint-hearted. She was expected to be as fit as the men and take the rough with the smooth. "Let's be honest, it was tough," she says. "I was very young, so I didn't care. I loved it so much that I didn't worry. It took a lot out of me, though. I lost weight. It was hard work. You had to put on a good show. We used to do six nights a week, five hours on stage. We got buttons for it. When I look back now, we should be multi-millionaires. I had no social life. It was just bed-to-work all the time. But I loved it. If you didn't, it would be hell. We looked really glamorous on stage. I think people used to imagine that we were having wild parties and a wonderful time. It wasn't glamorous. It was hard work. You really had to love it to stick it. You didn't get home until eight or nine in the morning, and we used to see everybody else going to work. We were actually going to bed then. You'd get up about one or two in the afternoon and travel to Kerry. You could be up in Belfast one night, and down the other end of the country on the next night." Conditions were terrible in many places. The Cadets, like other bands, were at the mercy of gombeen proprietors. Eileen reflects: "The ballrooms were very cold; there was no decent dressing room. You had to go across the border up north to get a decent dressing room. That's a fact. There was no soap or toilet rolls, or anything. It was primitive really. The boys would get ready and they'd go on stage. Then I'd get ready. I used to go down to the ladies' toilets to change: that is, if there was a proper ladies toilet. It was a grueller."

1963 brought public exposure for the Cadets, and a string of TV "firsts" for an Irish showband. They appeared twice on the BBC TV *625 Show*, as well as on the top rating *Thank Your Lucky Stars* ITV show, sharing a bill with Helen Shapiro. At home, the band made their Telefís Éireann debut on *The Showband Show* and recorded four broadcasts for Radio Eireann's *17 Club*. The Cadets had struck a blow for feminism in a chauvinistic business by opting for a female lead vocalist. This bold departure made them different to the rest. Another original concept was to reject the conventional showband suits. They chose instead to wear naval-type uniforms. This tactic helped to assert some individuality. The uniforms were easily the most distinctive in the business: well-tailored blue jackets cut in the naval style and embellished with gold buttons and badges; an anchor in a shield on the upper arms; an embroidered crest on the lower sleeves; white trousers with a blue stripe; and topped off with black peaked caps displaying the familiar anchor crest.

Designed by Pat Murphy, the colourful uniforms quickly became the Cadets' trademark on the ballroom circuit. *Spotlight* hailed the band as the most impressive yet on *The Showband Show*: "They treat every number as though it's an opener. Their show swings and drives from start to finish. I particularly liked their interpretation of 'Merseybeat' — they've got that 'shake,' or whatever that Beatle inspired new dance is called. Eileen Reid, the lead vocalist, has terrific range and power in her voice... pretty too." The Cadets delivered the usual mix of country'n'western, pop, dixieland, and anything else 'punters' wanted to hear. They built up a huge following in Dublin and in the North. The other members were: Pat Murphy, leader and founder, harmonica player; Jas Fagan, trombone; Gerry Hayes, piano; Paddy Burns, trumpeter and Presley-style vocalist; Willie Devey, drummer and country'n'western vocalist; Brendan O'Connell, lead guitarist; Jimmy Day, tenor saxist who doubled on clarinet and guitar; and Noel McGann. As leader, Murphy called the shots. An Irish champion harmonica player, he was the first Irish musician to appear on UTV. He held the harmonica championship of Ireland for a decade: one of his pupils was John Stokes of The Bachelors. Murphy, regarded as a perfectionist, insisted on long hours of rehearsals for the Cadets.

The Cadets made their first record for Decca, *Hello Trouble*. It didn't make the charts, but got a few plays on Radio Luxembourg at least. All later recordings were made for Pye. Indeed, the Cadets became one of Pye's top recording showbands. The band went on a four- week U.S. tour in November '63, playing in New York, Boston, Chicago, Philadelphia, Dallas, Hollywood, San Francisco and Las Vegas. They played Vegas at the invitation of Johnny Cash. When Cash toured Ireland earlier in '63, he was impressed enough to offer them a stint as guest stars at The Mint in Las Vegas. The first big break of '64 came when the Cadets made a thirteen-week series of programmes for Radio Luxembourg, sponsored by Marlowe Cleaners. They were given their own lunchtime programme on Radio Éireann every Thursday at 2.30pm, titled *Carnival Time With The Cadets,* and it ran for twenty-six weeks. In 1964, Eileen won national fame as the Irish pop girl who made it to number one. She went to the top of the charts with her revival of the old Jim Reeves favourite,

Fallen Star. It hit No. 1 on May 29, and stayed in the charts for eight weeks. The success took her by surprise: "I'd have been satisfied if it got to number five." The Cadets joined the exclusive ranks of chart-topping showbands. At the same time, the band also released a single, *We Shall Remember*, Eileen's singing tribute to assassinated President Kennedy. The song, sung to the traditional air of *Kevin Barry*, was completely overshadowed by the chart success of *Fallen Star.* Both discs were released on the same day, and marketed simultaneously. The Kennedy tribute sold reasonably well, despite not being broadcast. Radio Éireann refused to include it in any programmes. As a result, it never made the Radio Éireann Top Ten — but did figure in the Northern Ireland Top Ten.

One of the mysteries of Irish showbusiness in 1964 was why her next release, *I Gave My Wedding Dress Away*, never went to No. 1. It certainly sold enough, but reached only No. 4 in October and stayed in the charts for seven weeks. For some showbands, chart-rigging was part of the game. "Why it didn't go to number one is beyond me," reflects Eileen. "I don't know what way the charts were worked. It sold more than any of the other records. That's the gas part. It should have stayed at number one for weeks. I don't know what happened. We didn't even buy one of those ourselves. Normally bands helped their records by buying a few themselves. We never bought one. We felt this was going to be a genuine hit. Maybe that's why it didn't get to number one."

Reid would forever be associated with *I Gave My Wedding Dress Away*. Nostalgic references to Ireland in the '60s invariably include mention of Eileen and the wedding dress. During the late '50s, Kitty Wells had a hit in the American country charts with *Wedding Dress*. It was difficult to locate American country albums here then. Brendan O'Connell, the Cadets' guitarist, had a country collection. Eileen heard the song on one of his albums. She thought it was great. Her famous dress was bought at the French Shop in Wicklow Street — the best place in Dublin for bridal wear. It cost £40 — a lot of money. Factory workers earned only three or four pounds a week. Eileen wore the dress on stage six nights a week for nearly a year: "Can you imagine the state of the dress after that time? I put my foot down

(Photo: Sunday World)

and refused to wear it any more. Everywhere we went people expected to see it. I used to hate going out in it after a while because it got so dirty. That's why I put my foot down. They wouldn't invest in another dress. I wouldn't wear it any more. All those stages were dirty. It was a big long dress, streaming along the floors every night. Hundreds of people stood beneath the stage watching me as I walked out to sing the song. Nowadays, I'd probably be sponsored by a bridal shop to wear it. I'd even get a few of them."

The dress was eventually raffled for charity. The idea was that the winner would get a new one at the French Shop. Thousands of tickets were sold in ballrooms all over the country. A penny a ticket: a shilling a book. The raffle went on for months. The band got enormous mileage out of it. Everybody who came to dance bought tickets. Engaged couples snapped up books of them. "A million pounds in pennies must have been made on the wedding dress," says Eileen. "In every ballroom we went to, boxes of tickets were thrown onto the front of the stage. I mean, thousands of tickets. They'd be gone in ten minutes. The whole thing went on for a long time because we were only back in a ballroom about every three months. People hadn't seen you. They were taking books of tickets. Talk about Lottery fever!"

But the big raffle had an embarrassing anti-climax. The dress was won by a middle-aged married man who hadn't even bought the ticket: somebody gave it to him. He was named and asked to approach the stage at the Fiesta Ballroom in Letterkenny. Eileen chuckles at the memory: "I couldn't believe it. There were so many people getting married — so many people I knew getting married. I'll never forget when he walked up the dance floor with a cap on his head. He must have been in his fifties. He said that he didn't want the dress. He wanted the money instead. When Pat Murphy told him that it was worth £40, he laughed and said it was worth a lot more than that, like hundreds of pounds. He just wouldn't believe us." What happened to the original wedding dress? "It was probably dumped. I didn't want it."

1964 had been a special year for many reasons. Eileen became the only Irish girl, so far, to break into the Top Ten —

and the first to have a No. 1 hit. By Christmas '64, the Cadets released an LP. It featured fourteen numbers which were closely associated with the band. Like other top band leaders, Murphy of the Cadets dreamed of conquering Britain. "1964 saw the emergence of the showbands as big recording and international propositions," he said in a Christmas message to fans. "We ourselves have three major British agencies seeking to represent us. My ambition for the band is to get a recording into the British charts." Eileen and the Cadets were back in the Irish charts during June '65 with *Right or Wrong* which reached No. 7. They entered the British charts — a rare achievement for a showband — on the same month with *Jealous Heart*. It only managed to get to No. 42 for a week...but that was sufficient to generate valuable publicity at home. The record was boosted in the charts by sales in Northern Ireland. The Cadets were getting a lot of plays at the time on Radio Caroline, the pirate station established on a ship in the North Sea by Ronan O'Rahilly.

Showband women found it almost impossible to maintain relationships with boyfriends because they were away from home so much. "The men in showbands had women chasing them," says Eileen. "Nobody could deny that fact. We knew about particular bands that were into 'bonking', as they say today. That's probably a nice way of putting it. I wasn't on the chase. I was just interested in the singing end of it. I never chased anyone, or singled anyone out in the crowd. I suppose it sounds peculiar, but I was very shy that way. Yet, I know it didn't look like that on stage. Once I went on stage, I was mad. I was raring to go. I saved all my energy for the stage. I wasn't interested in anything else. I didn't want to know about fellas or going with anyone. That would stand in the way. Anyway, you couldn't have a relationship with anyone. I mean... you'd never see them."

Eileen observed it all from the sanctuary of the stage. "I saw girls refusing to dance with fellows with drink taken. It would be nearly a mortal sin if a fella came in tipsy: the girls wouldn't go for him. But the pioneers were in great demand: the pin suggested that you were a good living person — the boy or girl next door. You had to be a Daniel O'Donnell type... and they're slagging him today. That's true. If you smelled drink off someone, that was it, taboo... *oh no, he doesn't go to Mass or get Holy Communion.* Don't get me wrong. The boys or girls weren't all innocent, either. They were never innocent. It wasn't as open as today, though. There was more subtlety. Today, more people seem to be out for only one thing. They're not thinking about marriage; they just want to go to bed with one another. You often hear girls saying that it's all fellas want today. Of course, there were nice fellas and girls back in the '60s as there are now. But it's so easy today to get a woman or man to go to bed with. The temptations are greater. Girls are under more pressure to have sex. They think to themselves, 'well, if I don't go to bed with him, he'll think I'm a wall-flower'. They don't realise that by saying 'no,' you're being strong: it's not being weak. Today, when a girl is chasing a guy, and she knows that he can get it off other girls, she's caught in a very difficult situation. Even though she wants him, she knows that if she doesn't give in, he can go elsewhere. It wasn't the same in the '60s. Fellas would like to know then that a girl wasn't sleeping around, or wasn't with anyone else. Nowadays, guys don't seem to mind. A lot of them are sleeping around. In the '60s, if a girl said to a fella, 'come on, let's go to bed', she definitely wouldn't be the one he'd want to marry."

Eileen returned to the Irish charts in February '66 with a song called *If I Had My Life To Live Over*, which reached No. 4. That year also marked a launch on the charts by another band member, 'Gregory', who had a No. 1 hit on July 25th with *More Than Yesterday*. This was followed by another Top Ten hit by Gregory and the Cadets in November, *At the Close of a Long Long Day* which went to No. 9. Next, in '67, came two further releases — *Best Part of Loving You*, and *Land of Gingerbread*. The latter record went to No. 9 in July. The Cadets broke up in 1970, but that didn't spell the end of the road for Eileen Reid. She had married Jimmy Day two years earlier, and they have three grown-up children. Today, she's an actress and remains a household name in Irish showbusiness. Although a '60s survivor, her head isn't buried in the past: "The sixties period was my apprenticeship in the business. It was very hard, but stood to me years later. I'm having a much better time these days. I'm delighted with myself. I think life is great... I can wear my hair the way I want to now!"

As the Cadets took top billing during the late '60s, a school-girl trio, Maxi, Dick and Twink, served their apprenticeship on the dancehall circuit. They learned valuable lessons — on and off stage. By the age of twenty-three, Maxi was already a veteran when she won the National Song Contest with *Do I Dream* in 1973. Maxi (Irene McCoubrey) began her career in showbusiness at fifteen while attending the Holy Faith Convent in the Coombe. She never left home for a 'gig' at the end of the '60s without her 'survival kit'. That consisted of a hot water bottle, flask, sandwiches, blanket and cushion. It made life bearable while travelling in a van in the dead of night. She huddled under the blanket with the hot water bottle to get some sleep so that she could get up for school next morning.

Maxi recalls: "I wouldn't go anywhere without them. Often, I'd ask the ladies who made tea in the ballroom to fill the bottle for me. Sometimes they'd say, 'yes' — and sometimes they'd even say, 'no'. All it took was boiling a kettle. I just wanted to be warm in the van on the journey home. I tend to block out the bad memories. Many years later, I travelled as a DJ — just me and a driver. He'd been with me for years. He'd say to me — 'do you remember this place?' — and I'd say 'no.' He'd say, 'but do you not remember whatever' — and I'd eventually say, 'yes; but I'd prefer to forget about that'. If I prod my memory enough I will remember it. But if it's a particularly annoying thing, then I don't want to spill it into now."

Maxi appreciated her early education... outside the class-rooms. "Look, I was wised up about life by seventeen," she reflects. "People often ask me if I think I wasted time. I think it was the best education. I was being educated bookwise as a teenager and educated in life at the same time. Some people might ask — 'my God, what were you doing out so late?' On the other hand, I was streets ahead of my other seventeen-year-old friends when it came to being ripped off. I could spot a chancer a mile away, so I was being educated on both sides of the counter and I didn't even realise it."

An outstanding memory is the lack of compassion by ball-room proprietors for three teenagers who just wanted to be paid so they could go home to bed. Frequently, proprietors delayed till long after the dance was over before dipping their hands into their pockets. Maxi, Dick and Twink were paid a fee for their feature spots in the dancehalls. As soon as they went on stage, their road manager went in search of the proprietor in order to sort out money. Since the girls had school next day, they couldn't afford to hang around for long afterwards. "We were delayed a lot by uncaring people," says Maxi. "They'd say that they hadn't got the money counted yet. This was all very good training for me in later life. It used to annoy me being hassled over money. I couldn't understand why these people would do that. They would keep you waiting, knowing in their heart and soul that you were uncomfortable and that you had worked hard for them. After all, we delivered the product. It annoyed me that a promoter, who had far too much money anyway, would just delay you for his little moment of power. He knew that we had travelled down from Dublin. He knew that we had to leave at a certain time. He knew we were only sixteen or seventeen. They had to pay us in the end; but if they could keep you waiting an hour, they would be very pleased.

"I remember my mum often asking me why I got in so late, especially if the ballroom wasn't all that far away. I'd say — 'but, mum, the guy didn't pay us until whatever time'. I didn't understand why they couldn't have cash ready for the acts, and then figure out the finance later. I mean, the ballroom owners were making money. The halls were full. We had a saying in those days that 'you never saw floorboards' — it was always just people. They didn't keep the artistes happy. When the downfall came, I drove past as a DJ and saw the ballrooms, one by one, become supermarkets. I knew the reason why."

It wasn't all bad, and there were many hilarious memories. One concerns the ballroom 'macho man' who impressed girls apparently by taking the top off a mineral bottle with his teeth. He bought a mineral earlier in the night, took the top off with an opener, replaced it and left the bottle on the front of the stage. At an opportune moment, while dancing, he reached out his arm, took the bottle, stuck it in his mouth and removed the top. Maxi once played a trick on him by switching bottles. A loud yelp was heard as far away as the car park. Maxi laughs: "As he grabbed the bottle from the stage as usual, I said to myself — 'go on, deal with *that* macho man.' He forgave me for it afterwards, and we remained friends."

The girls had a hectic schedule: home from school, homework, make-up and out to work. "My parents were very sensible," says Maxi. "My mother was a schoolteacher. She could see that I might be influenced by all the glamour and the few bob. She said — 'the first exam you fail, then the singing stops'. It was good psychology. I had to make sure that I passed my exams — otherwise what I really wanted to do would be taken away from me. My parents were very rock solid on the thing."

Conditions were abysmal in many ballrooms; dressing rooms nothing more than sheds. "The proprietors were making an awful lot of money," says Maxi, "but my complaint was that they didn't put anything back in. That's why, in time, the punters got dissatisfied and ended up in the pubs and singing lounges where at least they were more comfortable. The proprietors put a few bob into what you saw on stage — but definitely not backstage. I was offered one dressing room that actually had a stream running through it — a kind of outside shed where beer crates were stored. It was freezing cold. The stream flowed through it." Maxi faced the prospect of changing into her stage clothes with trepidation that night. She called the owner, and said: "Look, don't you have anywhere that's dry?" He snapped: "It was good enough for others — so it's good enough for you." Maxi changed "with one on leg either side of the stream." She sums up: "You weren't treated like a human being. You travelled five hours sometimes to get to these places. When you got there, they just wanted to make the money fast. They didn't stop to think that if they made the punters and the artistes more comfortable, maybe the business would have lasted longer. It was all about a quick buck..."

The Blonde Bombshell

Cork, Saturday, October 6th, 1962.

Girls rush towards the stage at the Arcadia Ballroom to shake the hand of Brendan Bowyer and collect his autograph for posterity. The dance is over. It's a nightly event for the handsome showband star and, as always, he obliges. Manager T.J. Byrne approaches a teenage girl who stands alone. Her friend joins the other girls who swarm around the glamour boy, but she can't pluck up the courage. Byrne asks: "Why aren't you down getting an autograph like everyone else?" The reluctant fan replies: "It's my first time coming to see Brendan." He asks: "Would you like to meet him?" She says: "Yes." Byrne makes the introduction and the youngster is lost for words. It's a dream-come-true, made sweeter by an invitation to attend his birthday party that month in Tramore. Bowyer had just met Eileen Kelly, a teenager who, within a few years, would become a showband star herself and, later on, share the stage with him under the neon lights of Las Vegas.

Nearly three decades on, her eyes light up at the memory of that first meeting with Bowyer and of the night when she fell in love with showbusiness. She says: "It was my first experience of bands. I was too young for dances. I ducked out with a friend. We queued to see the Royal Showband for the first time. I stood in front of the stage and idolised Brendan all night. We were totally amazed by him. To us, he was Ireland's answer to Elvis Presley. I thought he was absolutely superb. He had everything. He was the big hunk. He was the biggest pop star in Ireland. When all that is moulded into one person, you've got everybody's idol." It was the "greatest thrill" to be invited to the birthday party. She told all her friends, but her parents wouldn't allow her to go. It was a major disappointment. Eileen telephoned Bowyer at his party to apologise for her absence. "In fairness, he did remember me," she says. "He said that the party was fantastic and told me all about it. That was nearly as good as being there. It was big deal to even speak to him on the phone."

Eileen maintained contact with the Royal and, together with her friend, Helen O'Leary, met the band every time they came to Cork. The pair were their guests at the dances. Parental permission was eventually granted for trips to Waterford where they stayed with Eileen's uncles and aunts who lived in the city. Her mother, Bridie, whose maiden name was Dalton, came from Waterford. It was an "added thrill" to see Bowyer and the Royal in action in their home town. "There was fantastic hype about them in Waterford. They were stars." The girls were introduced to band members' families and friends. They shared the lime-light, offstage, and had the time of their lives.

Eileen was born in Cork, the second eldest of four children whose parents, Cecil and Bridie Kelly, settled at Magazine Road, south of the River Lee. The family moved to the northside — first to St. Lukes, then Cathedral Road, Dominic Street, and back to St. Lukes. She first raised her voice at the age of five: "I remember being put up on a table and asked to sing. I was shaking, completely terrified. I sang with this terrible quiver in my voice." Eileen was interested in music growing up, and sang along to the pop songs she heard on the radio. She bought records and studied the words. She practised standards like *Summertime* and was ready when called upon at parties. Her favourite singers were Brenda Lee, Connie Francis, Sandie Shaw, Cilla Black and Dionne Warwick. "If you didn't sing at parties," she recalls, "then you weren't part of what went on. I always had one or two songs." Eileen read about the glamorous world of film stars and models in glossy magazines, and she longed to be part of it. Her head was full of dreams; her thoughts a million miles away from the hills of Cork's northside.

In the real world, she passed exams at the North Presentation secondary school. Next came a commercial course at Miss Haynes secretarial college in the Grand Parade. She mastered 120 words shorthand per minute and 100 at typing. The skills provided a passport to an office job at local tea merchants. At the same time, Eileen took a deportment course with the Marie Woods agency. "Thank God I did it," she reflects, "because it stood to me later in showbusiness. I knew all about fashion, the correct application of make-up and hairdos. It gave me a great grounding." Girls who completed the course were selected as ramp models, photographic models or show comperes. Although Eileen had stunning good looks, she was unsuitable for the ramp at five foot two inches in height. As a photographic model, she was a natural. Pictures of the glamorous Cork girl began to appear in newspapers and magazines. The blonde "look" was a trademark. Her sex appeal was undeniable. She became a familiar face...and a familiar figure. The mini-skirted sex-kitten image would follow her all the way to the bandstand. Her first assignment as a model was to advertise Phillips televisions. Part-time modelling was an antidote to the office. She spent her extra earnings on clothes and make-up: "That's where all my money went, and my father was always giving out to me."

In 1963, while still on a weekly wage as a secretary, she was recommended to a local band, the Music Makers, by the Prendergast brothers, Peter and Phillip. The band was well-rated, although Cork was ruled by the Dixielanders. Della Heslin left the Music Makers, so they needed a female singer. Eileen was going out with Phillip at the time. "He thought I was terrific," she says. "He thought I was the best thing since cheese. With the Prendergasts, there were always parties. I used to sing Ketty Lester's *Love Letters*. Phillip heard that Della had gone from the Music Makers, so he and Peter put my name forward for the job." One of the band members, drummer Joe Horgan, knocked on Eileen's door and said: "We believe you can sing." He invited her to audition at the Shandon Boat Club. She was dumbfounded and said: "I haven't a clue. I don't even know how to hold a microphone." Horgan replied: "Look, come along anyway." Eileen did and sang Brenda Lee's *All Alone Am I* and Sandie Shaw's *Always Something There To Remind Me*. She got the job.

Eileen fronted the Music Makers in '64 and '65. She learned the fundamentals of the business and maintained her high profile in the press. Musically, she had a versatile repertoire and made songs that entered the Eurovision Song Contest her speciality. She can still recall the words of an Italian entry. "I didn't have a clue of Italian," she laughs. "But, I was so interested that I sat down and listened to every word over and over until I had it off. One of the lads in the Music Makers told me later they knew I wasn't going to stay with them. They thought I was too good. They felt all along they weren't going to keep me."

Meantime, Maisie McDaniel, who had fronted the Fendermen, was transferred to the Nevada by manager George O'Reilly who handled showband acts from his office in Pearse Street, Dublin. He decided that the Nevada needed the glamour of a female lead singer. He picked McDaniel, a big showband name who appeared weekly on the RTE *Jamboree* show and on Radio Éireann's *Maureen Potter Show*. O'Reilly publicised McDaniel and the Nevada as Ireland's "greatest double attraction." The association was short-lived because McDaniel was injured in a road accident. T.J. Byrne recommended Eileen Kelly as her replacement with the Nevada.

"T.J. and George were close friends," she recalls. "I was talking to T.J. one day and he told me that the Nevada were looking for a girl singer. He asked me if I was interested, and I said that I was. He went back and told George. They made plans to come down and hear me at the Showboat in Youghal, but these never materialised. They decided to bring me to Dublin to audition for the Nevada. I auditioned at the Radio Éireann studios in Henry Street. I remember Bill O'Donovan saying, 'she looks the part... now all she needs to do is sing'. When he was satisfied, everybody was satisfied." She passed the audition, and Kelley and the Nevada became the latest showband 'sensation' in '65/'66.

Eileen took to the road fulltime, although the Nevada were not yet rated in the upper echelon of showbands. "We were a pop band," she explains. "In hindsight, I feel that if I had continued on where Maisie left off, in the country'n'western vein, I'd have been better off. But, I wanted to be Dusty Springfield. At that stage, she was my idol. I wanted to be just like her. I had blonde hair too, and I thought she was the bees knees. I wanted to sing all of her stuff, even though I don't think I did a very good job of it. I probably should have stuck to country'n'western." She became known for her covers of Springfield's hits like *I Only Want To Be With You, I Just Don't*

(Photo: Sunday World)

Know What To Do With Myself, and *You Don't Have To Say You Love Me.*

Her stage name was Kelley, and she became known as the "blonde bombshell." The nickname stuck throughout her career. It was novelty at first, but she grew to hate it. She explains: "I absolutely loathed it. I got an awful lot of press and newspapermen were always looking for a tag. Because I was blonde, they printed it once and it stayed forever. I suppose I had a sex symbol aura. There was no way I was ever going to get away from that nickname. I always dressed in the latest fashion. When miniskirts were in, I wore them. Then, when hot pants were in, I wore them too. It was probably the minis that led to the blonde bombshell. I always thought it was a tag that could be attributed to somebody who was dumb. Just a dumb blonde...but I wasn't that."

Kelley was the focus of clever image management. The simple country girl became a sex symbol. The sexy image provoked the wrath of the conservatives in Irish society. After being photographed once in a mini-skirt, a newspaper clipping of the picture was sent to her family in Cork. The anonymous sender wrote the word 'disgusting' across the paper. Pictures of the "blonde bombshell" even appeared in English newspapers and magazines.

"I already had a lot of publicity before I came into the business," she says. "All that experience helped enormously with regard to dealing with the press. I was always in the papers. I was going to lunches and receptions and well used to meeting the press. George O'Reilly, who managed the Nevada, knew every pressman and photographer. He had great connections in the business." As part of the publicity splash to launch Kelley, O'Reilly arranged a photo-opportunity for her in London with Bing Crosby. O'Reilly was a friend of Crosby. Kelley was flown to London where she met him at the Savoy Hotel. "Bing graciously agreed to do the pictures," she recalls. "He was a lovely man, very easy going. He made you feel at ease straight away. We had a great chat and he spoke about his affection for Ireland. In fact, he began to sing... 'does your mother come from Ireland.' I got great press as a result of that meeting. I linked up with him again years later on a film set here."

At the height of her fame, Kelley met the biggest stars of the entertainment world... among them Frank Sinatra, Jack Jones, Susan George and Telly Savalas. She describes Savalas — the actor who became known years later for his role as the tough TV cop, *Kojak* — as a "real charmer." While attending the Louis Prima Show at the Tropicana Hotel in Las Vegas, Kelley was invited to sit at Sinatra's table, a rare honour, and she chatted to him throughout the evening.

Another legendary story concerns her relationship with Tom Jones. Kelley met him on his first Irish tour, and they renewed the friendship on his second visit to Dublin. When Jones flew in on the second occasion, he refused to speak to waiting reporters. When they pressed him for a few words, he asked: "How's Kelley?" The reporters replied that Kelley and the Nevada were "just fine." She says of their relationship: "We became quite close when he was here. We went for meals and drinks together. I liked him very much. I liked everything about the guy. When I first heard him singing I thought he was tremendous. I said to myself, 'if he looks anything like his voice, he's going to be massive'. I was dying to see a photograph of him. When I got one, I said to myself, 'perfect... the photograph matches the voice'. I wanted to meet him. I hoped that he'd be as nice as he looks. Then, when I met him, he knocked me flat.

"He was everything that I hoped he was going to be. A nice down-to-earth guy. I knew nothing could come of it. It couldn't have developed into a serious relationship because he was married at the time. I didn't set out with the idea...'Tom Jones is married. I'm going to get him'. Of course, I accepted that he was married. I just wanted to meet and befriend him. There was absolutely no way it could have gone any further. I knew that. How far can you go with somebody like Tom Jones who's a huge superstar and who's a married man? I didn't fall in love with him. Mind you, he was the type of guy I could very easily have fallen in love with. If you ask me that out straight, I would have to say yes, I could have fallen in love. No doubt about it. I could have fallen flat on my heels in love with him."

Kelley and the Nevada did the dancehall circuit in Ireland, Britain and the U.S. as well as the American bases in Germany.

She was idolised by men, in the same way that women worshipped Bowyer. The hysteria was such that she travelled with
a chaperone to 'mind' her. Her free time, according to the
publicity machine, was spent mountaineering, water ski-ing and
horse riding. In reality, she had little free time, and spare hours
were spent at hairdressing salons. The band clocked up high
mileage. Even though Kelley may have felt tired, she was
always expected to look well. The image had to be perfect...
twenty-four hours a day. Kelley enjoyed showbusiness, despite
the strains. "It was the most marvellous part of my life," she
says, "even though you had to be tough to survive. The hours
were crazy — going to bed at all hours, getting up at all hours
and back on the road again. I must have been tough to stay in
the business as long as I did. Some girls who couldn't stick the
business got out of it. To me, they were the best years. I wouldn't
have stayed if I didn't enjoy it." Kelley, like other showband
girls, found it almost impossible to maintain steady relationships. "We worked so hard we didn't have time to meet guys,"
she says. "You didn't meet people in ballrooms. You spent most
of your time travelling to ballrooms. We had one night off a
week and, sometimes, not even that much."

Kelley recounts familiar stories about deplorable conditions
in the ballrooms. She frequently had to share dressing rooms
with her male colleagues in the Nevada. She developed the art
of beach-style dressing and undressing without revealing any
flesh. She also used the wagon to change, or else asked the
ballroom owner for permission to change in his own bathroom.
The biggest task was to make herself look glamorous in the
"breezeblock ballrooms" that consisted of no more than four
walls and a roof. She says: "Yes, the conditions in some places
were rough, but you took the rough with the smooth. It was all
new and exciting to us, and we looked upon it as a great
adventure."

The worst memory is of breaking down on lonely country
roads in the dead of night and waiting for hours to get the wagon
fixed. Kelley, in common with the others, hated the marquees
where promoters managed to provide dancers with even less
than the basic minimum of four walls and a roof. Kelley was
once stranded, literally, in a sea of mud between a gate and the

marquee. "We had to dress in the wagon and then get from the gate to the marquee. The field was full of muck. I was destroyed by the time someone rescued me and brought me inside." Kelley and the Nevada indulged in drinking sessions, poker games and "great crack." They played pranks on other bands who shared the same hotels.

The "blonde bombshell" was occasionally hauled offstage by leering male fans for whom the excitement proved too much. The band had to drop their instruments and wade through the crowd to help her back up. Kelley knew the ballrooms where extra care had to be taken — most of them in the west of Ireland — so she never went too close to the edge of the stage. She recalls the madness: "Being pulled to the ground made me very nervous. The west was a devilish place for me, because there always seemed to be a group of guys around the stage. They always looked treacherous. They looked as if they were going to dive on me any minute. It was very nerve-racking. If they didn't succeed in pulling me off the stage, they might catch my leg. I'd lose balance and fall. Once, when I was dragged to the floor, they tried to tear my clothes off. I was never attacked or assaulted as such, but attempts were certainly made. There was no such thing as bouncers or security that time."

Kelley attracted a coterie of determined male followers who, clearly infatuated by her, wrote letters, made telephone calls and waited on after dances for autographs. There were many marriage proposals and gifts. She remains friendly with some fans to this day. One landowner in the North always brought along presents of sacks of potatoes to his local ballroom when Kelley and the Nevada topped the bill. The potatoes were heavy, and she had to get help loading the sack aboard the wagon. He was a country gentleman...'cravat, check shirt, beautiful jacket and fawn trousers.' He frequently told Kelley: "You're going to be the lady of the manor some day." In Dublin, her greatest admirer was a coloured boy who studied at the Royal College of Surgeons. He never missed a dance. He met Kelley backstage one night and gave her an expensive tiger's eye brooch. It turned out that he came from a wealthy African family.

The Nevada gradually increased in popularity. Kelley recorded her first single in London for RCA, titled *Be My Man.*

The band's profile was raised by the presence of Roly Daniels in 1969. Daniels, born in India, had toured with the Memphis Showband and the Jim Farley Big band. He was hyped as Ireland's answer to Tom Jones and had all of the famous hip-swivelling gyrations off to perfection. He made a name for himself singing *The Green Green Grass of Home*, *Detroit City*, *Funny Familiar Forgotten Feelings* and other Jones' hits. Daniels, who later switched to country music, was replaced by Red Hurley in 1971. Tommy Hayden took over management. At that stage, says Kelley, the Nevada were "huge."

Hurley had two No. 1 hits with the band in '71 — *Sometimes* on July 31st, which stayed in the charts for fifteen weeks; *Kiss Me Goodbye* on November 18th, in the charts for eleven weeks. '72 was a pivotal year for Kelley, Hurley and the Nevada. They dominated the annual *Spotlight* Awards: top male vocalist, top female vocalist and top band. Hurley's song, *Hold Me*, went to No. 3 in the charts during May. At Christmas, Kelley reached the Top Ten with a song called *How Great Thou Art*. It reached No. 2, beaten for the top position by Thin Lizzy's *Whiskey In The Jar*. The BBC filmed a one-hour documentary on the Nevada, titled *The Best Years Of Our Lives*, as part of a series of programmes called *The Entertainers*. It featured a typical day for the band.

Hurley had two Top Ten hits with the Nevada in '73 — *Arkansas* and *I Never Said Goodbye*. Kelley's other big hit, *The Wedding Song* — not the Julie Rogers version — reached No. 3 in June 1974. That year marked the departure of Kelley and Hurley. Kelley was given the opportunity to replace Twink in Bowyer's Big 8 and move to Las Vegas. Kelley had previously visited Vegas on a five-day trip with Hurley and Hayden. She loved the resort. Twink, who was resident there with the Big 8 at the time, saw Kelley off at the airport and asked her: "Would you like to stay?" She replied: "I'd love to." Kelley says she never imagined that she would replace Twink some years later. "That was never on my mind. I loved Vegas and everything that went on there... the big shows, the glamour."

The Big 8 returned to Ireland in the summer of '74. Word on the grapevine was that they wanted Kelley to fill the gap left by Twink. "It seemed that I was the obvious choice," says Kelley, "even though they were auditioning other girls. The lads in the Nevada said to me, 'they'll probably want you for the Big 8'. I wasn't sure about whether I really wanted to leave the Nevada because I'd been so long with the band." Bowyer, Dunphy and the Big 8 came to watch Kelley perform at the Tara Club in Dublin. Kelley takes up the story.

"Various chats were going on among them. Suggestions were made to me that I might like life in Las Vegas and would get on well there. They couldn't really ask me directly because the Federation of Musicians were cracking down on poaching in bands. Eventually, Tom Dunphy called out to my house. He said, 'it's like this Kelley, we need you for the Big 8.' I said, 'Tom, it's the first time in my life that anybody has ever told me that they need me. I'll consider the job'. Then, Tom added, 'okay, I'm not supposed to be approaching you. I just want you to think about it'."

Kelley decided to leave the Nevada and join the Big 8 in Las Vegas. Kelley says that Las Vegas was 'terrific' — 'fabulous'. She took the opportunity to watch Elvis Presley perform at the Hilton Hotel. The King was her hero. She was bitterly disappointed by what she saw. "I couldn't believe it," recalls Kelley. "Elvis was grossly overweight. He was obviously heavily drugged and didn't have any control. He'd start a song and decide not to finish it half way through. There were ten bodyguards on each side of the stage. I was sitting up front and put my glass of champagne on the stage at one point. It was quickly taken away by the bodyguards. My lasting memory is of Elvis reaching out to girls seated behind me. He leaned over my head. He had a huge tummy. I felt so sorry for him."

Kelley was part of the Big 8's showband programme at the Stardust Hotel. However, the novelty wore off. She tired of having to sing the same two songs — *Amazing Grace* and *Viva Espana* — for three performances a night. Although the shows were well choreographed, she became bored with the nightly routine. Kelley explains: "When I was with the Nevada, I worked very hard. We did more numbers and I was more involved in what went on. But singing the same two songs over and over finally got me down. Doing the same thing three shows a night, eighteen shows a week, for six months, monotony sets in. It's very hard to overcome that. It got to the stage where I'd go to Brendan and ask for a change. He'd reply, 'why should we change when we're going so well?' Towards the end of the six-month stint in Vegas, Brendan offered to drop a show for me. He knew I was losing interest. It meant that instead of me doing three shows a night, I'd just do two. But I couldn't very well drop a show, because everyone else in the band was doing three. It would have looked terrible. It wouldn't have been fair to the others. I decided that was it. I had enough. I came home with the Big 8 in '75. That was the time when Tom died. After we did the circuit here, I decided not to return to Vegas. Brendan made me several offers... less shows. But I didn't think that was a good idea anyway. Another reason for the decision was my health. I hadn't been feeling well in Las Vegas. A doctor there told me I had diabetes. When I came home, my doctor here tested me and gave me the all clear. He suggested that a change of diet in the States might have made me ill. Anyway, because of that problem and the stage monotony, I decided to stay in Ireland."

Kelley was left in a 'limbo' situation during the second half of the '70s. She decided to launch her own group, called Kelley with Klass. "It was very expensive," she says. "There were four lads in the group. It was either have a big band in the ballrooms, or go into cabaret. It worked for a certain amount of time, but not for too long. So, I ended up doing cabaret on my own, which I'm still doing." The hysteria once generated by Eileen Kelly, the "dolly bird" who built a career from St. Luke's to Las Vegas, is long dead. The nickname that once fuelled the fantasies of young men means nothing to today's generation. Other bombshells have taken her place. She lives with her memories. She never married. "I've been engaged twice — once officially, and once unofficially," says Kelley with the giggle of a schoolgirl. "I came close to marriage, but never took the final step...not yet."

The First Lady Of Showbands

Brighton, Saturday, April 6th, 1974.

It's a sweet Eurovision victory for ABBA while sixteen other entrants, among them Ireland's Tina, met their Waterloo. A little- known foursome delivered Sweden's first win and sang their way to a successful international career. Conductor Sven Olof Walldoff dressed up in the garb of Napoleon as Benny Andersson, Bjorn Ulvaeus, Agnetha Faltskog and Frida Lyng-stad captured the votes of Europe. TV commentators who shared the excitement with 500 million viewers worldwide couldn't resist the temptation to report that Napoleon reversed the course of history when his quartet of marshals crushed the troops of European nations, including the British.

Tina, who sang *Cross Your Heart*, written by Paul Lyttle of Chips, came joint fifth with Israel. She performed well in the teeth of strong competition from Britain, the Netherlands, Italy, Norway and Luxembourg. Tina's appearance in the contest was a personal triumph because she was recuperating from a major road accident in '73 in which she nearly lost her life. The first lady of showbands fought back against serious head injuries that threatened her career to take her place in Brighton. On the eve of the contest, she rehearsed the Irish entry four times without a hitch as Colman Pearce conducted the orchestra. She spoke frankly at a press conference later about the accident and ad-mitted that the resultant effects of amnesia had worried her. "For a while," she said, "I thought I might have to write down the words of the song to glance at on stage."

For an earlier performance on *The Late Late Show*, Tina wrote some of the words on her hand. She praised the make-up by Maureen Carter of RTE — a task that required much delicacy because there were still scars on her face. Tina agreed to grant photo sessions for foreign journalists as well as radio and press interviews during that hectic week in Brighton. Tina had a slight touch of "throatiness" but seemed to be the most relaxed of all seventeen singers. Her only worry was whether her memory would let her down. The betting odds put Britain's Olivia Newton-John at 7/2 favourite, and Tina at 10/1.

Tina, dressed in a beautiful silk gown designed by Dublin designer Thomas Wolfangel, proved a worthy representative. The partisan audience at the Dome in Brighton hoped for a British victory, but England's fancied entry finished joint fourth. Tina told Irish journalists: "Apart from the day I got married, it turned out to be the happiest day of my life. I'm not disappointed that we did not win." Her father, John Quinn, commented: "Tina did very well. She really put the song over, especially considering what she had to go through after the car accident last year."

Preparations for the Brighton finale had started in early 1974, even though Tina wasn't fully recovered from the accident. She sang all eight Irish entries in the National Song Contest every week on the RTE programme, *The Likes of Mike*. The public was asked to vote by postcard. Paul Lyttle's song won the contest on Sunday, February 10th. Tina's *Cross Your Heart* was No. 1 in the Irish charts during the week of Eurovision in April, but replaced afterwards by ABBA's *Waterloo*. Her record sold well abroad. It was the only Euro song picked by Polydor for general release in Britain. It was a chart hit in Germany where Tina sang the German version on a TV show within weeks of the Eurovision final. Offstage, Tina was a popular contestant in Brighton. As she boarded a coach to Heathrow Airport afterwards, a special best wishes telegram was handed to her. The message came from six Sussex CID men who had guarded her for a week. It read: "You're still tops with us."

Eurovision imposed strains on her health, yet she was determined to take part. "I was off the road recuperating when asked to do it," she recalls. "I wasn't sure whether I'd be able for it. It was an ordeal, but I decided to go ahead anyway. I wouldn't have been able to accept it within myself if I turned it down. Eurovision was something I just had to do, and it was wonderful. Going to Brighton to represent Ireland was the highlight of my career and something I wouldn't have missed for anything."

Tina's career was marked by tragedy, and her private life by personal trauma. Two serious road accidents left scars for life. Physical injuries forced her off the stage just as her career was blossoming. Her marriage broke up. She suffered acute depression. All these things took a heavy toll. Tina's battle to achieve peace of mind was waged for years. Nobody knew of her nightmare. It was a struggle against incredible odds. Tina found comfort in prayer. She returned to the Church. She prayed for help to St. Jude. She thanks God for having raised her from the depths of despair. The physical scars remain, but the psychological ones are healing. "I thank the Lord I'm past it, but I feel that I had to go through it," says Tina. "I feel I'm a much stronger person now."

Tina was, of course, a stage name, an invention of showbusiness. Her real name is Philomena Josephine Veronica Quinn. She was the youngest of four children. She was born with TB and spent her first four years in hospital. Her mother was seriously ill with TB and had to be cared for in a sanatorium at Newcastle, Co. Wicklow. Philomena was raised in an orphanage, the Sacred Heart Home of Drumcondra, from age four till nine. Her father went to work in England. Her mother came home from hospital and made a home for young Philomena and her two sisters and brother in Greystones, Co. Wicklow. It wasn't easy, and the head of the household was bedridden most of the time by sickness. Philomena was educated during the '50s at St. Brigid's national school, and later at St. David's secondary school. She loved to sing in school choirs and at Feiseanna and disliked study. In her own words, "I didn't have one little brain in my head." She frequently had to take time off school to look after her ill mother at home. Her brother and sisters won school scholarships, but Philomena left school, at the age of fourteen.

Her life changed course after her mother died in Britain during early '64. Philomena, accompanied by her mother, had travelled over to attend the wedding of her sister, Mary, in Cambridge. Mrs. Anne Quinn took ill and passed away. At just sixteen, Philomena decided to stay in Britain. She got a job as a telephonist in Cambridge. Opportunity knocked for Philomena, as for so many others, at Butlins. While on a holiday to Skegness in the summer of '64, the Red Coats asked her to perform one night, so she sang *Danny Boy*. One of them entered her for the week's heat of the talent contest. She agreed, although reluctantly, because she was nervous of singing before a big audience.

She won hands down and returned for the final. She sang her way into second place with the Springfields hit of 1963, *Island of Dreams*. "That's how it all started for me," she reflects.

Meantime, her Butlins success was reported in the columns of *The Wicklow People*. The story was read by Tom Cranny who managed the Mexicans. His son, Alan, was band leader and played guitar. Cranny senior sent Philomena a telegram and said they were about to switch to a showband format and needed a girl singer. Was she interested? "I never gave it a second thought," she says. "I gave in my notice at work and told Tom I'd be home in two weeks." A stage name was suggested by her brother, Kevin. He told her: "If you ever want to sing professionally, then get rid of Philomena. You need a small name that's easy to remember... Tina."

She turned professional with the Mexicans at the end of 1964. They developed a versatile showband repertoire and played the full range from *Danny Boy* to rock'n'roll. "We were a showband, so we did absolutely everything. We even did dance steps." The band traipsed around the ballrooms north and south, playing as relief to the top billing bands. Tina was a glamour girl. The Mexicans toured the circuit of German clubs, and returned home to resume a busy schedule across the country. Although the travel was horrendous, Tina, in her late teens, had the stamina and loved all the excitement. "There was so much happening," she says. "Everything was so new and different. I loved it. Nothing was too much for me. We were young and full of enthusiasm. If we had to be in Cork tonight and Belfast tomorrow we wouldn't give it a second thought."

Tina, like other females who made a living in showbandland, suffered the slings and arrows of people who felt that her way of life was not appropriate for a young woman. Gombeen ballroom proprietors made them feel cheap too. "We were looked down on," she says. "I mean, we were women on the road with male bands, and that hadn't happened before in Ireland. Some people, mostly promoters, thought so little of us. They couldn't see that you had a profession and worked hard to perfect your talent as a singer. Whatever about the way they treated the men, the proprietors didn't have a clue when it came to women. Ladies in bands were looked down on, but that didn't put me off." Tina can vividly remember the dingy dressing rooms... and sometimes even the absence of changing facilities. The marquees were the worst. They had to change in the 'ladies'... a field behind the big tent. "It was very unfair. They wouldn't get away with it today."

In 1968, after four productive years with the Mexicans, Tina joined Jim Farley's band who had a residency at the Top Hat Ballroom in Dun Laoghaire. She went on the road with the Real McCoy in '69/'70, and her career took off. Tina and the Real McCoy had a No. 1 hit on December 9th, '71 with the song, *I Don't Know How To Love Him*, from the *Jesus Christ Superstar* musical. The record was in the charts for eight weeks and made her name nationwide. The success represented a highlight of her career. Tina and the band broke into the charts again in '72 with *Tell Me What's The Matter* and in '73 with *When Morning Has Come*.

The first accident happened in 1973 outside Portlaoise as Tina and the Real McCoy returned to Dublin during the early hours from a dance in the country. It was a head-on collision. Tina says she was asleep at the time and can't remember what happened. She was told later that the band gear fell on top of them in the impact. Tina suffered multiple injuries, the most serious to her head. She was rushed to hospital unconscious. She woke up a week later, and spent another five in hospital under intensive care. The injuries caused a loss of memory. "I wasn't a pretty sight," she recalls. "My head was shaved. There was a big scar across the top of my head and it's there to this day. I was really badly smashed up and was lucky to escape. I came home afterwards and spent a year and a half recuperating. When I was offered Eurovision, I wasn't sure what to do. I missed the stage and decided to do it, even though I didn't know whether I was doing the right thing or not."

Eurovision '74 catapulted Tina back to the top of the charts. There was valuable TV exposure in the run-up to the national contest as RTE bosses broke with tradition and asked Tina to sing each of the eight songs. It was a high honour, and just the tonic she needed to restore her confidence after the accident. Then, in April, she took centre-stage at the Dome in Brighton and sang for Ireland. Even though ABBA won convincingly,

Tina was euphoric. Two months later, however, she came back to earth with a bang. Her marriage collapsed. She says she had no idea it was crumbling: "I wish I knew why it broke up. I wish I knew the answer to that question. If I had any inkling, I wouldn't have allowed it to happen like that. I don't think that my career impinged on the marriage because my husband was also in the music business and just as career- minded. I could have given it all up in the morning."

In the months that followed, Tina displayed a smiling face, but her world was really falling apart. "I just went downhill. I wasn't feeling well anyway at the time. I came back from Eurovision and we separated. I got depressed and couldn't seem to pull out of it. That was the worst I've ever felt in my whole life. I didn't have anybody to turn to. Although I had loads of friends in the business, I needed a different sort of friend...somebody I could share my feelings with. My dad and all my family were in England. I just wanted to end it all," she says. "I didn't want to live any longer. I took tablets... anything that I could find in the house. I said to myself, 'what's the point in going on?' I took an overdose. That's how bad I was." Fortunately, Tina was discovered in time and rushed to St. John of Gods.

In 1975, she took the advice of her sister-in-law, Mary Quinn, and attended a prayer meeting at the shrine to St. Jude at the Carmelite Church of Our Lady of Mount Carmel in White Friar Street. "You pray to St. Jude when you feel like a hopeless case," says Tina. "That's how I felt at the time. I decided to go to St. Jude for one night. Since then, I've experienced a draw there like a magnet. If I'm not working, then that's where I am. I feel that my week wouldn't be complete without going. God reached out and helped me in those moments of despair. Very much so. It was through going in to St. Jude that I've met the most genuine people in my life."

Tina attempted to get her career back on the rails. She joined the Nevada and, in November '76, achieved a Top Ten hit with a song called *I'll Do It All Again*. It was in the charts for eighteen weeks. Fate dealt Tina another blow in 1977 when she suffered more injuries in a second accident. The Nevada was involved in a collision with a car at Enfield, Co. Meath, on the way back to

Dublin from Galway. Tina, who was sitting in a back seat of the wagon, suffered mostly leg injuries. She was wearing a seat belt, and says it saved her life. She had multiple fractures of one knee, underwent surgery and spent five weeks at Elm Park Hospital in Dublin. Tina's career was again thrown into disarray.

After a prolonged period of recuperation, she went into cabaret. She regards the two high points of her career to have been the No. 1 hit with the Real McCoy at Christmas '71 as well as the Eurovision appearance of '74. Tina has happy memories of a month's stay in Las Vegas where she sang in the lounges of the Landmark Hotel. "I learned everything during the weeks of Eurovision and the month in Vegas," she says. "I was treated like a star and I felt like a star."

Tina still sings professionally, and says "it's what keeps me going." The hard knocks would have been enough to leave most with feelings of bitterness. But Tina isn't bitter and says that her faith has taught her to accept the will of God. "I've pulled out of both of the accidents. It was a fight, but it was up to me to help myself. I thank the Lord that I'm past it, but I had to go through it. I believe so differently now that if it's to happen again, I would say to myself, 'this is what the Lord wants'. I still sing because the Lord gave me a gift to bring happiness. It took years to pick myself up after everything that's happened to me. But I'm so together now, it's great. I'm not wonderful all the time. Sometimes, I do get a down day if I'm not well. But I'm getting through. I really believe that the Lord decides everything. If he wanted to take me tomorrow, then I'm ready."

Like many showband people, Tina says she once lost the Lord: "When you're young going around the country singing and playing to crowds, you don't have time to think about God. You're so immature that you lose the Lord. I stopped going to Mass and Confession. I lost the Lord. I discovered the Lord again through everything that's happened. I needed that within myself. The Lord wasn't getting through to me in another way. I don't think that he said, 'I'll get this lady and knock her about,' but he did come back into my life. I really thank God for coming through to me. I'm not gone in the head or anything. I just feel so at peace within myself."

Rebel With A Guitar

Telefís Éireann Studios, Dublin, April 1965.

Rory Gallagher causes a big upset on *Pickin' The Pops*, Telefís Éireann's Saturday evening music show, by dropping a pre-arranged Buddy Holly number, *Valley of Tears*. Instead, he plays a Larry Williams' R&B classic, *Slow Down*. A panel of guests, invited to predict showband disc hits and misses, is shocked at the sight of a rocker with long hair breaking the rules. The studio audience loves it. "Rory made a great impression," recalls DJ Larry Gogan who succeeded Gay Byrne as compere of the half-hour pop show in '65. "He surprised everybody by doing something completely different. He had a style that was unique. He was one of the people who changed the showband scene."

Gallagher and the Impact band had just made a demo disc of *Slow Down* in London when they were given a valuable TV spot. It wasn't typical showband material — but neither was Rory. "The Impact rehearsed the Buddy Holly track before going on *Pickin' The Pops*," recalls his brother, Donal. "The show had a Juke Box Jury element. The panel listened to the latest releases, gave their verdict, and guest showbands came on. The Impact appeared on the same night as a Dublin band, the Young Shadows, a kind of cover version of the Shadows. The emphasis was on showbands. When Rory switched to *Slow Down* at the last minute, there was a bit of consternation at first. But there wasn't anything anybody could do about it. They said, 'you can't do that sort of thing.' But it was great for viewers who were dying for some rock on television. Instead of listening to the usual dross, Rory got people up from their seats and rocking."

Gallagher had a habit of doing it his way, regardless of convention, in an age when rock was frowned upon. While he served an apprenticeship in the ballrooms, he refused to be governed by showband conventions. *Pickin' The Pops* was one of many acts of defiance. As 'relief' act to the top bands, he regularly provoked the wrath of managers and promoters by working the crowd into such a frenzy that they stopped dancing to watch him. Support bands like the Fontana — later renamed the Impact — risked losing work by trying to upstage headliners such as the Royal, Capitol or Dixies. "We were often warned, 'either you quit doing these numbers, or else no more gigs,'" says Declan O'Keeffe, rhythm guitarist with the band. "Rory didn't go along with that, and neither did we. You weren't supposed to put the pressure on in the final lap of your set. Keep it simple. Don't play anything from the Top Ten, or put on stoppers. But we didn't hold back for any of the top bands. Our attitude was: if they were better than us, so be it. If they weren't: then tough luck."

Some top bands never wanted the support acts to sound too good, and they discovered ways of keeping them in their place. 'Relief' bands were allowed to use the equipment of the headliners, since the logistics of having two sets of gear on stage were impractical. One important gadget was a Binson echo chamber that enhanced the sound. It was beyond the financial reach of the smaller bands. A common trick played by some top bands was to alter the settings so that the 'relief' failed to achieve the same powerful sound. "They'd have changed the echo off into different weird sounds, and you'd spend the night trying to find the right level and balance," says O'Keeffe. "That confused a lot of relief bands. But we had one of our own and knew how to use it properly. So, when we went on stage to use theirs, we just changed the settings back straight away. That's why they could never catch us."

Irish popular culture of the mid-'60s was suspicious of rock: it was a musical form that conjured up images of sex and drugs. In this climate, Gogan upset the powers-that-be in RTE by playing Gallagher on his sponsored radio programmes. "I was one of the few DJs who followed his career. It was dicey because they didn't like me playing things that were 'too noisy.' They used to say, 'a lot of the stuff you're playing is too heavy'."

Gallagher's musical values were tested against the tide. His devotion to the blues never wavered. Defiantly, he did it his way. "It would have been very easy to take the £50 a week gig with the showband and enjoy an easy life. But it didn't enter my mind," he says. His flowing dark hair set him apart from the showband establishment, even before he played a single note. When Gallagher appeared on *Pickin' The Pops*, it was the first time anybody had seen a showband musician with long hair. Offstage, it exposed him to public criticism, particularly in Cork. People even lost their tempers in the street. "Rory took a lot of stick," recalls Donal, who has stayed at his brother's side throughout his career. "That used to infuriate me because when it comes down to it, your brother is your brother, and I used to look up to him. Rory was a pacifist and never allowed anybody to faze him. A lot of people wanted to provoke a reaction and they wouldn't get one. That made them even more angry. My temper made up for both of us."

Nobody knows precisely when Rory Gallagher first displayed a love of music. Donal's earliest memory is of his brother, aged four or five, making a small toy banjo with the aid of a round cheese box, a ruler and some elastic bands. Rory was born in Ballyshannon, Co. Donegal, on March 2, 1948. The Gallaghers moved to Cork, where the boys spent their schooldays. The family home was at MacCurtain Street. Play for the boys and their friends meant pretending to be musicians. Rory was the ringleader. "He wanted us to be in a band instead of in a gang," says Donal. "He gave us all different duties to do and instruments to play. They were supposed to be little skiffle bands which were popular at the time. We made a double bass with a tea-chest, broom handle and string. I remember him telling me about Chuck Berry and Woody Guthrie when he was only eight because he'd listened to all the Lonnie Donegan stuff."

Rory discovered Leadbelly and Guthrie through Donegan. Radio was his lifeline to the music of the '50s. Later, he listened to blues radio recordings of Leadbelly and Big Bill Broonzy on American Forces Network and the BBC. With the exception of BBC jazz programmes and AFN who played the odd Muddy Waters track, Donegan was the only source to hear such material. Other influences were Berry, Eddie Cochran, and Jimmy Reed. Young Gallagher listened to Radio Luxembourg at night, and tuned in to jazz and blues on the American forces.

At nine, Rory got his first acoustic guitar, and never put it down. He taught himself to play, using tutorial books. He practised folk, skiffle and early rock'n'roll numbers. Inspiration came from the blues, his first love. He saw photographs in *Melody Maker* of the Chris Barber Band touring with Waters and Big Bill Broonzy. He was fascinated by the blues, and couldn't play traditional Irish music like jigs or reels nearly so well. In his own words, he had a 'good ear' for blues. That motivating force would remain constant throughout his career.

At ten years of age he began entering talent competitions and playing at variety shows, charity concerts, school fetes and community events. At twelve, his picture was published in the press. He won a talent contest at the City Hall, Cork, and the photo made the front page of the *Evening Echo* — he was still in short trousers. Rory played a lot of shows around Cork: it was the only vehicle to perform on stage before an audience and gain experience. He acquired his first electric guitar at twelve, and tried to emulate the great American musicians he'd heard on the radio. He had natural flair and ability. Amateur shows dictated that he play "tame stuff," but he didn't always comply.

He once took part in a week-long student variety show at school, North Monastery C.B.S. For the first few nights, he played *The Four Legged Friend*, a quiet cowboy tune. One night the show was disrupted when the tape recorder broke down. The Brothers asked Rory to go back out and keep the crowd entertained while it was being fixed. Rory said: "I've run out of material." The Brother-in-charge replied: "Play anything you like." He launched into rock'n'roll. The Brothers "went absolutely insane," recalls Donal. "That's how severe it was. Rory was taken out of the show from that moment. The Brothers had asked him basically to save the show, which he did. Now they felt that he'd played the devil's music."

At thirteen, Gallagher formed his first band. They played a couple of dates at the Cork Boat Club in Blackrock. "A lot of it involved just getting little groups together to rehearse, rather than play serious dates," he says. "To get a group together in those days was just about impossible." Gallagher knew what he wanted, but the outlets were limited. He was going nowhere. The pop culture of the early '60s was dominated by showbands: if you wanted to be a musician, you joined up. Gallagher answered an advert in the *Cork Examiner*: 'Guitarist wanted for showband'. He was hired by the Fontana. "I wasn't a fan of showbands, but at fourteen or fifteen you don't quibble. I was betwixt and between, but I decided to reply. Luckily, they had a reasonable amount of work around Cork, Kerry and Limerick. I thought it would be better to play a couple of nights a week than get nowhere with make-up groups. The idea of jumping into a van, doing gigs in other counties and playing through an amplifier appealed to me."

At fifteen, Rory bought the Fender Stratocaster which he still plays. "It's a 1961 model," he explains. "I got it second-hand. It was £100, an absolute fortune at the time. It was in good condition then, but it's got so battered now it's got a kind of tattoo quality about it. I just like the sound of it. It's also a good luck thing. It was stolen one time and it came back. It's kind of a lucky charm." In '64, aged 16, he took to the road with the Fontana. While studying for his Leaving Cert at St. Kieran's College, Camden Place, Cork, the band played the ballroom circuit an average of four nights a week. Gallagher now had regular gigs and got paid for doing what he liked best. It wasn't always easy to find time for schoolwork. "I was able to cope because, at that age, you can live without sleep. I'd come home early in the morning after a journey in a slow van. I managed. By some miracle, I did get as far as my Leaving Cert. I did the one-year version at St. Kieran's. I scraped through the exam."

The Fontana had its origins in West Cork: leader Bernie Tobin and his brother, Oliver, another member, were from Drinagh. The line-up was: Gallagher, lead guitar; John Lehane, saxophone; Eamon O'Sullivan, drums; Declan O'Keeffe, rhythm guitar; Oliver Tobin, bass guitar; Bernard Tobin, trombone, and later saxophone. Bernie Tobin was the force behind the Fontana and worked hard to keep the show on the road. The band either played or rehearsed every night. There was regular work at the Arcadia, Cork. They played 'relief' there to the top showbands and visiting British groups such as the Animals and Searchers. Says O'Keeffe: "We covered a lot of road. We often left Cork at one o'clock, drove to Westport, played from ten until two and drove back. I remember arriving into Cork at half-seven in the morning. I'd still be at work in Egans Jewellers by eight. It was crazy."

The Fontana (later Impact) built up a wild reputation and made some of the bigger bands look subdued. "We went mad on stage," recalls O'Keeffe, "we were a total loony band. We'd be up on each other's backs playing guitars, twisting over.

(Photo: Cork Examiner)

Most bands that time had the Shadows-style moves. But we went bananas, shaking and jumping around. Bernie used to hang by the heels of his boots from a railing over the old stage in the Arcadia. One of the heels fell off once and he came tumbling down. I suppose we were more than just a showband. We were mad — but we didn't go as far as shoving guitars through speakers like the Who. Most of the bands were regimented, but we freaked out on stage. Rory was fairly wild like the rest of us."

Gallagher agrees it was all great fun, but teenage exuberance did not quench his desire to accomplish much more musically. He was a purist who wanted to play the kind of music that touched his soul. Box office returns were not his yardstick of success; he didn't believe in showband publicity strokes to grab headlines and he was never ruled solely by commercial values.

In the beginning, he had to play by the rules, however reluctantly. "I didn't like doing stock copies of pop and country and western tunes," he says, "I was keen to get the band aiming towards more rhythm and blues properly. That was my preoccupation. But when you had to play three, four or five hours at a dance, you couldn't be that high-minded. You just got on with it. In the early stages, it was the usual showband mix: you'd learn the hits of the day, and then add some popular songs from different styles. After a while, I was allowed to do a couple of rock 'n roll numbers by Chuck Berry, Fats Domino or Eddie Cochran. But you wouldn't be allowed to do rock-and-roll all night. You'd have to do whatever was popular in the charts, even Jim Reeves covers. My main influences were all the American rock and rollers plus, at that stage, the Beatles and Rolling Stones. I hated doing the novelty numbers most of all: things like the Paul Jones and waltzes. You had to play whatever the people wanted, or whatever the band leader wanted. I don't think we were the corniest showband around. It was fun in a showband, although it was frustrating too. You'd get a great jazz saxophonist having to play *The Twist* by Chubby Checker, and you'd get a drummer who really wanted to be playing in a ceili band or you'd get someone like me who just wanted to play Chuck Berry and R&B. But you do it for a laugh at a certain

364 *Send 'em Home Sweatin'*

point. Some of the bands had quite a serious attitude. They'd spend a lot of time getting good uniforms and hoping to make it in Las Vegas. I had a uniform, God forbid. I actually wore the jacket with the group Taste for a bit. It had double buttons, kind of like a Beatle jacket. But I knew from Day One that I was just passing through."

Unlike most musicians on the circuit, Gallagher did not look up to the top-earners. In his own words, he wouldn't "sit in the balcony and be in awe of the big showbands." He thinks that the Freshmen were the best, and speaks highly of Arty McGlinn, the Platters' lead guitarist who, years later, worked with Van Morrison. The Fontana joined the showband exodus to Britain during Lent. For Gallagher, it was a welcome break from the limitations of the ballrooms and it exposed him to new influences.

In 1964, Gallagher saw how the Beatles had established the idea of rock bands as independent, self-defined units who performed their own songs. He was influenced by the phenomenon, and began to lobby for an image change for the Fontana. He went to see the Rolling Stones in London, whom he had already watched in action in Cork a year earlier. At that time, Brian Jones came to Gallagher's hometown along with the other Stones. He vividly remembers Jones' skill as a guitarist. "It was the first time I'd seen anyone playing the slide guitar. A very underrated musician."

Gallagher listened to upcoming groups at the Marquee Club, London, on his nights off during British tours in '64. Musically, London was moving at a faster speed. It was a culture shock for the Fontana: they ran foul of the police when their flashing showband lights gave an unexpected clear path through busy Oxford Street. Many showbands had their name illuminated in lights on the wagon roof. In London, police warned the Fontana that only emergency vehicles could display flashing lights.

The period '64/'65 marked a turning point for Gallagher and the Fontana: the band changed their name to the more upbeat Impact and secured a six-week summer residency at an American air base outside Madrid, while Gallagher made his debut in the clubs of Hamburg. Pressure for a name change came from Gallagher who wanted to move away from the showband genre towards a rhythm-and-blues style group. He met with resistance. "I wanted to get away from the showband tag, but some members were quite happy to remain in the showband scene," he says. "We still had to go out and make a living and play gigs. Instead of the usual showband suits, with little bow ties and things, we'd dress in black polo neck sweaters and Beatle jackets. That doesn't seem very adventurous by today's standards, but at the time it was unusual. More and more, we started doing a couple of original songs, a lot of Chuck Berry or whatever we'd get away with. Obviously, we had to do a couple of hits of the day to get through a set. You played whatever was required at a dance. The Impact would be classed as a beat group, but to some people we were still a showband...that's the bit I didn't swallow too well."

The name change coincided with a minor reshuffle in the ranks: John Lehane's brother, Michael, joined on organ for a period, and in came Johnny Campbell on drums. Philip Prendergast — whose brother, Peter, ran the Arcadia in Cork — took over as manager. It was a time of transition, and Gallagher was fast approaching a crossroads. "The Impact wasn't totally into the Beatles style, but we did Beatles numbers," says Declan O'Keeffe. "We were a cross between the real old showband and the incoming beat groups. We did a lot of Rory's stuff. But then if you were out in the country you'd have to do a few old time waltzes. We tended more towards the beaty side than to showbands. However, back in that era, you had to play the showband stuff."

For Gallagher, the Spanish trip was a welcome break from the limitations of the ballrooms. The American airmen wanted to hear rhythm and blues and rock'n'roll. "It was tantamount to living in the States," he recalls. "It gave us some freedom." A military policeman called Nero was bowled over by Gallagher's spontaneous rocking and regularly joined the band on stage to sing his own personal party-piece, *Great Balls Of Fire*. Gallagher had more in common with Americans who understood his love of the blues than with ballroom dancers who only wanted to be entertained.

On their return home, Gallagher became increasingly disillusioned with the circuit and thought of starting his own group.

His talents were obvious to the rest of the band. "Rory had something special from day one," says O'Keeffe. "As a guitarist, he was streets ahead of anybody else. You could feel it coming out of him. We once went to see the Byrds in England, and they used a twelve-string guitar to get the intro of *Mr Tambourine Man*. Rory found the same effect on his Strat by plucking two strings at one time. He found the harmonies himself. I was just a basic three-chord-trick player, but his chord formations were way ahead. It was all his own work. I can't ever remember him getting lessons. He studied a lot of books, and worked out chords."

When Prendergast once prepared a press release for the Impact, he asked each member to state their favourite composer. O'Keeffe named Gallagher who had written several compositions for the group. "I can't remember all the titles," says Gallagher. "I wrote *You Fooled Me All The Time*, and *I Want You To Be Happy*. I'd only written about a half dozen. It was a start anyway. They were fairly derivative of the beat groups of the time."

In late '65, the Impact returned to London in search of work. The cracks widened as they prepared for a stint in the clubs of Hamburg, Germany. Gallagher finally went his own way and the group split up. He decided to honour the three-week commitment in Hamburg and packed his bags, along with drummer Johnny Campbell and bass player Oliver Tobin. Most clubs demanded a four-piece beat group, so Gallagher got a friend to pose with an organ for a publicity photograph. Back home, a three-piece would only be regarded as a brass section. On arrival in Hamburg, Gallagher informed the club owner that the organist had taken ill with appendicitis on the ferry journey.

The sleaze-pits of Hamburg opened his eyes to a world far removed from that of the showbands. He was out on a limb, and he knew it. He remembers times when there would be nobody left in the club at 3.30am.

The trio played six sets a night with fifteen minutes off every hour. It was hard-gained experience, but paved the way for dates there with Taste later on. It also marked his rock'n'roll liberation. "The whole atmosphere was still very Beatle-esque. The beauty of it was that, aside from playing forty-five minute sets a night, you could play as much Chuck Berry as you wanted, and do as much jamming as you wanted. You still had to play a couple of pop hits every so often to keep the dancers happy and avoid the beer bottles. I never felt that my life was to do six nights a week around the Irish danceband scene. I basically had enough of it. I just wanted to get into a serious group. The band had only limited success apart from anything else. My main reason for quitting was that I felt I'd compromised enough. It was time to get a bit more serious about the whole thing. It wasn't my goal in life to smash the showbands. I wanted to play my own style of music. I probably helped to break the kind of attitude of some of the dancehall owners about letting beat groups in to play. I could live with showbands doing their thing and playing for their audiences. But I didn't want them to rule the whole roost entirely, which they did for a long time. It was very much tied-up: there was a strong ballroom management thing going on."

Meantime, the rest of the band re-grouped, reverted to the original showband concept and even resurrected their old name, Fontana. At the time of the break-up, some members were keen to go back to being a band, rather than attempt to be a beat group. The Fontana returned to the circuit and continued to tour Britain. They recorded an album of Irish songs, which sold well. A combination of little money, uncertain gigs and a lack of acceptability for a three-piece rock band put an end to Gallagher's own experiment. It would take time to alter the balance of power.

Gallagher may have been ahead of his time, but he wasn't giving up easily. In 1966, he returned to a more active beat scene in Cork. Among the most popular clubs were the 007 in Drawbridge Street, formerly known as the Cavern, an army club in MacCurtain Street and another club in the St. Luke's district. Gallagher decided to experiment with a trio once again, teaming up with Eric Kitteringham (bass) and Norman Damery (drums) during the final days of the Axills, a local beat group. He played some remaining dates with them, filling in for one of the guitarists. "Naturally, when the drummer and bass player and myself formed a new group, people thought that I had been with the Axills, too. But that's only minor confusion. Once the last dates with the Axills were over, that was the end of the group.

We got on well together, so we decided to form a new group and call it Taste."

This embodied Gallagher's vision: bass and drum instrumentals and lyrics were based around his guitar. Gallagher played the blues and kept his musical integrity intact, despite the poor financial returns. The group collected £30 a night, a fraction of what could be made in the showbands. Gallagher was content stubbornly doing it his way as long as he earned enough to keep the van on the road. Unlike other musicians, he wasn't tempted to retreat to the sanctuary of a showband. Taste played their own material. "We made a serious attempt at not doing too many covers. We started doing original material as well as a lot of Chuck Berry, rock'n'roll and blues. We wouldn't do anything that was pop as such, or danceband stuff."

Taste went to Germany in early '67 where they worked a punishing seven-hour-a-night schedule in Hamburg. At home, Taste played in the ballrooms, but there was strong opposition from the showbands in '67: promoters met three musicians and thought they were being short- changed when told there was nobody else in the band. The Federation of Irish Musicians laid down rules about the minimum number of musicians required — usually seven or eight — and even sent representatives to the halls to count heads. Smaller bands and groups found a way around the rules by asking friends to stand-in at keyboards or on trombone. Donal Gallagher was occasionally called on to perform the task. "For fifteen or twenty minutes, you'd stand there in embarrassment pretending to play an instrument when the Fed guy came in," he says; "it was easy to get away with standing at the keyboards."

The Fed came down hard on Taste when they got their first booking at the Arcadia, Cork, and tried to prevent the dance going ahead. The controversy split the union locally. Showband elements who felt threatened were against allowing a 'three-piece' perform. However, they were opposed by younger musicians in the beat groups. The showbands were under pressure in '67: many semi-pro outfits found it difficult to survive with so many musicians in their line-ups. The dispute had other implications: the Arcadia had booked Taste and weren't going to be pushed around by the Fed. In the end, an extraordinary union meeting was called at the Metropole Hotel one Sunday morning. A compromise offer emerged: if Taste agreed to do an audition for the Fed, then they would consider giving the 'gig' their blessing. Rory replied: "I've been in a showband long enough and I've proven myself. I'm not going to do an audition for anybody." The union backed down and the performance went ahead. It was a significant victory.

Gallagher brought his music to halls around the country and built up a strong following in Cork and Dublin throughout '67. "At that stage, some ballroom owners would accept the odd 'beat night', so to speak, or they'd have us as 'relief' for a showband," he recalls. "The smaller dancehalls would take a chance, but the bigger ballroom owners were dubious about anything that was non-showband. They'd prefer more adult dancing. They were just a bit scared of the idea of a beat group, the fans and the image."

Promoters may have been blind to Gallagher's talents, but accomplished touring musicians, who shared dance dates with Taste in Cork, recognised his flair. The Dave Glover Showband from Belfast were impressed when Taste played support to them at the Arcadia. Bass player George Jones, who had previously played with Van Morrison in The Monarchs Showband, advised Gallagher to aim north of the border. Jones recalls: "We weren't due on stage until ten or half past ten, or even later. So there was always a warm-up group. We turned up early and sat up in the balcony. There was a three-piece on stage, Rory Gallagher and Taste. Rory was doing his thing, leaping in the air and playing brilliantly.

"We were knocked out by this guy. We thought he was tremendous. The funny part about it was... these guys were making unbelievable music which we were really into, but yet the crowd down the front were shouting 'we want the Dave Glover showband,' simply because we were the name then. Whatever showband was on that week was the big name. We just laughed. We couldn't believe it. We spoke to Rory afterwards and complimented him on his guitar playing. He was advanced for that period. I had come back from Germany where I'd been playing blues and rock'n'roll with Van Morrison.

"I was really into blues. I found it very hard to believe that a young guy down in Cork had immersed himself so much into the blues. On the showband scene, you didn't see that, especially when you went so far down below the border. It was all country'n'western or typical showband material. But to hear this guy in Cork — who had obviously been training the other two boys in the group how to play the blues and rock'n'roll — was amazing. His guitar playing was so far advanced, it was unbelievable. You're talking about the same standard as Jimi Hendrix. We were knocked out. I said that he should get over to England. He thought it would be very difficult. I said, 'at least get up to Belfast where there's a blues scene'. The Maritime blues club, where Van started his career, was happening. I contacted Rory when he came up for the first gig and we continued to meet afterwards. I was totally delighted for the young lad because he had a great way with him. He was a very polite young man."

Belfast made Taste feel at ease. The city was more in tune with the Corkman's obsessional love of the blues. It was a more sophisticated scene than Dublin or Cork: Van Morrison and Them had already converted audiences to rhythm and blues and made the music industry sit up and take notice. Belfast, says Gallagher, "took to us." Taste secured a regular residency in '67 at the Maritime Hotel, an old Belfast dancehall turned R&B club, where Morrison and Them had been the house band four years earlier before they left for London and got a recording contract with Decca. Gallagher and Morrison shared a blues tradition and their careers followed similar paths. Morrison also started his career in a showband, and wanted to steer their programme to R&B. He, too, served his time in the ballrooms before taking the club trail to Germany and sweating through seven-hours-a- night "gigs." Both were free spirits who put their heart and soul into their music. Their values were forged by live performance.

Gallagher soon acquired the status of a top-class blues guitarist and launched a prolific recording career in the '70s. As the showbands faced extinction, rock bands began to take over, and Gallagher led the way. The youth of the '70s revered the long-haired crusader for the blues, especially for his Fender guitar, and storming performances at open air festivals. The rocker not only became respectable; but was acclaimed as one of the greatest ever blues guitarists. Gallagher hauled a battered Stratocaster, a bass player, drummer and minimal road crew across the European festival circuit. *Messin' With The Kid* and *Bullfrog Blues*, from the *Live In Europe* album of 1972, were anthems of the new generation. Millions of record sales have been notched up since Gallagher first applied for a job in a showband. The passage of time has not changed his views.

"I have mixed feelings about the showbands. It was a start. I learned a lot and had good fun. But I was always restless to do my own thing. It will always be that way. The Freshmen were excellent at what they did. But, ultimately, what's the point in being a copy band? That was the sad part. In fairness, you'd find excellent musicians in some of the bands. But they were wasted really because they just had to play covers and copies. Billy Brown was one of the better musicians. You could say that showbands, at least, brought some different music to the dance-halls and gave young people a chance to play. That's the positive side of the story."

Gallagher — who never married and lives in Chelsea, London, where he runs his operation with younger brother and manager, Donal — remains true to his deep-seated philosophy. He lives by the tough standards of the working bluesmen who did what they did best, and kept on doing it... Muddy Waters, B.B. King, John Lee Hooker and Albert King. His last release, *Fresh Evidence*, one of his finest blues albums, confirms that dedication to the great tradition. The guitar playing remains as potent as ever. Critics praised the album as yet another sturdily dependable collection of high grade boogie music that sustained his career down through the years. The compass, says Gallagher, has come around again for blues.

Gallagher, at forty-two, the indefatigable rock'n'roll journeyman, plans to carry on...just like his blues heroes. He won't be beaten into submission by commercial values in an age of stage pyrotechnics and video packaging...just as he refused to be caged in by the showbands. Genius, after all, is boundless.

Van — The Showband Man

Lyceum Ballroom, The Strand, London, May 1964.

It's an unlikely combination: Butch Moore and the Capitol Showband, supported by Van Morrison's Them. The bands — music worlds apart — are drawn together by impresario Phil Solomon in a bid to get the Capitol into the British market. Them, a distinctly unglamorous bunch, reflect Morrison's love of the blues: their material is drawn not from mainstream pop, but from American folk-blues. Their taut rhythm'n'blues sound supports Morrison's aching voice. The performance is intense. The lead singer — a brooding son of East Belfast with bright blue eyes, a surly expression and mop of sandy red hair — is watched from the wings by the Capitol. His voice is harsh. It brims with emotion and impresses the other band. "We thought Morrison was terrific, but nobody was really interested in him because it was our big night," recalls the Capitol's sax/clarinet player Paddy Cole.

The Capitol were promoted by Solomon following their first performance at the London Palladium. He invited club owners and booking agents along to the Lyceum. Them, the warm-up act managed by Solomon, left the stage after an hour to make way for the star attraction. A crowd of 2,500 got their money's worth. The Capitol, a commercial product, were slick, well-rehearsed and delivered tried and tested material from the pops, country'n'western, to dixieland with characteristic showmanship.

"We were a showband with the brass sound, clean-cut, dressed in brightly-coloured stage outfits," says lead singer Moore. "Them were totally different. They were a kind of rock group. To be honest, we didn't have much contact. We did our thing and they did theirs. I met Morrison once or twice in Solomon's office. He was a quiet, retiring person. I really didn't think he was going to be that famous." Morrison's musicians told Cole they'd just returned from a gig in Scotland that paid

£35. "Whenever I hear of Van Morrison," jokes Cole, "I always remember the thirty-five pounds."

The Capitol could be forgiven for failing to take their scruffy support band seriously. The feeling was mutual. Like Rory Gallagher, Morrison was no fan of showbands. He also compromised to make a living, served an apprenticeship in a showband, the Monarchs, but then cut loose. The Capitol represented the establishment. Morrison had spent his teenage years fighting the system. By 1964, Them had mastered the basics in Belfast and wanted to join the musical revolution in Britain: playing a date with the Capitol didn't fit their game plan. They had nothing in common...with the exception of Solomon. The Capitol were offered a six-month contract at the Palladium after the Lyceum show. They turned it down because they were making more money at home. Their diary was already full. Ten years on, the Capitol were a spent force. Morrison left the Lyceum that evening to continue a brief problematic stint with Them that yielded, nonetheless, two British hits, and provided the springboard to an extraordinary international career.

Before breaking into the British Top Ten, Them had built up a following in Belfast clubs, particularly The Maritime Hotel. Morrison later claimed that their records never matched the intensity of their early Maritime performances. They were regarded as curiosities in the ballrooms. Before achieving recognition in their short and turbulent '60s heyday, the group was laughed off stage when they hawked their rhythm'n'blues act around the dancehalls of Ulster. Morrison's performance was seen about this time by Robert Ballagh of the Chessmen at the Stella Ballroom, Mount Merrion, Dublin.

"We were quite impressed," he recalls. "They presented the Rolling Stones kind of image as distinct from the Beatles' image. They were the nasty boys of rock, rather than the cuddly boys. I don't think anyone realised the significance of the group at the time." Them, of course, had nothing to do with rock, as Morrison told *In Dublin* magazine in March '88: "That wasn't rock. That was called rhythm'n'blues in those days. There was rock and pop. The Beatles were pop, Little Richard was rock, or rock'n'roll. We were rhythm'n'blues...that's what it was called."

Morrison went out on a limb while his contemporaries played safe in the lucrative showbands. In his mid-teens he, too, had been a showband musician. He didn't have a choice. It was either put up or shut up. Like Gallagher, he couldn't afford the luxury of pondering his options from the outside. Morrison and his mates wanted to find work as musicians, so they added the showband trimmings that gave their group, the Monarchs, access to the dancehalls. Strictly speaking, the Monarchs were not always a showband, and their repertoire shifted from pop hits of the day to a solid programme of rhythm and blues. Nobody, least of all Morrison, imagined that this early experience with the Monarchs would lead eventually to recognition as the foremost popular Irish artiste of the past thirty years: the first Irish musician to influence American rock; a singer/songwriter ranked with Bob Dylan and John Lennon; a man whose vision — whether expressed through jazz, blues, gospel or soul — produced some of the finest work in contemporary music; an inspirational force who influenced Bruce Springsteen, Mark Knopfler, U2 and Elvis Costello as well as a new generation of artistes including the Waterboys and Hothouse Flowers.

Typically unimpressed by his own success, Morrison says the professional point of view is that you learn an instrument, play it and go through an apprenticeship. He told *In Dublin* : "When I pick up the paper and read that I'm a rock star, I find it unbelievable. If they can call me a rock star, they can call anybody that. That's just another meaningless word. The people who wrote that don't even know what it means." He summed up his approach in a *Hot Press* interview of November 1987.

"A lot of people say to me, well you're really lucky. I'm not lucky. At certain times, I had to do certain things and that's really the way it was. I didn't have a choice. It was either A or B. I did the one thing that happened to get me through. It wasn't a matter of sitting up in an ivory tower and saying, 'I wonder whether I want to do A or B or C.' In the sixties, you didn't have a choice. You were either in the van going up and down the M1 doing gigs, or doing nothing. When the singer/songwriter thing appeared, there wasn't a choice. You had to do that a certain way and the people in charge did things a certain way. If you wanted that, you had to compromise. There was a lot of compromise and a lot of hard graft. But it got me to a point where I did have a choice. I didn't really have a choice about any of it until I was twenty-eight. It was a struggle financially. I didn't even start making money until I was twenty-eight. All I did from the time I was eighteen to twenty-seven was work. I worked my way from Belfast to New York and didn't even know I was there because it was work."

There wasn't any grand master plan. Everything was based on survival, as he explained in his last *Rolling Stone®* interview in August 1990. "The fact is, sometimes you do something because you've got no money, okay? Sometimes you're starving, sometimes you do things for that reason. It all comes down to survival, and you can't intellectualise survival, because either you survive or you don't. That's the way life goes, and I'm not going to intellectualise it, because that's only going to spoil it. That's a job for writers, not for me."

Like Gallagher, Morrison developed a love of the blues early: he was brought up on Leadbelly, "and heads like that." Musical inspirations can be traced back to his childhood in East Belfast, enriched by ready access to his father's weighty collection of blues records — the finest in Ulster. He listened to treasured recordings of such artistes as Muddy Waters, Ray Charles, John Lee Hooker, and Bobby Bland. His mother was a jazz singer who specialised in gospel and country music. His parents were Jehovah's Witnesses, and he was brought up with those beliefs. George Ivan, an only child, was born on August 31st, 1945, into a working class home at Bloomfield, East Belfast. He was one of the War Children... "the wild children, born 1945, when all the soldiers came marching home, love looks in their eyes."

His Belfast background moulded an approach to life that guides him to this day. Childhood references feature regularly in his output: the Belfast he sings of is a special place. He reveals glimpses of his working class roots in autobiographical flashbacks through his music. *Cleaning Windows*, for example, portrays life in Belfast terms of "Jimmy Rogers records in my lunchbreak," "five Woodbines" from the corner shop, "lemonade and Paris buns" before knocking off for tea, "blowin' sax at the weekend." He wrote: "I'm a workin' man in my prime cleanin' windows." In *Got to Go Back*, Morrison recalls his years at Orangefield School, gazing out the classroom windows, dreaming, and then going home to listen to Ray Charles. Other songs — such as *Orangefield* — reflect a childhood innocence. Emigration leads to "pastures not greener, but meaner." His writing conveys feelings of loneliness and homesickness. There are Belfast reminiscences in songs like *Cypress Avenue*, a wealthy part of the city.

Asked by *Rolling Stone®* how he first got interested in music, Morrison replied: "I remember my father took me into town one day. There was this jazz band playing on the back of a truck. I was, like, five. I got into it because I saw people blowing horns and saxophones and singing. I thought it was great that people could do that. So I suppose in terms of why I got into it, it would be for all the wrong reasons. It wasn't about being a star or wearing certain clothes or having a certain image. It was just the idea that people could get up and sing and play. Then everything changed. Maybe jazz musicians are still like that now. But because of my age group, I got put into the pop field. I was doing blues really. I came out of a blues club when this record company came over and we made a record, and that somehow put me into this other pop thing. But that's not at all where I was at."

As a youngster, he was shy and didn't mix easily. His schooldays were spent at Elm Grove in Bloomfield, and later at Orangefield. It was Ray Charles, more than any other singer, who inspired him to turn to music. He listened to Cliff Richard on Saturday Club... and, twenty- five years later, he recorded a duet with Richard, the pop-gospel *Whenever God Shines His Light On Me* on the *Avalon Sunset* album of '89. (That hit provided the unlikely spectacle of Morrison on Top of The Pops). His schoolfriends — among them George Jones, who also lived in Bloomfield — became interested in guitars during the late '50s. They were influenced by Lonnie Donegan and skiffle music. In 1958, at the age of thirteen, Morrison took saxophone and guitar lessons. Jones, now a BBC producer and radio personality, formed a skiffle group, The Javelins.

In '56, Jones was drawn to the guitar sounds he heard on the radio. His sister, who was in one of the original Glee Clubs in Belfast, arranged to get him an acoustic guitar on hire purchase.

His father, a haulage contractor, thought it a waste of time. Only eleven at the time, Jones taught himself to play the guitar, practising under the blankets into the early hours at home in Greenville Street. Jones and his friends decided to form a group: "Another guy on the street who played guitar was more advanced than any of us. We picked out the three chords that he knew. Before long, we all knew the three chords. We got a tall guy who was prepared to play tea chest bass. That's just an old tea chest with a brush pole and string. Someone else volunteered to play the washboard. It was a basic skiffle line-up. We finished up with seven people in the Javelins." That included five guitars — only one of the guitarists could extend his range beyond three chords — as well as a tea chest bass and washboard. Later on, a girl singer joined up, and so the group became known as Dainie Sands and The Javelins in the period '58/'59. They won an award for their performance at Minors Matinee, a children's club which met every Saturday at the Strand Cinema. The Javelins played a couple of tunes and earned ten shillings. "We thought we were wonderful then," says Jones.

Morrison joined The Javelins shortly before they broke up in '59. He lived at Hyndford Street, Bloomfield, and already knew Jones and the others. "We were all mates," says Jones. "We knocked about together the way that kids hang out on the corner. Except that we hung out in my father's backyard where he kept the lorries, and we rehearsed there. Van played guitar." Morrison summed up this first part of his career in the *Rolling Stone®* interview: "It was a small scene in Belfast, but it was enough. It developed around certain record shops. There was a place called the Smithfield, where you'd go in for a certain R&B side and they'd already have it out for you. I sort of came out of the jazz scene because my father used to take me into these places where all these jazzers hung out. When I left school, I played with showbands, rock bands, whatever was going. I just took anything because I was a professional musician."

During the period of Dainie Sands and The Javelins, a transition occurred from skiffle to pop or rock'n'roll. When Morrison came along at the final stage of the group, they were still playing skiffle and Bill Haley numbers. He told them they should be playing John Lee Hooker, Chuck Berry and Jerry Lee

Lewis. "We never heard of these, but Van did because he had all the records," recalls Jones. "Van could really rock a tune. He didn't sing as much then. He was a very quiet lad — very much within himself. Musically, he was very talented. He could turn to any instrument. His father bought him a saxophone, and he was playing it in a few weeks. With a mouth organ, he could just play it right away. He played guitar, but not brilliantly. Van could feel an instrument more than just technically play it. He had a feel for music." The group changed its name to The Thunderbolts in '59: they specialised in instrumentals playing material by the Shadows, the Ventures, Johnny and the Hurricanes, and Duane Eddy. It was a basic line-up of drums and three guitars — bass, rhythm and lead. Dainie Sands left the group. Morrison discovered his inner voice through the saxophone, and his flair for the instrument was a great asset to the group. Morrison introduced the sax as the group practised Duane Eddy's big hit, *Peter Gunn*. Jones asked him: "Can you play it?" Morrison replied: "Yeah, I can play a few notes."

The Thunderbolts were short-lived. The name was changed again to The Monarchs in 1960 to coincide with another transition, from instrumentals to more vocals, especially rock'n'roll vocals. The new name was chosen because Jones could get crown transfers from a friend who worked in the post office and whose job was to place them on post office vans. "We put one of the crowns on the front of the drum. We put another couple on the amplifiers. We called ourselves the Monarchs and thought it was a great idea."

Jones worked in the post office as a messenger boy where he met Wesley Black, a fine Jerry Lee-style piano player. Black, also from Bloomfield, was recruited to the band. The line-up was: Black, piano; Jones, bass guitar; Billy McAllen, lead guitar; Morrison, sax, and Roy Kane, drums. Initially, they had no wish to become a showband. But the Monarchs failed to get enough bookings. "Dancehall owners used to ask us, 'how many are in the group?'" says Jones. "When we said five, they shook their heads and said, 'no'. In those days, groups played as warm-ups and at little hops. There wasn't as much work for groups. Showbands had all the business. For instance, we couldn't play in the big Belfast ballrooms. We'd be lucky to get a warm-up job. Everybody wanted to hire showbands in those days."

In 1960, Morrison, aged fifteen, left school to play saxophone with the Monarchs. The outlook was bleak, and money scarce in the face of the showband colossus. Morrison supplemented his small earnings in the group by doing manual work. Inevitably, financial pressures dictated that the group adopt a showband format. That meant finding more brass instruments to achieve the "big sound." Jones sums up: "We felt that a five-piece wasn't enough because all the popular showbands had seven or eight musicians. We went one step further and got nine."

THE MONARCHS SHOWBAND

Can you spot Van the Showband Man?

Morrison was supported in the brass section by David Bell, another sax player; Leslie Holmes, on trumpet, and by trombonist Ronnie Osborne, who joined from a brass band. To complete the showband line-up, the Monarchs recruited a lead singer, Jimmy Law, who worked for British Airways (then BEA). "He couldn't sing all that well," says Jones. "But he was talented at business and finance and organising bookings. He put us on a proper business footing. He sang soft little songs of the time that were recorded by Bobby Vinton, Johnny Tillotson and Craig Douglas. Thanks to his efforts, we started getting bookings locally as The Monarchs Showband. He was able to deal with the promoters, convince them that we could do a complete night on our own, and then get money out of them. We weren't a group anymore. We didn't go to the Republic because we had a fair amount of work in the province."

The Monarchs remained a showband until '62. Morrison was never happy as a showband musician: neither dancehall owners nor audiences were ready for his brand of rhythm'n'blues. The band at least provided him with a platform during an early stage of his apprenticeship when he needed to gain as much experience as possible. "He had to do it to eat," says Jones. "The thinking in those days was... if you didn't get paid for playing music, it wasn't worth it. I think that's why showbands took over. You had to play for money. Van was reluctant to do the showband steps. He did it. He thought it a big laugh. He would have preferred to leap in the air, do a Jerry Lee Lewis or Chuck Berry's famous guitar walk.

"Jumping and diving off stage in rock'n'roll frenzies was Van's kick. He wasn't really one for standing in a uniform symmetrical line, doing steps and singing *Send Me The Pillow That You Dream On*. I mean, he did it. There was no other outlet. He had to conform and play in the band to earn money to live. He could certainly never be called a classic showband man. He knew from the start that it wasn't what he wanted. We had to do it as well. We looked upon being in a showband as having another job. Plus, it was handy money to help meet the HP payments on all the expensive instruments we kept buying. Sometimes the money wasn't great, so most of it went on HP payments."

By late '61/early '62, Morrison wanted a rhythm'n'blues repertoire and tired of having to reproduce the stock showband material to entertain dancers. He wrote his first song in 1961, "a very simple sort of country'n'western thing. Nobody was writing their own songs then; it was just doing covers." Jones and McAllen shared Morrison's preference for blues and rock'n'roll. About this time, Morrison and Jones met two Glasgow musicians, Lawrie McQueen and George Hetherington, who were on a visit to Belfast. They spoke of the changing music scene across the Channel. They were rock'n'roll and blues men.

"The trick is to go to Scotland first, and then head down to London. You're bound to make it," advised McQueen. Jones, Morrison, McAllen and Black decided to have a go. The rest of the band opposed a move to Scotland. As Jones puts it: "We said to the others, 'we're heading off. You can come with us if you want to.' We knew that they wouldn't, so it was a good way of trimming down the band." In the new line-up, McQueen played drums and Hetherington, much to Morrison's satisfaction, was a great blues singer. They brought in a baritone sax player, Harry Mack. As a musician, Mack was average, but he had a minibus. The Monarchs were now a seven-piece: Black, McAllen, Jones, McQueen, Hetherington, Morrison and Mack.

They travelled to Glasgow when promised that an agent there could get work for them. Instead of getting five or six weeks' work, they only had enough for one weekend. Undaunted, they continued to seek work all over Scotland. It was a tough grind. "We bummed around," says Jones. "We starved a lot. We were starving once up in the Highlands. We had enough money for petrol, but couldn't afford food. We picked up hitch-hikers, two Indonesian girls. They were exhausted and delighted to get the lift. We told them of our plight. They said, 'okay, stop the wagon'. We did. They had a few eggs in their rucksacks. We boiled some water from a stream. They made us egg soup. Believe me, it was like a banquet. We'd have eaten anything." Their luck improved with a run of work that lasted for ten days and earned them badly-needed income. They decided to pool the money and head for London. Following the last gig in

Scotland, at the Beach Ballroom in Aberdeen, they drove straight to the capital.

"As young lads, I suppose we were naive," recalls Jones. "We felt that just being in London was enough to make it." They washed in public toilets and slept in the minibus at car parks. They were ordered out of parks by the police. On one occasion, they unknowingly picked an off-limits location to stop for the night after being moved on from several parks. Jones tells the story: "We were driving around on a misty summer's night. It was smoggy. We were really tired. We just kept driving to try and find a place to bunk down. We felt dejected. We were ready to go home, but didn't want to give in to our parents. We saw this sign for a car park and turned down to the right, down a hill. The car park doubled back on to a high wall that led back up to the road level. So we parked the minibus against the wall. It had a side-door and back-door. Lawrie McQueen, a big man, stretched out, with his legs sticking out the open side-door. It was a warm night. We'd been living in this bus for two weeks. No clothes or socks had been washed. We took the socks and shoes and lined them along the roof.

"Van couldn't stick it inside any longer. He stepped out in his underwear, threw a blanket on the ground underneath the minibus and lay there for the coolness. The rest of us curled up in the bus around the gear as best we could and tried to get some sleep. Suddenly, we were rudely awakened by a huge gonging sound. We all woke up with a start and jumped up. We looked out and couldn't believe what we were seeing. Parked beside us were Rolls Royces and Bentleys. We looked up to the road level where we saw a row of men in bowler hats, staring down at us, trying to fathom this ghastly sight of people packed in a minibus in their underwear with shoes and socks laid out on top. We'd actually stopped in the peers' car park at the House of Lords. As you can imagine, we made a quick exit. My memory is of the minibus speeding off, Van running behind holding the blanket, and shoes and socks flying to the wind. We laughed about it for hours later."

When they were about to give up, in late summer '62, the Monarchs met Don Charles, a one-hit-wonder, whom they had backed in one of their Scottish dates. He bought them a meal and got their band suits cleaned. He introduced them to an agent, Ruby Bard, who managed Georgie Fame, The Temperance Seven and Kenny Ball and The Jazzmen. She lined up auditions — one of which took place at The Flamingo Jazz Club in Soho where The Blue Flames had a residency. "We did a good set there," says Jones. "We impressed quite a few people — among them a couple of German agents who liked the band. Lo and behold, within a month, we were packed off to Germany...the first English speaking band to play in a club in Heidelberg. We found ourselves in the middle of this town in Germany, trying to find our way to the club. We were just naive young lads from Ireland."

The Monarchs played the circuit of U.S. army bases, and at clubs in Heidelberg, Frankfurt and Cologne. They were the first Irish musicians on the round of German clubs, nicknamed the "work camps." It was a hard slog: seven-hours-a-night, seven-nights-a-week. Professionally, this period marked a significant turning point: Morrison fell in with black GIs who understood his commitment to the blues. The nightly routine was punishing, but Morrison relished the freedom to express himself, and the appreciative audience. Jones recalls his delight.

"For the first time in his life, Van witnessed coloured Americans in the U.S. sector in southern Germany. Van thought all this was unbelievable because they were talking about Ray Charles and all the real blues music that he'd listened to on his father's records. We all really got into this, but especially Van. The GIs started gigging with us on stage. That was wonderful. The songs went into extended jams. It broke the monotony of the routine into the early morning hours. They dropped in at all times of the night. They taught us great r'n'b, blues and rock'n'roll stuff."

Morrison in those days, according to Jones, was "shy, too shy to bother with girls. He was so enveloped in his music that I think this was the guiding force throughout these years. At the same time, he loved local Belfast humour and liked a joke and good laugh. He wrote poetry. It was deep... most of us didn't know what he was talking about. He was just one of the lads. We accepted him the way he was." Onstage, Morrison was a "good busker." He wasn't a brilliant musician, but could play any instrument adequately. His songwriting abilities were developing slowly. "You didn't have to write in those days," says Jones. "There was such good rock'n'roll coming out, as long as you reproduced it well, you were in."

Meantime, the Beatles were performing at British army bases in Germany. "We heard that this group from Liverpool were making it in the British sector," says Jones. "Suddenly, when we moved from Heidelberg up to Cologne, we were confronted by the British. They were screaming for this Beatles and Gerry and the Pacemakers stuff. We'd been so locked away down south that we only knew American rock'n'roll and rhythm'n'blues. We now had to rehearse all this Beatles and British chart stuff." The Monarchs worked in the armed forces clubs in Frankfurt and Cologne in '63. The group made a record for CBS in Germany during this period, titled *Booh-zooh-hully-gully*. It went into the local charts. Jones was lead singer on the record. A CBS executive was impressed, and wanted him to stay on for further recording. He promised to make Jones a "star." The Monarchs were homesick. "When he made me that offer, I said, 'no thanks, I'm going home with the lads.' We went home. He sent us telegrams later and told us that the record made the charts. We were amazed. We really kicked ourselves."

Morrison became aware of the changing music scene while touring Germany with the Monarchs. "I remember we were playing in Heidelberg for GI's there," he told *Rolling Stone*. "One of the guys came up to us and said, 'have you guys ever heard the Dave Clark Five?' I hadn't. I remember coming back on the train from Germany on my way to Dover thinking 'everything's going to change now'. Sure enough, when I got back to London all the bands were dropping the horn sections. It was all pop groups." After more than a year of seven-days-a-week performances for little money, the Monarchs broke up in Belfast.

While Jones and other members of the Monarchs returned to showbands after the break-up, Morrison went back to London in '63 with the hope of establishing a hard core rhythm'n'blues group. Morrison wanted to find an outlet for his music in London, but opportunities were slow to come his way. He was influenced by groups who had long hair and wore outlandish clothes. It was a rebellious image. Morrison found little support for his new thinking back in Belfast. He failed to stir interest among former members of the Monarchs. Nobody wanted to return to the uncertainty of the poorly-paid group scene. Most musicians were earning steady money in showbands. Morrison refused to be drawn back into them, and supported himself by cleaning windows. Eventually, persistence paid off when he found a little-known band who were ready to go along with his ideas, The Gamblers.

"They were just a group who played everything from country'n'western to pop," says Jones. "He discovered them in a local rehearsal room, and he talked them into it. They all grew their hair long. They were seen hanging out together wearing weird clothes. He changed their name to Them. They became a rhythm'n'blues group and played local colleges and 'in' clubs where showbands didn't go." They gradually built up a following and secured a residency at Belfast's Maritime Hotel, owned by the Seamens Institute. They played in a dancehall run as an R&B club on a few nights of the week by promoter Eddie Kennedy. Them could be described loosely as the city's answer to the Rolling Stones or Pretty Things.

Ballrooms across the North were not yet ready for the alternative offered by Morrison and his anarchic-looking bunch. The number of venues receptive to their raw sound was very limited. "The image was fine when they played to like-minded people in the Maritime," says journalist John Trew, who wrote the showbusiness pages for *City Week* magazine in Belfast. "But when they were booked into some places in the country, the punters were astounded by the presence of guys who were long-haired, smoked and drank on stage and wore dirty jeans. They certainly didn't present themselves in the manner of the Royal or Capitol." When Them went on stage at one of the best known ballrooms in the north-west, they were pelted with pennies and anything that dancers could lay their hands on. The group was taken off by the proprietor after the first few numbers. He refused to pay Morrison and the others because they had not finished a a full programme. However, the group stayed on until they were paid.

Them were eclipsed by the big name showbands. "They were nobody... literally: they weren't at the match, as we say up here," explains Trew. "Some of the more sophisticated showband musicians admired Morrison because they recognised his talent. Whereas, to the country bands, Morrison was probably as much of a freak as they saw the Stones, though commercially it paid them to put in a couple of Stones' numbers in order to please the punters." Finally, their potential was spotted by the Solomon brothers: Mervyn, managing director of the Irish label, Emerald Records, and director of Solomon & Peres (Irish distributors for Decca Records) and Philip, a London-based music publisher and agent who handled a stable of artistes. Phil stepped in to manage the group. In '64, Them signed a contract with Decca and moved to London.

As with Gallagher, Morrison's apprenticeship in the '60s meant compromise in the showbands, acquiring stamina and resilience, taking the knocks in a shark-infested business and developing the skills to handle both the creative and business levels of his career. In his own words, he "paid the price to be where I am. There is no such thing as luck." The first stage — as a teenager experimenting in the Javelins, Thunderbolts and Monarchs — taught him lessons in survival. "I think he learned to knuckle down and play the music of the era to earn money," says Jones. "It was a lot for him to take, but he had to do it. I think he learned first and foremost it wasn't the music he was brought up to play. He learned comradeship and how to fit in with a band. This was important. Van was known as a loner: a quiet, retiring guy who kept to himself and got enough satisfaction out of the music he was listening to. He was accepted as one of the guys in the Javelins and Thunderbolts. He fitted in. Other people hadn't given him the chance to fit in."

The later phases of his apprenticeship taught Morrison how to take care of business, drawing on experiences in the '60s at the hands of the wide boys of the pop world. As he explained to *Hot Press* : "You have to be able to deal in all angles. If you're just dealing say on the creative level, and not bothered about how things operate when you're dealing with hardcore facts of the business world, then you're sort of walking into walls. You have to be aware of that as well. What you're in is a tough business and you have to be very aware. The way I put it: I don't suffer fools gladly. That's not always been the way. To get where I am, I've had to fight. It's still a struggle. It's still a fight.

"I'm not playing the same game I played twenty years ago. I've gone through the rock and roll stars... I've been a star I don't know how many times. I was a teenage star. So, I went through being a teenage star. Then I went through being a twenty year old star. Then a singer songwriter star. I went through that one. I found out what that was all about. I learnt my lessons and took my blows. By the time I was twenty-seven, I'd done that one. I'd gone through my second phase of being a rock star. That's what they called it in those days. But I didn't call it that. I'd already wrapped that up by the time I was twenty-eight. I started a whole new career."

At forty-five, Van Morrison — a superstar no matter how much he deplores the tag — ploughs a singular furrow and his music remains all the articulation he needs. One wonders how he feels today about those early showband roots. "I think he looks back and laughs," says Jones. "If somebody asked him now to stand up and do the steps on stage, he'd probably do it for a joke..."

The Lights Go Out

The showband was invincible — or so everyone thought. By '65, a boom year, there was no room for pessimism. The future looked rosy. 'Nobody saw floorboards' — bands, managers and ballroom proprietors laughed all the way to the bank. The scope and potential of the showband seemed limitless. Observers proclaimed that showbands had not yet reached their full potential. They predicted that the business would settle into a very profitable industry complete with tycoons, executives and publicists.

But all the confident predictions were wrong. Few were inclined to consider what the '70s would bring. Albert Reynolds saw the writing on the wall in 1966 and turned his back on a business that had made him a wealthy man. The Royal looked to Las Vegas and a new world to conquer — but most bands covered the same territory and played the same old tune. The first half of the '60s were the halcyon days — the second half marked the beginning of a gradual decline. The slide towards oblivion started in '67/'68 and continued in the early '70s. At some indefinable point, the glitter faded. The men in the mohair suits became vulnerable for the first time in over a decade.

It was a lingering death. There were last-gasp efforts to stay alive: re-shuffles and re-launches amid the usual publicity campaigns. By '70, most bands were fighting a losing battle. There was nothing fresh in the business anymore: what seemed exciting in '60 was now old hat. During the boom years, the Royal led the way, and a multiplicity of bands chased behind. There were only about half a dozen top bands still on the circuit during the early '70s. Most of the middle-range acts had disappeared. The old formula was no longer sufficient to close the doors and yield pots of money. Habits were changing: mid-week dancing all but vanished in rural Ireland in '70/'71. Dancing was on a three-day week, and even shorter in parts of winter. The big bands looked to overseas markets: the Royal and Dixies went to Vegas; the Capitol to Canada, Joe Dolan to Europe, and beyond.

By the mid '70s, the Big 8 had settled into the entertainment lounges of Las Vegas, and the American market became their bread and butter. Their loss for a greater part of the year had a psychological impact on the bands left at home competing in a dwindling market. They had a feeling that time was running out while, in enviable contrast, the Mainliners and Mighty Avons held a firm grip on the country music market.

North of the border, the business was already dying. The 'troubles' contributed to the downfall. Journalist John Trew, who had covered the showband scene for *City Week* Magazine in Belfast, can recall a moment in '73 when he knew the business was finally lost. Trew, then features editor of the *Newsletter*, was approached by Harry "Trixie" Hamilton who wanted publicity for a special showband concert at the Ulster Hall. "All the big names will be there," said Hamilton, "but we need some promotion." Trew was shocked to learn that only 170 tickets were sold. The Ulster Hall could hold 2,000. He reflects: "I remember saying to myself, 'my God, how times have changed. Things will never be the same again.' I thought back on times when crowds packed the Orpheus to see the Royal Showband. The doors used to open at half past eight, but people were standing in line at half past six. The change happened in the space of ten years."

Ballrooms, the natural habitat of showbands, were losing ground all the time to new forms of entertainment... discos, lounge bars and hotels. In the beginning, there was the ballroom, and nothing else. Now alternatives existed. When profits began to fall, the money men turned to greener pastures. The business was swamped by too many bands and too many managers/owners. "Fellows were coming out from under motor cars and down from trees to become showband managers overnight," says Des Kelly of the Capitol. "The new idea was to pay a lead singer a big wage, and you got abused and ill-paid musicians to back him. All these managers decided that the best concept was to get an image man, and pay him good money. The management would own everything. From that day on it all changed. There were some money-grabbing managers who had no talent and no tradition in the business. They had no love for the business. It was just money, money, money... and dog eat dog."

Investors began to think twice about putting their money into showbands when the market shifted to the hotels and lounge bars. "It would be very difficult for a new band to start up today," said Jim Hand in 1970. "The expenses are too heavy in advertising and publicity, equipment and organisation. As well as that you must have the connections to make the bookings. It's the managers who've been a long time in the business who are best able to do that. If an advertising agency spent £10,000, they could create a successful showband. But with £10,000, who'd want to start a showband?" There was a lack of new bands to breathe life into the business. Band managers saw a change in the licensing laws as a way to combat the exodus from the ballrooms.

"People are drinking at cabaret shows, so why can't they do it at dances?" asked T.J. Byrne at the time. "This showband business is really a big industry. There must be £500,000 coming in on taxes each year, maybe more. We bring people into the towns where we play... 400 to 500 cars at a time. We're entitled to a better deal than we're getting at the moment on this issue. We need better ballrooms as well. Some of them are not so hot. And we need better presentation of the lads in the bands. I think some part of the decline is due to the way some of them dress themselves up. It's alright to dress up with long hair, psychedelic shirts and beads when you're in the city but ninety per cent of the business is in the country now and the country people don't want that. If you look at the scene, it's the collar and tie bands who are doing all the business." Social patterns were changing, too. Alcohol became more acceptable, particularly for women. "Ten years ago, you'd never see girls drinking on their own", said Hand. "Now you can see them any night at cabaret spots. Fellows can meet girls at cabaret shows in lounges and hotels. And they can have a drink there and something to eat as well — which they can't do in ballrooms."

Bands fought to protect their monopoly. Managers campaigned against the hotel discos that served alcohol. They even picketed the RTE studios when the station took a decision to transmit *Top of the Pops*. Why did a business that employed many thousands — musicians, managers, ballroom owners, PR men, record companies, journalists — collapse with no apparent attempt to save it? Today, if an industry giving employment to 10,000 people went to the wall, there would be a public outcry. Amid government apathy, the business was allowed to slowly but surely bleed to death.

Who was to blame? Ballroom proprietors blame the bands and bands blame the proprietors. The truth is that both parties contributed, but that's not the full story: factors over which neither had control conspired to kill the golden goose. First, take the part played by bands and dancehall owners. Bands outlived their usefulness. Their *raison d'etre* in the late '50s and first half of the '60s was to give dancers a visual representation of their favourite stars and the hits of the day. By the '70s, the media — especially TV — made the showband copycats redundant. Television brought the stars into the living room. The recording industry expanded, and the hits were widely available in record shops. Travel became faster and easier, and more international stars toured Ireland. Teenagers' tastes were changing. Their expectations were higher: a night out with a favourite showband was once exciting and relatively inexpensive. It was good value at 7/6, or ten shillings. By '70/'71, dancers of the late '50s and early '60s were married with children of their own. The new teens liked rock music and adopted new idols.

As the covers wore thin, there was nothing of substance to carry the showbands into the '70s. There were some notable exceptions like Bowyer, Rock and Dolan who adapted to cabaret and found a new market. But the 'show' had gone out of the showbands. There was no effort to move with the times. They were now competing in an age that preferred the singer/songwriter and original sound. The emphasis switched to the quality of the music, as distinct from sheer glamour and entertainment. Youth in the early '70s were susceptible to other influences: folk and traditional music, rock and even Celtic rock. If a musician wanted to earn a decent living in the '60s, he was invariably roped into a showband. He may have preferred to experiment beyond Jim Reeves' covers, but daren't bite the hand that fed him. Many talented musicians undoubtedly preferred jazz and rhythm'n'blues, but played safe in the showbands. They experimented during rehearsals and jam sessions, but had to stick rigidly to the band's programme on stage in the ballrooms. Big money compensated for the lack of artistic freedom.

The beat boys — who played in basement clubs and disliked the showbands — didn't command the same general acceptability. Rory Gallagher, Phil Lynott and Brush Shields rejected the showbands and played what they liked. At the same time, many innovative beat groups were forced into submission by the system. The Chessmen with Alan Dee, broke new ground by playing in basements as well as ballrooms. Dee wrote his own songs but, as bass guitarist Robert Ballagh said later, originality was seen as something of a crime: "If we ever managed to record some of Alan's songs, they were hidden away on the back of records. We were playing in the ballroom circuit and the audience just wanted to hear the latest Top 20 tunes. The money was enormous." Originality was a feature of the Chessmen who were always known for their progressive style of music. "We did our own thing," says Dee. "We didn't pander to the tastes but, at the same time, had to make a living."

Their early records were original songs by Dee, three of which entered the charts — *Michael Murphy's Boy*, *Fighting*, and *What In The World Has Come Over You*. The most successful was *Michael Murphy's Boy*, a ballad about emigration, which climbed to No. 4 in the charts in August 1966. The Chessmen rose above other bands by playing and recording their own material. They gradually adopted a showband line-up, complete with a brass section. Dee left the band. He says: "I was disillusioned with life on the road." Ballagh quit shortly after a performance at a country ballroom: he realised there wasn't a single tune played all night that remotely interested him. He sold his equipment to Lynott, "and watched it on the telly for years until it was pinched somewhere."

Ballagh recalls the frustrations: "The Irish people seem to like that kind of country and western light-entertainment thing, especially in rural parts. Daniel O'Donnell is basically the showband concept resurrected. When I was playing, the country and western thing hadn't come in at the start. A lot of people think it's something that's always been there. I remember bands like the Royal and the Clippers, and all the early top showbands, had very few country and western songs in their repertoire. It was really only when Larry Cunningham and Big Tom started that the phenomenon grew. Showbands played a mixture of old favourites, top twenty tunes, some instrumentals, and a little bit of the country and western sentimental thing. But that changed. This was one of the reasons for me leaving. I've nothing against country and western in principle, but the variety that became popular in Ireland was possibly the worst aspect of it. Musically, it was fairly uninteresting, and so were the lyrics. We were professional musicians; you had to play what the public wanted. Gradually, over a period, I found that we were playing this material almost exclusively and weren't playing any of the kind of music that I liked. That change happened over the period from '64 to '67. I didn't notice it happening for ages because, obviously, a programme doesn't change radically overnight. But, you start dropping songs that aren't going down so well and including more popular ones.

Over a few years, I discovered that we dropped all the songs that I liked. We were fine when we played in cities like Dublin, Cork, Belfast, Galway, because the musical tastes were slightly more sophisticated. But if you were professional you couldn't earn a living by just playing city venues. You had to play rural venues as well. That meant adopting a programme. It was almost impossible to have two entirely different programmes. All sorts of compromises had to be made. I was only in it while there was fun in it. When the fun evaporated, I lost interest. Also, I think the travelling finally gets you down. It's a pretty exhausting affair... going to Cork in a van from Dublin was a six hour journey. You were six hours going down, playing for four hours and then six hours coming back. It was a long haul."

The beat scene flourished from '64 to '68 and groups dabbled in rhythm and blues, soul, Tamla and pop. English beat outfits toured Ireland because the money was better. As well as the beat craze, there was a folk boom in the mid '60s with Johnny McEvoy, Danny Doyle, the Dubliners, Wolfe Tones and We 4. While Bob Dylan was breathing revolution into the air of San Francisco, preaching anti-war sentiments through his songs, armed with only a guitar and harmonica slung around his neck, McEvoy was the young Irish 'Dylan' who bore similar weapons.

He brought the music of Dylan and his own songs to Irish audiences who were being urged by their showband leaders to do the *Hucklebuck*. McEvoy recorded a song called *Mursheen Durkin* that went to No. 1 in the charts in '66; *Boston Burglar* was No. 1 in '67 and stayed in the charts for twenty-three weeks; *Nora* was No. 1 in '68. These hits established him as a top box office attraction. The familiar lone figure with the guitar and harmonica shared top billing with Bowyer, Dolan, Rock and O'Brien. McEvoy paved the way for other 'acoustic' performers like Danny Doyle who had a No. 1 hit in '67 with *Whiskey On A Sunday*, as well as Jim McCann and Paddy Reilly.

Showbands had it all their own way until '68 — and then the electric guitar sound reached Ireland, expressed by Jimi Hendrix, Eric Clapton and Rory Gallagher. (Electric guitarist Henry McCullough, from Portstewart, began with showbands, the Sky Rockets and Gene and the Gents. He later toured with Hendrix, performed at Woodstock and joined Paul McCartney's Wings). The Irish yearned for home-grown rock. That hunger was satisfied by Brush Shields and Skid Row, Rory Gallagher and Taste, Phil Lynott and Thin Lizzy. The pioneering Celtic rock group was Horslips from '71 to '75. They and Thin Lizzy adapted indigenous Irish music, and these trends helped, in part, to break the showbands. Lynott had earlier formed a group called The Orphanage. He was joined, in '70, by a gifted guitarist, Eric Bell, who quit The Dreams Showband. Thin Lizzy was born that year. Horslips were the first band to seriously dent the showband monopoly. They merged traditional Irish music with glam and pomp rock. They came up with a version of Celtic rock that won widespread approval. Horslips played in the ballrooms, where they upstaged showbands with their flamboyant costumes, shamrock-design guitars and Celtic-type stage props. The first single, *Johnny's Wedding*, and first album, *Happy to Meet — Sorry to Part*, brought a new sound in 1972. Eamon Carr, the drummer, recalls: "If you were Irish and young — which I was in the '60s in Dublin — it was so depressing. Everything seemed black and white. There was something exciting going on somewhere else — in Liverpool, in swinging London. We were plagued with God-awful showbands. By and large, the showbands weren't original. It was more a show: you had the men dressing up in daft skirts and acting the maggot. It was vau-deville, but it had nothing to do with the essence of rock and roll. Now and again the older guys would show that they could play trumpets, and they would do a little bit of dixieland or something. Dixieland was old hat."

There is no doubt that the bands played a part in their own downfall. The top acts jacked up their take from 60, 70 to 80% in the boom years while, at the same time, cutting back their performances to two hours... or even less. 'Relief' bands per-formed from 9 till pub closing time. Publicans realised that they could hold customers by staging their own entertainment. The use of relief bands was abused. It was a Catch 22 situation: top bands claimed there was little point playing from 9pm in half-empty halls while the pubs were full. Albert Reynolds says: "I always believed it was the showbands themselves that killed the golden goose. They used to play a full five-hour programme. I remember queues in Roosky and Moate at eight o' clock on a Sunday evening in the middle of summer. The bands pulled back and only played two hours or less. People drifted into the pubs and from that grew cabaret.

"I saw this trend. I said it to the bands, and I said it to T.J. Byrne. I remember the night T.J. said to me, 'you'll have to charge 12/6'. Ten bob was tops. But the Royal always wanted to be that bit higher. I said, 'that's bad value for money. It's wrong for the customer. Over the top'. I think the rot started with the showbands playing less and less time every night and charging more and more money. Peoples' tastes began to change. They were demanding better facilities. Cabaret rooms grew up. I felt that the whole thing was on a downward trend. The customer wasn't getting value for money. I was proven right later. I got out in time and moved into industry."

Showbands do not accept all the blame. T.J. Byrne points the finger at taxation, the failure to grant drink licences to ballrooms, and the failure of ballroom owners to upgrade their premises. "It was a self-made industry," he says. "It was going so well that the government started to put a tax on the box office. They put so much tax on the admission. Then they started over-taxing the bands. VAT was put on the fees. Then VAT on advertising. They actually started to kill off the business. Hotels started up entertainment. Bars started with ballad groups; then, hotels ran dances with bars. People wouldn't come into a ballroom until pubs closed. The ballrooms didn't get occasional licences to compete with the hotels who were taking their business away. All the hotels ran discos because of the bars. All the ballrooms closed down because the proprietors couldn't get a licence and the local vintners would object in the courts to a licence being put into ballrooms. In addition, ballrooms didn't keep up with the times because they had no incentives. If the government allowed them to have a licence, then it would have encouraged them to modernise. To spend money on something with no bar would have been crazy.

"Also, showbands didn't put in the same effort as in the early days. They sat back, relaxed, and were overtaken." Nearly two decades after the ballrooms closed, surviving managers, agents and promoters, as well as newcomers to the business, formed an association to plead with Finance Minister Reynolds for a cut to 10% in the 23% VAT rate applied to dances and cabarets. They urged him to levy a retention tax — as in Britain — on the fees paid to big rock and pop acts who can avail of the zero-rating for VAT on theatre and concert tickets to make vast profits on fleeting visits to Ireland.

Says Phil Coulter: "Everybody was just falling forward. Nobody really knew what the hell was going on. This phenomenon was exploding all over the place. Big halls were being built. There was money to be made. You didn't have to be all that great a musician to be involved. Then, suddenly, it was all gone."

Gay Byrne believes that the showband boom, in microcosm, was a repetition of the big band era in the '30s and '40s. "This era gave rise to Benny Goodman, Woody Herman, Count Basie, Glenn Miller, Artie Shaw and Tommy Dorsey. They were big sit-down bands who toured America and played for dancing. That big band thing continued in Ireland until the showband scene came along. During the '50s and '60s, the showband thing in Ireland was a smaller microcosm of what happened in America. Just as they rolled through the fashion, so the showband lasted for ten or fifteen years. They went out of fashion because of a combination of circumstances. In the same way, probably disco will go out of fashion in time."

The general attitude was take-the-money-and-run. "Very few bands re-invested in their act or tried to elevate themselves past that situation," says Coulter. "The Capitol were one of the few exceptions. They tried to do other things: they had a shot at the English charts; they tried recording original material; they brought choreographers in; they were investing in tailors in London making their suits. Eventually, the whole scene became more and more mediocre. It was perceived by a lot of guys of minimum talent as a way to get their hands on bucks. There were some excellent musical operations like the Capitol, the Freshmen and Johnny Quigley. For example, the Freshmen obviously gave a lot of care getting their harmonies correct and worked very hard at it. Quigley's arrangements for his band were superb. Most bands who rehearsed pop records were content with getting down the words and the chords. But that was just the start-off point for Quigley.

"At one of their rehearsals, I remember Mickey Quigley and Johnny Peel actually listening to the phrasing. For example, while rehearsing the Coasters' *Yakety Yak*, other bands would just have repeated the words. But Quigley listened to the way that the Coasters did it. So when his band went on stage, it was as close as you could get. Certainly, one can slag the showbands and point to their copies and lack of originality. But the best of them had the copies off superbly well. A famous story is told of the Freshmen blowing the Beach Boys off the stage in Dublin. But, having said that about a handful of bands, a lot of the others were very un-together in every department, in particular musically. Anything over and above three chords was a mystery package. The bigger bands peaked naturally: that's in the nature of popular music. I don't think they were ever replaced. In the second wave of showbands, there was never that same magic or kind of innocence as in the first flush of the Royal, Capitol, Miami. When the second wave came, it seemed more like a cynical exercise. The attitude was... put a band together to make money. A lot of Dublin impresarios put seven guys together, invented a name and paid them thirty quid a week."

Gay Byrne, too, retains a sense of perspective about the showband days: "As in so many aspects of life, we look back now with rose- tinted spectacles and think weren't they wonderful and marvellous days. In fact, people were going to grotty, dirty, filthy ballrooms around the country with no amenities at all and, by and large, with a few exceptions, listening to fairly indifferent musicians banging out their few chords. But we were all young, vigorous, in love or on the hunt, or whatever, and all that has an effect when you look back. The ballroom people were so short-sighted they didn't realise that they would have to improve the surroundings. As the lounge bars became better and better and more comfortable, so the ballrooms became grottier and grottier. Not a single penny was spent by the ballroom owners to improve them, so people just stopped going. People got a bit more sophisticated, and time caught up with the ballroom owners."

Property developer Robin Power, chairman and chief executive of the Power Corporation, who is a former dance promoter, reaches a similar conclusion. "The business could still be going," he says, "if the hall owners spent money and moved with the times by providing facilities."

The ballroom barns were now following the paraffin-lit parochial halls into oblivion, and the love story setting moved from the upstairs mineral bar to the deep-pile lounge bar. For the young lady of the '70s, Dwan's was a mixer — not a mineral. The fashion-conscious girl who looked to Mary Quant was not to be found in the cattle mart environment of the ballroom where her unliberated sister once stood, back to the wall, waiting for inspection by some boy-jobber. Girls no longer tolerated the boys' bad manners: they refused would-be suitors who barked at them, grabbed their arms and headed for the floor.

Showbands ushered in an age marked, on one level, by extremes of innocence and euphoria and on another, by ruthlessness and greed. Some bands lingered into the '70s — largely unwanted and out of step. Finally, the wagons stopped rolling. Instruments were sold off or stored away. Yesterday's heroes returned to nine-to-five day jobs. The dream was over. A chapter of Ireland's social history closed. The lights dimmed on the ballrooms that are now derelict, demolished or being used as bingo halls, workshops, factories, supermarkets, garages or furniture stores. Most of the great landmarks of the era exist in memory only.

The showbands' legacy was the introduction of live contemporary music to people who could not experience it in any other way. "Look, there is a great premium on originality now," says Ballagh. "From U2 down, all the bands play original material. That was impossible in my day. Showbands were not seen as purveyors of originality. They were purveyors of entertainment. In fact, the public didn't like to hear original music. I believe that every developing music culture has to go through that phase. I've seen it in Eastern Europe where they're a few years down the line from producing Soviet U2s or Bulgarian U2s. I think they have to go along this road. You have to find your own voice and identity. You can't force it. It would have been absolutely impossible for a U2 band to develop in Ireland in the '60s like the Beatles did in England. That's because the English had done all of this a decade before. Every American record that came out was covered by an English artiste in the '50s. Tommy Steele was a classic example. Cliff Richard was one of the few who did original numbers. But all the Marty Wildes and these people just copied the American records exactly like the showbands. I think it's a phase that has to be gone through before a society finds its own voice. And then the originality comes."

Michael O'Riordan, of Ritz Records, sums it all up: "The sad thing is that there were no writers or producers in Ireland during those days. There were no songwriters that reflected the era. But if we had writers and producers, it probably would have gone on and developed. So the bands did cover versions. People say the showbands were only imitators who never developed into anything. They didn't because it was easier to get a song from an obscure album, do a cover version, and have a hit. The Freshmen tried to do something different, but it never really worked as much as it would now. There were some good record producers. With original songs, they would have had to create original sounds like in the UK and America.

"It was a shame that this didn't happen. It contributed to the death of the era because bands continued to do cover versions of hit records. Then, suddenly, these records were available; their tours were available and the acts started to come to Ireland. The homegrown thing died off. Joe Dolan is still very popular and puts on a great show, even for young people. But it's not the same thing as when he was seventeen. A sixteen-year-old can't gaze on him admiringly like girls might do with Bros or boys might do with Kylie Minogue. I always wished that there were writers we could have supported at the time. There wasn't enough money in songwriting unless you won the National Song Contest. We didn't have time to develop; we didn't have the recording technology or equipment."

But the showbands did produce enduring talents. Bowyer, Dolan and Rock, that irrepressible trio of Irish superstars, were the outstanding examples who outlived all contemporaries. No other Irish entertainers have come close to achieving that kind of longevity...